BRAZIL IMAGINED

THE WILLIAM & BETTYE NOWLIN SERIES
in Art, History, and Culture of the Western Hemisphere

BRAZIL IMAGINED

1500 TO THE PRESENT

Darlene J. Sadlier

UNIVERSITY OF TEXAS PRESS   AUSTIN

Requests for permission to reproduce material from this work
should be sent to:
    Permissions
    University of Texas Press
    P.O. Box 7819
    Austin, TX 78713-7819
    www.utexas.edu/utpress/about/bpermission.html

∞ The paper used in this book meets the minimum requirements
of ANSI/NISO Z39.48-1992 (R1997) (Permanence of Paper).

Library of Congress Cataloging-in-Publication Data
  Sadlier, Darlene J. (Darlene Joy)
  Brazil imagined : 1500 to the present / Darlene J. Sadlier. — 1st ed.
    p. cm. — (The William & Bettye Nowlin series in art, history,
and culture of the Western Hemisphere)
  Includes bibliographical references and index.
  ISBN 978-0-292-71856-2 (cloth : alk. paper) — ISBN 978-0-292-71857-9
(pbk. : alk. paper)
  1. National characteristics, Brazilian. 2. Brazil—Civilization.
I. Title. II. Series.
  F2510.S24 2008
  306.4′20981—dc22   2008005572

For Jim

CONTENTS

ACKNOWLEDGMENTS

I was fortunate to receive a number of grants from Indiana University to support the research and writing of this book. I want to thank the President's Office for an Arts and Humanities Research Award and the College of Arts and Sciences for an Arts and Humanities Institute Fellowship, both of which provided me with time away from teaching. A New Perspectives Grant from the Office of the Vice Provost for Research and a second College of Arts and Humanities Institute grant supported a research trip to Brazil in 2005. In Brazil I gave lectures on "the Good Neighbor Brazil" at the Universidade de São Paulo and the Universidade Federal Fluminense in Rio and received valuable feedback from colleagues and students there that contributed to my development of Chapter Six in this volume. I wish to thank Professors Esther Hamburger and João Luiz Vieira for inviting me to speak at their universities. My former Indiana University colleague Silviano Santiago brought to my attention important contemporary sources on the colonial imaginary, and I want to thank him for his advice and friendship. While I was in São Paulo, journalist Leila Gouvêa invited me to an exhibit at the Ateliê Amarelo, where I was fortunate to meet artist Vinicius Berton, who allowed me to represent one of his works in this book. The Rio artist Laerte de Sousa was equally generous in allowing me to include his work in this study. I am also grateful to Carmen Teixeira, who has been a great help whenever I visit the Cinemateca Brasileira in São Paulo.

Although not as exciting as places like Rio or São Paulo, Bloomington, the home of Indiana University, does have the world-renowned Lilly Library. The Charles R. Boxer and Bernardo Mendel collections there contain rare materials on Brazil, some of which are reproduced in this volume. It was a privilege to teach a course on images of Brazil in the Lilly in 2004, and I want to thank librarian Becky Cape for her knowledge and wit and for taking time out of her busy schedule to talk to my students about the Brasiliana materials. Having a *pied-a-terre* a few blocks from The Newberry Library in Chicago has been a joy, and I was fortunate to discover in the

William B. Greenlee and Edward F. Ayer collections there additional rare materials, including the little-known Frankfurt edition of Hans Staden's 1557 account of his captivity in Brazil.

Throughout the writing of the book, my longtime colleague and friend Heitor Martins shared with me his encyclopedic knowledge of Brazil, especially in the areas of literature and broadcast and print journalism. There are no words to thank him adequately for his time, counsel, and good fellowship. My colleague Juan Manuel Soto provided me with vital technical support, and I appreciate his time and efforts. Fellow Brazilianist Jon Tolman graciously allowed me to reproduce images from a Brasiliana collection that originated in the Latin American and Iberian Institute at the University of New Mexico. Finally, James Naremore encouraged me from the beginning to the end of this project, reading everything that I wrote and providing scholarly critique and editorial advice, all the while being the best companion in life a gal could ever have.

BRAZIL IMAGINED

This book originated in a plan to write a large-scale history of Brazilian literature, showing how different authors have contributed to ideas of Brazilian national identity. Had I followed through with my initial aims, the result might have vaguely resembled Peter Conrad's *Imagining America* (1980), which describes how certain nineteenth-century English writers who visited the United States imagined the country for their respective readerships. (Niagara Falls, for example, was a mandatory stop for Oscar Wilde, H. G. Wells, and others, and it assumed iconic status in their works.) My plan changed, however, when in the course of researching in the Lilly Library and Newberry Library's Brasiliana collections I began to realize the importance of early cartographic iconography to the formation of the Brazilian colonial imaginary. From cartography, it was a short step to studying early woodcuts and copperplate engravings, a topic that I had addressed in an earlier study of Nelson Pereira dos Santos's 1971 *Como era gostoso o meu francês* (*How Tasty Was My Little Frenchman*), a tongue-in-cheek film about sixteenth-century European expansionism and indigenous anthropophagy. Before long, my book had grown to include not only literature but also maps, book illustrations, architecture, painting, films, and broadcast media, and my history of the nation ranged from the sixteenth century to the present.

Although my study is broad, even panoramic, I should perhaps make clear at the outset that it is focused on various forms of art or mass communication and takes a particular approach to the question of national identity. By using this last term I mean to designate anything that contributes to the individual subject's sense of belonging to a nation. Does national identity therefore actually exist? Yes, but as I hope to show, it always exists discursively, as a representation or as an *idea* that is open to contestation and change over time. How does it take shape in Brazil? In many ways— for example, we can observe its workings through a study of law, politics, religion, and even historical linguistics. My own interests, however, are slightly apart from these matters and indeed from the economic relations, technologies, and institutions that determine ideology. Unlike Benedict Anderson's valuable and highly influential *Imagined Communities* (1983), which explores many of the material conditions that gave rise to ideas of nationhood, my book exclusively addresses imaginary representations; thus I speak only about the cultural superstructure and allude indirectly to certain concerns of historians, political scientists, and anthropologists. For instance, I have little or nothing to say about constitutional law, definitions of citizenship, geographical-territorial boundaries, industrial economies, or popular customs. I do not deal, except obliquely, with the development of print cultures or representational technologies, and I do not write about the formation of "public spheres" such as the ones that have been theorized by Jürgen Habermas. My subject is the relatively manifest ideological effect of fine art, literature, architecture, film, and television on the shaping of "Brazilianness." The modes of cultural expression I have chosen to analyze are obviously determined by economic and political forces, but in themselves they contribute to the shaping of national identity and give us a window onto political and social struggles. They are worthy of study in their own right and have been given relatively little attention, at least in the academic world, along the lines in which I have tried to discuss them.

The process of selecting writers, artists, and works was challenging, partly because I was covering five hundred years in a changing culture. In lieu of an encyclopedic survey of the arts, I constructed a series of historical moments in which one or more art forms become dominant or strongly influential. Thus my discussion of the colonial period focuses chiefly on cartography and visual arts, while in my chapter on the nineteenth century I give most of the attention to literature. When I reach the twentieth century, the materials under consideration are increasingly public, so that I discuss modern architecture, city planning, films, and television. I have also tried to explore the ways in which both foreigners and native-born Brazilians have imagined the country.

Anyone who has studied Brazil knows that there are myriad accounts of the nation written by foreign travelers. In recent years, scholars José Carlos Barreiro, Felix Driver, and Luciana Martins have focused attention on nineteenth-century illustrations and writings by such individuals as the French painter Jean Baptiste Debret and various British subjects, including the diarist Maria Graham and naturalists William Burchell and Charles Darwin. The nineteenth century is particularly rich in foreign materials on Brazil because shortly after arriving in Rio de Janeiro in 1808, Dom João VI opened the country's ports to commerce. Curiously, the image of Brazil produced by Brazilians themselves has received far less critical attention. This may explain why most of my Brazilian colleagues and friends assumed that I was focusing exclusively on the outsider or "imperial" gaze. My aim instead is to concentrate on Brazilian materials, occasionally showing the relationship between local and foreign imaginaries. In all cases, I have indicated the sociopolitical and economic interests and concerns that played a part in the image-making process.

Although I have attempted to provide as many examples of national imagery as is feasible, by no means is the material exhaustive or complete. The wealth of materials from which to choose is an indication of Brazil's importance as a New World territory of vast proportions, bountiful resources, and indigenous peoples; as the new home of a transplanted European royal court; as a bourgeois society eager for national independence; and as a modern nation of seemingly endless potential, dubbed by a spellbound Stefan Zweig "the land of the future."

Faced with a massive archive, I have necessarily been selective and tried to be mindful of what Raymond Williams described in *The Long Revolution* (1961) as the "selective cultural tradition":

> Within a given society, selection will be governed by many kinds of special interests, including class interests. Just as the actual social situation will largely govern *contemporary* selection, so the development of society, the process of historical change, largely determine the selective tradition. . . . We tend to underestimate the extent to which the cultural tradition is not only a selection but also an interpretation. We see most past work through our own experience, without even making the effort to see it in something like its original terms. What analysis can do is not so much to reverse this, returning a work to its period, as to make the interpretation conscious of showing historical alternatives; to relate the interpretation of the particular contemporary values on which it rests; and, by exploring the real patterns of the work, to confront us with the real nature of the choices we are making. . . . Every element that we analyze will be in this sense active: that it will be seen in certain real relations, at many different levels. In describing these relations, the real cultural process will emerge. (68–70)

To the best of my ability I have documented and examined representations of Brazil "in something like their original terms." By this I mean that

I study specific images in their historical contexts and alongside other images to give a sense of their significance in what Williams refers to as the "lived culture." My study includes canonical texts as well as other works that, for whatever reason, have been neglected or dismissed. A case in point is the poetry of the nineteenth-century African-Brazilian Luís Gama, a gifted writer who was a contemporary of Castro Alves and Joaquim Nabuco. Unlike Alves and Nabuco, who wrote celebrated (and canonical) anti-slavery works during and after the abolitionist movement, Gama focused on the issue of race itself in Brazil. Among his poems are *tour de force* satires directed at middle- and upper-class Brazilians of African descent who try to pass as white. Perhaps for that reason, Gama never gained entry into the Brazilian literary canon.

My book is concerned with a great variety of nationalistic themes in distinct historical periods and at different cultural levels. I have attempted to show how national identity is shaped in the colonial and postcolonial eras, in times of dictatorship and democracy, and in response to modernity and postmodernity. At certain junctures I also indicate how the image of Brazil has been influenced by the politics and culture of other nations, particularly France and the United States. In addition, I realized during the course of writing the book that for the entire time span of its existence, Brazil's imagined identity has been strongly affected by at least two important concepts that can sometimes take on different qualitative implications at different historical junctures. The first of these is race, which becomes an important issue from the moment European colonizers encounter indigenous peoples and which lies behind the present-day recognition that the nation is made up of a multiracial population, much of it black. The second theme is nature, meaning in this case the flora and fauna of the place, and its value as a "natural resource." From the beginning of the European "discovery" of Brazil, the vast and varied landscape has been seen alternately as an exotic Eden, a savage wilderness, and a source of valuable commodities. The contrast in these views of the natural world is vividly evident today in the long-unequal distribution of landownership and especially in the ever-increasing conflict between ecology and commerce. Both sides of this conflict tend to cultivate a rhetorical technique called *ufanismo*, which praises to the point of exaggeration Brazil's resources. Although largely a characteristic of sixteenth-century texts by Portuguese writers who were eager to promote the country's colonization, *ufanismo* continues to inflect contemporary writings about the nation.

At the outset I emphasize the importance of historiography, cartography, engravings, and woodcuts to the construction of the first images of Brazil. As I show in Chapter One, among the best-known representations of Brazil were Belgian-born Johann Theodor de Bry's sensational engravings of indigenous cannibals, images that circulated throughout Europe at the end of the sixteenth century. Those engravings not only refuted earlier images of Brazil as a paradise populated with Edenic inhabitants, as recorded by the Portuguese royal scribe Pero Vaz de Caminha and others, but also helped to bolster and justify an aggressive colonial campaign to enslave and ultimately rid the Brazilian coast of the native presence.

In Chapter Two, I show how the contrasting images of Brazil as terrestrial Eden and barbarous land continued to be explored in Dutch paintings by artists who accompanied Prince Johan Maurits von Nassau-Siegen to Pernambuco in the seventeenth century. Although scenes of anthropophagy appear on Dutch maps and in other works of the time, they are relatively few and always subordinate to images of passive if not friendly natives, happy African slaves, and an energetic commerce—all of which was devised to encourage Dutch colonization. The paradise described in writings by early Dutch visitors is especially evident in the work of Frans Post, who is regarded as the first landscape artist of the New World, and in Albert Eckhout's ethnographic-style paintings of Indians, flora, and fauna. The Edenic vision became a major topos in the earliest literature written in Brazil, and nativist works by poet Manuel Botelho de Oliveira and the Jesuit Vicente do Salvador, among others, extolled the country's natural beauty and abundant resources. Renowned for his satiric verses, the Bahian poet Gregório de Matos took a different approach by criticizing his bountiful homeland for enriching foreigners at the expense of locals. The discovery of gold and diamonds in the mid-eighteenth century confirmed early prophesies of Brazil as a land rich in precious stones, which resulted in representations of the country along the lines of a tropical Eldorado. That image contrasted sharply with pictorials and accounts of the brutal treatment and death of African slaves who were brought to Brazil to work the mines and plantations. If Brazil was a paradise on earth for some, it was at best (in the words of the Jesuit Antônio Vieira) a "sweet hell" for those enslaved.

Chapter Three focuses on the flight of the Portuguese royal court from the Napoleonic invasion and their arrival in Rio de Janeiro in 1808. Early writings by the newly arrived immigrants complained about the lack of civilization in Brazil and drew unfavorable comparisons between the country and the homeland left behind. Following various proclamations and projects to lift the profile of the new royal capital, in 1816 the monarch Dom João VI invited a group of French artists and architects to Rio to train local talent and design buildings in keeping with Brazil's newly appointed status as part of the kingdom with Portugal and the Algarve. The opening of Brazilian ports to overseas commerce in 1808 encouraged the arrival of various foreign scientific expeditions that documented flora and fauna and produced ethnographies of its people. Travelers like the British-born Maria Graham and John Mawe kept diaries of their visits that described in detail the problems and impact of imported notions of civilization on a people and nation eager for independence.

With the proclamation of Brazil's independence in 1822 and the beginning of the Brazilian empire, a new image came to the fore; and the Indian, who was no longer visible, having died or fled into the interior, became an icon of the recently independent nation. As I discuss in Chapter Four, although the Indian had appeared earlier in Brazilian literature, the European romantics, including the Portuguese poet Almeida Garrett and the French Brazilianist Ferdinand Denis, encouraged their Brazilian cohorts to adopt the figure of the noble savage as a national symbol. Meanwhile, as Antônio Gonçalves Dias and José de Alencar were writing popular epic-style works about valiant indigenous warriors and maidens in the wilderness, other intellectuals and artists were beginning to write works about life in the city.

The desire to forge a national literature moved from discussions of the Indian to debates among urban novelists such as Joaquim Manuel de Macedo and "regional" writers such as Franklin Távora, and by the latter part of the nineteenth century, the literary image of the nation was split (albeit unevenly) along geographic lines. On the one hand were works of limited circulation about the Brazilian interior with its "exotic" flora and fauna and regional types such as farmers and storekeepers, muleteers and bandits. On the other hand were the more widely published books about the city and the urban middle class. Blacks rarely figured in either genre; when they did appear, they were usually cast as slaves. However, the image of the slave took on new meaning in abolitionist writings and oratory of the period, efforts toward emancipation that were finally rewarded in 1888. Despite emancipation, the suffering slave continued to be evoked in speeches and writings as a metaphor for a nation eager to wrest its freedom from the imperial monarchy. The freeing of the slaves anticipated by one year the overthrow of Emperor Pedro II and the establishment of the republic. At the same time, novelist Machado de Assis was charting a new course for Brazilian literature that shifted emphasis from romantic nationalism to a more cosmopolitan, proto-modernist sensibility with which he dissected the values and foibles of the growing bourgeoisie.

Chapter Five focuses on the images of modernist Brazil, beginning with the Modern Art Week in São Paulo in 1922. Held in the Municipal Theater during the centennial celebration of Brazil's independence, the week's events were an attempt by writers, artists, and musicians to expand on the nation's cosmopolitan image while emphasizing the importance of its regional character. Once again the Indian was called forth as a national symbol. Instead of the romantic *bon sauvage,* however, poet Oswald de Andrade summoned the anthropophagous figure as part of a modernist counter-colonialist strategy: the local culture would ingest (as oppose to emulate) foreign sources in order to strengthen what was endemic to the nation. The desire to "make it new" was especially evident in painting and architecture, in which classical forms gave way to futurism, expressionism, cubism, and other modernist schools. This radical shift in the arts and architecture culminated years later with the construction of the futuristic capital, Brasília. The "new way" also produced bossa nova, a cool, hip music whose impact was felt far beyond Brazil.

In Chapter Six I examine the 1940s, when Brazil's national identity was shaped not only by its own artists but also by the U.S. Good Neighbor policy, which fostered cultural exchanges and an emphasis on both modernity and exoticism. During this time Hollywood transformed Carmen Miranda into a colorful, amiable, and tropical Latin icon—an image that endured long after the end of World War II. In the same period Orson Welles functioned as a goodwill ambassador from the United States; through his aborted film, *It's All True,* and his radio programs broadcast from Rio and New York, he emphasized a very different image of Brazil as a racially diverse, culturally rich, and respected wartime ally of the United States.

The early oscillating images of Brazil as Edenic and barbarous reemerge in the later part of the twentieth century as Cinema Novo films about the utopian possibilities of a poor but developing nation accede to darker pictures of a dystopia plagued by corruption, drugs, and violence. I explore these contrasting media images in Chapter Seven, and in many ways they remain at the heart of the country's view of itself today. The media coverage of Brazil's growing poverty, violence, and corruption coexists with reports on the country's emergence as a global economic power—a contradiction that seems more extreme with each passing year. The contradiction is especially evident in the major cityscapes, where towering multinational buildings and high-end shopping centers appear alongside modest housing and sprawling *favelas,* or slums. It is impossible to predict what lies ahead for a nation still referred to as "the land of the future"; nevertheless, an examination of the ways the nation has been represented over the centuries should provide us with a better understanding of the imaginary that has shaped Brazil and may shape it in decades to come.

CHAPTER 1

Edenic and Cannibal Encounters

When the Portuguese nobleman Pedro Álvares Cabral and his armada of thirteen ships left Lisbon on March 9, 1500, his mission was to sail to the port city of Calicut in India and bring back spices, silks, porcelains, and other valuable commodities.[1] Vasco da Gama had opened the sea route to India two years earlier, and the Portuguese monarch, Dom Manuel I, was eager to send a much larger expedition to keep Portugal in the forefront of maritime trade with the East.[2] Onboard Cabral's ship was the royally appointed financial administrator from Oporto, Pero Vaz de Caminha, who was attached to Cabral's ship as scribe. It was on that trip that Caminha wrote his famous letter of May 1, 1500, to Dom Manuel, in which he describes the founding of a land that eventually would be called Brazil.

There are different hypotheses about why Cabral sailed so far west of Vasco da Gama's Atlantic route to India that he ultimately sighted Brazil. In his *Tratado da terra do Brasil* (Treatise on the Land of Brazil), written in 1574, the Portuguese chronicler Pero de Magalhães Gândavo attributes the fleet's southwesterly turn to doldrums that forced Cabral to seek better sailing winds far off the Guinea coast. This course took his armada directly west to Porto Seguro and the coastline of what is today Bahia. According to Brazilian cultural historian Luís da Câmara Cascudo, for a long time the discovery of Brazil was attributed to a storm that caused Cabral to change direction and head south-southwest. But neither Caminha's letter nor nautical charts of the period refer to any inclement weather that might have driven Cabral off course.[3]

Portuguese literary historian Jaime Cortesão argues that imperialism, and not nature, was the real reason for Cabral's westerly turn. He contends that with the Spanish already in North America and with the redrawing of the Line of Tordesillas in 1494 to a more favorable position for Portuguese expansion (370 leagues west of the Cape Verde Islands), Cabral's imagination was fueled by the possibility of new Atlantic conquests (Cortesão 1967, 90–91). The German-born medievalist scholar Carolina Michaëlis de Vasconcelos argues that Caminha's letter to the king makes Cabral's intentions clear, for instead of using the term *descobrimento* (discovery) when referring to the "Land of Vera Cruz" claimed for the Portuguese by Cabral,[4] Caminha used the word *achamento* (finding). Vasconcelos infers from Caminha's word choice that the armada did not make a chance "discovery" as the result of weather but a "find" while searching for new territory.[5] Her interpretation supports at least one other theory that Cabral had prior knowledge of the new land from earlier navigational sources and that he journeyed westward from Africa to claim it officially for the Portuguese empire.[6] Whatever the actual case, together the various speculations about the events and intent surrounding Cabral's voyage have transformed the "discovery" of Brazil into something akin to legend or myth—as if the "find" in and of itself were somehow insufficient to convey the extraordinary nature of Cabral's maritime achievement.

Given all the different theories and speculations, Caminha's description of the sighting of Brazil seems almost matter-of-fact: "On this day [April 22], in the evening hours, we sighted land: first of a very high, large and round mountain, and of other, lower mountains to the south of it, and of flat lands with giant groves of trees. The captain gave the name of Monte Pascoal [Easter Mountain] to the tall mountain and to the land he gave the name the Land of Vera Cruz."[7] One might infer from his description that the "finding" was less important to Caminha than what was actually found. Unlike the customary brief messages written to the king by Cabral and other ship captains about the sighting, Caminha penned a lengthy missive (fourteen folios, front and back) that is remarkably detailed and ethnographic in its descriptions of the land, the people (Tupiniquims, or Tupis), and their customs. Caminha is modest about his abilities as a scribe, telling Dom Manuel that he is the least equipped to put these matters into writing; nonetheless he assures him that he will strive neither to play up (*aformosentar*, to make beautiful) nor play down (*afear*, to make ugly) what he has seen. His letter has long been recognized as the official record of the first contact between the Portuguese and native Brazilians. No indigenous documents exist on this or any other encounter between the two groups.

As for Caminha's objectivity, it should be noted that his letter concludes with a petition to the king to grant clemency to his son-in-law, Jorge de Osório, who had been exiled to São Tomé off the west coast of Africa.[8] Although petitions of this kind were not uncommon, especially when a servant of the King provided him with good news, one cannot help but wonder the degree to which Caminha's request affected his objectivity. It seems unlikely that he would pen anything "ugly" that might displease his sovereign, while he would have every reason to curry favor and write a positive if not exuberant account. Historian José António Costa Idéais has observed that the custom of the *alvíssara* (a gift given to a bearer of good tidings) was an incentive for the embellishment of events: the better the news received, the more valuable the gift given (in Amado and Figueiredo 2001, 113–114). For centuries, maritime accounts of new lands and peoples were regarded along with charts, maps, and illustrations as historical documents and, therefore, as truth. But Caminha's reference to the *alvíssara* is an important reminder that even the most apparently straightforward narratives are produced not in a vacuum but within a context that can bring to bear forces as widely divergent as a family member's plight, a religious conviction, or a broader ideological position, which in sixteenth-century Portugal was steeped in imperialism and the desire for territorial conquest and global commerce.

It should not come as a total surprise, then, that Caminha's letter offers a very favorable impression of Brazil. Although the armada had landed in one of the more humid areas in the tropics, he described the weather as cool and temperate and compared it with the climate of northern Portugal. He praised in particular the bountiful forests filled with different species of trees (including the dyewood, also known as brazilwood, which would become the first commodity exported by the Portuguese), the vast mountain ranges, and the sweet and plentiful waters of the rivers. He was amazed by the abundance of shrimp of a size he had never before seen and by the macaws and vibrantly colored parrots of multiple hues. Although he did not see many other birds while on shore, he inferred from the number of trees and forested areas that they were many. Not unlike some ancient and medieval myths about remote Atlantic islands, one of which was called Brazil,[9] Caminha's account describes the "island of Vera Cruz" along the lines of the classical *locus amoenus* (gentle place)[10]—in this case, a tropical Eden with comely and innocent men and women who are curious about yet shy of the European. This image of a paradise on earth was not unique to Caminha's letter; indeed, as scholars such as Henri Baudet, E. Barlett Giamatti, Sérgio Buarque de Holanda, and Laura de Mello e Souza have pointed out, the biblical garden was repeatedly evoked in writings about the New World.[11] It is perhaps not surprising, then, that the name "Brazil"—long associated with an imaginary island paradise, not to mention the valuable and coveted dyewoods indigenous to the land—would ultimately replace "the Land of Vera Cruz."

Although Caminha discusses in some detail the topography and wild-life of the new land, most of his narrative focuses on the human inhabit-ants, many of whom carry bows and arrows: "In appearance they are brown, somewhat reddish, and they have good faces and well-shaped, good noses" (folio 2, verso). Here Caminha defines the native Brazilians' facial features in terms of their similarity to Europeans; there is also the suggestion that they are different from the west coast African, whose broader, flattened nose was deemed unattractive by the Portuguese. Caminha remarks more than once on the native inhabitants' cleanliness, their unusual fitness, and their complete lack of awareness or shame about their nakedness. At one point, he compares their total innocence to that of the biblical Adam, and he praises them over "civilized man" for their personal hygiene and purity of mind. What is particularly interesting to note is Caminha's use of neu-tral terms, such as "men," "young women," "girls," "people," and "gallants" to describe the local population. These non-racial, non-ethnic terms would soon be substituted by either tribal designations, such as Tupiniquim and Tupinambá, or by the generic "Indian" (used by Columbus to refer to the Caribbean populations that he believed to be East Indians), or by the depre-catory "savage," "beast," and "barbarian."

The ethnographic feel of Caminha's account is especially evident in his detailed descriptions of the indigenous culture. He refers on various occa-sions to the different dyes used to tint the inhabitants' bodies. For example: "This one . . . was tinted with red dye on his chest, shoulder blades, thighs, hips, and down to the lower part of his legs, while his stomach and other places were of his own color. And the dye was so red that it would neither wash off nor dissolve in the water. On the contrary, when he came out of the water, he looked even redder" (folio 5). Later on he observes: "[There was] one with her thigh from knee to hip and buttock all tinted with black paint and the rest of her in her own color; another had both knees and calves and ankles so painted, and her private parts were so naked and exposed with such innocence that in this there was no shame" (folio 7).[12] Caminha also commented on the male tradition of wearing decorative bone fragments and stones in the lower lip, and at one point he seems amused by an old man's attempt to provoke Cabral, if not silence him: "This old man had his lip bored so deeply that a large thumb could fit into the hole; and in it he wore a large and worthless green stone that closed the hole from the outside. The Captain made him take it out. I know not what devil spoke to him, but the old man took it directly to the Captain in order to place it on his mouth" (folio 7).

Caminha noted that like their European counterparts, the men were not circumcised, while the young women's genitalia were remarkable for their lack of pubic hair. He gave considerable attention to the inhabitants' hair (or lack or it) as well as to their headdresses and other adornments, many of which were made of bird feathers. Caminha also commented on their basic foodstuffs of seeds and yams and their fear and suspicion of unknown animals such as lambs and chickens that were brought on the ships. When two men were invited to board the captain's vessel, Caminha described their being treated as if they were visiting royalty. Following a welcome ceremony, they were given food and drink (which they tasted and subsequently spit out); when night fell, they curled up on the floor and fell asleep, and the captain ordered his men to cover them with blankets, and pillows were eased beneath their heads. There is no question that Caminha regarded the native inhabitants as primitive and "other"; in at least two places in the narrative he refers to "taming" the population, and he calls them "bestial" on another occasion. In most instances, however, he preferred to draw comparisons between them and animals of a benign nature—especially with birds whose prized feathers decorated the natives' heads and bodies.

Although the Portuguese and indigenous peoples were unable to understand each other's language (unlike the African experience, no interpreters were available to the Portuguese on this expedition), Caminha nevertheless commented on the Tupiniquim's purported lack of religious belief. He gave special attention to their curiosity about the Catholic masses conducted while the Portuguese were on shore and approved of the ways they imitated the Europeans by remaining silent during the services and standing and kneeling at different parts of the ceremony. As important as gold, spices, and other precious commodities were potential converts to Christianity who could help the Portuguese empire deter the spread of Islam. Indeed, the Treaty of Tordesillas was enacted specifically to allow the Portuguese and Spanish to claim territories for their respective kingdoms as long as the native inhabitants were non-Christian. For Caminha, the goodness, passivity, and simplicity of the native people and their receptivity to ceremony made them ideal candidates for Christian conversion: "And I believe that were Your Majesty to send someone here to stay longer among them, they will all be converted according to Your Majesty's desire" (folio 13). He concluded his account of the New World by drawing links between Christianity, colonization, and commerce. After praising the vast lands, plentiful waters, and gentle climate, he wrote: "However, it seems to me that the best fruit to be taken from this land would be that of saving this people. And this should be the principal seed that Your Majesty should cast here" (folio 13, verso).

As the expedition's leader, Cabral wanted to prove the potential commercial wealth of the new land to Dom Manuel, and he immediately dispatched a ship back to Lisbon with a small cargo of brazilwood (Marchant 1942, 28–29).[13] The vessel also carried Caminha's letter as well as other communications about the discovery. The rest of the armada continued its voyage to India, where Caminha died in December during an attack by Hindi locals on the Portuguese trading post in Calicut. Although his letter remained unpublished until 1817, it is a prototype of an emerging literary sensibility known as *ufanismo,* whose rhetoric is characterized by glowing and often highly exaggerated descriptions of New World lands and peoples. In his 1500 missive, Caminha lays the foundation for subsequent descriptions of Brazil as a tropical Eden—an idea that would become a major trope in sixteenth- and seventeenth-century representations of Brazil.[14] This image confirmed and bolstered the sense of good fortune and accomplishment that was associated with Portuguese expansionism; at the same time, it ultimately persuaded the monarchy to engage in a more rigorous colonization enterprise.[15]

As mentioned earlier, Caminha was one of several who wrote to the king, but only two other documents from the 1500 voyage have survived. In the *Carta do mestre João* (Letter by Master João), the armada's surgeon-astronomer writes briefly about the newfound "islands" but reserves most of his comments for a discussion of the *estrelas da Cruz,* or Southern Cross.[16] In a much longer document known simply as the *Relação do piloto anônimo* (Account by the Anonymous Pilot), the unnamed author wrote that they had landed on *terra firme,* an observation that confirmed Cabral's belief that they had encountered a continent and not an island as posited by Caminha in his letter's closing. This is an important observation because history has long credited the Florentine Amerigo Vespucci as the first navigator to recognize that the territory was a continent. The anonymous report differs from Caminha's account in one other, significant way. While Caminha only focuses on the new land and its people, the nameless author places the founding of Vera Cruz within the much broader context of the fleet's expedition to India, and he writes about negotiating trade as well as about the loss of men and ships in the battle at Calicut. Although his report is positive in its description of Brazil, it lacks the breadth and ethnographic specificity that makes Caminha's letter so fascinating to read. The anonymous letter suggests that the discovery of Vera Cruz, albeit fortuitous, was of minor importance in comparison with the fleet's arrival in India, whose precious commodities were the objective of the voyage.

Although Dom Manuel forbade the publication of navigational charts and maps outlining the route to India (Marchant 1945, 297), in the summer of 1501 he wrote to his Spanish in-laws, the Catholic royal couple Fernando and Isabel, to inform them of finding "Santa Cruz."[17] He was succinct in his account of the new land, stating that it provided logistical support for the expedition, which made repairs and replenished water supplies there. In fact, he made only one brief reference to the people of Santa Cruz, stating that they were nude, innocent, and peaceful. No mention was made of the natural beauty, wildlife, or other resources amply described in Caminha's narrative. Similar to the account by the anonymous pilot, Dom Manuel's letter gives far greater emphasis to Cabral's voyage around the Cape of Good Hope to India, the loss of ships and life in battle and at sea, trade with the East, and the commercial success of the venture.

However, prior to writing to his Spanish relatives, Dom Manuel had commissioned the renowned cosmographer Amerigo Vespucci to make a second voyage to Brazil to strengthen Portugal's claim to the territory.[18] In June 1501, on his way to Brazil, Vespucci wrote a letter to his former patron and friend in Florence, Lorenzo di Pierfrancesco de Medici, from Cape Verde, where he encountered ships from Cabral's fleet on their way back to Lisbon.[19] This letter and subsequent correspondence with Medici brought word of Brazil and Portugal's successful commercial enterprise in India to the Florentines, and from there, word spread to other parts of Europe. From Cape Verde, Vespucci traveled from what was believed to be the mouth of the Amazon River to the Rio de la Plata region, helping to establish with greater exactitude the line that separated Portuguese from Spanish holdings. In a second letter to Medici written after he returned to Lisbon in

1502, Vespucci described the new land in Edenic terms: "sometimes I marveled so much at the delicate scents of the herbs and flowers, and the tastes of those fruits and roots, that I thought I must be in the Earthly Paradise . . . What is there to say of the quantity of birds, their plumes and colors and songs and how many kinds and how beautiful they are? (I do not wish to enlarge upon this, for I doubt I would be believed)" (in Formisano 1992, 30–31).

Although Vespucci was clearly moved by the riches of the land, he was far more judgmental than Caminha in his assessment of the native population. Having lived among native Brazilians for nearly a month, he reported on their "pagan" custom of body piercing and wearing large bones and stones in their facial holes for the "brutal business" of making themselves look fierce. Caminha's description of New World inhabitants seems almost pastoral compared to Vespucci's narrative,[20] which comments on their cruelty in warfare and their anthropophagy:

> And at certain times, when a diabolical frenzy comes over them, they invite their relatives and people to dinner, and they set them out before them—that is, the mother [enemy captive] with all the children they have got from her—and performing certain ceremonies kill them with arrows and eat them; and they do the same to the . . . male slaves and the children that have come from them. And this is for certain, for in their houses we found human flesh hung up for smoking, and a lot of it. (In Formisano 1992, 33)

A text often attributed to Vespucci entitled *Mundus novus* (1503) enjoyed wide circulation—twenty-two editions of the Latin version appeared by 1506 (Amado and Figueiredo 2001, 325), and sixty-six editions in six other languages were available by 1529 (Lestringant 1977, 28])—spreading even greater affirmation of Brazil as a tropical Eden. In both Vespucci's private correspondence to Medici and in the apocryphal *Mundus novus*, attention is given to the temperate climate, the bountiful flora and fauna, and the miraculous life spans of the native population.[21] Like later narratives about Brazil, certain editions of *Mundus novus* were illustrated by artists who had never even traveled there. Woodcuts represented native Brazilians as transplanted classical Greek or Roman figures with long, curly, golden tresses, and a few men even sported beards. One of the earliest of these woodcuts of indigenous Brazilians appears in the 1505 Basel edition of *Mundus novus*.

Attributed to the German Johann Froschauer, it is a broadside, and its inscription reads:

> This figure represents to us the people and island which have been discovered by the Christian King of Portugal or by his subjects. The people are thus naked, handsome, brown, well-shaped in body, their heads, necks, arms, private parts, feet of men and women are a little covered with feathers. The men also have many precious stones in their faces and breasts. No one also has anything, but all things are in common. And the men have as wives those who please them, be they mothers, sisters, or friends, therein make they no distinction. They also fight with each other. They also eat each other and even those who are slain, and hang the flesh of them in the smoke. They become a hundred and fifty years old. And have no government. (In Eames 1922, 27)

In the center foreground of the woodcut a woman is seated and seems content to watch the children around her, one of whom suckles at her breast. To the far right of the woodcut, two men, one bearded, the other clean-shaven, appear to be in friendly conversation, while another bearded man and young boy are looking back at the nursing mother. In the left corner and behind the mother figure is a group of four people standing around a headless body that is stretched out on its side. Although the body has little definition and could be that of an animal, one of the men is clearly chewing on a limb that has a hand and fingers attached. In the center background of the illustration and hanging from a makeshift rack over an open fire are human body parts, including a head, an arm, and a leg. Although cannibalism is far from an Edenic activity, the image in the woodcut has a certain benign, almost pastoral look. In fact, the face of the severed head is turned in the direction of the two men in amiable conversation—as if it were somehow partaking of their fellowship.

Despite the fact that *Mundus novus* and the woodcut's inscription refer to the people's nakedness, the men and women are depicted wearing headdresses, skirts, and other adornments made of feathers. Moreover, all male and female sexual organs are concealed—even those of the children. It is not clear if the artist had actually traveled to Brazil, but the physical representation of the local population is in many ways more realistic than some later illustrations. Like an iconic signature, two caravels appear in the upper right corner to mark the European presence. This single woodcut

1.1 Early woodcut of native Brazilians (1505). Basel edition of *Mundus novus*. Spencer Collection, New York Public Library, Astor, Lenox and Tilden Foundations.

consolidates a number of tropes emerging in the early part of the sixteenth century: the comeliness of the native inhabitants, the egalitarian or utopian nature of the community, their warring tendencies, and their practice of anthropophagy.[22]

The popularity of *Mundus novus* cannot be overemphasized: it announced to readers that a "new world" existed, a faraway utopia of extreme natural beauty—not unlike the Atlantic islands described by myth and lore over the centuries. The German Martin Waldseemüller's 1507 map pays homage to Vespucci by affixing the name "America" to the South American continent. And although the descriptions of a cannibal people were disturbing if not terrifying, the emphasis given to the land's real and potential natural wealth piqued public and private interests about still other riches and wonders that the New World might hold. A greater focus on commerce was evi-

dent within just a few years. In his *Décadas da Ásia* (Decades on Asia), published in 1552, Portuguese historian João de Barros was extremely critical
of the people's substitution of the name Santa Cruz for the commercially
oriented name Brazil:[23]

> Santa Cruz was the name given to that land in the first years, and the cross
> made out of trees lasted for some years in that place. However, like the devil,
> the sign of the cross lost its power over us . . . So much of the red wood, known
> as brazil, came from that land that this name has been taken up by the people
> and the name of Santa Cruz was lost. It is as if the name of a wood to dye cloth
> were more important than the name of the wood that gave tincture to all the
> sacraments by which we are saved and that was spilled on it by the blood of
> Jesus Christ. And since on this matter I cannot avenge myself of the devil, I
> advise, on the part of the cross of Jesus Christ, and to all those who read this,
> that they give to this land the name that was so solemnly bestowed upon it.
> For under penalty of that same cross that has to be shown to us on our final
> day, we may be accused of being more devoted to brazilwood than to the cross.
> And in honor of such a great land, let us call it the "Province of Santa Cruz,"
> which sounds better than "Brazil" among those who are prudent, since the
> common people are inconsiderate and unqualified to name properties of the
> royal Crown. (1945, 1:111)

Nearly fifty years would pass before Dom João III, the successor of
Manuel, initiated the process of religious instruction and conversion that
Caminha enjoined his monarch to consider in 1500. In the meantime, the
luxurious brazilwood on the coastline became the object of growing commercial interest for the Portuguese—as well as for the French, who, refusing to recognize the Treaty of Tordesillas, sent expeditions to harvest the
trees with the aid of the Tupinambá.[24] Because of its aggressive overseas
expansionism from Africa to the Far East, Portugal lacked the manpower
to prevent other nations, particularly France, from extracting the precious
hardwoods whose red dye, used in making the vibrant garments worn by
the French royal court, was in increasing demand by the European textile
industry (Hemming 1978, 8). The dye also was used to make illuminated
manuscripts, and the tree pulp had medicinal properties that cured ills
such as inflammation of the eye (Emert 1944, 19).

One of the woodcut illustrations in Franciscan André Thevet's *Les singularités de la France Antarctique* (The Singularities of Antarctic France),

published in 1557, depicts a Huguenot community founded off the coast of Rio de Janeiro in 1555. In the woodcut, a brazilwood tree is being chopped down by two naked Indians, while a third, attired only in headdress, carries a piece of timber on his shoulder in the background. This is not the first illustration to show the commercial importance of brazilwood. In fact, the Portuguese Cantino's world map of 1502, which is regarded as the first to illustrate the Brazilian coastline, identifies the territory as both "Vera Cruz" and "Brazil" and uses figures of large parrots and gold, green, and brown trees as symbols of its resources. Nicolau Canério also used trees on his map of Brazil (1505–1506), and brazilwood appears in a legend on charts as early as 1508 (Emert 1944, 18, 95). The Portuguese Lopo Homem-Reinel map of 1519, whose remarkable detail of the coast was no doubt provided through descriptions by Portuguese sailors and merchants, is decorated with tree-toting native Brazilians who serve as iconographic ornaments alongside drawings of tropical birds. A similar image of indigenous inhabitants appears on sixteenth-century wood carvings located in Rouen, a French city that had strong ties to the brazilwood industry (Marchant 1942, 42).

Until the measuring of longitude became an accurate science, maps tended to vary in their interpretations of where the Line of Tordesillas was located and consequently where Portuguese possession stopped and Spanish dominion began. A map drawn in approximately 1574 by the Portuguese Luis Teixeira and another by the Spaniard Lopes Velasco about the same time show very different territorial divisions. Not surprisingly, Teixeira's interpretation gives far more land to Portugal than Velasco's map—the latter of which shows the southwestern part of Brazil belonging to Spain. The Portuguese Vaz Dourado's map of 1568 is also generous in its representation of the land under Portuguese control. A much earlier and far more accurate map of Brazil and the placement of the line were produced by the Portuguese Diogo Ribeiro about 1525.[25]

Yet despite Brazil's depiction on maps as a Portuguese possession, the reality was that in the first half of the sixteenth century the French were quite successful in extracting timber from Brazil—so much so that in 1516, King Manuel sent an armada to drive off French ships. However, most French vessels did not even need to touch land, because the Tupinambá rowed out to them to initiate trade. In some ways, the French were more effective than the Portuguese in negotiating with the native inhabitants. They learned the local languages, and a few even took up residence among the Tupinambá

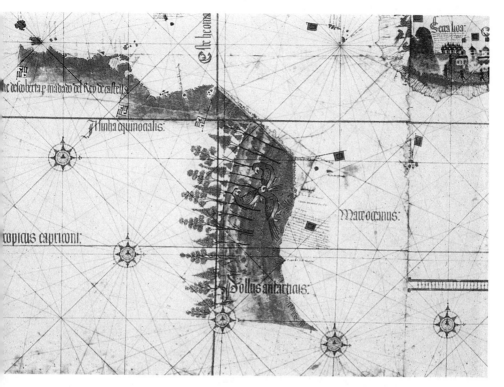

1.2 Brazil as parrots and trees on Cantino's world map (1502). Courtesy of the Lilly Library, Indiana University, Bloomington.

and practiced their customs. In exchange for carrying the heavy tree trunks, often over great distances, native Brazilians were given clothing, knives, scissors, tweezers, tools, and trinkets. Somewhat like what occurred during the American Revolution, skirmishes between the Portuguese and French in Brazil resulted in the formation of different tribal allegiances to the two European groups. For example, the Tupinambá, who inhabited the area around Rio de Janeiro, aided the French, while the Tupiniquim, whose lands were in the area of São Paulo, allied themselves with the Portuguese.

The success of France's commercial enterprise in Brazil brought about a change in priorities back in Lisbon. In 1534, Dom João III divided the territory (known and unknown) into vast strips of land called *capitanias* (captaincies), which were given to *donatários* (generally individuals of the lesser nobility, the middle class, or court favorites) in exchange for which they

1.3 Nature and commerce on Lopo Homem-Reinel's map (1519). Courtesy of the Lilly Library, Indiana University, Bloomington.

would begin the process of colonization: growing crops on *fazendas* (plantations) or *roças* (smaller farms), building towns, recruiting settlers, producing offspring, and generally expanding commerce in the New World. However, the barter system employed for so many years by the Portuguese gradually lost its appeal to the native Brazilians, who were no longer interested in exchanging hard labor for trinkets. Increasingly, Portuguese farmers and tradesmen took to enslaving indigenous populations, which, in turn, led to resistance and warfare.[26]

Battles between the Portuguese and the Indian, between the Portuguese and the French, and between rival indigenous groups created an instability that proved disastrous for the *capitanias,* nearly all of which failed by 1548. One year later, in 1549, the monarchy decided to establish a royal government in Brazil and sent Tomé de Sousa as the territory's first governor-general. That same year, the monarchy took up Pero Vaz de Caminha's suggestion and sent the first Jesuit priests to Brazil in an attempt to proselytize the native population.

Interestingly, it was neither the Portuguese nor the French who produced one of the most widely disseminated images of Brazil in the mid-sixteenth century. The person responsible was a German by the name of Hans Staden, who wrote a riveting eyewitness account of life among the native inhabitants following his capture by the Tupinambá in 1553. What made Staden's 1557 chronicle, *Warhaftig Historia und beschreibung eyner Landtschafft der wilden, nacken, grimmigen Menschenfresser Leuthen in der Newenwelt America gelegen* (True History and Description of the Land of the Wild, Naked, Fierce, Man-Eating People in the New World of the Americas, translated to Portuguese as *Viagem ao Brasil*), so engaging was his detailed account of the customs and habits of a cannibalistic people, who were made even more sensational by a series of woodcuts that accompanied the text.

It should be noted here that the woodcuts we have come to associate with the Staden text published in Marburg in 1557 and the "Great Voyages" engravings by Theodor de Bry, which will be discussed later, are not the illustrations that appeared in the Frankfurt edition also published in 1557. The Frankfurt images are more elaborate and deserve a brief commentary. For example, although Staden was writing about his capture by the Tupinambá, the Frankfurt illustrations have nothing to do with Brazil. They are largely orientalist in appearance, depicting turbaned sultans and merchants, camels and elephants, and an occasional figure that might be an Amerindian.

There is no king in Staden's account, yet the image of a king appears at different junctures in the illustrations: in one scene he is sitting in a dining room in a castle, and in another, he is outdoors with various animals. Whether it was Staden (which seems unlikely), the publisher, or someone else who incorporated these images into the text is not clear. What is certain is that at some point they were deemed appropriate and desirable for the book, and no distinction was made between the New World and Europe or the Far East.

One of the woodcuts stands in ironic juxtaposition with Staden's description of mutilations and anthropophagy in the chapter titled "How the Tupinambá Treat Their Prisoners upon Their Return" and was used on the cover of the book. It is one of the only images that has some relation to the narrative, and yet instead of a Tupinambá, it depicts a European male who looks like a sailor clothed in knee breeches, open vest, and a head band, holding a cleaver in his hand, and standing over a headless body. The illustration is all the more ironic because it includes still other European types who look like castaways, seemingly unfazed by the act of dismemberment.

In a note to his preface for the 1930 Portuguese translation of the German edition, Alberto Lofbren tells us that a Dr. Dryander proposed new woodcuts be made for the text, since the original Frankfurt ones had nothing to do with the narrative. His point is certainly true, even though the illustration of mutilation has at least a tangential relationship to the text. But one can imagine that that image in particular was troubling to Dr. Dryander. It was one thing to represent mutilation at the hands of an Indian; it was quite another to suggest that a European was capable of such an act—even though that was historically true.[27]

Among the woodcuts supplied for the Marburg edition are depictions of village life, tribes combating one another, a naked European captive (presumably Staden) in the company of his naked hosts, and the preparation (depilation, killing, cutting up, roasting) and consumption of enemy prisoners. Staden is graphic in his description of the Tupinambá's anthropophagy, and the woodcuts, though crude and lacking in detail, show grotesque scenes such as a man's body being slit up the back and a human head sticking out of the top of a roasting pot. Several other woodcuts portray the community's preparation and ingestion of the captive-meal. What is perhaps most startling about the illustrations is that, with the exception of the captive's execution, which was always carried out by a male, all oth-

Warhafftig Historia

vnnd beschreibung einer Landtschafft
der Wilden/Nacketen/Grimmigen Menschfres=
fer Leuthen/in der Newen welt America gelegen/vor vnd
nach Christi geburt im Land zu Hessen vnbekant/biß auff dise ij. nechst ver=
gangene jar/Da sie Hans Staden von Homberg auß Hessen
durch sein eygne erfarung erkant/vnd jetzund
durch den truck an tag
gibt.

Dedicirt dem Durchleuchtigen Hochgebornen Herrn/
H. Philipsen Landtgraff zu Hessen/Graff zu Catzen=
elnbogen/Dietz/Ziegenhain vnd Nidda/seinem G. H.

Mit einer vorrede D. Joh. Dryandri/genant Eychman/
Ordinarij Professoris Medici zu Marpurgk.

Inhalt des Büchlins volget nach den Vorreden.

1.4 Cover of the Frankfurt edition of Hans Staden's witness-captive account, *War-haftig Historia* (1557). Courtesy of the Newberry Library, Chicago.

1.5 Woodcut of women and children eating, in the Staden Marburg edition (1557). Courtesy of the Lilly Library, Indiana University, Bloomington.

er aspects of the cannibalist act are generally associated with women and children (who receive relatively little attention in Staden's narrative). For example, a woodcut of women and children shows them consuming the contents of two large platters placed on the ground. There is a certain irony in this picture: without knowledge of the text, one could easily interpret the image (which lacks a certain detail) as yet another representation of the idyllic life—this time of harmless naked mothers with their naked children at their side who are joyously partaking of a meal in the out-of-doors.

As we have seen, Staden's account was not the first to describe cannibalism in the New World, but his narrative certainly had the greatest impact of any of its time. Ultimately, the internecine feuds between tribal groups, their participation in the Franco-Portuguese struggle, and their resistance to slavery resulted in another image of the indigenous people as savages, in the minds of many Europeans, despite the violence and brutality practiced by the Portuguese and French in their battle to profit from the land. Moreover, woodcuts such as those in Staden's book often circulated independently of the written text, and the dissemination of images of naked beings engaged in anthropophagy became even wider. By mid-century, a discourse had emerged based on reports and woodcuts of savages and cannibalism, and this discourse appeared alongside accounts and images of docile residents in a tropical Eden.

Perhaps nowhere were the contradictory images in evidence more than in an engraving titled *Figure des brèsiliens* from a 1551 French manuscript that describes in detail a simulacrum of Brazilian indigenous life constructed in 1550 on the banks of the Seine in the city of Rouen.[28] The occasion for this lavish construction was King Henri II and Queen Catherine's official arrival and entry into the city. Apparently it was common for towns to stage reenactments of significant historical events to honor the arrival of the royal court. In this case, it appears that Rouen chose to fashion a unique

1.6 A Tupi village in Rouen (1551). Courtesy of the Newberry Library, Chicago.

spectacle based on its special relationship with an exotic land that served its (and the king's) commercial interests.

The spectacle required considerable investment: fifty native Brazilians were imported for the event; foreign-looking trees and shrubs were planted to simulate a tropical forest; two complete Indian villages were constructed; 250 French sailors and prostitutes role-played in the nude in order to fill out the native cast; and parrots and monkeys were released into the faux-wilderness set. In his essay "Strange Things, Gross Terms, Curious Customs: The Rehearsal of Cultures in the Late Renaissance" (1988), Steven Mullaney describes the various scenes portrayed in the 1551 engraving, which is the only pictorial representation of the spectacle. Most interesting for our purposes are his descriptions of a man and woman who "strike a pose that recalls period illustrations of Genesis" (71); a few others who are walking hand in hand or engaged in making love; and many more who are making war with clubs, spears, and bows and arrows. Mullaney observes:

> Along with its version of Edenic pastoral [the engraving] reveals a land of un-biblical license and enterprise. Some of the couples are partially obscured in the underbrush, taking advantage of the cover to indulge in relatively unabashed foreplay; men are hewing trees, then carrying them to the river to build primitive barks. The soft primitivism of biblical tradition coexists with a harder interpretation of pagan culture, akin to the portraits of barbaric life composed by Piero di Cosimo. (71)

As for the various representations of warring tribes in the engraving, Mullaney informs us that a battle between two rival indigenous groups was staged upon Henri's arrival and that in the course of the simulated struggle one of the villages was burned to the ground. An encore performance of the battle was staged the next day in honor of Catherine's arrival, during which the second village was torched and destroyed (72). In his book *Cannibals* (1997), Frank Lestringant comments on a watercolor miniature of the spectacle that shows Henri observing a battle staged between French and Portuguese ships on the Seine. He also calls attention to a verse that appears alongside the miniature, which celebrates the French king's rule: "Thy power to the cannibals extends: / Faithless to others, they remain our friends, / And in those islands we may safely dwell" (42).[29]

Whether it was for religious purposes alone or because the French had fostered such close alliances with indigenous groups that they rigorously challenged Portugal's political and economic sovereignty or because there were increasing reports and illustrations circulating about pagan acts in the New World, Dom João III sent the first group of Jesuits to Brazil to begin their crusade to convert the Indians to Christianity. In a letter written to his reverend superior in the spring of 1549, the Jesuit Manoel da Nóbrega was optimistic about the new land, stating that it was "good and healthy" and that the Jesuits themselves were in good health, in fact, "in better health than when [they] left [Lisbon]" (1988, 75). His first impressions of the indigenous community were also quite positive. According to Nóbrega, the natives were eager to learn Christian doctrine, and they wanted to be like the Europeans (72).[30]

Nóbrega's observations seemed to agree with Caminha's earlier remarks about the docility of the native Brazilians and the potential ease of Christian conversion:

> If they hear the call for mass, they respond and . . . do everything, kneel, beat their chests, [and] raise their hands to the Heavens. One of their principals is already learning to read and he takes lessons with great care every day, and in two days he learned the entire ABCs. And we have taught him to cross himself, and he takes in everything eagerly. He says that he wants to be a Christian and no longer eat human flesh, nor have more than one wife, and other things . . . These are people without any knowledge of God. They have idols and do everything that they tell them to do. (72–73)

Ironically, Nóbrega's accounts of Europeans in the New World were less positive: "they live in mortal sin, and there isn't a one of them that doesn't have many black [indigenous] women by whom they have many children and it is a great evil" (72). It has long been established that because Portuguese women did not participate in the early colonization of Brazil, interracial relationships between European males and Amerindian females were common, and many mixed-race children were born. Nóbrega condemned the colonizers' libidinous acts,[31] and he encouraged his superior to send Portuguese women—even if they were *erradas* (wayward), stating that "they will marry well" (80)—but the monarchy did little or nothing to respond to the Jesuit's complaint.[32] Regardless of how it came about, active procreation meant more royal subjects in the colony, and this fact alone was enough to please the Crown.

Nóbrega's letters praised the new land and its people. The air was good, few of the people fell ill, and there were delicious fruits and excellent fish in abundance. He commented on the unusual and plentiful wildlife, "almost all of which was unknown to Pliny" (89), and he described the extraordinary variety of herbs—far more diverse than what could be found in Spain. With regard to the territory's size, he wrote in terms that were clearly *ufanista* in spirit: "The region is so large that, they say, of the three parts into which the world is divided, [Brazil] would occupy two parts" (89). His descriptions of the Brazilian natives focused on their innocence, their warlike activities (which, he was quick to point out, were based on blood vengeance and not greed), their ritual of bringing captives to live in their communities before killing and consuming them; and their practice of burying the dead in an upright position with a clean hammock and plates of food placed on top of the grave (91, 100).

Nóbrega acknowledged that the process of religious conversion was not without its challenges and problems; he articulated this most effectively in 1554 in his *Diálogo sobre a conversão do gentio* (Dialogue on the Conversion of the Indian), an important early work of Brazilian literature about the need to find unity of purpose between the often antagonistic lay and religious groups in the colonial community.[33] In 1550, he wrote about a war being waged by a former convert who convinced a tribe in the interior that the governor-general was out to enslave or kill them and that the Jesuits were using conversion to turn more of them into slaves (104)—all of which ultimately proved to be true. Tensions also steadily grew between settlers and the Jesuits because of the latter's desire to spare the Indians from the labor forced upon them by colonizers who, according to Nóbrega, were lazy and practiced all kinds of vices (110). At the same time, the Jesuits were not loathe to use converts to tend their missions' crops and to carry out other tasks. Salvation came at a price—as the renegade convert's acts made clear. And while Nóbrega and other Jesuits condemned the enforced slavery of Indians by the settlers, he was not hesitant to ask his superior in Portugal to send African slaves to work in the missions (130).

In later letters, Nóbrega expounded upon the sins of the settlers, the difficulty of retaining converts in the mission, the desirability of converting as many of the children of the enslaved as possible, the need for more white women in the colonies, and the continuing battles among Europeans under the command of a later governor-general, Mem de Sá. In one of his final letters, addressed to the Infante Dom Henrique in 1560, he described Mem de Sá's expedition to Rio de Janeiro with the Portuguese allies, the Tupiniquim, and the subsequent Portuguese victory over the French, who had built settlements in the region. Nóbrega was part of that expedition, and he was pleased to report the victory over the Calvinists, the French Huguenots, and their Indian allies, who were living in a fortified settlement called Fort Coligny on an island in Guanabara Bay. Early residents of that community included the French Admiral Nicolas Durand de Villegaignon, the founder of the island colony, and religious leaders Jean de Léry and André Thevet, all of whom wrote about life in the New World's "Antarctic France."

In 1556, Villegaignon had obtained permission from Henri II, by way of the admiral of France, Gaspard de Coligny, and the cardinal of Lorraine, to establish a colony that would be a religious haven for Catholics and Protestants alike.[34] Apparently Henri II was favorably disposed to the request because it opened the possibility of increased brazilwood trade between France and Brazil (Whatley 1990, xx), and French Protestant theologian and Reformed Church founder John Calvin sent a group of missionaries to the island community to provide instruction. But just as the island experiment got under way, fierce theological debates broke out between the two groups—debates that were exacerbated by Villegaignon's tyrannical leadership. Lacking material support from the indigenous population and with the Portuguese pressing for control, Villegaignon ultimately abandoned Fort Coligny, which came under Portuguese control in 1560—as noted by Padre Nóbrega in his letter of that same year.

Villegaignon's letter to Calvin is a fascinating document: it makes clear the Huguenot community's general lack of preparedness for living in Antarctic France, as well as Villegaignon's personal dissatisfaction with the land and particularly the native inhabitants:

> The country was all wilderness, and untilled; there were no houses, nor roofs, nor any use of wheat. On the contrary, there were wild and savage people, remote from all courtesy and humanity, utterly different from us in their way of doing things and in their upbringing; without religion, nor any knowledge of honesty or virtue, or of what is just or unjust; so that it seemed to me that we had fallen among beasts bearing a human countenance. (In Léry 1990, xlix)[35]

Among those who accompanied Villegaignon to Brazil was the Franciscan friar André Thevet, who served as the community's chaplain. However, after just ten weeks in Brazil, he returned to France, where he published

Les singularités in 1557—the same year that Staden's captive-witness account appeared. Thevet's book had a tremendous impact on readers not only because of its detailed descriptions of New World inhabitants and their customs, which included accounts of cannibal rituals, but also because of several woodcuts and the first engravings or *taille-douce* images ever to appear in a Paris publication (E. Pinto 1944, 19). Thevet was exceedingly proud of having contracted the finest engravers from Flanders to illustrate his text, and the book sold well despite reservations by critics that his narratives were exaggerated if not outright fanciful.

In his preface to the Portuguese translation of the book, Estevão Pinto notes that critics especially objected to Thevet's literary pedanticism or attempts to make matters of little consequence seem polemical, his excessive quotes from Greek and Latin philosophers, and his lack of common sense (20). At the same time, Thevet's ethnographic descriptions of indigenous life, as well as his commentaries about animals such as the *preguiça* (sloth) and *javali* (wild boar), various birds (Thevet apparently gave the large-beaked toucan its name), and plant life were instructive and highly regarded.

In his book, Thevet remarked on the cordial welcome the Huguenots received from the New World inhabitants, whom he referred to as "savages" throughout the text and who offered the a range of local foods, including *farinha*, a diet staple made from manioc. He compares the banquet of food to the feast described by Virgil in his description of Dido's offerings to the Trojans—except that the Trojans had a "good and old wine," while the French were only given drinking water (163–164). Accompanying this account is an artful drawing of one of the primary foodstuffs of the country, a large, leaf-covered manioc root whose design clearly resembles a phallus. In the following chapter, Thevet discusses the abundance of fish in the waters off the island, including "monstrous" species such as the *panapaná*. The accompanying engraving of this unusual fish must have impressed readers. Like the manioc root, the *panapaná* drawing takes up an entire page; its two blunt-shaped heads are attached to a long body with fins that is distinctly phallic in shape. Other engravings of a long potato, a huge pineapple, and a toucan with an immense beak are similarly phallic in design. It is as if nature were reigned by a large and potent penis, which was also a metaphor for the uninhibited nature of the indigenous community.

In other discussions of the native inhabitants, Thevet seems to repeat Pero Vaz de Caminha's commentary when he stated that they had neither

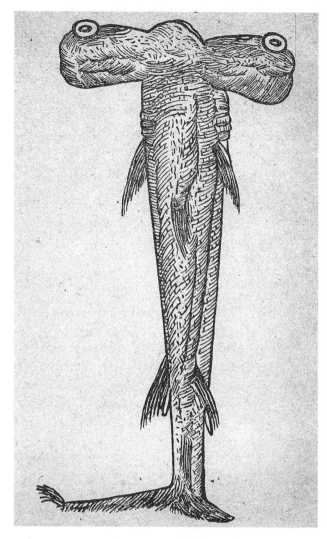

1.7 The *panapaná* in Thevet's *Les singularités* (1557). Courtesy of the Lilly Library, Indiana University, Bloomington.

faith nor religion; he further contended that they had neither law nor civilization (culture). Later on, he contradicted himself by describing the Indians' belief in the god Tupã and commenting that divine representatives among the tribe were known as *pajés*. At one point in the narrative, Thevet gives thanks to his God for his being given the ability to reason, and he expresses even deeper gratitude for being of a race distinct from that of these "brutes" (175).

Although Thevet's accounts and judgments make clear his uneasiness with the indigenous people and their "barbarous" ways, he does challenge certain popular beliefs based on iconic representations of the "savages" as hirsute beings:

> Many believe, unwittingly, that these people, whom we call savages, have bodies covered with hair like bears, deer and lions because they live almost like animals in the woods and fields. And this is the way they [outsiders] paint them on their rich canvases. In other words, whoever wishes to describe a savage must attribute him with abundant hair from his toes to the top of his head—a characteristic as much his as the color black is to the raven.
>
> Such an opinion is entirely false, although some individuals, whom I have had occasion to hear, obstinately insist and vow that savages are hairy. If they are so certain of this fact it is because they have never seen a savage. But this notion is the general consensus.
>
> I, however, who have seen them, know and confidently affirm the opposite. The indigenous inhabitants . . . leave the maternal womb as beautiful and clean as children born in Europe. If with the passage of time hair appears on certain parts of the body, as it happens with any person—they pull it out with their fingernails, maintaining only the hair on their heads. This is a custom to which they attach much honor—the men as much as the women. (191)

This passage is intriguing because while Thevet decries the falseness of popular and painterly images of native Brazilians as hairy beings, he offers equally questionable visual representations of the native population. This is especially true in the engravings entitled "Tobacco Smoker and Maker of Fire," in which the male figure, who is smoking a large, phallic-looking roll of tobacco leaves, closely resembles a figure out of Greek mythology, and "Massacre of Prisoners" and "Amazons," in which indigenous women resemble Greek warriors with bows, arrows, and shields.[36] The engraving "The Preparation of Cauim" looks more like a pre-Raphaelite drawing in which women with long, wavy tresses bend gracefully over a kettle while two males in the background resemble Roman senators (albeit unclothed) in private conversation.

Although Thevet is interested in authenticity, the Flanders artists whom he had employed had never been to Brazil and were as unknowledgeable as

1.8 Amazons in Thevet (1557). Courtesy of the Lilly Library, Indiana University, Bloomington.

the painters whom Thevet critiques. Yet unlike the 1505 graphic representations of the New World, these have a greater authenticity if only because they depict the native inhabitants in their nakedness. There is also a definite distinction in the way the illustrations portray the naked body. Several of the illustrations, like the ones described in the paragraph above, make clear that for some Europeans artists the naked body, regardless of whose it was, needed to conform to notions drawn from canonical art. Thus, certain figures in Thevet's book are classical in design, with muscular thighs and buttocks and long, flowing tresses. In "The Smoker of Tobacco" engraving, the naked "maker of fire" resembles a satyr out of Greek mythology. A few more crudely drawn illustrations, like those in Staden's text, depart somewhat from this style of representation. In "The Harvest," naked men and woman are more narrow than muscular in physique, and there is a clear attempt to draw a comparison between the human form with its headdress and the birds and trees with their feathers and fronds that appear in the surrounding natural setting.

One of the most powerful and detailed illustrations is a head-and-shoulders portrait of the Tupinambá leader Cunhambebe, whom Thevet describes as the "most feared of the country's principals" (318). He adds: "This leader considers himself so powerful that he passes the time recounting his great feats, considering it the highest honor and glory to have decimated and devoured numerous people—some five thousand, as he affirms. There is no human memory of such a cruelty" (320). Perhaps it is because Cunhambebe's bodily lower stratum is not shown, but the illustration is very different from others in the book. He appears with the executioner's club in hand—a pose similar to a king with his scepter—yet his large eyes with dramatic dark circles underneath have a vaguely hostile look. The portrait

1.9 Tupinambá leader Cunhambebe, in Thevet (1557). Courtesy of the Lilly Library, Indiana University, Bloomington.

is even more unusual because of the heavy eyebrows—a feature that was rare for native Brazilians, as they were very particular about removing all facial hair. The artist has also given him a slightly bulbous nose, while a round plug juts out from his chin just beneath his fleshy lips. He is bald, and his furrowed brow is partially covered by a crown made of short feathers; an earring dangles from a hole in his ear, and a short shell necklace is wound twice around his strong-looking neck. The portrait makes clear that he is the dominant force in his land, for even the mountains and trees in the engraving appear small and subordinate to his presence.

An equally compelling engraving depicts a *sariguê* (a marsupial) that looks more like a mythical creature with its gargoyle-like head, its long and exaggeratedly narrow back, and its enormous plume-like tail (329). But while the image suggests a fierce and fantastic creature, Thevet's description shows that there is little connection between word and image: "[The animal] is a little larger than a kitten, its fur is fine like velvet with gray, black and white markings. Its feet look like those of an aquatic bird" (327).

The part of the book that most captivated readers was Thevet's description of the battles between enemy tribes and the cannibal ritual following the capture of prisoners. In one of the few references to Villegaignon, Thevet informs the reader that the French admiral, unlike the Portuguese monarchy, forbade under penalty of death the coupling of his followers with the local populations, stating that "it was an act unworthy of Christians" (254). It is not clear if Villegaignon's law was meant to protect the local inhabitants or simply another instance of his puritanism and racial intolerance. The engravings that accompany this part of the text are fascinating in their grotesqueness.

In the foreground of *Scene of Cannibalism,* an Indian male chops apart a headless corpse while an Indian woman pulls out a long piece of entrails from the body cavity. In the background various activities are taking place: two men are roasting body parts over a rack while two other men carry the severed leg of another captive, whose decapitated head is the object of interest of two small children. There is a certain irony in what is being illustrated, which harks back to one of the original woodcuts mentioned earlier. Because of their partially shorn heads and European features, the males who are hacking, cooking, and carrying body parts look more like monks or friars who just happen to be naked than like representatives of the Amerindian population.

1.10 Cannibalistic activity in Thevet (1557). Courtesy of the Lilly Library, Indiana University, Bloomington.

Despite the skeptical critical reception of *Les singularités,* the book was popular with readers, and poets of the period hailed Thevet as the new Jason of the Argonauts and modern-day Ulysses (Whatley 1990, xx). Nearly twenty years later, in 1575, he published *La cosmographie universelle,* a revised version of his first book that contains an added commentary in which he attacks the Calvinists for conspiring against Villegaignon and for causing the collapse of the religious experiment.

Among the Calvinist missionaries who were sent in 1556 to participate in the island experiment was Jean de Léry, who was dubbed the "traveling Montaigne" (E. Pinto 1944, 29) after the publication in 1578 of his *Histoire d'un voyage au Brésil,* one of the most important accounts of New World colonization in French. Following the execution of four Calvinists by Villegaignon for purportedly plotting against him, Léry and the other Calvinists fled the island colony and settled on the coast, where they lived among the Tupinambá. Léry stayed there for nearly a year, until 1558, when he returned to France to find Thevet's *Les singularités* in print. Published twenty years after his own Brazilian adventure, Léry's *Histoire* partly rebuts Thevet's work in a long preface that charges the friar with making false accusations against the Calvinists. Léry further claims that Thevet's revisions in *La cosmographie* are even more fanciful and fallacious than his original accounts in *Les singularités*.[37]

Léry's book is remarkable for its detailed descriptions of the island experiment and his firsthand account of life among the native Brazilians—parts of which seem to have been influenced by earlier writers, including his Franciscan rival Thevet. Like Staden and later Thevet, Léry also refutes the notion that the "savages" are covered with hair.[38] Léry reported, as did Vespucci several decades earlier, that the native Brazilians enjoyed an unusual longevity, and he discussed many topics that already had been covered by Staden—not all that surprisingly, as both men lived among the native Brazilians for considerable periods of time. However, Léry's rhetorical style is more engaging than that of Thevet or Staden. He is especially adept at drawing readers into his remarkable narrative, helping them to imagine what New World inhabitants looked like through detailed descriptions and an accompanying engraving:

> [I]f you would picture to yourself a savage . . ., you may imagine in the first place a naked man, well formed and proportioned in his limbs, with all of the hair on his body plucked out; his hair shaved in the fashion I have described; the lips and cheeks slit, with pointed stones or green stones set in them; his ears pierced, with pendants in the holes; his body painted; his thighs and legs blackened with the dye that they make from the *genipap* fruit that I mentioned; and with necklaces made up of innumerable little pieces of shell that they call *vignol*. . . . To fill out this plate, we have put near this Tupinambá one of his women, who, in their customary way, is holding her child in a cotton scarf, with the child holding on to her side with both legs. Next to the three is a cotton bed made like a fish net, hung in the air, which is how they sleep in the country. There is also the fruit that they call *ananas* [pineapple], which, as I shall describe hereafter, is one of the best produced in this land of Brazil.
>
> For the second contemplation of a savage, remove all the flourishes described above, and after rubbing him with a glutinous gum, cover his whole torso, arms and legs with little feathers minced fine, like red-dyed down; when you have made him artificially hairy with this fuzzy down, you can imagine what a fine fellow he is.

[. . .] Finally, if you add . . . the *maraca* in his hand, the plumed harness that they call *araroye* on his hips, and his rattles made of fruit around his legs, you will then see him . . . equipped as he is when he dances, leaps, drinks and capers about.

As for the rest of the devices that the savages use to bedeck and adorn their bodies . . ., you would need several illustrations to represent them well, and even then you could not convey their appearance without adding painting, which would require a separate book. (Léry 1990, 62, 64)

The illustration that complements Léry's description is a full-length portrait of an Edenic family that appears loving and contented. Only the male is displayed in full nakedness, and although his head with its shorn hair and adornments have an indigenous look, his body and its pose are reminiscent of Michelangelo's David. The woman and child are equally interesting: her body is largely concealed behind the man's; nonetheless, we can see part of a plump leg and her European features and light, wavy tresses. Like her, the chubby child in her arms looks more European than indigenous, and his pose is classic—almost religious, as he gazes at the viewer with his hand gently cupped under his mother's chin.

Although not as puritanical as Villegaignon or Thevet, Léry also wanted to correct the official record about the libidinousness purportedly provoked by the nakedness of the Indian women. He observes: "While there is ample cause to judge that, beyond the immodesty of it, seeing these women naked would serve as a predictable enticement to concupiscence; yet, to report what was commonly seen at the time, this crude nakedness in such a woman is much less alluring than one might expect" (Léry 1990, 121). The comment may have been true for the Calvinist but certainly not for the Portuguese, who, according to Nóbrega, were drawn to and mated with as many local women as possible. Even the illustrations in Léry's own text contradict his assertion, although like most of the engravings of sixteenth-century Brazil, they were at least as much the product of imagination as a reflection of any reality.

Léry is especially effective in describing the rituals of honor and blood vengeance that involved anthropophagy. Personal anecdotes appear throughout his account of the capture, execution, and ingestion of the enemy. Emphasis is on the ritualistic aspect of the event: both captive and captor performed a series of acts and pronounced words that were expected

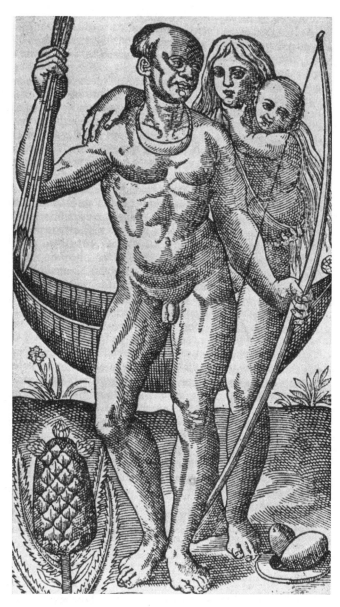

1.11 Tupi family in Léry's *Histoire* (1578)

by both parties. Léry recalls attempts by himself and other Frenchmen to save both Portuguese and indigenous captives. His comments are interesting on this matter and show that despite the war between the French and Portuguese at the time, Europeans often banded together against the Indian. In fact, once the French were driven out of Brazil in 1560, the Portuguese attacked and killed not only the French allies, the Tupinambá, but also the Tupiniquins, their own allies against the French. As for indigenous captives, Léry recounts that he once saved a woman by purchasing her from her enemy-captor. But when he told her that he would ensure her safety by sending her to Europe, she told him she preferred the honor of being a prisoner and a swift execution over a prolonged, empty life in a foreign land (201).

What distinguishes Léry from others at the time who wrote about cannibalism was his observation that European readers should not be overly judgmental about descriptions of anthropophagy and other indigenous practices. In his view, Europeans, out of greed or intolerance, regularly engaged in atrocities far worse than cannibalism:

> In the first place, if you consider in all candor what our big usurers do, sucking blood and marrow, and eating everyone alive—widows, orphans and other poor people, whose throats it would be better to cut once and for all, than to make them linger in misery—you will say that they are even more cruel than the savages I speak of. . . .
>
> Furthermore, if it comes to the brutal action of really (as one says) chewing and devouring human flesh, have we not found people in these regions over here, even among those who bear the name of Christian, both in Italy and elsewhere, who, not content with having cruelly put to death their enemies, have been unable to slack their bloodthirst except by eating their livers and their hearts? And without going further, what did we see in France? (I am French and it grieves me to say it.) During the bloody tragedy that began in Paris on the twenty-fourth of August 1572— . . . among other acts horrible to recount, which were perpetrated at that time throughout the kingdom, the fat of human bodies (which, in ways more barbarous than those of the savages were butchered in Lyon after being pulled out of the Saône)—was it not publicly sold at auction to the highest bidder?—an act far more barbarous than that of the savages? . . .
>
> There are thousands alive today who beheld these things never before heard of among people anywhere, and the books about them, printed long since, will bear witness to posterity. (132)

The Jesuit José de Anchieta, who arrived in Brazil in 1553, seemed to agree with Léry's assessment in his *Informação do Brasil e de suas capitanias* (Information About Brazil and Its Captaincies), published in 1582. Author of the first grammar of the Tupi language as well as poetry and plays called *autos* and written in Tupi, Anchieta was impressed by the valor and honor of the indigenous peoples in war, in contrast to the cruel and inhumane ways of the European: "They [the Indians] are naturally inclined to kill, but they are not cruel: Ordinarily they do not torment their enemies, and if they do not kill them in battle, they treat them very well, and then content themselves with striking the enemy's head with a club, which is an easy death. At times they kill with a single blow or at least they knock their enemies out. If they practice any cruelty, even rarely, it's because of the example given to them by the Portuguese and French" (1988, 337).

It may be interesting to speculate a bit here why Nóbrega, Anchieta, and Léry were so eager to take up the cause of native Brazilians against the European settlers. On the one hand, we know that Portuguese Jesuits were constantly writing to their superiors in Lisbon about their success in converting Indians—which became their main reason and purpose for being in Brazil.[39] The letters of Anchieta and Nóbrega take pains to argue that any pagan custom practiced by the Indian was neither an obstacle to conversion nor any worse than the far more lascivious and cruel acts of their colonizer compatriots. Anchieta's plays are all about the goodness to be achieved by Indians who relinquish their old ways, a lesson that scores of them followed—unlike the Portuguese colonists, who tended to ignore the Jesuits' teachings on Good and Evil.[40] We know, too, that the Jesuits became increasingly at odds with the settlers, who looked to the indigenous peoples as free slave labor for their farms and plantations. Proselytization also meant that new converts would be "free" to work for the missions.

On the other hand, Léry's favorable attitude toward the Indian serves to highlight his much larger differences and disagreements with his compatriot enemies Villegaignon and Thevet. Moreover, the illustrations in Léry's book focus on the noble and even docile character of the native population. In addition to the family portrait, there are engravings that show two males posed with the traditional maraca, bow and arrow, and club; the "greeting of tears" practiced by the indigenous women upon the arrival of an outsider; and a "sickroom" scene with various women crouching and crying or embracing one another. The only image of violence in any of the illustra-

1.12 Two Tupi males in Léry (1578)

tions is the dead man's head that appears on the ground and at the side of the two males. In a corresponding engraving, two men are performing a dance. The emphasis on docility in this image seems evident: one man seems to be leaning down to pet a monkey that sits at his feet, while the other has turned his head in mid-step to gaze at a parrot on a perch.

One of the best-known defenses of the Brazilian native and the anthropophagic act was written by Michel de Montaigne in a 1580 essay titled "Des cannibales" (Of Cannibals). Montaigne takes a proto-Enlightenment position in this essay, criticizing those who "cling to vulgar opinions" and judge things from "common rumour" as opposed to "the light of reason" (1927, 202). His main argument is that "sophisticated men" who have traveled and lived in Brazil always elaborate or "glose" what they see and "never describe things as they really are" (204). He based his critique on what he had read about Brazil, in comparison with what he had learned from a "simple" houseguest who resided in Brazil for some years:

> Now we need either a very truthful man, or one so simple that he has not the art of building up and giving an air of probability to fictions, and is wedded to no theory. Such was my man; and he has besides at different times brought several sailors and traders to see me, whom he had known on that voyage. So I shall content myself with his information, without troubling myself about what the cosmographers may say about it. (202–203)

There is little doubt that Montaigne's attack here and elsewhere is directed toward André Thevet and his *La cosmographie,* which features descriptions of a barbarous people accompanied by sensationalized iconic representations of indigenous warfare and anthropophagy. In critiquing "cosmographers," Montaigne rejected all references to barbarism, arguing that the word was regularly employed to describe "that which does not fit with our usages" (203). He further stated that, based on what he has heard about the new land, he saw "nothing barbarous or uncivilized" (203) about it and regretted that Plato, who regarded all things produced by Nature or chance to be the greatest and most beautiful, had no knowledge of nations such as Brazil:

> [I]t seems to me that what we have learned by contact with those nations surpasses not only all the beautiful colors in which the poets have depicted the golden age, and all their ingenuity in inventing a happy state of man, but also

the conceptions and desires of Philosophy herself. They were incapable of imagining so pure and native a simplicity, as that which we see by experience; nor could they have believed that human society could have been maintained with so little human artifice and solder. This is a nation, I should say to Plato, which has no manner of traffic; no knowledge of letters; no sciences of numbers; no names of magistrate or statesman; no use for slaves; neither wealth nor poverty; no contracts; no successions; no partitions; no occupation but that of idleness; only a general respect of parents; no clothing; no agriculture; no metals; no use of wine or corn. The very words denoting falsehood, treachery, dissimulation, avarice, envy, detraction, pardon, unheard of. How far removed from this perfection would he find the ideal republic he imagined! (206)

Montaigne marveled at the obstinacy with which the Indians fought their wars and the valor of both the captor and the captive, the latter of whom was "dispatch[ed] with a sword" and then roasted and eaten "not as one might suppose for nourishment, as the ancient Scythians used to do, but to signify an extreme revenge" (209). Similar to Léry and Anchieta, he blamed the European (in his case, he focused exclusively on the Portuguese, who by this time had ousted the French) for far greater atrocities that the local inhabitants then proceeded to imitate. Montaigne specifically mentioned burying captives up to the waist, shooting the upper part of their bodies full of arrows, and then hanging them. He goes on to state:

I think there is more barbarity in eating a live than a dead man, in tearing on the rack and torturing the body of a man still full of feeling, in roasting him piecemeal and giving him to be bitten and mangled by dogs and swine (as we have not only read, but seen within fresh memory, not between old enemies, but between neighbors and fellow citizens, and, what is worse, under the cloak of piety and religion), than in roasting and eating him after he is dead. . . . We may therefore well call those people barbarians in respect to the rules of reason, but not in respect to ourselves, who surpass them in every kind of barbarity. (210)

As the Brazilian literary historian Afrânio Peixoto observed in his *Panorama da literatura brasileira* (1940), which includes a transcription and translation of indigenous lyrics that appear in Montaigne's essay, Montaigne constructed an image of the Indian as noble savage some two centuries prior to Rousseau (27). This image was not unique, for as we have seen, Léry was also sympathetic toward his indigenous hosts, and he and earlier writers such as Caminha, Nóbrega, and Anchieta often regarded the Indian as superior to the European colonizer in certain customs and habits. But despite the various portrayals of Indians as a simple people whose violence was directly related to notions of honor and valor and despite the prominence of an author like Montaigne, those who could read and even more who saw the illustrations were increasingly inclined to imagine Brazil as a land of naked savages who spoke strange languages and indiscriminately committed heinous acts, which included eating local and foreign enemies. The place that was once represented by trees and parrots and was often referred to as "the Land of Parrots" was now better known as the land of eaters of human flesh.[41] Diogo Homem's 1568 map of Brazil features the words "Cannibals" and "Anthropophagic land" in large letters. The main figure on the map is a man grilling a leg over a fire, while other body parts hang from a rack. The only other illustrations are of a few trees and a monkey.

Similarly, narratives became even more preoccupied with the idea of the fierce man-eater, as seen in sixteenth-century Portuguese chronicler Pero de Magalhães Gândavo's *Tratado da terra do Brasil*:

> One of the things that is most repugnant to mankind about these Indians, and by which they seem to represent the extreme opposite of other men, has to do with the great and excessive cruelties that they practice on anyone who falls into their hands, as long as he does not belong to their fold. For not only do they impose a cruel death . . . but to satisfy themselves after this, they proceed to eat the flesh and carry out crudities so diabolical that in these they even surpass brute animals, which have neither reason nor were born to perform acts of mercy. (1995, 113)

Gândavo also remarked on the extreme fierceness of the Aimoré tribe, who resided in wooded areas near Ilhéus in southern Bahia and who, like guerilla warriors, ambushed unsuspecting settlers and other Indians. He goes on to discuss still another community called the Tapuias, who, he said, carried out rituals even more vile than anthropophagy: "When someone becomes so ill that death seems a possibility, the person's father, or mother, or brothers, or sisters, or other close relatives, kill him with their own hands . . . And the worst is that after this they roast, cook, and eat him, saying . . . that there is no more honorable burial that they can give him than ingesting him, thereby giving him eternal shelter in their intestines" (119–120).

While images of indigenous communities tended to fluctuate between

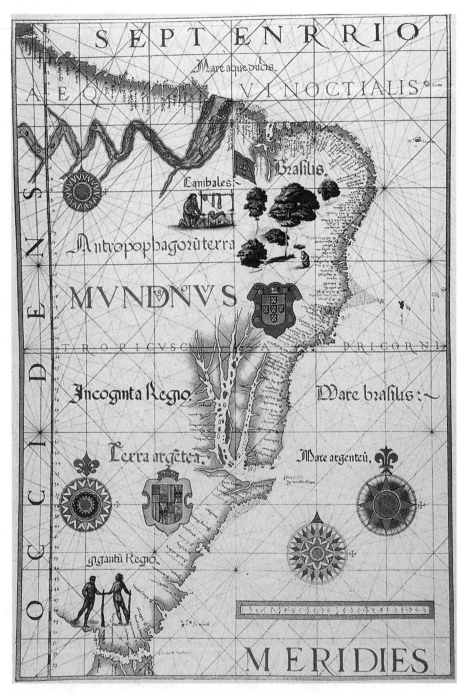

1.13 Land of cannibals, Diogo Homem (1568). Courtesy of the Lilly Library, Indiana University, Bloomington.

the docile and the demonic, the land continued to fascinate those like the Jesuit Fernão Cardim. Recently arrived from Lisbon in 1583, he sent glowing letters back home to his reverend superior: "It's a thing of great joy to see the many flowing rivers and fresh forests with the tallest trees imaginable that are green year-round and filled with the most beautiful birds" (1980, 146). Cardim produced two tracts that are encyclopedic in their information about the land and the people. One calls attention to "some notable things that can be found on land as well as in the sea"—a phrase that serves as subtitle for the piece. The work is divided into twenty-five sections that cover a range of topics, including animals, poisonous and non-poisonous snakes, birds, fruit trees that have medicinal properties, fish, shellfish, and freshwater rivers. Each section is subdivided and gives information on specific varieties or kinds of trees, fish, and so forth, and nearly everything is described in positive terms—even venomous snakes like the *igbigboboca,* which is deadly but "very beautiful," and the *jararacas,* which give off a "good and fragrant scent" (31), along with rats, which are "tasty, the large ones similar to rabbits" (29).

One of the most important sixteenth-century writings on Brazil is Gabriel Soares de Sousa's *Tratado descritivo do Brasil em 1587.* Sousa had spent several prosperous years in Bahia as a *senhor de engenho* (plantation owner). Beginning in 1580, Portugal was governed by the Spanish King Felipe II, and Sousa went to Madrid, where he waited six years for official concessions to a silver mine in Brazil (Moisés 1976, 404). During that time he began writing a treatise arguing for greater royal investment in the new territories. Its *ufanista* language was undoubtedly a means to achieve the desired *alvíssara* from the king: "All the care that Your Majesty sends to this new realm for repair and improvement will be well used, for it is capable of building a great empire . . . [It will be] one of the States of the world because it has more than one thousand leagues of coastline . . . whose land is very fertile and healthy, whose good airs are fresh and cleansed, and whose waters are cold and refreshing" (Sousa 1971, 39). Sousa praised the many large and safe ports; the abundance of timber, which exceeded that in any other part of the world; the animals, fish, fruits, and sugar that rivaled those of Spain; and the plentiful precious metals and stones.

Interestingly, the court historian Damião de Góis—who, unlike João de Barros before him and Gândavo shortly after, never traveled to Brazil—recounted the discovery of Brazil in far greater detail in his *Crônica do felicíssi-*

mo rei D. Manuel (Chronicle of the Very Felicitous King D. Manuel) in 1566. There is no question that he was well served by documents in the Torre do Tombo in Lisbon, where he was curator for several years; but he was also familiar with Staden's and Thevet's texts, and his work exemplifies the borrowings that often took place when writing about the New World. He was a consummate practitioner of the *ufanista* style, as can be seen in his description of "Santa Cruz": "The land is very lush, very temperate and with very good airs, very healthy, so much so that the majority of the people die from old age rather than sickness. It has many great rivers and many good ports, and many sources of very good waters" (1926, 1:119).

However, Góis's lengthy and detailed description of the inhabitants is often less than complimentary; in this sense, the affinities with Staden and Thevet are greater than those with the Jesuits, Léry, or Montaigne. Of course by the time Góis was writing, the Portuguese had already defeated the French in Rio, and they were well on their way to displacing and eradicating the indigenous population, who proved a less hardy and resilient workforce than the slaves imported from Africa. In a form that Hayden White has called "self-definition by negation" (1978, 152), Góis's description of the Amerindians becomes a litany of what they did not do: "The people of this province are pale in color and they have long, straight black hair, no beards and are of medium stature. They are so barbarous that they believe in nothing, nor do they worship, nor do they know how to read or write. They have no churches or idols of any kind before whom they worship. They have no law, no weights or measurements, nor money, nor king, nor master" (Góis 1926, 1:119).

At another point in the narrative, Góis appears to take a different approach by commenting on Amerindians' accuracy with bow and arrow. He adds an eyewitness account of an event that occurred in a Portuguese village in 1513. Here three natives performed their archery skills for King Manuel— a performance far less elaborate than the one showcased in Rouen, but still a good example of the entertainment that New World "exotics" provided to royals and others. At a later juncture, Góis returns to the topic of their extraordinary talent, but what he formerly presented as simply a remarkable display of accuracy and skill is now linked to the destiny of the empire:

> They are so dexterous in shooting that, in their wars with the Portuguese, they aim their arrows just around the guns. For this reason [the Portuguese] have

taken to using protective outerwear made of linen that is lined with cotton which covers them from head to foot and is so thick that the arrows lose their force. But for this very reason, these archers no longer shoot them except in the eyes, and they are so accurate in this that they kill many. (1:119)

Góis includes commentary on other aspects of the indigenous culture, including the various preparations for killing and consuming the enemy. He concludes by abruptly shifting focus from anthropophagy to Christianity. In a single sentence, he seems to want to reassure readers about the greater powers that are at work in Brazil, stating that many of the local inhabitants have been converted to the Christian faith, have married in the church, and live exactly as the Portuguese do.

Although Góis basically restated what Jesuits like Nóbrega and Anchieta believed and hoped to achieve in their missions, his comments overall foreshadowed the subordination if not nearly displacement of images of docile, innocent natives by images of their savagery and perdition. As his summary statement suggests, conversion and assimilation were now the necessary course of action for the community to secure a "proper" existence—an existence that was far removed from that blissful and Edenic lifestyle recorded by the first travelers to Brazil. His statement also worked both with and against arguments raised at the time about the primary objectives of the colonial enterprise. On the one hand, Góis believed that proselytization had priority in the New World over commercial ventures. His critique, like those of Barros and Gândavo—who expressed dismay at the renaming of the country for a commodity—supports this view. And there is no question that in order for the Crown to promote and benefit from the New World—a desire that increased substantially once trade with India became less profitable—potential immigrants needed to be assured that they would not be killed and consumed once they touched land.

Knowing that Christianity could transform a barbarous people into civilized human beings who "live in the same way that we do" was incentive to many who sought a better life outside Portugal. A better life was understood not only in the Christian sense of living in a place that offered a plethora of resources (something that most sixteenth-century chroniclers agreed upon, repeated, and further exaggerated in their retellings of already fantastic accounts),[42] but also in economic terms. As historian Alida C. Metcalf has pointed out, despite the royal decree of 1570 that freed the native inhabitants, the settlers and Jesuits did not want to relinquish their rights and continued to battle over the Indian, who was an essential property in their respective colonial interests.[43] Ultimately commercial interests came to the forefront, especially when it became clear that the country had far more to offer than just brazilwood and when the French and later the Dutch tried to profit from the bounty. Any resistance by the "savages," whose numbers were reduced not only by wars but also diseases brought by the European, was addressed by the local militia and settler population. Not surprisingly, as the dwindling indigenous population became more problematic than useful to the colonizers (especially once Africans proved to be a more desirable workforce), representations of a gentle, honorable people were replaced by images of man-eaters who either had to submit and "live like we do" or be killed off.

One work that undoubtedly surpassed all in promoting the beastly over the Edenic Brazil was engraver Theodor de Bry's *Historia Americae,* an illustrated multivolume series begun in 1590, that is also referred to as the *Grands et petits voyages.* The third part of the "Great Voyages," *Americae tertia pars,* was published in both Latin and German in 1592, and it is dedicated to Brazil.

It is important to note that the Belgian-born Protestant de Bry had never traveled to Brazil and that his remarkable copperplate engravings were largely based on illustrations that appeared in early travel narratives. For his volume on Brazil he fashioned striking engravings based on the woodcuts that appeared in Staden's and Léry's texts, and he presented the illustrations alongside the narratives. In contrast to the original works, where the image was subordinate to the text, de Bry's volumes featured the text as a kind of backdrop for the image. The engravings are not only exceptional for their detail but also striking in size, being many times larger than the originals and often occupying nearly a full folio page. De Bry's illustrations for Brazil, especially those based on scenes of anthropophagy from Staden's book, were the most sensational to appear in his multivolume series; and it is not surprising that they comprise one of the single most powerful iconographies associated with the discovery of the Americas.

Whether by coincidence or by design, de Bry produced his sensationalist engravings of cannibalism in 1592, the very year that he decided to become a bookseller as well as publisher. Anthropologist Bernadette Bucher writes that de Bry's project was highly successful, attracting a wide range of readers that included the European aristocracy, educated people and collectors, the rising class of merchants and artisans, and individuals even of more modest means who purchased shares in maritime companies like the Dutch East India Company (1977, 11). The books' copious illustrations made them attractive to those whose literacy was limited or even nonexistent. As a promotional device, frontispieces to the different volumes circulated separately and were displayed in streets or by itinerant peddlers as well as in marketplaces and fairs (ibid.). Somewhat like today's movie posters, de Bry's frontispieces piqued the imagination because they were so provocative. This was particularly true for the artwork in his volume on Brazil.

In creating the frontispiece that introduces the engravings and text based on Staden, de Bry appropriated the "hybrid" approach used in earlier illustrations that combines classical design with New World–cannibal motifs. But de Bry's frontispiece is also allegorical and far more daring, with its classically inspired man-eating New World inhabitants set in an architectural façade whose design resembles an altar and whose niches are normally occupied by religious figures. Like many earlier woodcuts, the engraving shows different activities taking place in a single image, although here they are represented in a vertical as opposed to horizontal pictorial—as if conveying a hierarchy of meaning. For example, at the very top of the façade two natives in ceremonial attire are kneeling while reaching out and upward as if in prayer or praise. The focus of their attention is twofold: the one on the right, whose frontal nudity is totally exposed, looks at the ceremonial maraca that appears at the top of the structure, while the other, whose frontal nudity is concealed, looks over his shoulder in the direction of the viewer. Their position and stance are reminiscent of angels who often adorned the upper corners of religious painting and architecture, and the maraca appears at the center top, which is normally occupied by the figure of the cross. On the tier immediately beneath the two figures are New World icons in the forms of a large conch shell and clusters of different fruits. Hybridity is suggested by the combination of these icons alongside what looks like a Greek or Roman urn.

The most dramatic images in the frontispiece are the figures in the middle tier who are chewing on dismembered limbs: the male figure's importance as a leader is suggested by the executioner's club that he holds in his hand. The female figure is drawn from the various accounts and illus-

1.14 Frontispiece for *Americae tertia pars,* by Theodor de Bry (1592). Courtesy of the Lilly Library, Indiana University, Bloomington.

trations that depict mothers and children during the anthropophagic act. Here de Bry retreats a bit from the traditional image of mother and son by placing the baby (who resembles a little adult) clinging to the woman's back rather than to her side. He also shows the child to be merely a spectator to his mother's delicate nibbling—as if a child's participation in the meal, which was shown in many early woodcuts, would exceed the limits of propriety for the viewer. The bottom tier is two-dimensional: the niches on the structure return to the New World and classical motifs of shells, fruits, and urns that appear in the higher tier, while the recessed archway in the center, like a proscenium, opens onto a Danteesque vision replete with smoke, fire, and individuals roasting and eating body parts. De Bry's "story" in images is built around a placard that gives the title of the book and a short, enticing description of its contents.

The large engraving that introduces Léry's text in the second part of the volume is another hybrid image but totally different in content and design. Here de Bry portrays an anguished Adam and gently smiling Eve against the backdrop of a wooded landscape where a peasant tills the earth while a mother sits with her child. A menagerie of animals appears in the foreground that includes a lion, a mouse, and a bizarre-looking creature typical of the fantastic beasts that often appeared in early illustrations of the New World. There is nothing obviously "Brazilian" in the illustration, although there is a symbolic relationship between the man and woman in the Staden frontispiece, who are eating flesh, and the Adam and Eve figures, who are about to taste the forbidden fruit. And although it is not clear what the exact relationship is between the biblical figures and Léry's narrative, one could speculate that de Bry's provocative portrayal of the loss of innocence, as suggested by Adam and Eve's enticement by the tempter and the snake, is emblematic of the "fall" of another population once perceived as innocent and Edenic. As far as sensationalism is concerned, while biblical images (unlike those depicting anthropophagy) no longer shock modern-day sensibilities, de Bry's subtly sensuous interpretation of the temptation and impending loss of paradise must have fascinated, if not titillated, more than a few.

As mentioned earlier, the woodcuts in Staden's text are simple and crude in design—so much so that captions were sometimes inserted in the Portuguese translation to comment on the image, as was the case of the illustration of women and children seated on the ground and "eating the prisoner."

1.15 *Adam and Eve,* by de Bry (1592). Courtesy of the Newberry Library, Chicago.

De Bry tended to rely on Staden's chapter titles to serve as captions for his engravings. For the most part, special captions were unnecessary because de Bry's image vividly depicts not only who is eating but also what is being eaten. In the case of Staden's "Eating a Prisoner," de Bry goes beyond artistic detail by making certain crucial modifications that move Staden's crudely "pastoral" setting in the wilderness to a more specifically indigenous setting that is separated from nature by a series of huts. We might say that the *locus amoenus* of the original is transformed into a *locus terribilis* by de Bry, who adds a platter with a decapitated head to the image and a mother figure who pulls entrails from another platter as the child bound to her back looks on, somewhat aghast. De Bry adds other children to the picture, one of whom is eating a phallic-looking intestine.

De Bry also combined individual woodcuts to achieve more complex and startling images. In Chapter 27 of Staden and just prior to the image described above, two separate woodcuts show Indians preparing a captive body for consumption. In one, a group watches as a man places his hand in the flayed back of a body with a head but no appendages; certain individuals in the group are holding dismembered limbs in the air. The follow-up image shows men and women tending to a head being roasted in a large pot while a bearded man (presumably Staden) looks on with his hands together in

1.16 Women and children eating, in de Bry (1592). Courtesy of the Lilly Library, Indiana University, Bloomington.

prayer. The backdrop to all of this is crudely drawn nature with bushy trees, a cloud, and a setting sun with a face and long beams that look like hair.

De Bry takes other liberties as he combines these two illustrations. For example, once again he moves a scene from the original woodcut out of the wilderness and into the village with its huts and fortress-like fence. Two men work on dismembering the body, whose head has been chopped off and is being held as if for display by a child who looks more like a little old man than a youth. Added to the original scene of dismemberment is a woman who is bent over while holding a platter for the entrails. Her gaze is directed downward—as if she were appraising the quality of the meat. The scene also shows women holding large appendages aloft: somewhat like the woman with the platter, one female is holding and judging a sturdy leg limb, and another is running with a severed arm to the cooking pot. De Bry's more savage representation clearly depicts a woman who holds a man's limb in the air as she symbolically nibbles away at her own hand. This nibbling is described by Staden and others as a prelude to consumption. De Bry also modifies the bearded figure (Staden) by crossing his arms over his chest as if in a defensive pose instead of with his hands folded in prayer.

1.17 Flaying a captive, in Staden Marburg edition (1557). Courtesy of the Lilly Library, Indiana University, Bloomington.

1.18 Cooking pot, in Staden (1557). Courtesy of the Lilly Library, Indiana University, Bloomington.

1.19 Flaying and cooking captives, in de Bry (1592). Courtesy of the Lilly Library, Indiana University, Bloomington.

The most startling image of anthropophagy in the de Bry volume takes even greater liberties with Staden's woodcuts. The illustration shows a barbeque of sorts: men, women, and children are feasting on a variety of body parts as other limbs cook over a long, raised wooden rack. De Bry seems to have reveled in providing detail here: we can see the fat globules dripping from the various grilled limbs and the curl of fingers that appear to be gripping the rack as they roast. Several of the men's bodies are covered with either tiny feathers or hair. Especially provocative are de Bry's figures of three older women with sagging breasts who lick their fingers.

Bernadette Bucher, who has written extensively on the "hag" in de Bry's work, states that

> we can see that the use of the motif of the woman with the sagging breasts . . . cannot be interpreted as an opposition between benevolent woman and ma-

1.20 Cooking and eating, in de Bry (1592). Courtesy of the Lilly Library, Indiana University, Bloomington.

levolent woman, for our young cannibals of the statuesque bodies and Roman profiles appear equally demonic and sinful as the old women who have lost their charms. In a certain degree even, their voracity is even greater, as they devour the human flesh without restraint, while the old women, more discreet in their pleasure, are satisfied to collect the drippings from it. (1977, 49)

It is important to note that this particular aspect of the engraving is based on Léry, who seems intrigued by the "gluttonous older women" in the cannibal ritual: "they get together and collect the fat that runs through the branches of these large and tall wooden grills; and, urging the men to continue so that they will always have such treats, they lick their fingers and say: *iguatú* which means 'it's very good'" (Léry 1990, 199).

Anthropologist Ronald Raminelli reminds us that chroniclers like Léry and Staden were careful to emphasize the division of labor whereby men killed and cut up the captive and ingested large body parts, while women were involved in cooking and partook primarily of the entrails, blood, and fat. Perhaps de Bry's decision to incorporate the old women, who not only lick their fingers but also brandish body parts, was his way of pictorially suggesting the downfall of the community, which is analogous to Eve's eating the apple. Bucher makes an especially perceptive observation about the significance of the older women when she says that "conceiving the 'savage' state as the aging and deterioration of a more perfect state is the contrary of all ideas of the original goodness of nature and the 'savage'" (1977, 53).

A few years after Cabral returned from his famous voyage to Brazil, the Portuguese artist Grão Vasco painted a fanciful portrait titled *Adoração dos magos* (The Adoration of the Magi) in which the figure of the black wise man, Baltazar, is substituted by an adoring Tupinambá in full ceremonial regalia. By the end of the century, this kind of imagery would be eclipsed by equally fantastic images of a population that existed only to eat flesh. At the same time, Brazil would continue to be touted as a land of riches and opportunity. Portuguese seafaring ultimately gave way to the colonization of the Brazilian coast and the exploration of the interior, and new ways of imagining the country would emerge based on new discoveries of a vast mineral wealth in the interior.

1.21 *Adoração dos magos*, by Grão Vasco (Vasco Fernandes) (circa 1505)

CHAPTER 2

Paradise (Re)Gained

Dutch Representations of Brazil and Nativist Imagery

Although images of anthropophagy continued to appear on maps and in other texts about Brazil in the early seventeenth century, it was during the Dutch occupation of the country that a discernible return to images defining Brazil as a paradise or *locus amoenus* can be found. This shift can be explained by a variety of factors: unlike the Portuguese, the Dutch established friendly relations with the indigenous populations in the Northeast, including the Tapuias, who were greatly feared by the Portuguese; enslaved Africans had largely replaced Indian labor in the fields, and indigenous peoples either assimilated or fled into the interior; and perhaps most importantly, the Calvinist military leader of the Dutch expedition to Brazil, Prince Johan Maurits von Nassau-Siegen, went to great lengths to forge and market a seductively bucolic image of Brazil that would not only attract other Dutch settlers to Brazil but also celebrate his accomplishments as a colonial administrator.

The iconography on five maps of Brazil produced by the Dutch between 1585 and 1640, a period when Portugal and its colonies were under Spanish rule, sheds further light on the image of Brazil constructed by cartographers from abroad. Scenes of dismemberment, execution, and anthropophagy hold prominence in Dutch representations of the country on maps by Jan Van Doet (1585), Arnold Florentin Van Langeren (1630), and Clemendt de Jonghe (1640). Josse Hond's map (1598) rivals most previous cartographic representation thus far mentioned with its bizarre image of a headless man with eyes set in his shoulders and a bow and arrow in his hand. Standing alongside this man-monster is an Amazon warrior who, in comparison, looks more real than mythic and various animals, including a deer, a dog, and a boar. In stark contrast to this illustration is Harmen Janss and Marten Janss' map (1610), in which we see an imagery of trees and animals that harks back to the earliest cartographic iconographies of Brazil. Although a scene of dismemberment appears on Jonghe's map, it is subordinate to a much larger engraving of a king being carried on a litter by indigenous inhabitants. The scene is unusual because instead of portraying Indians as cannibals, it depicts two large groups of comely and attentive natives gathered at each side of the litter, somewhat like Roman senators united around their Caesar. A palace appears in the far background of the engraving, apparently the home and destination of the traveling regal figure.[1]

Much like early Portuguese explorers and writers, the Dutch were excited by the bounties of Brazil, in particular by the vast sugarcane regions in the Northeast. Following the union of Spain and Portugal under the Bourbon Crown in 1580 and especially following the Twelve Years' Truce, a treaty between former enemies Spain and Holland and other "Low Countries" that lasted from 1609 to 1621, Holland's relationship with Portugal changed dramatically from a mutually beneficial trading partnership to one of territorial aggression in both Africa and Brazil. The emergence of the Dutch West India Company in 1621 spurred the invasion and occupation first of Bahia (1624–1625), then more successfully of Pernambuco and areas to the north,

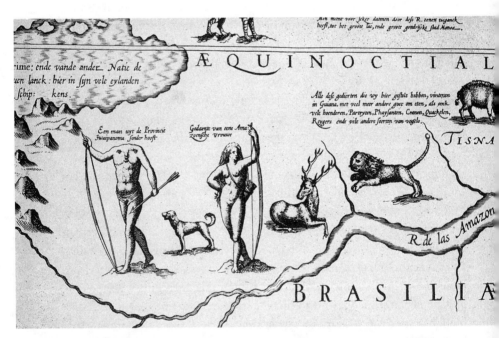

2.1 Headless man and Amazon, on Josse Hond's map of Brazil (1598). Courtesy of the Newberry Library, Chicago.

2.2 Pastoral Brazil, Harmen and Marten Janss's map of Brazil (1610). Courtesy of the Newberry Library, Chicago.

where the Dutch ruled from 1630 until they were ousted in 1654.[2] During this period, Brazil was the focus of numerous Dutch cartographic studies as well as histories, travel literature, and the first paintings of the country by Dutch artists Frans Post and Albert Eckhout.

The maps described above are important to consider for what they do and do not represent pictorially. For example, although brazilwood was still in abundance and exported to Europe in the late sixteenth and early seventeenth centuries, sugar had become a more valuable and desirable commodity. As historian Boris Fausto notes, in the sixteenth century, sugar was a luxury item in Europe and was becoming increasingly popular in haute cuisine (1999, 34). Portugal was eager to take advantage of the rising market demand by encouraging sugar production in the environmentally conducive area of the Brazilian Northeast, where the country's first capital, Salvador, was established in 1549. A labor-intensive industry, sugarcane plantations required large numbers of workers, the majority of whom in the mid-sixteenth century were native Brazilians who had been forced into slavery or, as converts from the Jesuits missions, worked for slave wages.[3] However, with the Dutch intervention in both the African slave trade and the sugar economy of Brazil, the percentage of African slaves on northeastern plantations rose dramatically, to the point that by the end of the *monarquia dual* (dual monarchy) or Iberian Union in 1640, Africans and African Brazilians constituted 100 percent of the workforce (Fausto 1999, 36–37).[4]

Interestingly, however, the early Dutch cartographers, who had never traveled to Brazil, continued to represent the country primarily as a primitive world associated with trees, animals, and cannibal rituals. Although there was a graphic tradition in seventeenth-century Dutch art to create the "illusion of verisimilitude" (Nguyen 9), art historian Paulo Herkenhoff has found that the European public was far more interested in such exotic representations of Brazil as cannibals, Amazons, fantastic creatures, and unusual if not horrific native customs (1999, 136).[5] Josse Hond's map is only one example of how the cartographic imagination was fueled by century-old myths and legends about the New World. His headless man is a forerunner of the famous Acephali (headless men) engraving that appears in Sir Walter Raleigh's 1599 account of his trip to Guiana. This fantastic image was based on what Captain Laurence Keymis later documented as a legend created around a people who retained their shoulders in a raised, hunched position, believing, for whatever reason, that it gave them a more aesthetically pleasing countenance (in Gheerbrant 1992, 48–49).[6]

Hond's inclusion of an Amazon is equally consistent with the continued emphasis on New World wonders—even those that, like the warring Amazons, were increasingly considered more fantasy than fact. In *Les singularités*, André Thevet devoted an entire section to the female fighters that includes the provocative engraving of warrior women with shields and bows and arrows. In this section he documented the history of the Amazons and then turned his attention to their culture, writing that the warriors resided in little huts or caves and regularly killed male offspring while nurturing the females.

Thevet was far from the first to write about the Amazons. In fact, a cartoon-like drawing of the legendary warriors appears as early as 1509 in Amerigo Vespucci's *Disz büchlin saget wie die zwe durchlüchtigsté herré Her Fernandus K. zu Castilien vnd Herr Emanuel. K. zu Portugal haben das weyte mör ersuchet vnnd findet vil Jnsulen, vnnd ein Nüwe welt von Wilden nackenden Leüten, vormals vnbekant* (This Book Tells How the Two Noblemen Fernando K. of Castile and Manuel K. of Portugal Have Searched Through the Wide Ocean and Have Found a Hitherto Unknown Island with a New World of Wild, Naked People). In the drawing, three naked Amazons successfully distract a European male dressed in full colonial regalia, as a fourth Amazon, who stands behind him, is posed to strike him down with a club. In their *Reise in Brasilien* (Voyage Through Brazil), dated 1823–1831, the Austrian naturalists Johann Baptist von Spix and Karl Friedrich Philipp von Martius stated that it was a characteristic of New World literature (and I would add, New World cartography) to shock the sensibility of the Old World by emphasizing the dangers (monsters, anthropophagy, and so forth) faced by travelers and explorers (Spix and Martius 1938, 3:199). Thevet ultimately retracted what he wrote about the Amazons in his revised *La cosmographie,* stating that they were simply unfortunate women who endeavored to preserve their lives, children, and property while their husbands were away. Nonetheless, writers like Simão de Vasconcelos in the late seventeenth century, Charles Marie de La Condamine in the eighteenth century, and Alexander von Humboldt in the early nineteenth century were not prepared to totally discount the possibility that communities of warrior women did exist.

The significance of the engraving of a king on a litter and his indigenous followers that appears on Jonghe's 1640s map is more ambiguous. Generally, Portuguese reign in the New World was iconographically represented by ships off the coast or fortresses on land. In some ways Jonghe's engraving is reminiscent of those early woodcuts of kings and castles in the extremely rare 1557 Frankfurt edition of Hans Staden's travel narrative, which had absolutely nothing to do with his captive-witness account. Since no monarch had ever been to Brazil prior to Dom João's arrival in Rio de Janeiro in 1808,

2.3 Vespucci's Amazons (1509)

the engraving could simply be documenting sovereign European rule supported literally and figuratively by the native inhabitants. But what is the relationship between this central engraving and the smaller image of Indians practicing dismemberment that appears on the map near the coastline? And whose rule, Holland's or Portugal's, did Jonghe intend to represent?

We might conclude that Jonghe's juxtaposition of "civilized" and "savage" natives is simply a continuation of two of the major tropes about Brazil that were developed in the sixteenth century and discussed at length in Chapter One. However, Jonghe makes a further stylistic distinction by using a far smaller scale to represent an individual act of dismemberment while utilizing a richly detailed and large engraving to portray the courtly image of the king and his followers. The larger engraving suggests a microcosm—an ordered world where royalty sits secure in its position of power above the serf (or Indian) and where civilization (in the form of the palace) presides over a vast wilderness. The dismemberment iconography makes clear that not all people and activities are part of this microcosm; nonetheless, these are portrayed as marginal and not at all threatening to the social order.

Whether Jonghe was representing Portuguese or Dutch imperialism is not clear. The fact that Jonghe was a Dutchman would seem to support the latter. At that time in Brazil, Dutch imperialism was represented by the enlightened and relatively peaceful rule of Prince Maurits, who had good relations with the indigenous populations.[7] The engraving might also rep-

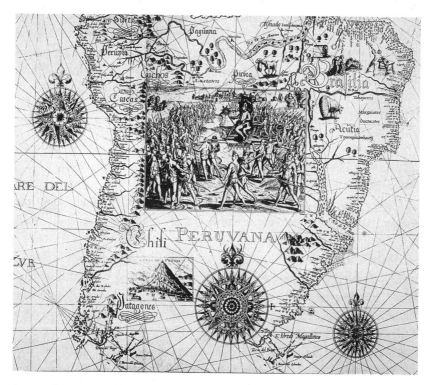

2.4 Acclamation and anthropophagy, on Clement de Jonghe's map of Brazil (1640). Courtesy of the Newberry Library, Chicago.

resent the Portuguese push into the interior at a time when the Dutch were in full command of Pernambuco and the African slave trade. The Portuguese took advantage of the dual monarchy and the more relaxed attitude of Spain toward the Line of Tordesillas and expanded Portugal's territory westward into the interior.[8]

To better understand Dutch perceptions of and interest in Brazil, one need only read Jan Andries Moerbeeck's proposal *Spaenschen Raedt* (1626), which was translated as *Motivos porque a Companhia das Indias Ocidentais deve tentar tirar ao rei da Espanha a terra do Brasil, e isto quanto antes* (Reasons Why the West India Company Should Try to Take the Land of Brazil from the King of Spain, and as Soon as Possible). Moerbeeck had presented his study in April 1623 to the prince of Orange and lords of the Low Countries; he enumerated more than a dozen sometimes questionable and contradictory reasons that not only the Northeast but all of Brazil should be conquered by the Dutch. For example, Moerbeeck contended (point 1) that the local Portuguese and Brazilian inhabitants had no military experience and would be easily won over in battle. He further contended (point 2) that the Portuguese Jews who resided in Brazil at the time were secret enemies of Spain (because of the Inquisition) and would support Dutch intervention. He stated also that by capturing the two vital cities of Bahia (Salvador) and Pernambuco (Recife/Olinda), the Dutch would in effect have seized control over the entire nation (point 3) and that the costs of war would be slight (point 13) compared to the economic returns in lands and commodities, such as sugar, brazilwood, tobacco, and cotton (points 9, 10, 12, and 14).

Moerbeeck argued somewhat disingenuously that a large-scale Dutch invasion was defensible and warranted because Spain, Holland's longtime enemy, had illegally taken control of Portugal, its former trading ally with Brazil (point 7). He concluded less disingenuously by stating that the Dutch occupation of Brazil would bring an end to the Portuguese empire. Moerbeeck bolstered his proposal with an appendix that listed everything that Brazil could produce annually and that inventoried the monetary gains the Dutch could expect by taking control of the sugar trade in northeastern Brazil.[9]

Moerbeeck's assessment of Brazilian and Portuguese resistance was initially accurate in the sense that Salvador was taken quite easily in 1624; however, his reasoning about the ease with which the Dutch could defend their foothold failed to take into consideration the will of local residents—

especially plantation owners and farmers, who banded together and ousted the Dutch after only a year. That defeat did not prevent the Dutch from raiding Pernambuco in 1630 and successfully defending its occupation during seven years of local resistance.

The end of the dual monarchy three years later, in 1640, had absolutely no impact on the Dutch occupation—which goes to show the degree to which Moerbeeck's argument about Spain's illegal seizure of Portugal and consequently Brazil was a bit of a red herring. But the Dutch West India Company's status as a semigovernmental organization supported by individual stockholders meant that leaders and the populace alike were not at all disposed to relinquishing their lucrative Brazilian possession to their former ally, Portugal. Moreover, Brazil was increasingly a part of the Dutch imagination and culture as a result of the works of an expedition of artists, scientists, and writers who accompanied the newly appointed governor-general Prince Maurits to Brazil. These are the individuals who constructed an image of Brazil as a paradise gained by Holland and the Dutch West India Company, and Prince Maurits effectively marketed this image over a number of decades.

Art historian Robert C. Smith regarded the Dutch artist Frans Post as the first landscape painter of America, stating that prior to Post there were only cartographers who might or might not have traveled to the Americas or European artists who tended to paint fantastic landscapes (1938, 246). Post was part of the cultural entourage that sailed with Prince Maurits to Brazil in 1636, and he was specifically commissioned to paint representative scenes of Brazilian agriculture, especially sugarcane plantations and processing mills, as well as scenes depicting the Dutch seats of government and places of worship. During his seven years in Brazil, Post completed eighteen landscape paintings that became the property of Maurits, who later gave them to King Louis XIV of France, supposedly for future political favors. But Post also made hundreds of drawings and sketches during his stay in Brazil, more than two dozen of which appeared as engravings in the Dutch poet Caspar van Baerle's monumental 1647 history in celebration of Maurits' Brazilian administration, titled *Rerum per octennium in Brasilia* (History of Events During Eight Years in Brazil).

Post continued to paint landscapes of Brazil long after his return to Holland, producing more than one hundred pictures over the years. Robert Smith points out that although Post's paintings became more stereotyped and nostalgic in his later years, he easily capitalized on the ready market for Brazilian artwork and extracted good prices for his paintings (256). Art historian Joaquim de Sousa-Leão estimates that Post's corpus of work includes at least 140 paintings of Brazil (1973, 21) and that his clientele back in Holland included people he had met in Brazil, as well as merchants, sailors, sea captains, and directors and shareholders of the Dutch West India Company (17).

Post's paintings have a sweeping, almost cinemascopic quality; their vast skies and sprawling yet highly detailed flora and fauna seem even more majestic as a result of the miniature human figures and animals that populate his landscapes. Plantations houses, churches, water mills, sugarcane mills, and ox carts are among his most popular subjects, along with the African slave. Very few of his paintings depict native Brazilian inhabitants, which is likely the consequence of the African slave trade that had effectively dispensed with indigenous servitude in the cane fields. Nor does Post depict the harsh realities of slave life;[10] in fact, his African figures, when they are not riding ox carts or dancing and singing, look more like serene country peasants or industrious mill laborers.

Two excellent examples of his paintings about blacks in the countryside are Brazilian Landscape with Natives Dancing and Chapel, which shows a group of colonists heading for church while a few slaves dance in the foreground, and Oxcart, in which blacks take the guise of country peasants in a pastoral setting. Although mills, plantations, and slaves are regularly portrayed in Post's work, emphasis remains on the skyline, vegetation, birds, and other wildlife found on riverbanks, the sea coast, and in the interior. His paintings support the topos of Brazil as a vast tropical paradise—a paradise that so astonished Prince Maurits when he arrived that he is quoted as saying that had he not seen it with his own eyes, he never would have believed it (in Boxer 1973, 72).

Like early-sixteenth-century Portuguese chroniclers, Prince Maurits was eager to attract settlers to the colony, and Post's landscapes, which were displayed in Maurits's palatial residence in Recife, conveyed to visitors the beauty, bounty, and civilization that awaited them. Post also contributed to Baerle's volume mentioned earlier with a magnificent map of the Dutch territory in Brazil. Back home in Holland, Maurits disseminated the images of Brazil created by Post and others by giving parts of his Brasiliana collection to leaders of other countries in exchange for titles, lands, and political favors. The three main recipients were Prince-Elect Frederick Wilhelm I of Brandenburg, Frederick III of Denmark, and most importantly, Louis XIV of France.

One cannot discuss Post's work without at least mentioning its relationship to a canonical piece of historiography titled *Diálogos das grandezas do Brasil* (1618; *Dialogues of the Great Things of Brazil*, 1986) and attributed to the Portuguese "new Christian" author Ambrósio Fernandes Brandão, a successful sugar mill owner in Paraíba in the early part of the seventeenth century. Divided into six parts, the work is structured around a conversation between Alviano, a Portuguese newcomer to Brazil who is learned and often skeptical if not cynical about the New World, and Brandônio, a Portuguese settler who is well-informed and enthusiastic about the possibilities of his adopted homeland. The book reflects the *ufanista* rhetorical style that characterized much of the historiography written during the previous century. A good example of the image of Brazil as a tropical as well as commercial Eden appears early on in the book's third dialogue, as Brandônio outlines for Alviano the various riches to be found in Brazil:

> Now to begin, I will say that the wealth of Brazil consists of six things, from which its settlers grow rich, and these are: first, the production of sugar; second, trade; third, the wood they call brazil; fourth, cotton and timber; fifth, the growing of food crops; sixth and last, cattle raising. Of these things, the principal nerve and substance of the wealth of the land is the production of sugar. (1986, 132)

In this same dialogue, Brandônio makes a compelling case for Portugal to plant pepper in Brazil to challenge the Dutch East India Company, which was the principal supplier for Europe at the time. The Portuguese did not implement this idea at the time, and the Dutch moved aggressively to lay claim to the highly profitable sugar industry in Brazil—a move that might very well have been influenced by Brandão's myriad observations about the wealth to be earned in that industry.[11]

Although he was painting more than two decades after Brandão wrote the *Diálogos*, Post was, in the words of Joaquim de Sousa-Leão (1973, 5), the visual chronicler of the sugar industry in seventeenth-century Brazil, and his work constitutes a "pictorial counterpart" to the *Diálogos* in the sense that both men focused on the natural beauty and bountifulness of Brazil's natural resources. Brazilian historian João Ribeiro suggested that the Dutch knew the *Diálogos* because a copy of the manuscript was found in Leiden (in O. Lima 1997, 5). Post's 1655 painting titled *Plantation Scene* might be regarded as a visual rendition of the book's basic structure, since the focal point in the painting is a plantation house where two men are engaged in a conversation on the veranda. The idyllic surroundings include a brilliant blue sky with white clouds overhead and lush tropical trees in the background; in the foreground, black slaves wear vibrantly colored clothing and appear to be dancing and singing.

Although there is much to critique in Post's bucolic renderings of plantation society, his rural and river landscapes are convincing pictorial tributes to the verdancy of the Brazilian Northeast. Writing two centuries later, English traveler Maria Graham rightly observed in her diary, *Journey of a Voyage to Brazil* (1824): "Nothing can be prettier of its kind than the fresh green landscape with its broad river winding through it. . . . I doubt not that the flat meadows and slowly flowing water, were particularly attractive to the Dutch founders of Recife" (104). This was surely the case with Post,

2.5 *Plantation Scene*, Frans Post (1655)

whose broad, serene landscapes of sea, sky, fields, forests, and streams suggest what Aldous Huxley once described as the "profusion that exists in tropical reality" (1960, 262). According to Huxley, "the painter of the average tropical scene would have to begin by leaving nine tenths of reality out of his picture." To this he added: "If [Gauguin] had not, there would have been no seeing the wood for the inordinate quantity of the trees" (ibid.). Whether this was true of Post or not, he constructed an image of Brazil that has much in common with the *ufanista* spirit of prose writing of the time; and his hundreds of sketches, drawings, paintings, and engravings remain among the most important documents of the Dutch presence in Brazil.

A less-known figure in Prince Maurits's artistic entourage was the artist Albert Eckhout, who was commissioned to paint the peoples, flora, and fauna. Art critic Paulo Herkenhoff contends that Eckhout was the first person to document pictorially the different racial and ethnic types anywhere in the Americas (1999, 146). In his essay "First Visual Images of Native America," William C. Sturtevant states that Eckhout produced the "first convincing European paintings of Indian physiognomy and body build" (1976, 419). There is also the point that because Eckhout's portraits of native Brazilians, Africans, mulattoes, and *mamelucos* (offspring of the European and Indian) were regarded as ethnographic studies, he was rarely included in discussions of Dutch art in Brazil until quite recently.[12]

Eckhout's large portraits of Tupi and Tapuia males and females are stunning and rich in meaning. Although painted only forty years after Theodor de Bry's famous engravings of the nude, fierce, and anthropophagous Tupi, Eckhout's Tupi male and female figures are docile in comparison—but not in the same way that Pero Vaz de Caminha wrote about them in his 1500 letter on the founding of Brazil. As art historian Ronald Raminelli notes, Eckhout illustrates the once brave Tupi as a figure conquered by civilization (1996, 106). In his portrait of the male, there are none of the traditional body piercings or scars associated with the former warrior; his hair is no longer shorn, and he appears to sport a small European-style goatee. He wears a skirt made of cloth rather than birds' feathers, and he carries a knife in his waistband—a symbol of the European presence. The bow and arrows that he holds in his hands look more like decorations or artifacts than hunting or killing weapons. A gigantic manioc root sliced open at his feet suggests the transformation of the former hunter-warrior into a gatherer—a role traditionally carried out by Tupi women.

2.6 Tupi man, by Albert Eckhout (1643)

Eckhout's portrait of a Tupi woman holding a child is similar to his depiction of the Tupi man: she wears a white cloth skirt belted at the waist and reaching almost to her knees, and instead of body parts, she is posed with a manioc root, a folded hammock, and a basket on top of her head. Unlike the traditional flowing tresses of de Bry's Tupi women, her hair is tightly woven with ribbon into two long braids. While still linked to the natural world, represented by a banana tree at her side and a large frog at her feet, she has been pacified by the European and integrated into civilization, which appears in the form of a plantation house with crops and workers in the background of the painting. The gaze of the male and female Tupi figures is similar in that their eyes are cast slightly downward—perhaps Eckhout's way of suggesting their gradual domestication and submission. Only the small, naked child clinging to the woman's side looks directly at the viewer, although other body language—the child's expression and her firm hold on her mother's breast—suggests an uncertainty or uneasiness with what she sees.

Eckhout's portraits of a Tapuia man and woman are quite different from his Tupi figures. Unlike the Tupi, who lived on the coast, the Tapuia inhabited the interior and often joined the Dutch to fight the Portuguese and their Indian allies. In his 1647 study of the period, Baerle wrote of the Tapuias' threatening countenance and reputation for cruelty and that they were all cannibals who terrorized other savages and the Portuguese (in Herkenhoff 1999, 117). Unlike the Tupi figures, Eckhout's Tapuia figures are still part of the wilderness landscape. Almost naked and showing no sign anywhere in the portraits of the colonizing presence, the man carries in one hand the ceremonial executioner's club and arrows and in his other hand a second club. He wears a feathered headdress and *enduape,* or traditional cluster of feathers, attached to a cord wrapped around his waist. His ferocity as a warrior is enhanced by the long, narrow spikes that pierce his cheeks and by the stone that rests in the hole in his chin. Unlike the Tupi male, he looks directly at the viewer with an emotionless gaze. The nature that surrounds him is yet more dangerous and daunting—particularly a tarantula and a large boa constrictor with huge teeth.

Eckhout's portrait of a female Tapuia is even more sensational because of the contrast between her serene semblance and the ferocity symbolized by the body parts she carries in her right hand and a basket strapped to her head. With the exception of a small cluster of leaves covering her pubic

2.7 Tupi woman, by Eckhout (1641)

2.8 Tapuia man, by Eckhout (1643)

2.9 Tapuia woman, by Eckhout (1643)

area, she is naked, although her skin is blemished with dirt, and like the male figure, she wears roped sandals on her feet. Unlike her Tupi counterpart, her hair is loose, and she wears a simple headband. Her face and body, like those of Eckout's other indigenous figures, are in keeping with the artistic representation of the European nude; at the same time, her pose with the body parts is made even more provocative by the presence of a wild dog with sharp teeth that laps at a stream running at her feet. In the far background, a line of Indians on the distant horizon appears rather suggestively further up and between her legs. This phallic symbolism of nature portrayed in earlier sixteenth-century engravings such as those found in Thevet is repeated here in the form of a tree with long, narrow pods that dangle above her head.

Eckhout was a master of the still life, a popular genre in seventeenth-century Holland, and all of his portraits with the exception of his dynamic *Dança de tapuias* (Dance of the Tapuias) have a certain still-life quality. Although he often painted shells, periwinkles, and ivory—all of which were favorite subjects of Dutch audiences because of their beauty and economic implications, he also painted pictures of manioc roots, leaves, and fruits, which are captivating for their brilliant color, simplicity of line, and sensuality. Like Post, Eckhout continued to make a living long after his return to Europe by painting Brazilian flora and fauna on canvas as well as in the interiors of castles and stately homes. Among later artworks inspired by Eckhout's paintings, none is more impressive than the 1687 tapestry series on America by the Paris-based company Manufacture des Gobelins, whose works hung in various palaces in France. According to Charles Boxer, these tapestries were so popular that the series was reproduced on the original looms for the next 120 years (1973, 153).

Prince Maurits also brought to Brazil the physician and naturalist Willem Piso, who with his assistant, the physician, astronomer, and cartographer Georg Marggraf, and Joannes de Laet produced the first natural history of South America, titled *Historia naturalis brasiliae* (1648). Two other figures deserve mention. The first was illustrator Zacharias Wagener, a German who was living in Brazil prior to Maurits's arrival and who served as butler in the prince's residence. He wrote an unpublished manuscript, *Their Buch Darinnen,* translated and published as the *Zoobiblion: Livro de animais do Brasil* (Book of Animals from Brazil), which contains more than one hundred watercolors of different Brazilian species, including human

2.10 *Indian Hunter,* by Manufacture des Gobelins (1692–1700)

figures copied from Eckhout's earlier paintings. The second noteworthy visitor to Brazil, Johannes Nieuhof, arrived after Maurits's departure. Published posthumously in 1682, his memoir of his nine years in Brazil, *Gedenkwaardige brasiliaense zee- en land reis,* reaffirms the fascination that the land held for foreign travelers. A Dutchman in the employ of the West India Company, Nieuhof was initially impressed by Brazil, and his memoir is *ufanista* in its descriptions. As in the *Diálogos das grandezas do Brasil,* the praise once heaped upon brazilwood has been transferred to the more lucrative sugar production:

> Brazil is a country excellently well-qualified by Nature for the producing of all
> Things, which are generally found in the West-Indies, under or near the same

climate; except that hitherto no Gold or Silver-Mines have been discovered here worth taking note of. But next to Gold and Silver, Sugar claims precedency here before all other commodities . . . for the situation of Brazil . . . is such as could not be more conveniently contrived by human Art or Nature for the Transportation of so general and agreeable a Commodity, as Sugar, into all the other parts of the World. (1703, 31)

Art historian José Roberto Teixeira Leite finds that all but two of the illustrations in Nieuhof's book were based on designs by Marggraf, Eckhout, and Wagener. The two executed by Nieuhof are interesting to contemplate. *A Brazilian* is the title given to a picture of a naked Indian whose arrow has just pierced a bird in flight. Another naked Indian appears in the near background with hands raised as if to catch the bird as it falls. In the far background is a small scene depicting the anthropophagic rite. The other illustration by Nieuhof, *Blacks Dancing,* shows a mostly naked African man and a seminude African woman playing instruments while a small group enjoys the music in the background. Like Eckhout's Tapuia woman and the iconography on certain maps, *A Brazilian* shows that anthropophagy was still a topos in Dutch Brazil but had been recessed or marginalized (when not completely erased) in the vast majority of representations. Rural and pastoral images of Brazil now assumed iconic status, and the African slave was introduced as a decoration and a festive image in harmony with the tropical scenery, associated less with labor than with music, song, and dance.

Protonationalist Imagery

What historian Charles R. Boxer calls the "promotion literature" of the seventeenth and eighteenth centuries can be divided into two types: the *ufanista,* associated with the hyperbolic language of sixteenth-century traveler-chroniclers, and the *nativista,* a later phenomenon that emphasizes the superiority of things Brazilian. The latter form is generally written from the perspective of those born in Brazil or who have resided in the country for some time.

The Franciscan Vicente do Salvador, regarded as the first Brazilian historian, is a good example of a fusion of *ufanista* and *nativista* styles. In his *História do Brasil: 1500–1627* (1627), we see the same exaggerated prose about Brazilian woodlands found in some of the nation's earliest documents:

2.11 *A Brazilian,* by Johannes Nieuhof (1682)

2.12 *Blacks Dancing,* by Nieuhof (1682)

In Brazil there are huge forests of wild trees, cedars, oaks, mimosas, angel-woods, and others unknown in Spain. Their woods are extremely strong and exceptionally sturdy galleons can be constructed out of them. . . . The woods from Brazil are no less beautiful than they are strong. They are of all colors: white, black, red, yellow, purple, pink and jasper-colored . . . They are so es-teemed for their beauty that they are used to make beds, chairs, desks, and buffets . . . Other trees called myrocarpus provide the very smooth balsam that is used in healing and that the Holy Father has declared a legitimate material of the holy unction and anointing. (1965, 67)

At the same time, Salvador writes in the "nativist" mode about what Brazil can offer that other countries cannot: "Brazil has a greater wealth of foodstuffs than all the other lands in the world combined because in it can be found the foods found in all the others" (ibid.). At another point, he reiterates that in order to survive, Brazil requires absolutely nothing from beyond its borders: "of all the praises to be bestowed upon Brazil, the great-est is that it can sustain itself with its ports closed, without any help from other lands" (ibid.).

In *História da América portuguesa* (1730), published more than two cen-turies after the founding of Brazil, the Bahian Sebastião da Rocha Pita showed how *ufanismo* and *nativismo* continued to be cultivated in histories of the country. His book is filled with superlatives, swooning commentary, and lyric descriptions:

[Brazil is an] incredibly vast region, the most felicitous land, on whose surface are fruits, whose center is filled with treasures, whose mountains and coastlines are filled with aromas. Its fields produce the most practical foods; its mines, the finest gold; its timber, the softest balsam; and its seas, the most select amber. . . . In no other region is the sky more serene, nor is there anywhere a more beau-tiful dawn. No other hemisphere has more golden sun rays or more brilliant nighttime reflections; the stars are the most benign and they always twinkle happily. The horizons, whether at dawn or dusk, are always clear; the waters, whether from country fountains or city aqueducts, are the purest: Brazil is an earthly paradise, where the greatest rivers are born and flow. (1880, 2)

Similarly, the Jesuit Simão de Vasconcelos's 1668 *Notícias curiosas e nece-ssárias das coisas do Brasil* (Curious and Necessary News of Things from Brazil) combined *ufanista* and *nativista* sentiments in his descriptions of the land:

The incredible height of these shapeless mountains is proportionally similar to its accomplishment: they seem to want to compete with the Heavens; neither the Pyrenees, nor the Alps, nor any others known to us can compare with them. Clouds serve them as a belt that wraps round the middle of their huge bodies, the upper part totally free of terrestrial vapors and exhalations. Those who climb them tread on clouds from the middle part on up: and when they arrive at the top, it seems that the very same clouds drift over the land. Rains, winds, storms, rainbows, exhalations, and meteorological impressions—everything that they see from above seems superior and, at the same time, they enjoy the Sun and fine weather. It is as if they were in another world, free of the jurisdiction of the times. (2002, 69)

Critic Wilson Martins notes in his multivolume *História da inteligência brasileira* that Vasconcelos's *ufanista* zeal harks back to early-sixteenth-century notions about Brazil, especially when Vasconcelos argued at various points that the country is a terrestrial paradise. His position on this subject was so extreme and contrary to religious beliefs of the time that his Jesuit superiors suppressed what they found to be most objectionable in the book, although not every reference to Brazil as an earthly Eden was omitted (1977, 1:162). As we have seen, Sebastião da Rocha Pita was not at all reluctant to equate Brazil with the biblical paradise, although fortunately for his purposes he was writing as a layman and not as a Jesuit.

The language of the *nativista-ufanista* sensibility was not limited to historiography, and, as mentioned above, it carried into the eighteenth century. Manuel Botelho de Oliveira, believed to be the first published poet in Brazil, wrote a lengthy lyric composition printed in 1705, "A Ilha de Maré: Termo da Cidade de Bahia" (The Island of Maré: At the Border of the City of Bahia), that provides a veritable menu of the incomparable and bountiful treats to be found in Brazil. Note in the following stanzas how the nativist rhetoric is used to empower Brazil over previous and present colonizing nations:

Lemons are not appreciated,
Being so many, they are disdained.
Oh, were Holland to savor them!
Not even for a province would she trade them.

The falling yellow citrons
Are beautiful,

Swollen and fresh,
It is good that they have fallen to the ground.
The muscatel grapes are so delicious,
So rare, so exquisite;
Had Lisbon seen them, she would imagine
Someone had robbed them from her garden;
The production of them is so copious
It seems miraculous,
Harvested twice a year,
They give birth two times, without fail, in twelve months.[13]

In *The Golden Age of Brazil 1695–1750* (1969), Boxer writes at some length and with considerable verve about the distance between the imagined utopia of Brazil and the realities that awaited emigrants:

> The majority of the emigrants were probably illiterate, but any who might have read such eulogistic works must have been cruelly deceived soon after their arrival. While extolling the variety of delicious fruits which Brazil afforded, the beauty of the evergreen scenery, and the serenity of the tropical nights under the Southern Cross, these writers discreetly forbore to mention the numerous insect pests which made any kind of agriculture a gamble, and which all the resources of modern science are still far from controlling. . . . Droughts ravaged some regions of the country for years on end; and elsewhere the capricious climate was likely to alternate between excessive rain and floods on the one hand and totally insufficient rainfall on the other . . . . The dearth of calcium was (and is) particularly serious, adversely affecting the nutritional value of such food plants as did grow. (13)

Boxer includes a citation from a letter written in 1687 by landowner João Peixoto Viegas in Bahia to the Marquis of Minas in which Viegas describes the precarious nature of farming in Brazil: "it is just like the act of copulation, in which the participant does not know whether he has achieved something, or whether the result will be a boy or a girl, sound or deformed, until after the birth is achieved" (13).

I do not mean to suggest that there was absolute silence about the difficulties one might confront in the New World. While Johan Nieuhof was enthusiastic about his close to a decade of experiences in Dutch Brazil, he was not reluctant to mention at least one drawback of living in the tropics: "Plague is a thing unknown in Brazil . . . thou' they are not free from continued putrid fevers, caused by the hot and moist Air, and the excessive use of raw Fruits" (1703, 32). A later traveler, Johan Brelin, the first Swede to publish a book on Brazil, praised the country but was far from impressed with its inhabitants. In his diary of a trip to Brazil in 1756 he notes: "Having been bestowed with many and great natural resources, [Brazil] could become the richest country in the World if it were in the hands of a more work-oriented people. But the innate vanity and grand imagination of the Portuguese have grown to such a point that even the humblest regard work to be a dispensable thing" (1955, 100).

A few pages later Brelin repeats this observation, remarking that "even the blacks are not humble" (104). His description of the indigenous peoples seems largely based on hearsay and myth—not surprising, since by that time fewer Indians lived in the coastal areas. His description of native women and breastfeeding might be better classified as miraculous: "Their breasts are so long that they throw them over their shoulders when they nurse their children, who are carried in hammocks on their backs" (102). However, at a later juncture he is frank about his scant knowledge of Indians, saying: "Of these kind of people I only saw two examples which were kept in iron cages in the Viceroy's palace, and it was said that they were to be shipped to Europe" (102)—a comment that provides additional insight into the mistreatment of Indians, who continued to be exported to Europe as exotica in the eighteenth century.

A far more searing indictment of Brazilians of nearly every caste and class can be found in the writings of the seventeenth-century Bahian-born poet Gregório de Matos, whose satiric verses were so personal and vicious that he was dubbed "Boca do Inferno" (Mouth from Hell). In Brazil, Matos witnessed the misery of the country under the increasingly hardened rule of royally appointed governors and other functionaries who diminished the ability of *câmaras,* or town councils, to operate. In his introduction to the poetry of Matos, José Miguel Wisnik lists the growing sugar crisis (owing to greater competition from areas like the Caribbean), the weakening of local governments, opportunism and the rise of the Portuguese businessman, and colonial oppression among the principal topics in the poet's works (Wisnik 1976, 15). In poems such as "Descreve o que era naquele tempo a cidade da Bahia" (Describing What Was at That Time the City of Bahia), Matos was not at all reluctant to point out the greed, dishonesty, and stupidity of his fellow Bahians, and he reserved a special disdain for people of color:

In every nook and corner a great counselor,
Who wants to rule us from shack to vineyard;
They don't even know how to run their own kitchens,
And they presume to rule the whole world.

In every doorway a habitual busybody,
Who scrutinizes, watches, spies on, and probes
The lives of his male and female neighbors
So they might be carted off to the public square.

Many shameless mulattoes,
Rise on the backs of noble men,
By knowing every dirty trick in the book.

Stupendous usury in the marketplace,
Destitute are those who fail to steal:
And there you have the city of Bahia. (Matos 1976, 41)

Having lost his post as an ecclesiastical tribunal appeals judge for, among other infractions, refusing to wear a cassock, Matos was especially critical of clerics. Among his best-known anticlerical writings is a long satire of the *pardo* (brown-skinned) vicar Lourenço Ribeiro, who ventured a public critique of Matos's verse (Wisnik 1976, 45). In the poem, Matos repeatedly refers to Ribeiro's mixed-race heritage, using terms such as *mestizo* and *mulato* in combination with variations on the word "dog."[14]

Boxer notes the considerable enmity between locals and emigrants, the latter of whom were given positions and other perks by government officials largely of European birth (1969, 12). Matos's ire was considerably piqued by the privileges bestowed upon the growing Portuguese mercantile class over the Brazilian plantation society into which he was born. His poem "Descreve com mais individuação a fidúcia com que os estrangeiros sobem a arruinar sua república" (Describing with More Precision the Insolence with Which Foreigners Rise up to Ruin Your Republic) focuses on the partiality shown to the outsider by his own city, which he personifies as "Lady Madam Bahia":

Lady Madam Bahia,
noble and opulent city,
stepmother to your own children,
and mother to those from abroad:

Tell me for your sake
on what do you base your reason
for praising those who come here,
and crushing those born here?

If you do that for your own interests
so that strangers might sing your praises,
well, that's something our own countrymen would do
to receive the same advantages. (49)

Matos's acerbic verses predate the 1731 decree of Dom José I of Portugal that banned the publication of all satires and libelous material. Nonetheless, his poetry was so controversial in its attacks against policies and officials—including the governor himself, that he was deported to Angola.[15] Matos was permitted to return to Brazil shortly before his death, on condition that he reside in Recife and refrain from writing satires. He wrote a number of religious and love poems during his lifetime, but his satiric verse best exemplifies his particular nativist approach. Unlike most nativist writers, his poetry did not focus on the wonders of Brazil, and his attitude toward Brazilians born of mixed blood as well as Portuguese Jews was undeniably prejudicial. Yet he was a nativist poet in the sense that he privileged the local over the foreign, and he sometimes adopted Tupi and African terminology in his compositions. His poems about the Bahia of his youth, such as his famous "Triste Bahia" (Sad Bahia), indirectly comment on the depth of his despair about his homeland; read in conjunction with other satiric poems, they reveal how truly great for him the differences were between a nostalgic (mostly imaginary) past and the present-day reality of Brazil.

The Jesuit Antônio Vieira, who spent many years in Brazil and was regarded as one of Europe's most compelling orators, shared some of Matos's concerns that Brazil had been handed to royal officials.[16] But Vieira's critique of Portuguese administrators was couched in the language of the pulpit, and his renowned linguistic dexterity, with its baroque turns of phrase and word play, made him less a target for retribution—at least in some matters. Among his hundreds of sermons is the "Sermão da visitação de Nossa Senhora" (Sermon on Our Lady's Visitation) given in 1640, the year of Portuguese independence from Spain, in which he compared the king's sending of administrators to Brazil with God's sending Adam to watch over and tend the earth. Vieira was quite pointed in his critique of their sins, stating that just as Adam took the apple that was not his, certain officials came to Brazil not for the country's welfare but to take its goods (2001, 2:217–239). Vieira's admiration and love of Brazil is apparent in his many sermons about the country. His nativism is especially evident in his "Sermão do bom ladrão" (Sermon on the Good Thief) of 1655, a linguistic *tour de force* on the terminology used for robbers, whom he described as the "active voice" who victimize the unsuspecting "passive" (2001, 1:387–413). Vieira was fond of prophesy, but even he would have been amazed at how accurate his sermons were in foretelling the extraordinary plunder of riches that would take place in Brazil a few years later.

The Gold Rush and the Seeds of a Revolution

The image of Portugal as a great seafaring nation was considerably changed by the mid-seventeenth century. As a result of sixty years of Spanish rule, the country was in a precarious economic state, and the loss of parts of the Brazilian and African territories to the Dutch had devastating effects on both the commercial and psychic well-being of the Portuguese. Despite António Vieira's famous "Sermão pelo bom sucesso das armas de Portugal contra as de Holanda" (Sermon for the Good Success of the Arms of Portugal Against Those of Holland) in 1640, the Dutch were ousted not by the Portuguese military but by guerrilla-style fighters who lived in Pernambuco.

Once the Northeast was back in Portuguese hands, new problems began to materialize for the mother nation. The Dutch withdrawal translated into an immediate loss of capital to support the sugar plantation economy; Brazil was no longer the sole exporter of sugar, and new markets meant lower prices; and the cost of slaves to work the fields and mills was so exorbitant that profit margins were at an all-time low. The reaction of the monarchy to its own ruined economy was to explore other possible sources of income in Brazil—in particular in the area of the *sertão,* or backlands, where it was long believed an Eldorado existed.[17] To this end, *bandeirantes* pushed even farther into the interior, and in 1695 word spread of the discovery of massive deposits of gold in the central interior, known as Minas Gerais (General Mines). The discovery of gold and later silver and diamonds launched a major land rush that lasted more than fifty years. Although many Brazilians' fortunes changed dramatically because of the mines, much of the wealth from precious metals and stones went directly to Portugal as a result of a heavy tax. The 1703 Treaty of Methuen between England and Portugal virtually ensured that the wealth from Brazil passed from Portugal to Britain, whose industrial revolution was bankrolled by it.[18]

One of the most intriguing documents to appear in this period in Brazil was *Cultura e opulência no Brasil* (Culture and Opulence in Brazil) by the Italian-born Jesuit Giovanni Antonio Andreoni, who published his book in 1711 under the pseudonym André João Antonil—and for good reason. This straightforward and highly detailed chronicle of the agricultural and mineral wealth in Brazil was the source of considerable consternation back in Portugal. Any information about the Brazilian mines, especially their whereabouts and lucrative contents, was considered confidential to the Crown. Shortly after Andreoni's book was released, the government immediately seized all available copies. The book's existence was generally ignored until some 150 years later, and it took another half-century after that for historian Capistrano de Abreu to uncover the identity of the pseudonymous Antonil.

Andreoni wrote the book to honor the memory of his predecessor, the Jesuit José de Anchieta, who was renowned for his lifelong dedication to missionary work and for his many writings, which included the first poetry ever written in Brazil. From Andreoni's standpoint, Brazil owed so much to Anchieta that it was only right to celebrate his life and memory with an inventory of the many riches that God had bestowed upon the land. He also alluded to generous rewards that would accrue on earth and in heaven for even the smallest contributions to the Church in Anchieta's name by those "plantation owners and sugar and tobacco farmers and those who extract gold from the mines in the state of Brazil," to whom Andreoni addressed his book (Antonil 1955, 9).

While news of the bounties offered by Brazil in the sixteenth century was ultimately deigned by the Crown to be a way to increase migration to and commerce with the New World, the experience of fighting off nations such as France and Holland because of resources such as brazilwood and sugarcane resulted in Portugal's attempt to prevent any announcement about the mines. Unlike the historiographies written by Salvador, Pita, and others that focused on the past, Andreoni's narrative furnished precise, up-to-date information on the locations of and specific processes involved in the sugar, tobacco, and mining industries, giving exact accounts of how much was produced, how much was taxed by the government, and the total (and generous) revenues that were collected by Portugal. Andreoni not only compiled an extraordinary set of data but also used the information to make a plea to the Crown to boost aid to plantation owners and workers, who were the human factors behind Portugal's new source of wealth. His requests included expediting landowners' and miners' petitions in the courts, paying punctually those soldiers who kept the peace in the frontier towns of the interior, and supporting the church by educating more priests for missionary work (Antonil 1955, 252–253).

Andreoni begins his account of the mines by stating that the search for precious metals in Brazil was most likely delayed because of the visible and more easily obtainable bounties offered by the countryside, which included fish, fruits, and timber, as well as Indians, who were hunted down and captured for slave labor. His narrative includes a description of the discovery of gold:

> They say that the first discoverer was a mulatto who had been in the mines of Paraná and Curitiba and who went to the backlands with some Paulistas to hunt for Indians . . . he lowered a small wooden vessel to scoop up some water from a brook that today is called Ouro Preto [Black Gold]. After placing the vessel in the water and scraping it along the river bottom, he noticed some steel-colored granules in it, but he didn't know what they were. Nor did his companions, to whom he showed the granules, know enough to realize what he had so easily found. They merely thought that it was a well-formed but unknown metal. When they arrived in Taubaté, they continued to ask what kind of metal it might be. Without further examination, they sold some of the granules to Miguel de Souza . . . not knowing what they were selling and without his knowing what he was buying, until they decided to send a few of the grains to the governor in Rio de Janeiro, Artur de Sá. The results of the examination showed that it was the highest grade of gold. (Antonil 1955, 179–180)

Andreoni devoted an entire section of his book to the people who ventured into the area to search for gold—an account that shows that even prior to his book, the Crown had been unable to keep the discovery a secret:

Each year ships bring large numbers of Portuguese and foreigners, who move on to the mines. From the cities, villages, coastal lands, and interior of Brazil come whites, mulattoes, blacks, and many Indians who serve the Paulistas. The mixture includes persons of all kinds: men and women, young and old, poor and rich, noble and plebeian, laymen, clerics and religious people from different institutions, many of whom have neither convent nor home in Brazil. (186–187)

His account of the different sites and varieties of gold and silver hark back to the first chroniclers' descriptions of the flora and fauna of Brazil:

First of all, silver mines are for the most part found where the earth is red and white, free of trees and with little grass. . . . Silver found in veins is varied in color: . . . white, black . . . the color of yellow gold, blue, light green, brown, liver-colored, orange, tawny. Other kinds of silver are completely silver in color. . . . All these stones are called metals by the Castilians, and a few bear names. Covered metal is a stone that has a green appearance, is very heavy, salty in taste, thin, and it shrivels the mouth because of the mix of acrid antimony and vitriol. Powder-fine metal is a stone that is slightly yellow, more solid than the one just mentioned, and at times the silver is harder toward the bottom. Blackened metal of the best kind is a black stone with highlights from thick iron filings; however, it not very solid when mixed with salt and second-grade black metal. (230–231)

As a good Jesuit, Andreoni was not reluctant to moralize about the dangers incited by the lust for gold:

There is no good that cannot be the occasion for bad because of those who do not use it well . . . . How is it that despite being such a beautiful and precious metal, so useful for human commerce and so worthy of vases and ornaments for Temples of the Divine, gold continues to be the cause of men's insatiable greed and the instrument for so much danger? The fame of bountiful mines invited men of all castes and from all parts: some with means, and others without. For those of means, who withdrew large quantities of gold, it meant haughtiness and arrogance, and always to be accompanied by troops of armed guards who are ever ready to carry out violent acts and great and thunderous revenge, without fear of the law. Gold has seduced them to gamble widely and to spend extraordinary amounts without any notice on trifles, buying (for example) a black trumpet player for a thousand *cruzados*; and a mistreated mulatta for double the price, so he can multiply his continuous and scandalous sins with her. Those vagabonds without means, who go to the mines to take out gold . . . carry out inexcusable treacheries and even crueler deaths that go unpunished. Even Bishops and Prelates of some religions ignore taking blame for letting their numbers in the convents and priesthood diminish because so many clerics and other religious persons scandalously roam about the interior with resolve or as fugitives. And because the best of everything one could want goes to the mines, the price of everything for sale has gone up. So much so that plantation owners and workers have mortgaged themselves to the hilt, and because of the lack of slaves, they cannot take care of the sugar nor the tobacco fields—the true mines of Brazil and Portugal—as they did so happily in the past. And the worst part is that most of the gold taken from the mines passes in dust and coin to foreign realms. And the smallest part goes to Portugal and cities in Brazil—except for what is spent on hat cords, earrings, and other gew-gaws which today one sees mulattas of ill-repute and black women wear much more than ladies. There is not a prudent person who hasn't confessed that God allowed so much gold to be found in the mines in order to punish Brazil—just as he is punishing so many Europeans with wars as a result of the discovery of iron. (236–238)

It is difficult to imagine the fortunes extracted from the interior regions. In his 1979 study, *O ouro brasileiro e o comércio anglo-português* (Brazilian Gold and Anglo-Portuguese Commerce), Virgílio Noya Pinto estimates that nearly one thousand tons of gold (in addition to three million carats of diamonds) were taken from the area between 1700 and 1800.[19] One conse-quence of these riches was the architectural splendors of places such as Vila Rica, the capital of Minas Gerais (later to be called Ouro Preto), whose opu-lence was so great that it was called the "precious pearl of Brazil." Among the best pictorial documents of the period is the collection by Carlos Ju-lião of forty-three watercolors of whites, blacks, and Indians. Several of his paintings are set in the mining area of Serro do Frio, where diamonds were discovered; a few others feature wilderness landscapes. A captain in the royal artillery in the mid-eighteenth century, Julião was a master of detail. His portraits of black slaves in the interior are especially interesting because they portray different aspects of the difficult manual labor required by the mines. One of his watercolors of slave rock crushers bears a slight resem-blance to 1930s social realist paintings with their roundish and muscular laborers. The important difference between the two styles is that instead of being stoic, content, or even heroic workers, Julião's figures are slaves who wear poignantly unhappy expressions. Another watercolor, titled *Serro Frio*, depicts a proto–assembly line composed of slaves who are washing and retrieving diamonds. In this portrayal of management and labor, Julião features a row of white overseers sitting on high stools with small chests at their feet, while slaves in another, larger row carry out the backbreaking work of extracting stones and placing them in the boxes. The contrast be-

2.13 *Serro Frio,* by Carlos Julião (circa 1780). Courtesy of the Lilly Library, Indiana University, Bloomington.

2.14 *Two Overseers Search a Slave,* by Carlos Julião (circa 1780). Courtesy of the Lilly Library, Indiana University, Bloomington.

tween the two sets of figures is placed in greater relief by the expression of the first overseer, whose face is turned to the viewer and who appears bored and about to fall asleep. In a much simpler but no less dramatic painting, two white overseers examine a slave to ensure that he has not hidden any precious stones on his person. Julião effectively portrays the submission and vulnerability of the slave, who stands stripped of his clothes and holds his hands high in the air under the colonial inspectors' gaze.

Julião also portrays master and slave in situations whose urbanity is implied by their dress. Two drawings show black slaves in colorful uniforms carrying coach-style litters that bear upper-class women whose exquisite finery is partially revealed as they peek out from their curtained transportation. The wealth conveyed by these paintings of elegant coaches and brocaded servant uniforms that include hats and other fineries is subtly undermined by the depiction of the litter-bearing slaves' bare feet. Julião's figures of black vendors are beautiful in color and unusual in style. One particular figure of a black woman balancing a whole fish on top of her head has a vaguely surreal look. Her female companion, who carries a large basket of bananas and other fruits on her head, looks like the prototype for

2.15 *Two Black Vendors,* by Carlos Julião (circa 1780). Courtesy of the Lilly Library, Indiana University, Bloomington.

Carmen Miranda. Julião also painted Indians, but most of his figures, especially those with lots of hair covering their near-naked bodies, seem drawn more from the imagination than from any real-life model. (His watercolor of "civilized Indians" seems more realistic in its portrayal of a docile couple walking along and dressed in the plain white cotton garments worn by the poor.)

One of the most talented artists to appear in Minas Gerais was the sculptor and wood carver Antônio Francisco Lisboa, who came to be known as Aleijadinho (Little Cripple). The son of a Portuguese architect and his African slave, Aleijadinho created some of the greatest religious artwork of the Baroque era in Brazil. Although disabled by a disease that crippled his extremities, he was able to carve wood and stone by strapping tools to his hands. He constructed some of the most elaborate and beautiful altars, façades, and statues in Minas Gerais, including the Church of Saint Francis of Assisi in Vila Rica, the twelve prophets who represent the Stations of the Cross, and sixty-six life-size wooden statues that form scenes from the Passion of Christ in the town of Congonhas do Campo. The ornate, rococo style of his altars and entryways is a testimony to the vast wealth uncovered in the region. At the same time, his large wooden statues, which were unusual for the time because of their un-European-like imperfections, may have been his way of registering, like Vieira, a preoccupation with the future welfare of the nation.

The gold rush influenced not only painting, sculpture, and architecture but also the literature of the period. The Minas-born neoclassic poet Cláudio Manuel da Costa wrote "Vila Rica," an epic poem that is filled with descriptions of the processes involved in excavating metals. In the epic tradition, Costa bestows a heroic and even mythic grandeur on the leaders and founders of the city as well as on those who mine the hills. As critic Antônio Cândido observed, "of all the 'Mineiro' poets, [Costa] was perhaps the most deeply caught up in the emotions and values of the land" (1971, 1:88). By contrast, the Portuguese-born poet Tomás Antônio Gonzaga, who was sent to Vila Rica as an administrator, was unhappy with his experiences there and composed a long, scathing, and anonymous satire, Cartas chilenas (Chilean Letters), that focused on the base instincts and corruption of the governor, Luís da Cunha Meneses.

Although many Brazilian poets of the middle to late eighteenth century wrote in imitation of classical authors, their themes were often local and

2.16 Soapstone prophet, by Aleijadinho, in front of the Bom Jesus do Matozinho in Congonhas, Minas Gerais (1800–1805). Permission, Latin American and Iberian Institute, University of New Mexico.

focused on the Indian. For example, among the works of the Rio-born poet Antônio Pereira de Sousa Caldas is a long "Ode ao homem selvagem" (Ode to the Savage Man), which adopts a classical lyric form to lament the Indian's loss of his "former greatness" and freedom. The *mineiro* poet Joaquim José Lisboa wrote a series of quatrains to his muse Marília about "Os índios do Brasil" (The Indians of Brazil),[20] a poem whose imagery evokes sixteenth-century writings about the violence of the indigenous inhabitants:

> They have no homes, they produce nothing,
> They live off hunting and stealing,
> They are worse than wolves,
> Even worse than snakes.

The bombastic poem ends with an especially horrific image:

> If giants there were to be,
> Then giants are they;
> With force and heart
> Inexorable and evil. (In H. Martins 1982, 87–88)

Of all the poets of this period, Basílio da Gama was unsurpassed in his lament for the fate of the Indian in his long epic-style poem of 1769 titled *O uraguai* (The Uraguay), which was translated and greatly admired by the explorer Sir Richard F. Burton. Characterized as victims of the Jesuit missionaries, Gama's indigenous figures are endowed with a warrior nobility quite different from the binary docile/savage imagery created by earlier writers. One of the most-cited sections of the poem about a young Indian couple focuses on the suicide of Lindóia in the "green theater" of the Brazilian wilderness. Following the death of her husband, who was betrayed by a Jesuit priest, Lindóia prefers death by poisonous snakebite to marriage with another man. The poem strikes a plaintive note in the description of her body in repose; the image of her beauty in death has a Petrachean quality and anticipates the *bon sauvage* creation of later prose writers and poets:

> Lying there, as if asleep,
> On the soft grass and amidst mimosas,
> With her face on her hand, and her hand resting on the trunk
> Of a funeral cypress that sheds
> A melancholic shade. Looking more closely,
> They discover a green serpent coiled upon her body,
> Which has wrapped itself around her neck and arms and is licking her breast.
> . . . .
> Her pallid semblance still preserves
> Some kind of sorrow, a sadness
> That softens even the hardest hearts.
> So very beautiful was the death on her face! (80–81)

The nativism that characterized much of the writing of the early eighteenth century became more pronounced and proto-nationalistic in the latter part of the century. *Cartas chilenas* was only one example of the increasing dissatisfaction with the economic noose that Portugal had placed around Brazil's neck. Brazilians were buoyed by the successful 1776 American Revolution to the north, and the French Revolution offered additional hope for a budding independence movement. On October 2, 1786, a Brazilian student at the university in Montpelier named José Joaquim de Maia penned a letter to then envoy to France Thomas Jefferson, whose support he attempted to enlist for a revolutionary movement forming in Minas Gerais. The letter begins:

I am a native of Brazil. You are not ignorant of the frightful slavery under which my country groans. This continually becomes more insupportable since the epoch of your glorious independence, for the cruel Portuguese omit nothing which can render our condition more wretched, from an apprehension that we may follow your example. . . . Sir, we can with propriety look only to the United States, not only because we are following her example, but, moreover, because nature, in making us inhabitants of the same continent, has in some sort united us in the bonds of a common patriotism. On our part, we are prepared to furnish the necessary supplies of money, and at all times to acknowledge the debt of gratitude due to our benefactors.[21]

In this letter the "cruel" Indians have now been replaced by the "cruel" Portuguese, who would prove to be a far more formidable foe. Jefferson wrote to John Jay on May 4, 1787, about the visit paid to him by Maia and about his understanding of the situation in Brazil, mainly that while there were large numbers of individuals who would fight for the cause of independence, no one there would lead the revolution without the backing of a powerful nation. He further observed:

The person I am referring to [a resident of Rio de Janeiro] knows the city and former capital of Salvador well, and the gold mines that are situated in the interior. All these places are poised for revolution, and since they constitute the corpus of the nation, they will bring the rest of the country along with them. . . . They need artillery, munitions, ships, sailors, soldiers, and officers and for all this they are resolved to approach the United States, always with the understanding that provisions and services will be paid for. . . . I took care to impress on him, throughout the whole of our conversation, that I had neither instructions nor authority to say a word to anybody on this subject, and that I could only give him my own ideas, as a single individual; which were, that we were not in a condition at present to meddle nationally in any war; that we wished particularly to cultivate the friendship of Portugal, with whom we have an advantageous commerce. That yet a successful revolution in Brazil could not be uninteresting to us. That prospects of lucre might possibly draw numbers of individuals to their aid, and purer motives our officers, among whom are many excellent. That our citizens being free to leave their own country individually, without the consent of their governments, are equally free to go to any other.[22]

Brazilians revolutionaries, whose ranks included various intellectuals inspired by the French Enlightenment such as the poets Cláudio Manuel da Costa and Tomás Antônio Gonzaga, ultimately found a leader in the military officer and dentist Joaquim José da Silva Xavier, also known as "Tiradentes" (puller of teeth). But the conspiracy to overthrow the Portuguese government, or Inconfidência Mineira, was denounced in 1789; Costa presumably killed himself while in prison, and Gonzaga was exiled to Africa. Tiradentes suffered a much crueler fate: in a gruesome public spectacle, he was hanged and quartered, and his decapitated head was later displayed in Minas Gerais.[23] But he became a martyr and symbol of Brazilian nationalist pride, and two more attempts to overthrow the monarchy were tried: the Inconfidência Bahiana in 1798, which was quickly put down; and the revolt nearly twenty years later in Pernambuco, which was more successful. In 1817 Thomas Jefferson noted in a letter to Lafayette: "Portugal, grasping at an extension of her dominion in the south, has lost her great northern province of Pernambuco, and I shall not wonder if Brazil should revolt in mass, and send their royal family back to Portugal. Brazil is more populous, more wealthy, more energetic, and as wise as Portugal."

At the time, there was widespread discontent with the Crown's imposition of heavy taxes and fines on a Brazilian economy that was experiencing hardships in the agricultural sector as well in the interior, where the supply of gold and precious stones was dwindling. The marquis of Pombal, who was minister to Dom José I and ruled Portugal and the colonies with an iron hand, was especially concerned with maintaining complete control over the less-populated areas of Brazil. To that end, he confiscated the properties and income of the Jesuits and ultimately expelled them from Brazil in 1759. Two years earlier, he issued a decree that abolished the enslavement of Indians, believing, like earlier officials, that by encouraging population growth through the union of whites and Indians, the Portuguese government would have a more secure hold on regions in the interior. Discontent among the populace was exacerbated by an extraordinarily punitive degree in 1785, whereby Queen Maria I announced that industries in the interior would be disallowed because they drew too many workers from the cities, mines, and fields. Her decree was primarily directed at textile and clothing manufacturers who produced trimmings for clothes, gold and silver embroideries, velvet, taffeta, linen, and cotton. One concession was requested, for allowing the production of ordinary cotton garments (probably similar to the shifts drawn by Carlos Julião), which were used to clothe blacks, Indians, and the poor.[24]

Concurrent with the rise of dissent and revolutionary movements was Portugal's continued desire to explore the innermost regions of Brazil. Inspired by the ideas associated with the Enlightenment, in 1783 the Portuguese government mantled an epic expedition referred to as the Viagem Filosófica (Philosophical Voyage) through the central part of Brazil to collect, record, and illustrate animals, plants, and minerals from the interior. The expedition was led by the Brazilian-born naturalist Alexandre Rodrigues Ferreira, who was accompanied by artists José Joaquim Freire and Joaquim Codina. Among their 912 illustrations are riveting portraits of newly discovered indigenous peoples as well as some of the earliest paintings of tribal costumes and masks. The expedition, based in Mato Grosso, journeyed throughout the area now known as the Amazon Basin.

Ferreira, later nicknamed "the Brazilian Humboldt" because of his energy, erudition, and talent, spent nine years studying and collecting flora and fauna. His scientific reports along with a huge collection of drawings and paintings, including many of his own, were shipped back to Portugal, where they were housed until 1807. With the invasion of Napoleon's forces, the invaluable record of the Philosophical Voyage was confiscated by the French naturalist Geoffrey St. Hilaire, who apparently claimed credit for New World finds originally uncovered by Ferreira.[25] At the same time, the flight of the Portuguese court to Rio de Janeiro in 1807 and the subsequent opening of Brazilian ports in 1808 fostered a new era of exploration and discovery. With the royal family now ensconced in Brazil, the country was about to enter a new phase in its history and its cultural imaginary. It was leaving behind its status as colony to become a kingdom alongside those of Portugal and the Algarve—and finally an independent nation.

CHAPTER 3

Regal Brazil

According to historian Oliveira Lima in his *Formação histórica da naciona-lidade brasileira* (Historical Formation of Brazilian Nationality), the idea of transferring the seat of the monarchy from Lisbon to Brazil had been brief-ly considered in the mid-seventeenth century by the Spanish-born Luísa de Gusmão, who was the widow of Dom João IV and regent for her son, Afonso (1997, 106).[1] An energetic and ambitious monarch, she was the one to whom her husband had turned for advice when, as the duke of Bragança, he was offered the crown by leaders of the movement to restore Portuguese independence from Spain in 1640. Legend has it that her advice consisted of a single sentence: "Better to reign than to serve" (*Dicionário prático ilus-trado* 1979, p. 1759)—which was apparently enough to convince him to ac-cept the job. As discussed in the previous chapter, the years following the dual monarchy proved to be a difficult economic time for Portugal. Luísa's contemplation of moving to Brazil was precipitated by her fear that Spain might again challenge Portuguese sovereignty (Lima 1997, 106); and, like her husband, she sought counsel from the influential Jesuit Antônio Vieira, who was a passionate spokesman for Brazil.

In her book *Tropical Versailles* (2001), historian Kirsten Schultz reminds us that the British later suggested that the Portuguese monarchy move to Brazil when in 1762 an invasion by the Franco-Spanish alliance appeared possible (36n48). England was already benefiting enormously from the Methuen Treaty with Portugal, and its offer to transport the royal court was a means to increase its influence and have more direct commercial dealings with Brazil. In 1801, another proposal to move the court was made by two Portuguese statesmen, the marquis of Alorna and the count of Egas. They saw Brazil as a desirable refuge from the pressures and threats posed by France, which was intent upon destroying the long-standing Anglo-Portu-guese alliance. Two years later the royal treasurer Rodrigo Sousa Coutinho made an even more compelling case for the court's transference based on the escalating tensions between France and England and on Brazil's greater security and political and economic potential for the empire. But because the Portuguese noble and merchant classes had little or no holdings or investment in Brazil, they rejected Sousa Coutinho's proposal (Schultz 2001, 31n2).

It was only when Napoleon actually marched on Portugal in 1807 that the monarchy hastily took its leave. A small British fleet that had been standing by escorted the approximately thirty Portuguese ships and smaller merchant vessels that transported Prince Regent Dom João and his family. The ships also carried the royal library, a printing press, and treasury and other government records—all of which were loaded into seven hundred coaches and taken to the docks (Schultz 2001, 68). In addition to the royal family, passengers included as many members of the court, military, and clergy as could finagle and battle their way onboard. It is estimated that between 10,000 and 15,000 people sailed with Dom João to Brazil (Fausto 1999, 64), while the rest of his subjects remained in Portugal to face the invading French forces.

It is impossible to know what images the New World evoked in the minds of these unseasoned transatlantic travelers during the voyage, but one might suspect that the idea of Brazil conjured up visions largely based on descriptions and illustrations of primitives, forests, and exotic wildlife.[2] There was little exuberance about this transatlantic journey, which, for those accustomed to comfort, was crowded and early on plagued by strong storms. Indeed, in most ways the reaction of the passengers to Brazil was in striking contrast to those Portuguese who had first set foot on New World soil. Although these nineteenth-century voyagers admired the vistas of the former capital city of Salvador, where Dom João's ship was forced to stop for repairs, and the spectacular bay and mountains surrounding Rio de Janeiro, which was to become the home of the thousands of exiles, they complained bitterly about the heat, humidity, rain, insects, diseases, and lack of suitable housing. Whatever image of Brazil they might have had prior to their landing, the realities of life in the colony were hard for some to bear. Among these was Carlota Joaquina, the Spanish-born wife of Dom João, who had declined her request to allow her to return to Spain with their daughters rather than relocate to the tropics. Exiles wrote woeful letters to family and friends left behind in Portugal describing Brazil as a "sad and sickly land" populated by a less-than-civilized people (in Schultz 2001, 70). For many of those transplanted to Brazil, the motherland took on the guise of a *locus amoenus*—even though news from Portugal clearly indicated that there was nothing "gentle" about the war-torn situation there.

For his part, Dom João was eager to address the hardships in his new homeland, and in January 1808, shortly after arriving in Brazil, he reversed a royal decree that had kept Brazilian ports closed even to nations friendly with Portugal. Four months later, from his residence in Rio, he lifted the ban that his mother, Queen Maria I (who had been diagnosed insane in 1792 and no longer ruled), had placed on manufacturing in the colony. Later that same year, he repealed another decree that prohibited printing in the colony, and he immediately established a royal press that issued the country's first newspaper, the *Gazeta do Rio de Janeiro,* which was published until 1822.[3]

With the opening of the ports, Brazil became the destination of thousands of foreign travelers as well as numerous scientific expeditions, which were welcomed by Dom João. Expeditions led by naturalists like the German Prince Maximilian von Wied-Neuwied, who was greatly influenced by Alexander von Humboldt's research in South America, provided important information to Dom João about Brazil's resource potentials. Wied-Neuwied's expedition and others were critical to his plans for better communication and transportation systems (I. Leite 1996, 50, 54).[4] If it were the case that the Portuguese were no longer interested in exploring or having direct knowledge of still unknown parts of Brazil, this was far from true for other Europeans, who were responsible for a veritable "rediscovery" of the nation in the early part of the century (ibid., 47). For example, several historiographies of Brazil were published in England, most notably Robert Southey's multivolume *History of Brazil* (1810–1819), as well as travelogues by Henry Koster and John Luccock that inspired readers of English to see the vast and exotic land. Historian Ilka Bonaventura Leite gives an interesting example of how foreign travelers would venture into Minas Gerais to see the mines even though the extraction of gold and diamonds was largely over. Just the idea of the rich depositories that once existed in the area (and that greatly benefited England) was sufficient to compel visitors to travel difficult roads to reach the mining interior (1996, 52–53).

The opening of the ports and the various treaties signed with England in 1810 had both positive and negative effects on Brazil. The country's knowledge bank increased significantly with the freer circulation of printed news and the greater number of imported books. At the same time, the number of goods imported by Brazil rose dramatically—especially those from England, which was given a tax advantage. The flood of manufactured goods to Brazil caused unanticipated problems for the still inadequate customs services and storehouses in Rio. The British naturalist and mineralogist John Mawe, who stopped in Rio prior to traveling into the interior, described the confusion and absurdities that he witnessed in and around the port:

> The [Guanabara] bay was covered with ships and the custom-house soon overflowed with goods. Even salt, casks of ironmongery, salt-fish, hogsheads of cheese, hats, together with an immense quantity of crates and hogsheads of earthen and glass ware, cordage, bottled and barreled porter, paints, guns, resins &c were exposed, not only to the sun and rain, but to general depredation. The inhabitants of Rio de Janeiro, principally some Creoles and strangers from the interior, thought that these goods were placed there for their benefit, and extolled the goodness and generosity of the English, who strewed the beach to a great extent with articles for which their own countrymen had heretofore charged them but high prices. . . .
>
> To the serious losses thus occasioned by an overstocked flooded market, and by the sacrifice of goods at whatever price could be obtained, may be added another, which originated in the ignorance of many persons who sent out articles to a considerable amount not at all suited to the country; one speculator, of wonderful insight, sent large invoices of stays for ladies, who had never heard of such armor. Another sent skates, for the use of people who are totally unaware that water can become ice. A third sent out a considerable assortment of the most elegant coffin-furniture, not knowing that coffins are never used by the Brazilians, or in the Plata. . . . Large cargoes of Manchester goods were sent; and in a few months more arrived than had been consumed in the course of twenty years preceding. (1816, 333–335)

What Mawe's commentary tells us is that, regardless of the degree of absurdity in the selection of wares, British merchants and manufacturers viewed Brazil as a commercial paradise. Moreover, unlike in earlier colonial times, no longer was the principal direction of commodities going out from Brazil. As a consequence of the accessibility and volume of British manufactured goods, the industrialization of certain sectors in Brazil seemed less urgent—to the detriment of the nation as a whole. In the meantime, Brazil continued to rely on exporting agricultural products and leather goods, which were both plentiful and inexpensive.[5]

The installation of the royal government in Rio was both exciting and frustrating to the local inhabitants. On the one hand, the monarchy lifted bans, printed news, opened the country to foreign businessmen and scientific explorers, and established a national library, a theater, and a bank—all of which were welcomed by residents. There were also elaborate celebrations and processions held in honor of religious holidays, visiting dignitaries, and the like. On the other hand, the lack of local representation in the country's new government was deeply resented—especially by the merchant and upper classes. In 1810, José Hipólito da Costa, founder of the London-based opposition newspaper *Correio braziliense ou armazem literário* (Brazilian Courier or Literary Magazine),[6] which he published from 1808 to 1822, sharply criticized this situation and warned of its consequences while calling attention to the problematic image of Brazilian-born inhabitants long held by their European counterparts:

Government seats are a kind of monopoly. Those who traveled from Brazil to Portugal were looked upon as foreigners by the government and as monkeys by the people there. Now the government is in Brazil, and for the same reasons the local residents could regard the Europeans as foreigners. But not one of our compatriots from Brazil has been promoted to the State Council of the nation. Foreigners in their own house and foreigners outside of it. This proves not only the monopoly of which we speak, but also the lack of common sense by these monopolists. For if only to sweeten the taste in the mouths of the people from Brazil, they could have named one of the locals for the Council, even choosing some adulator or parasite, of which Brazil, as any other country in the world, abounds. But even this was not done. It is now three years that the foreigners sought refuge in Brazil, and whatever the opinion Europeans may have about the lack of talent and energy of local inhabitants, everyone should realize that Brazilians are not blind. It is enough to be able to see to understand the injustice of these proceedings, even more so as we watch the present circumstances unfold between Spain and its colonies. (In Inácio and Luca 1993, 182)[7]

With the defeat of Napoleon by the British in 1814, Dom João was free to return to Portugal, but he chose to stay in Brazil. Historian Neill Macaulay asserts that by remaining in Rio, the regent had a better chance of fending off British influence while "serving as a pillar of legitimacy on a continent wracked by revolution" (1986, 55). To this end, in 1815, Dom João raised the profile and status of the country by proclaiming it on par with Portugal and the Algarve in the newly formed United Kingdom of Portugal, Brazil, and the Algarve—an action that assuaged the exiles, who regarded their new home as less than civilized, while empowering Brazilian-born residents, who looked forward to a more central role in governing the empire.

But not everyone was pleased with Dom João's decree, particularly people in the Northeastern state of Pernambuco, where a slump in the area's agricultural economy was made worse by rivalry and competition between Brazilian-born and Portuguese merchants. New tax laws put even more pressure on Northeasterners to fund Dom João's unpopular efforts to annex Uruguay as a result of Spain's refusal to return the formerly Portuguese border town of Olivenza, which Spain had captured in 1801.

In the spring of 1817, a resistance movement made up of military, clergy, landowners, merchants and peasants took control of the Pernambucan capital, Recife, and a provisional government was formed that was to treat Brazilians and Portuguese alike. In March, a constitution was signed that announced the freedom of the press and religion. The twenty-sixth amendment specifically addressed the issue of equality among residents: "The naturalized and established Europeans among us, who have shown their allegiance to the party for regeneration and freedom are all patriots, can enter positions in the Republic for which they are qualified and able" (in Inácio and Luca 1993, 185). As Boris Fausto notes, however, nowhere in the constitution was there any mention of the hundreds of thousands of slaves who worked the cane and cotton fields (1999, 68). Two months later, the provisional government was attacked and defeated by the army of the governor of Bahia, a stalwart friend of the prince regent, and the governor ordered the executions of several revolutionary leaders. There was a certain irony about the events in Pernambuco: despite the tensions between locals and Portuguese in Brazil, the revolution gave heart to citizens back in Lisbon and throughout Portugal who hoped to rid themselves of the British regency of Marshall Beresford, who had led the troops in Portugal to victory against Napoleon's invading forces.

Although the desire for autonomy would increase steadily in Brazil in the next few years, the period between 1816 and 1821 was vibrant with cultural and scientific expeditions that opened up the country to discoveries and new ideas from various parts of the world—especially France. Once Napoleon was defeated, Dom João, through his ambassador to Paris, issued an invitation to a group of French artists to come to Rio in 1816. Members of what became know as the French Cultural Mission included one of Napoleon's favorite portrait painters, Jean Baptiste Debret. Along with fellow artists, Debret provided what Oliveira Lima has referred to as the "intellectual emancipation" of Brazil: "Looking through the beautiful works of Debret, whose curious lithographs record the great ceremonies of the Court of Rio de Janeiro in the first quarter of the nineteenth century . . . , one sees graphically where and how the country's national sentiment was formed" (1945, 268). In his essay "Why and For What Purpose Does the European Travel?" (2001), Brazilian cultural critic Silviano Santiago is skeptical about this and other "civilizing" missions that came from Europe (and elsewhere) to Brazil. He states: "It becomes the urgent requirement for the young nation to continue the process of westernization that it started on without requesting it" (17).

The specific assignment of the French Cultural Mission was to found an Institute of Fine Arts, where students would learn the fundamentals as well as latest trends in art and architectural design.[8] In addition to Debret, the mission included landscape painter Nicolas Antoine Taunay, his brother and sculptor Auguste Marie Taunay, architect Auguste Henri Victor Grandjean de Montigny, sculptor Marc Ferrez, engraver Charles Simon Pradier, and historiographer and leader of the mission Henri Lebreton, who brought with him an estimated sixty works that included paintings and engravings from France, Italy, and Holland. However, considerable controversy arose among the local intelligentsia about the significant role that France was being given in the development of the nation's cultural and scientific agendas. Oliveira Lima describes the French artists' discontent after Portuguese painter Henrique José da Silva was appointed to replace Lebreton as the head of the school. The artists complained that

> Portuguese intrigues were more actively heated, which was the reason the painter Taunay withdrew to France. In effect, the new director, in a highly nationalistic desire to reform even that which had yet to function, began to suppress positions and therefore to eliminate French artists, such as the copperplate engraver, two students from Architecture who also were teaching at the time, and the professor of Mechanics. (1945, 270–271)

As a result of the political maelstrom around this mission, a project that was expected to be accomplished in a couple of years stretched into a decade before the Institute of Fine Arts was officially opened in 1826. Debret stayed in Brazil for five more years, finally returning in 1831 to France, where he published his three-volume *Voyage pitoresque et historique au Brésil* (Picturesque and Historic Voyage to Brazil), regarded as one of the most important documents on the arts in Brazil.

Although Debret figures prominently in art histories on Brazil, little has been written about his historical and ethnographic narrative, which forms the background and context for the many illustrations in his work. There is no doubt that Debret was an enlightened figure and an enthusiast of Brazil, yet many of his ideas about the nation reflected notions espoused in the sixteenth century, with the source of wonder encompassing not only the indigenous peoples but also those of mixed race and African blood. For example, he marveled at the sight of a Botocudo Indian who has been brought to the city—an episode reminiscent of the spectacle and entertainment provided to the French by Tupis, who were transported to Rouen in the sixteenth century. He also called attention to the bravery of Europeans who traveled far into the interior and faced hardships and danger in order to study "primitive" indigenous communities. In lauding the valor of the European, however, Debret reminded his reader that three centuries earlier the ancestors of the native peoples lived largely along the coast and that they even welcomed the Portuguese when they stepped onshore. In other words, theirs was not a question of preferring the remote interior but rather of retreating to it as a way to resist European efforts to "civilize" them or to do away with them altogether.[9] In his account, Debret emphasized the instincts and ferocity of the indigenous male, who, in his view, was the incarnation of nature, while he described "civilized" (white) man as the bearer of science (1954, 1:13). He offered other current, albeit problematic, notions about race that were popular at the time, claiming at one point that Indian men regularly gave their daughters to white men as a way to improve the tribe's blood line (1:22).

Debret's account includes a "scientific" classification that apparently was established by the Portuguese government to chart the degree of civilization of peoples residing in Brazil—a classification that supports Hipólito da Costa's 1810 denunciation of how the Portuguese (or "those from Europe") continued to regard "Brazilians"—not to mention others—as inferior beings in their own homeland. The chart reads as follows (2:87):

1. *Portuguese* from Europe, legitimate Portuguese or *son of the Realm*
2. *Portuguese born in Brazil,* of a more or less distant ascendancy, *Brazilian*
3. *Mulatto,* mixed race, white male and black female
4. *Mameluco,* mixed race of white and Indian
5. *Pure Indian,* primitive male inhabitant; wife of Indian
6. *Civilized Indian, Caboclo, Tame Indian*
7. *Savage Indian,* in the primitive state, *Tapuia,* wild
8. *Black from Africa, Black born outside Brazil; moleque,* young black
9. *Black born in Brazil, creole*
10. *Goat,* mixed race of black with mulatto; *she-goat,* the female
11. *Curiboca,* mixed race of black with Indian

Debret often assumed a "scientific" posture, stating in his introduction to volume 2 that his intention was to "accompany the 'progressive march of civilization in Brazil,' [by] reproducing the 'instinctive tendencies of the indigenous savage' and emphasizing all of his progress in the 'imitation of the activity of the Brazilian colonialist,' who himself is the heir of traditions from the mother country" (2:85). Thus, volume 1 is dedicated largely to a discussion and illustrations of the indigenous population, as identified in numbers 5 through 7 on the chart, while volume 2 focuses on all other categories except the "legitimate Portuguese," who are the central focus of volume 3.

The stunning visual ethnography left by Debret undoubtedly had far greater impact on the formation of an image of Brazil than his narrative. But it is important to note that his discussions and portraits of racial groups such as "savage Indians" often conflicted with the pseudoscientific classifications that he used to give a certain order to his work. For instance, the lithographs of Brazilian "savages" seem less the product of a man of science than of a romantic who imagines the indigenous peoples of the forest, especially the men, in epic-heroic terms. His portraits of a Camacã man and woman are two excellent examples of a style of painting that focuses on the symbiotic relationship between a lush natural world and a larger-than-life indigenous people whose physical beauty, delicacy, and reserve contradicted prevailing notions of Indians as primitive and subhuman. In Debret's painting, the Camacã man has a proud yet slightly preoccupied look, and the multitiered feathers on his close-fitting headdress are unusually tall and seem to point toward the heavens. The strength of his body, posed in three-quarter profile, is conveyed by his muscular right shoulder and upper arm as well as by the broad fingers of his left hand, which tightly grasp a bundle of long, feather-tipped arrows. Different items that look like teeth and a seed pod hang from a simple beaded necklace around his muscular neck, while a strap decorated with teeth is slung in bandolier fashion across his upper torso. The overall effect of the portrait is quite powerful. The opulent headdress that serves as a crown conveys the ineluctable bond that Debret described between "primitives" and nature. This bond can be seen also in his portrait of a Camacã woman, whose beaded headband holds in place, on either side of her face, small branches adorned with tubular flowers and long, thin leaves. This festive head decoration lends a symmetry to the rest of her body, which is painted in full frontal pose. The woman's rather broad neck and substantial arms convey strength, while her large, round breasts emphasize health and nourishment. Her eyes, like those of her male counterpart, have a slightly Asian look; her demeanor, however, is more relaxed than the man's, and there is even a hint of a smile on her face.

Other lithographs in this section of Debret's work feature Indians from different tribal communities who are always portrayed in nature. In one painting, a Coroado leader, shown from the side and back striding up a hill and brandishing a spear, looks more like a figure out of classical mythology than a savage. The surrounding forest in this picture, with its detail of prickly cacti, ropes of vines, tree limbs, and dense foliage, appears as formidable as any human enemy. In fact, in his illustration of the Guaianases (also known as the Coroados), the Indians serve not as subject but rather as detail, and they provide a scale for the appreciation of the immense "green theater" that Basílio da Gama once described as Brazil. Debret's valiant Indian figures in the epic wilderness were undoubtedly forerunners of the popular "noble savage" of nineteenth-century Brazilian romantic literature—a figure who was later embraced by the nation as the symbol of independence.

There is inadequate space here to discuss the many observations Debret made about people of African descent in Brazil, although his commentary about the disdain that not only Portuguese but also Africans and Brazilian blacks felt for mulattoes is interesting, since the country's much later emphasis on the virtues of miscegenation (and the implicit whitening of the population) suggests that blacks have always aspired to be lighter in color. According to Debret, however, blacks regarded mulattoes as "mon-

3.1 Indian man, by Debret

3.2 Indian woman, by Debret

sters" and anathema to God's original creation of exclusively black and white peoples (1:108). The relative ease with which mulattoes gained their freedom or elided slavery—an ability that Debret attributes to their "parcel of intelligence" derived from the white race (ibid.)—was perhaps even more of a factor in the discrimination directed toward them by both blacks and whites.

3.3 A warrior, by Debret. Print Collection, Miriam and Ira D. Wallach Division of Art, Prints and Photographs, New York Public Library, Astor, Lenox and Tilden Foundations.

For his part, Debret seemed far more interested in the African population, and he gave a full account of the different roles carried out by slaves
as well as free men and women. In a lithograph titled *The Dinner,* two black
men and a black woman stand in attendance as a white couple dine at a
table heaped with food. The black woman is waving a fan of sorts, probably
to keep the air circulating or to drive away insects as the prosperous-look-
ing, fleshy couple eat their food. The two black men are pictured with their
arms crossed on their chests, as if standing at a kind of culinary attention.
The viewer's eye is immediately drawn to the two small black children, who
are naked and located in the painting's foreground. One child is standing
while being given a piece of food by the woman seated at the table as the
other child, who has already received his piece, eats in a seated position
on the floor. Debret's commentary on this scene draws a line between acts
of self-serving patronage and the hard future made even more difficult for
these children, who are coddled and fed like household pets:

> In Rio, as in all other cities of Brazil, it is the custom during the "tête à tête" of a
> conjugal meal, for the husband to silently busy himself with his business while
> the wife distracts herself with the small black children who stand in for pup-

3.4 *The Dinner,* Debret

pies, which today have almost completely disappeared in Europe. These little boys, who are fussed over until the age of five or six, are then handed over to the tyranny of other slaves, who tame them with whippings and get them in the habit of sharing their weary and unsavory labors. Outraged for no longer receiving succulent foods and sweets from the caring hands of their mistresses, these poor children try to compensate their loss by stealing garden fruits or battling with domestic animals for leftovers that their gluttony, suddenly frustrated, leads them to savor with true suffering. (1:137–138)

Debret's detailed chronicle of slave life in Brazil includes statistics that indicate that despite the abolition of the slave trade in England in 1808 and France in 1815, the business of transporting Africans to Brazil, which was to end officially in November 1829, was still in high gear in 1828, with 430,601 men, women, and children arriving that year alone (1:186). Debret mentioned that Africans brought to Brazil often believed they would be devoured not by savage Indians but by their future white owners—a fear that was not as fantastic as it might sound if one considers the all-consuming effects of slavery. Among Debret's lithographs are portraits of African "walking skeletons" (1:188) awaiting purchase by a wealthy proprietor, of slaves as workers in a shoe shop, as beasts of burden for grinding sugarcane, and as transporters of large casks and carts filled with cargo.

Debret also described and illustrated the lesser-known occupations of freed slaves who made their living as vendors, sidewalk surgeons, barbers, and guides for expeditions into the interior. He illustrated different forms of punishment experienced by slaves, including a snakelike iron collar that was placed around the necks of male and female runaway slaves, stocks that imprisoned the ankles and feet of other runaway slaves, a full-face iron mask that kept slaves from overimbibing, the *palmatória,* or paddle, used to beat a slave's hands, and the whip wielded by both white and black foremen who stripped slaves and trussed them up or tied them to stakes.

Similar scenes of work and punishment can be found in *Malerische Reise in Brasilien* (*Voyage pittoresque dans le Brésil,* Picturesque Journey in Brazil) by the German Johann Moritz Rugendas, who accompanied the baron of Langsdorff's 1822 scientific expedition to Brazil and published his observations and drawings during the same period that Debret's work appeared. But neither Debret's nor Rugendas's illustrations or narratives captured the harsh realities of slavery quite as effectively as the diary of the English travel

3.5 A master punishing a slave, by Debret

writer and illustrator Maria Graham, who lived in Brazil off and on between 1821 and 1823 and who was outspoken in her critique of the institution:[10]

> We had hardly gone fifty paces into Recife, when we were absolutely sickened by the first sight of a slave- market. It was the first time the boys or I had been in a slave-country; and, however strong and poignant the feelings may be at home [England], when imagination pictures slavery, they are nothing compared to the staggering sight of a slave-market. It was thinly stocked . . . Yet about fifty young creatures, boys and girls, with all the appearance of disease and famine consequent upon scanty food and long confinement in unwholesome places, were sitting and lying about among the filthiest animals on the streets. The sight sent us home to the ship with the heart-ache: and resolution, "not loud but deep," that nothing in our power should be considered too little, or too great, that can tend to abolish or alleviate slavery. (1824, 105)

In one diary entry, Graham reproduced a tally of the number of Africans who passed through Rio custom houses on a monthly basis between 1821 and 1822, and she included a table showing that of 1,574 Africans brought to Salvador in a three-month period, 374—more than 20 percent—perished at sea (151). She included information provided by an acquaintance, Captain Finelaison, who described to her how slavers would force African women into casks and throw them overboard whenever their ships were chased or how they would confine slaves in small, airless crates—often resulting in the slaves' deaths—whenever the ships were seized and searched (ibid.).

Graham noted that slaves who survived the transatlantic ordeal were far from safe on land and that female owners could be as abusive as males:

> This morning before breakfast, looking from the balcony of Mr. S's house, I saw a white woman, or rather fiend, beating a young negress, and twisting her arms cruelly while the poor creature screamed in agony, till our gentlemen interfered. Good God! that such a traffic, such a practice as that of slavery, should exist. Near the house there are two or three depots of slaves, all young; in one, I saw an infant of about two years old, for sale. Provisions are so scarce [because of the war between Portuguese and Brazilian-born over the country's independence] that no bit of animal food ever seasons the paste of manioc flour, which is the sustenance of slaves: and even of this, these poor children, by their projecting bones and hollow cheeks, show that they seldom get a sufficiency. Now, money also is so scarce, that a purchaser is not easily found, and one pang is added to slavery: the unavailing wish of finding a master! (107)

Although slavery was still practiced in the United States, in his travelogue, *Life in Brazil* (1856), the North American Thomas Ewbank was alarmed by the medieval-style torture devices used publicly on slaves in Brazil and the growing rate of suicide among them:

> I passed in the same street [in Rio] a short, spare, and feeble old woman, creeping along the pavement with a baril [sic] of water on her head. An iron collar grasp[ed] her shriveled throat, and from its prong a chain ran up and was secured to the handle of the vessel by a padlock—about as cruel a sight as I have seen yet.
>
> "Is it a cause of wonder that so many of your slaves emancipate themselves by death rather than endure life on such conditions?" "To treat them that way," replied my friend, "or to put masks on them, is forbidden, but laws respecting them are disregarded." Every day or two suicides are announced in the police reports, yet it is affirmed that not half are officially noticed. Those who plunge into the [Guanabara] Bay and float ashore come under the cognizance of the authorities. Of such as sink and never rise, and all that pass out to sea, or are devoured by sharks before they reach it, no account is or can be kept, nor yet

of those who destroy themselves in the secret places of the city or dark recesses of the neighboring forests. Many are advertised as runaways who have reached the spirit land. Suicides, it is said, have greatly increased during the last three years. (1971, 280–281)

Whether benign or shocking, images of slave life in travelogues and pictorials of Brazil were generally overshadowed by descriptions of flora and fauna and the occasional sighting of "savages," who had largely vanished into the interior. Maria Graham's diary is filled with observations that confirm Brazil's continuing fascination as a kind of Garden of Eden: "Every time I pass a grove in Brazil, I see new flowers and plants, and a richness of vegetation that seems inexhaustible" (1824, 286). Like Debret, she was intrigued by some visiting Botocudo Indians from the interior whom the city fathers tried to "civilize" by feeding them and giving them trinkets. Graham's description is reminiscent of the earliest narratives about the native inhabitants, whom she found comely if not handsome. However, like Léry and Montaigne, she was far less judgmental about practices such as cannibalism: "I cannot believe that any ever fed habitually on human flesh, for many reasons" (295n); and she firmly believed that atrocities claimed to be carried out by the Indians were actually fabricated by their "traducers," who used them as an excuse to capture and enslave the indigenous populations (294–295).

The period between 1816 and 1822 was a heady time for anyone who traveled or lived in Brazil. Debret recounted the country's celebrations surrounding the acclamation of Dom João VI after the death of his mother, the "mad" Queen Maria I. Debret's lithograph of this historical moment was followed one year later by another depicting the arrival of Brazil's new royal princess, the Austrian Archduchess Leopoldina, who was earlier married by proxy to Prince Pedro in 1817. A supporter of the arts and an amateur naturalist, Leopoldina sent her family in Austria numerous drawings of Brazilian plants and flowers that she collected on her daily walks, many of which were executed by Debret (Debret 1954, 2:174). Interest in local fauna led to the monarchy's decree in 1809 that established the Royal Botanical Garden, whose majestic palms appeared in late-century photographs and were a favorite motif for turn-of-the-century postcards produced in Brazil.[11]

Accompanying Leopoldina to Rio in 1817 was an expedition of natural scientists and artists known as the Austrian Mission, whose task was to collect specimens and illustrate the people and landscapes for a museum on Brazil to be established in Vienna. The mission remained in Brazil for nearly five years. At age twenty-three, the artist Thomas Ender also served as chronicler on the voyage over from Europe. Although he stayed in Brazil for only ten months, Ender alone produced more than one thousand drawings and watercolors; he was also influential for Rugendas, who traveled from Munich to Brazil shortly after the return of the Austrian Mission in 1821. The Austrian group also included the botanist Carl Friedrich Phillip von Martius and the zoologist Johann Baptiste von Spix, whose collaborative *Atlas sur Reisen in Brasilien* (Atlas of the Voyage Through Brazil), published 1823–1831, was as important to defining natural history as both science and art as Alexander von Humboldt and Aimé Bonpland's 1814 *Relation historique du voyage aux régions équinoxiales du nouveau continent (Personal Narrative of Travels to the Equinoctial Regions of the New Continent).*[12]

It is not by chance that both Debret and Rugendas used the term "picturesque" in the titles of their respective works. As art historian Philip Conisbee notes in *Painting in Eighteenth-Century France,* landscape artists were eager to take advantage of the public interest in copiously illustrated travelogues, a vogue that took root in the late eighteenth century (1981, 186).[13] Like sixteenth-century chroniclers, Debret and Rugendas produced works that capitalized on the visual grandeur and "foreignness" of the New World. As mentioned above, they also tended to play down or to avoid altogether the more difficult or problematic aspects of life in the tropics, perhaps because of the official nature of their expeditions. For example, although Rugendas's *Public Punishments* depicts the public flogging of a slave, the slave's back is conveniently turned away from the viewer. The viewer's eye is drawn away from the slave toward other actions and elaborately drawn figures in the square as well as to the mountains, trees, and celestial clouds that serve as a backdrop. Likewise, Debret's *Execution of the Whipping* shows a slave from the back, stripped from the waist down and bound to a pillar. Neither image conveys the brutality of whipping. There is even a voyeuristic quality to the scene Debret depicted: the tight bindings give inordinate emphasis to the slave's naked buttocks, which strangely seem to be the only target of punishment.

Rugendas's lithograph *Blacks in the Ship's Hold* depicts a relaxed, almost congenial atmosphere; the spaciousness of the hold contrasts sharply with blueprint-style engravings of the period that show slaves laid out side by side with no room to spare. In a similar vein, Debret's *Metal Mask Used on Blacks Who Have the Habit of Eating Earth* reduces the iron mask to the level of decorative ornament on a colorfully dressed slave, along the order of the enormous Grecian-style urn that he balances on his head.[14] To be fair, Debret's work does provides a good deal of information about the various devices used to punish slaves. But he regarded slaves among those most removed from the aristocracy of civilized human beings, stating at one point that "blacks are nothing more than big children, whose spirit is too narrow for them to think about the future, and too indolent to be concerned with it" (1954, 1:256). He commented rather matter-of-factly on whippings, observing that they were necessary to maintain discipline in the New World nation, where slaves were treated with the greatest humanity (1:264).

Debret was still in Brazil in 1821 when Dom João VI reluctantly returned to Portugal following that country's 1820 liberal revolution, which resulted

3.6 *Public Punishments,* by Rugendas

3.7 *Execution of the Whipping,* by Debret

3.8 *Blacks in the Ship's Hold,* by Rugendas

3.9 *Metal Mask Used on Blacks,* by Debret

in the ousting of the British regency. Portugal's first constitution, according to historian Tom Gallagher, made clear that the returning sovereign could reign but not rule (1983, 13). The French naturalist Auguste de Saint-Hilaire, who lived in Brazil from 1816 to 1822, keenly observed that the Portuguese had risen up

> perhaps not with the intent of weakening the royal authority as much as reestablishing control of its former colony, whose emancipation was an issue of great displeasure. In effect, such an emancipation relegated Portugal to a secondary status, resulting in the loss of one of its principle sources of wealth. Not only its national pride was wounded but also its interests. The assembly of the Courts of Lisbon judged that, in order to become popular, it was necessary to place Brazil back under the control of the metropolis. (In Inácio and Luca 1993, 191, 193)

Portuguese disdain toward Brazil in 1821 seemed as great as or greater than in 1810, when Hipólito da Costa complained of it in the *Correio braziliense*. Leaders of the Portuguese revolution now sought to curb constitutionally driven concessions given to Brazil by Dom João prior to his departure, and they publicly referred to the country as a "land of monkeys, bananas, and darkies plucked from the coast of Africa" (Fausto 1999, 70). *Deputados*, representatives sent to Portugal from Brazil, were scorned in the court and in the Lisbon newspaper *O contra-censor pela galeria: Semanário político* (The Gallery's Counter-Censor: A Political Weekly), which showed its disdain for the Brazilians by printing the word *deputados* upside down (*Brazil from Discovery to Independence* 1972, 36).

More troubling than name-calling or jibes in the newspapers was the real possibility that Brazil would lose the prince regent, Pedro, who had been left in charge by his father and was now ordered by the courts to return to Lisbon. Maria Graham's residency in Brazil coincided with the tug-of-war between Portugal and Brazil over Pedro and the actions and debates that fueled Brazil's mounting desire for independence. In her diary she copied a letter written by Brazilian officials to the prince regent in which they beseeched him to refuse the courts' mandate and remain in his adopted homeland:

> "How then dares a mere fraction of the great Portuguese nation [Portugal, Brazil, and the Algarve], without waiting for the conclusion of this solemn national compact [the constitution], attack the general good of the principal part of the

same, and such is the vast and rich kingdom of Brazil; dividing it into miserable fragments, and, in a word, attempting to tear from its bosom the representative of the executive power, and to annihilate by a stroke of the pen, all the tribunals and establishments necessary to its existence and future prosperity? This unheard-of despotism, this horrible political perjury, was certainly not merited by the good and generous Brazil . . . .

"... If Your Royal Highness, which is not to be believed, were to obey the absurd and indecent decree of the 29th of September, besides losing, in the world, the dignity of a man and of a prince, by becoming the slave of a small number of facetious men, you would also have to answer before heaven for the rivers of blood which would assuredly inundate Brazil on account of your absence: because its inhabitants, like raging tigers, would surely remember the supine sloth in which the ancient despotism kept them buried, and in which a new constitutional Machiavelism aims even now to retain them." (1824, 175–176)

According to historian Emília Viotti da Costa, popular verses were printed and posted in the streets advising Pedro that it was far better to be Pedro the First in Brazil than waiting to be Pedro the Fourth in Portugal (2000, 17); and a newspaper named for a hot red pepper, *A malagueta,* encouraged the prince to defy the courts' order for his immediate return (Macaulay 1986, 105). In January, the prince regent publicly declared that he would remain in Brazil, using the single first-person verb *fico* (I am staying)—which is how that important moment in history is often identified. Following a combative eight months during which Pedro ordered the withdrawal of Portuguese troops from Brazil and blocked the entry of ships from Lisbon bearing troop reinforcements, he proclaimed Brazil's "independence or death" on the banks of the Ipiranga River on September 7, 1822. He was pronounced Perpetual Defender and Constitutional Emperor of Brazil in coronation and acclamation ceremonies in Rio, the solemnity, pomp, and public celebration of which are expertly captured in historical paintings by Debret, who was among those in attendance.

As a result of the proclamation of independence, Hipólito da Costa closed the *Correio braziliense,* although debates continued between liberals and conservatives about the nation's future, and there were even attempts at secession and rebellion. But for the moment, the country was experiencing a patriotic euphoria that resounded in the speeches and poetry of statesman José Bonifácio de Andrada e Silva—whose work for the cause of emancipation (most notably his tutelage of and influence on his pupil, Pedro I) gained him the popular title "Patriarch of Independence"—and in fiery sermons about God and liberty by religious leaders like Friar Francisco de Monte Alverne, whom critic Alfredo Bosi regards as the true inspiration for Brazilian romanticism (1997, 95). But no text had as wide a dissemination as the "Imperial and Constitutional Hymn" published by the Royal Press, whose verses by Evaristo da Veiga on the joys of freedom and the "brave Brazilian people" were set to music composed by none other than the Emperor Dom Pedro I himself.

On November 16, 1822, a new symbol of the nation appeared in the form of the Brazilian flag, which was designed by the Frenchman Debret. Its green and yellow colors of the imperial houses formed the background for a coat of arms with a sky-blue circle containing nineteen silver stars that corresponded to the provinces of Brazil. The palm tree that for centuries was emblematic of Brazil was replaced with branches from coffee and tobacco plants that run beneath and alongside the crowned coat of arms, as if to reinforce their commercial importance and support to the nation. Following a procession that traveled throughout the city of Rio and was led by Dom Pedro I on horseback, a church service was performed at the Imperial Cathedral, where the flag was blessed. Shortly thereafter, in an even larger and more significant ceremony, the army took an oath to uphold the new flag. About this occasion Debret wrote: "That military act, whose energetic display proclaimed before the world the independent existence of Brazil, the former Portuguese colony so gloriously regenerated, concluded amidst the unanimous, enthusiastic cheer: *Long live D. Pedro I, perpetual defender and constitutional emperor of Brazil*" (1954, 2:222).

But it was one thing for a country to declare its independence and quite another to recognize and define itself as a nation. To a certain extent and in strictly political terms, the seeds for that process already had been sown with the unsuccessful attempt in Minas in 1789 to overthrow the monarchy and create a free and democratic Brazil. However, in cultural terms, the process of self-awareness and identification would be more gradual and extend well into the twentieth century. In 1873, fifty years after independence, the novelist and critic Machado de Assis remarked in his essay "Instinto da Nacionalidade" (Instinct of Nationality) that although there was a "general desire to create a more independent literature," this literature "still does not exist" and would not exist until the imagination became "engaged with the problems of the day and century" (1970, 131). But Machado's sense of what a Brazilian national literature should be was unique for its time. In the meanwhile, the country experienced one of the liveliest and richest periods in the history of its literature, a period in which the romantic-realist works about patriotic themes and heroic types are foundational to the idea of the nation.

CHAPTER 4

The Foundations of a National Literary Imaginary

Whoever examines present-day Brazilian literature will soon recognize, as its first trait, a certain instinct of nationality.
MACHADO DE ASSIS, "Instinto da nacionalidade," 1873

The Indian: Redux

In truth, these people are not of pure white blood and European pride looks upon them with scorn. But all the great qualities of their ancestors compete within them. The descendant of the white male with the Indian female resembles the mother more than the father. For him, liberty is everything. The mulatto is lively and filled with imagination. From both of these races great poets will emerge.
CARL SCHLICHTHORST, *Rio de Janeiro Wie Es Ist,* 1829

The sustained interest in the indigenous inhabitants by foreign travelers and scientific and artistic expeditions in the early part of the nineteenth century may give some indication why Brazil continued to be linked in the global imagination to the figure of the Amerindian.[1] Yet with some notable exceptions, Brazilian literature in the late eighteenth and early nineteenth centuries rarely looked to the indigenous inhabitant as subject.[2] This is partly explained by the neoclassical orientation of the lyric sensibility of the period and the disregard as poetic material of the poor and marginalized indigenous population in the cities.

Historian Nelson Werneck Sodré has observed that writers of this period "failed to offer anything specifically Brazilian and, therefore, should be considered part of the protohistory of our literary development" (1943, 28). His assessment overlooks the Indian protagonists created by Antônio Dinis da Cruz e Silva in *Metamorfoses,* posthumously published in 1814, and Cláudio Manuel da Costa in *Fábula do Ribeirão do Carmo,* published in 1768, which recall the Edenic hybrid figure of the sixteenth-century imagination.[3] But perhaps even more "specifically Brazilian" was the writing of

African-Brazilian poet Domingos Caldas Barbosa, who traveled to Portugal in 1763 and was celebrated in Lisbon society for his playful and witty *modinhas* and *lunduns*—poems inspired by African-Brazilian music, song, and dance. His "Lundum em louvor de uma brasileira adotiva" (Lundum in Praise of an Adoptive Brazilian Woman) is just one example of a consciousness of the land that was not readily apparent in Brazilian writing of the period. Somewhat like early nativist poets, Barbosa also used African-Brazilian terms such as *moleque* (black boy), *iaiá* (missy), and *nhanhanzinha* (little missy) in his lyric and comic-satiric verse. His success as a writer irritated Manuel Maria Barbosa du Bocage, Portugal's much-admired poet of the late neoclassical period, who satirized him more than once in verse, referring to him in deprecatory terms as "Orpheus with kinky hair" and even more violently as the "vile monster / that you produced, oh land / Where nature flattens noses" (1875, 185–186).[4]

Another potential exception to Sodré's observation is the 1784 "Ode ao homem selvagem" (Ode to the Savage Man) by the Reverend Antônio Pereira de Souza Caldas. Inspired by Rousseau, Caldas lamented the decline of a once proud and free people whose purity, he says, God made in his own image:

> Oh Man, what did you do? everything cries out;
> > Your former greatness
> Has been totally eclipsed; your golden peace,
> Liberty, finds itself in irons. (1821, 125)

Although Caldas may have been speaking about an Everyman in imitation of Rousseau's *Du contrat social* (*The Social Contract*), which declares: "Man is born free; and everywhere he is in chains" (1950, 3), his image of a shackled liberty was both a historical and contemporary reality for indigenous inhabitants, who, as the Swedish traveler Johan Brelin noted in 1756, were still being hunted, put on display locally, and shipped abroad as exotica.[5]

It is unclear at what precise moment the Indian emerged in Brazilian literature as a symbol of the newly independent nation,[6] but Caldas's elegiac ode about a noble savage in irons foreshadows the appearance of a literary movement whose nationalism had a liberal-populist flavor.[7] One might say that the rise of the Indian as a symbol of the nation-state is directly related to the sociopolitical and economic tensions that continued between Portuguese and Brazilians after independence. As we have seen, in the seventeenth century Gregório de Matos criticized the privileges bestowed upon the foreign-born in his poem "À Cidade da Bahia" (To the City of Bahia), and in the beginning of the nineteenth century, Hipólito da Costa denounced the prejudicial treatment of Brazilians by the Portuguese, especially in terms of political representation. Jean Baptiste Debret's transcription of the Portuguese government's hierarchy of civilized types, in which Brazilians are classified as inferior to the Portuguese, shows how this bias was made part of the official record.[8]

A far more subtle yet telling example of this conflict involves a large stage curtain that Debret was commissioned to paint for the royal theater on the occasion of Pedro I's coronation as emperor of Brazil. Debret recalled that his original design featured an allegorical figure representing the government, whose throne was placed in the midst of towering palm trees and covered by a rich tapestry canopy. Debret wrote that when he submitted the design to the emperor's prime minister, José Bonifácio de Andrada e Silva, for his approval, "he only asked me to substitute the natural palms for a standard architectural motif to avoid the idea of a savage state [estado selvagem]" (1954, 2:275).[9] Equally fascinating is Debret's description of the different figures who appear in the painting's foreground, the most prominent of which is "a white Indian woman" (2:276).

It is not surprising, then, that even after the proclamation of independence in 1822, most Brazilians still felt displaced and resented the titles, money, and commercial power that the Portuguese controlled. According to Boris Fausto, Brazilians were also fearful that Dom Pedro I, who ascended to the Portuguese throne in 1826, might reclaim Brazil as part of the United Kingdom (1999, 85). Debates over an absolutist versus constitutional monarchy fueled street demonstrations between Portuguese and Brazilian contingents, and protests grew to rebellious proportions. In an attempt to consolidate his powers, Dom Pedro created in just one year more than one hundred titles of nobility that he bestowed upon his wealthy Portuguese supporters. Angered by the preference and privilege accorded to Portuguese officers, the Brazilian rank-and-file military gradually withdrew its support for the king. Without solid military backing, the situation for Dom Pedro in Brazil became perilous—so much so that he abdicated on April 7, 1831, in favor of his five-year-old Brazilian-born son, also named Pedro.[10]

While these singular events between Portuguese and Brazilians were erupting on the sociopolitical scene, a few voices from a new literary generation from across the Atlantic were encouraging their Brazilian colleagues to discard the neoclassical model and to write about their recently independent nation. From a transatlantic perspective, this meant writing about the Indian. Among the voices advocating such literature was Almeida Garrett, one of the main exponents of Portuguese romanticism, whose introduction to the poetry anthology *Parnaso lusitano* (1826) became a touchstone for discussions in Brazil about what the national literature should be. In his commentary, Garrett expressed his concern that the European education received by Brazilians was destroying their national spirit: "it seems that they are afraid to show that they are Americans; and as a result, they suffer from an affectation and impropriety that detracts from their better qualities" (xliv). Garrett returns to this point in his assessment of the love poems in Tomás Antônio Gonzaga's *Marília de Dirceu* (1792, 1799):

> If I were to make a critique of his work, I would complain not about what he does but what he fails to do. Let me explain: instead of designing scenes of Arcadia in Brazil that are entirely European, would that he had painted his canvas with the colors of the country where he lives. Oh! . . . if that innocent Marília were, like Virginia of Saint-Pierre, seated in the shade of a palm tree . . . with the tender and melodious *sabiá* [songbird] . . . [and] the scaly anteater, . . . weaving for her lover and singer a garland not of roses, nor of jasmine, but of purple passion flowers and the white flowers with red berries of the lustrous coffee plant; what a painting Gonzaga's ingenious brush, with it natural grace, would create! (xlvi–xlvii)[11]

In his 1826 survey of Brazilian literature, the Frenchman and Brazilianist Ferdinand Denis regarded the land, the Indian, and the early colonizers as essential Brazilian literary topics. Four years later, in 1829, the German Carl Schlichthorst wrote that the Brazilian poet "will find in the traditions, habits, and customs of the people conquered by his race a rich source of motifs for the marvelous that is lacking in his verses" (n.d., 157). Schlichthorst further pointed out the poverty and incongruity of neoclassicism for the Brazilian writer: "Greek mythology, for the most part based on phenomena of nature, plays a pitiful role under the tropical sky . . . The initial attempts of the Brazilian muse already suggest that a more original flight will be taken and that Brazil will maintain its independence, whether poetic or political" (ibid.).

For two of these three influential writers, the idea of an authentic Brazilian literature was directly related to the Indian, although what Denis and Schlichthorst had in mind was not the anthropophagous Tupi of the sixteenth- and seventeenth-century imagination or the defiant and ultimately decimated community in Basílio da Gama's *O uraguai*, which was actually closer to contemporary reality. In his 1979 introduction to Denis's *Os maxacalis*, Jean-Paul Bruyas writes that Denis's conception of the Brazilian Indian was inspired by early chronicles, by Chateaubriand, and by the expeditionary works of Saint-Hilaire and Prince Wied-Neuwied, which were important to his chapters on the Masacali Indians in *Scènes de la nature sous les tropiques* (1824), the basis for the Portuguese translation *Os maxacalis*. One also might include the infamous spectacle performed in Rouen in 1550 in which Tupis brought from Brazil by French traders staged battles in a faux-tropical wilderness to honor the arrival of the French king and queen—battles that became the subject of Denis's later book, *Une fête brésilienne célébrée Rouen en 1550* (1850). Having lived in Brazil from 1816 to 1819, Denis was no doubt familiar with the French Cultural Mission and the "picturesque" work of his compatriot Debret, who painted stunning portraits of heroic Indian warriors in the wilderness. His comments on this subject suggest as much:

> [The New World's] age of mysterious and poetic fables will belong to the centuries in which lived the people whom we exterminated and who surprised us with their courage, and who invigorate perhaps the nations that came out of the Old World: the memory of their great savagery will overwhelm the soul with pride, their religious beliefs will animate the deserts; their poetic songs, preserved by some [indigenous] nations, will beautify the forests. (1944, 31)

Unlike Denis, Almeida Garrett had never been to Brazil, so his idea of the land and what Gonzaga should write about was stereotypical (palm trees, the *sabiá*, and so forth). However, both Denis and Schlichthorst directly associated the "marvelous" with the Indian—an attitude that conjured the earliest images of Brazil and its "exotic" inhabitants. Denis wrote: "The marvelous, so necessary to poetry, can be found in the ancient customs of these peoples" (1944, 31). Schlichthorst also refers to an engraving made shortly after independence that shows Dom Pedro I embracing the nation of Brazil, which takes the form of an Indian maiden apparently modeled after the emperor's mistress, the viscountess of Santos (n.d., 55).[12]

As I have pointed out in Chapter Two, there was no lack of nativist works in Brazil in the eighteenth century. However, the literary historian Sílvio

Castro argues that this protonationalist tendency was seriously affected in the late eighteenth and early nineteenth centuries by the expulsion of the Jesuits from Brazil in 1759 by the marquis of Pombal, the enlightened yet autocratic Portuguese minister whose dictatorial rule lasted twenty-two years.[13] Among the reforms that Pombal instituted to ensure Portugal's tight reign over the colony was a state-subsidized approach to education whereby the new curriculum in Brazilian schools was virtually the same as in Portugal. Castro states that the loss of Jesuit schools and the new direction in education under Pombal directly affected the course of Brazilian literature: "Whoever studied with the Jesuits in Brazil was always imbued with the idea of Brazil, as evidenced by the works of colonial poets and prose writers who were students of the priests" (392). He further contends that the writers involved with the 1789 revolt in Minas Gerais, namely Cláudio Manuel da Costa, Tomás Antônio Gonzaga, and Manuel Inácio da Silva Alvarenga, were the last to produce, prior to 1822, a literature that displayed any kind of identification with the nation or commentary on the Brazilian character (393). The American Revolution, the French Revolution, and the attempt to overthrow the monarchy by the Minas Gerais rebels fueled Portugal's anxiety about Brazil and prompted its greater stranglehold on the colony. Those who had the means to further their education were forced to study in Portugal and increasingly in France, where they followed the European models in vogue.

Portuguese authors like Almeida Garrett and his compatriot Alexandre Herculano, whose romantic poems and historical novels in the vein of Sir Walter Scott were greatly admired in Brazil, were inspired chiefly by the heroic past of the Portuguese nation. Revolutionaries in their own right who fought on the side of Dom Pedro I in the War of the Brothers, Garrett and Herculano celebrated the epic poet and soldier-adventurer Camões and national figures such as Frei Luís de Sousa, a Portuguese nobleman who defied Spanish dominion in the sixteenth century. For Brazilian writers of the 1830s and 1840s, most of whom were educated or traveled abroad and experienced firsthand the blossoming of the romantic movement there, it was clear that a truly Brazilian literature had to envision something more than a transplanted Arcadia.[14] In 1836, the Brazilian poet Domingos José Gonçalves de Magalhães, who was living in Paris at the time, issued a manifesto titled "Ensaio sobre a história da literatura no Brasil" (Essay on the History of Literature in Brazil), which appeared in the first issue of his Paris-based literary review, *Niteroi–revista brasiliense*. The manifesto declared that "each people have their own literature just as each man has his own character"—a proclamation that linked the idea of nationhood with Rousseau's idea of individual freedom.[15]

The young Brazilian poet Antônio Gonçalves Dias, who was studying and working in Portugal, wrote from Oporto to his friend Teófilo de Carvalho Leal in Coimbra that he was intent upon creating something "exclusively American—exclusively our own" (in W. Martins 1977, 2:348)—in other words, an attempt to break with the "shackles" of European neoclassicism. The result was a collection of poems in 1846 titled *Primeiros cantos* (First Songs), whose initial section, "Poesias americanas," opens with an epigraph from Chateaubriand's Indian novel, *Atala*: "Would the infelicities of an obscure inhabitant of the forests have less right to our tears than those of other men?" This is followed by a short patriotic poem that he wrote in 1843, "Canção do exilio" (Song of Exile), whose glorification of Brazilian nature is inextricably linked to the poet's *saudade*, or longing, for his homeland. In a sense, ideas from European literature were again being transplanted to Brazil but with the addition of Brazilian motifs:

> My homeland has palm trees
> Where the *sabiá* [songbird] sings
> The birds that sing here
> Do not sing as they do there.
>
> Our sky has more stars,
> Our meadows have more flowers,
> Our forests have more life,
> Our life, more loves.
>
> As I ponder alone, at night,
> More pleasure do I find there;
> My homeland has palm trees,
> Where the *sabiá* sings.
>
> My homeland has perfections,
> Of the kind I do not find here;
> As I ponder—alone, at night—
> More pleasures do I find there;

My homeland has palm trees,
Where the *sabiá* sings.

May God let me live,
Until I can return there;
Until I can relish the perfections
That I do not find here;
So I can behold the palm trees,
Where the *sabiá* sings.

The importance of this simple poem for an emerging national literature cannot be overstated. It was one thing for a Portuguese colonial subject to praise the verdant and fertile Brazil over the landscape of other countries, but it was quite another thing for that subject to speak as a Brazilian "in exile" for whom the "here" (the Portuguese city of Coimbra, one of the centers of higher learning in Europe) is imperfect and unsatisfactory compared to "there" (in Brazil).[16] The palm trees and birds that the poet celebrates are the very symbols that appear on the earliest maps and in the first chronicles of Brazil (and which Garrett recommended to poets in his 1826 essay). This poem resounded so forcefully in the imagination of Brazilians that certain verses were later incorporated into the Brazilian national anthem. The entire composition continues to be memorized and declaimed by schoolchildren—on the order of the Pledge of Allegiance in the United States.[17]

Gonçalves Dias published "Canção do exílio" six years after the young emperor Dom Pedro II came to power and at the beginning of the Second Empire. During the period, Brazil was still experiencing a tug of war between conservative landowners who lived near the capital and liberal landowners from more distant rural areas. In 1848, two years after the appearance of *Primeiros cantos,* a revolt took place in Pernambuco calling for the "expulsion of the Portuguese and the nationalization of all retail commerce" (Fausto 1999, 98). The revolt was put down that same year, but pockets of resistance in the northeastern state continued to fight for another two years. In "Canção do exílio," Dias makes repeated use of the pronouns "my" and "our," as if to insist that Brazil belonged to Brazilians—a picture of the nation that differed substantially from the actual economic one. As a Brazilian who embodied the mixture of the three races (Indian, European, and African), Dias also implicitly challenged Portugal's ideas about Brazilian "inferiority."[18] It is no wonder that readers were excited by this new "American" voice who championed the nation as homeland at a time when Brazilians, particularly those of mixed blood, felt hard-pressed to call the country their own.

Following "Canção do exílio" in the "Poesias americanas" section are three poems that focus on the Indian, a figure who "more than any other and better than any other, would [represent] Brazil" (Sodré 1943, 54). What is particularly important about "O canto do guerreiro" (The Warrior's Song), "O canto do piaga" (The Shaman's Song), and "O canto do índio" (The Indian's Song) is that all three are spoken from the Indian's point of view, "giving voice" to a population that over the centuries was seen and described but never heard. The three "songs" constitute a brief oral history of Brazil, focusing first on the valor of the Indian warrior, then on to the arrival of the Europeans and their exploitation of the land, and finally on the Indian's capitulation to the European.[19] The themes of the land, the Indians, and the colonizers are the very ones that Ferdinand Denis had recommended earlier to Brazilian writers. Although none of these early Indianist poems compares to Gonçalves Dias's later work "I-Juca-Pirama," which is regarded as one of his greatest compositions, they firmly establish the image of the Indian as a valiant warrior and as an *individual* capable of deep personal emotion and sacrifice—despite the fact that the Indian being represented in the poems was no longer alive in Brazil.

The "America" that Dias creates is a wilderness populated by a Rousseau-like community of proud and free individuals prior to their enslavement by the European, who appears as antagonist or *agent provocateur.* In "O canto do piaga," the devilish spirit that threatens the community takes the form of the colonist, who indiscriminately fells trees and rapes the land. "O canto do índio" portrays an Indian warrior who sacrifices his freedom for the love of a *virgem loura* (blond virgin). Although this poem may seem historically problematic (the dearth of European women in the early colonial period meant that interracial relations were usually between white males and indigenous females), Dias's portrait subverts the stereotypic representation of the Indian as bestial and savage and portrays him as a man in love, not unlike a hero of European romanticism. In fact, the figure can be traced back to the medieval troubadours who sang about women who were beyond their social reach. Dias is clearly knowledgeable of this tradition: he even refers to the troubadour in a later poem, and he places great emphasis on the theme of unrequited, unconsummated love. There is no real difference between the Indian in "O canto do índio" and the soulful speaker in his other, non-Indian poems such as "Amor! Delírio—engano" (Love! Delirium—Deception), in which we read of *coita* (sufferings from love) in the courtly tradition.[20]

The Indianist poems by Gonçalves Dias make up only a small portion of his overall production, yet literary histories and anthologies identify him as a writer of indigenous lyrics.[21] This is mainly because he was the major poet writing about Indians at the time but also because of the overwhelming acclaim for "I-Juca-Pirama" (1851), his epic-dramatic poem in ten *cantos,* which has the feel of a legend being told in verse. If ever there was a work that reinforced the idea of the Amerindian as the quintessential noble savage and symbol of Brazil, it was "I-Juca-Pirama," a story about a young Tupi warrior who is captured by the enemy Timbiras and asks to be released so he can care for his blind father. The story ends with the father returning his son to his captors so that the young man can die as a hero.

As compelling as the plot of the poem is the historic and ethnographic information that Dias provides about the Tupi and Timbira tribes and the ceremony that precedes the execution of the captive. Dias had access to the archives of the Instituto Histórico e Geográfico Brasileiro, which was founded in 1838 for the specific purpose of gathering information on Brazil, as well as its *Revista,* which, in the words of First Secretary Januário da Cunha Barbosa, was intended to "show the cultured nations that we also prize the glory of our country" (10).[22] In 1849, two years prior to the appearance of "I-Juca-Pirama," Pedro II commissioned Gonçalves Dias to write a comparative study for the institute about Indians of Brazil and of other American nations for the purpose of ascertaining which Amerindian nation offered the most to the "business of civilization" in the colonial period (in W. Martins 1977 2:415).

In "I-Juca-Pirama," Dias brings to lyric poetry the ceremony that sixteenth-century authors like Hans Staden, André Thevet, and Jean Léry had described in detail, but with the important difference that the narrator of Dias's poem, who remains anonymous until the end, is an old Timbira warrior who describes the ceremony not in the anthropophagic terms used by the outsider but rather in terms of a ritual about bravery and honor between noble enemies. The poem's initial five *cantos* interweave two narrative lines: an ethnographic description that includes references to the preparation of the *cauim* (drink), the women's decoration of the captive's body, their taunt-ing behavior toward him, and the arrival of the executioner-chief; and the questions surrounding the mysterious identity of the captive (whose only recognizable trait is his "Grecian-like" countenance).

When the Timbira chief asks the warrior to recount his valiant deeds and to prepare to defend himself in anticipation of the death blow from his executioner's club, the captive identifies himself as a Tupi and member of a tribe whose heroic past has been sullied by its association with "men who came as traitors"—in other words, the Portuguese. His tearful plea to be freed in order to guide his sightless father causes the Timbira chief to re-coil and then command his immediate release—as if the Tupi's tears were evidence of a contagious disease. The Tupi's humiliation is complete when the chief says scornfully, "We do not wish to weaken our braves with vile flesh"—the poem's only reference to the anthropophagic act.

The last five *cantos* of the poem focus on the drama of the father and son. The father senses his son's trembling and smells the acrid odor of the dyes used by the Timbira women to tint his body. When he touches the young man and feels the small feathers that are a part of the captive ritual, he asks if his son has escaped capture and defeated the enemy. After learning of his son's supplication to the enemy chieftain, he insists that they return to the Timbira camp. Once there, he sings of his own noble deeds and asks the chief to give him a guide from among the Timbiras who might serve him and who will "be honored to have [him] for a father."

Upon learning from the Timbira chief that his son cried, he recites a litany of curses that should befall him for his cowardice. In response, the son gives a warrior's cry and initiates a sensational battle against the enemy warriors, showing himself to be more than worthy of execution—which is the meaning of the title, "I-Juca-Pirama." The father praises his son's valor, saying, "Yes, this is my son," and of their tearful rejoicing, he says: "These tears do not dishonor." The poem concludes with the revelation that the poem's narrator is an elderly Timbira who informs his audience, who are children, of the veracity of his tale because, in his words, "I saw it." In addi-tion to its greatness as a literary work, the poem was an especially effective means to educate the country's children to fight to defend moral values.

The emphasis that the poem gives to truth in its final lines was in keep-ing with the *Revista do Instituto Histórico e Geográfico Brasileiro*'s desire to "re-suscitate the nation's memories from the unworthy obscurity in which they lay" (10) and to correct the historical errors of fact in the official record—much of which had to do with the Indian (11).[23] For example, the second issue of the *Revista* (1839) included information about the papal bull of 1537, which proclaimed that Indians were "rational and free human beings," and another study focused on the impact on Indians of the importation of the African slaves who largely replaced them as a workforce in the sixteenth century. A long, anonymous document written in 1587 about the Tupi as the first inhabitants of Bahia also appears in this volume.

In a sense, Gonçalves Dias was both reclaiming and rewriting a figure and culture that, according to the institute's *Revista* (not to mention individuals from abroad), already were being recognized as a symbol of the nation. There is absolutely nothing in "I-Juca-Pirama" about savagery or barbarism, unless we count the reference to the Europeans' treachery and ultimate betrayal of the Tupi, which was historically true and resulted in the tribe's decimation. Honor, ceremony, kinship, bravery, and sacrifice became the watch words for the nation's first peoples, whose rich, proud heritage is conveyed by Dias's incorporation of ethnographic detail and indigenous terms into an otherwise classical discourse.[24] In other words, Dias achieved a synthesis between the Indians and the "civilization" that ultimately did away with them.

Gonçalves Dias's death in a shipwreck off the coast of Brazil at the age of forty-one cut short his writings on the noble savage. In his works and others of his generation, however, we can see the intersection of national independence, patriotism, and literary romanticism that coalesced in the resuscitation and idealization of the Indian—who, in short time, would become a national icon. Indeed, so great was the Indian's popularity that Brazilians began to christen their children with indigenous names and to trace family histories in the hopes of discovering indigenous ancestors. But this Indian was quite different from the one who was living in the interior of Brazil at the time and about whom British traveler Gilbert Farquhar Matheson disparagingly wrote in his *Narrative of a Visit to Brazil, Chile, and Peru* (1825): "few or no benefits either do result, or can ever be expected to result, to Brazil, from this part of the population" (152).

In 1856, a few years before Gonçalves Dias's death, Gonçalves de Magalhães published his long-awaited *A confederação dos tamoios* (The Confederation of the Tamoyos), an epic poem about Brazil's earliest indigenous inhabitants that was sponsored by Dom Pedro II. This competent but sometimes tedious work sparked a polemical series of letters to the newspaper *Diário do Rio de Janeiro* in which the signator, "Ig," repeatedly attacked Magalhães as long-winded and clumsy. The true author of the letters was a lawyer and budding novelist, José de Alencar. In Alencar's estimation, it was not enough to write about the noble savage; it was necessary to write about him or her in totally new ways. Alencar elaborated on this point some years later:

> In later life, when I understood certain things better, I read works published on the indigenous theme; based on my study of the wilderness life of the autochthonous Brazilians, and to my way of thinking, they did not achieve the stature of a national poetry. Many of these works sinned by abusing indigenous terms that accumulated one over the other, which resulted not only in an unharmonious Portuguese language but also a less than intelligent text. Others were exquisite in style and rich in beautiful images; however, they were lacking in a certain guilelessness of thought and expression that should be characteristics of the indigenous language.
>
> Gonçalves Dias is the national poet *par excellence*; no one disputes the opulence of his imagination, the fine workmanship of his verse, his knowledge of Brazilian nature and indigenous customs. In his American poems he benefited from many of the most beautiful indigenous traditions; and in his unfinished poem *Timbiras,* he intended to write the Brazilian epic.
>
> However, the savages in his poem speak a classical language, which was criticized by Dr. Bernardo Guimarães, another poet of great inspiration. They express ideas appropriate to the civilized man and lack verisimilitude when spoken in the wild.
>
> Undoubtedly the Brazilian poet has to translate into his own language ideas of the Indians, no matter how crude and coarse; but it is in the translation that lies the greatest difficulty. It is necessary that the civilized language mold itself as much as possible to the primitive simplicity of the barbarous language; and that it represent indigenous images and thoughts only with words and phrases that seem natural in the mouth of the savage.
>
> Knowledge of the Indian language is the best criterion for the nationality of the literature. It gives the true style, as in the poetic images of the savages, their ways of thinking, the tendencies of their spirit, and even the smallest particularities of their lives.
>
> It is from this source that the Brazilian poet must drink; from it the true national poem will appear, such as I imagine it. (1865, 98)

As if to prove his point and in the midst of the polemic with Magalhães and his supporters (among whom was the emperor, Dom Pedro II, who heralded *A confederação* as the national poem of Brazil),[25] Alencar wrote the novel *O guarani* (1857), which was an immediate popular success. The novel's images of the brave Indian warrior could be found already in Jean Baptiste Debret's picturesque wilderness scenes, which, according to critic Thelka Hartmann, "contributed greatly to the erroneous and fantasy-like idea that is held of the Indian today" (1975, 73);[26] Alencar also drew upon the idea of the tragic-heroic warrior that Gonçalves Dias had introduced in "I-Juca-Pirama."[27] But the impact of *O guarani* was extraordinary, in large part because it was serialized in the *Diário do Rio de Janeiro* and reached a much wider contemporary audience than Debret or Dias could have achieved.[28] Alencar skillfully interwove a classic tale about lust and revenge with a traditional love story about a man and a woman in the wilderness—except that the man is an Indian and the woman is a Portuguese. Gonçalves Dias had already laid the foundation for Alencar's book in his short poem "O canto do índio," in which a warrior offers to sacrifice his freedom in exchange for the love of a blond and virginal European. *O guarani* retells Dias's story but avoids the sexual barter: the Indian protagonist, Peri, has left his tribe to serve Cecília, the fair-haired (and virginal) daughter of an honorable Portuguese administrator (based on the actual historical figure Dom Antônio de Mariz), who moved his family from the nation's capital into the interior of the state as an expression of his decision not to serve the Spanish Felipe, who was king of Brazil in 1604, the time the novel takes place. Although Peri does not pine for "Ceci" in the style of Dias's Amerindian "troubadour," she is his adored ideal. Peri is a knight errant or, in the father's words, "a Portuguese gentleman in the body of a savage." Peri watches over Ceci in the forest and as she is courted by suitors. He converts to Christianity (is given the name of Ceci's father) and later rescues her when the enemy forces (both Indian and European) attack the settlement.

Alencar's novel is filled with drama, intrigue, and sentimental relations among Europeans, Indians, and the biracial character Isabel, who is the secret love child of Ceci's father and an Indian woman.[29] Peri not only saves Ceci from capture (and more) by the novel's Italian villain, Loredano, who is a vengeful former Capuchin,[30] but he also rescues her from raging floodwaters by guiding her into the top of a tall palm tree and uprooting it. Alencar stops short of describing any sexual relationship between the two and

4.1 Cover from an undated edition of *O guarani*

literally leaves them clinging to the palm, which floats toward the horizon at the end of the novel. Nevertheless, by means of an indigenous tale of the great flood and the begetting of a new race of people that Peri recounts earlier to Ceci, the book points toward the eventual union of the two in a newly cleansed, Edenic Brazil.

Unlike *O guarani*, which Alencar classified as a "historical novel," *Iracema* (1865), his "legend" about the love between an Indian maiden and a Portuguese colonizer, received a rather chilly critical reception.[31] Machado de Assis was one of the only critics who wrote favorably of the book, claiming that ultimately it would be regarded as one of the major works of Brazilian fiction—a prediction that proved to be accurate. One hundred editions of the book were printed in the century following its publication. The name of the eponymous heroine, Iracema, appealed in particular to the large German immigrant community in southern Brazil, where many adopted it for their newborn daughters.[32]

Iracema, which is an anagram for "America," takes place in the mid-sixteenth century, prior to the events in *O guarani*. Alencar rewrote a legend from his birthplace in northeastern Ceará in order to tell the story of the encounter between a valiant European, Martim (based on the historical figure who established the first settlement near Fortaleza), and Iracema, the "honey-lipped" daughter of a Tabajara shaman. The girl's virginal status is essential to the well-being of her people. As in *O guarani*, the plot involves intrigues among various European and indigenous groups (Portuguese, Dutch, Tabajara, and Tupi), but the focus is on the romantic couple, in this case, Iracema and Martim. Their initial encounter in the wilderness (she grazes him with an arrow) quickly moves into a physical relationship that produces the child named Moacir—symbol of the coming together of the two races. Iracema instigates the first sexual encounter with Martim, which seems significant in the light of some early chroniclers' descriptions of indigenous females as libidinous. With this act, she is no longer able to serve her community, and the safety and well-being of her people are put at risk. When Martim is threatened by a defiant and jealous Tabajara warrior, Iracema decides to leave her tribe and follow him. Toward the end of the novel, she is left alone in the wilderness while Martim wanders about the interior with his Tupi friend, Poti. There he tries to resolve his feelings about his homeland (where he left a golden-haired fiancée) and his love for Iracema. The novel ends with the birth of Moacir, whose name means "son of sorrow," and the death of Iracema, who, like Basílio da Gama's tragic Lindóia, perishes from a broken heart.[33]

Significantly, just as Alencar idealized Peri and Iracema,[34] he also portrayed Portuguese figures such as Dom Antônio and Martim as noble and just, and he gives both races good and evil characters. Like Gonçalves Dias, Alencar was respectful of Portuguese culture, even though Iracema received unfavorable reviews from Portuguese critics, including Manuel Pinheiro Chagas, who complained that the language of the characters defied Portuguese rules of grammar and syntax (Biblos 1997, 2:1223). At heart, Alencar was writing about the synthesis of the two cultures that produced the first "Brazilians." We might say that the hybridity that characterized the early engravings of Brazil, in which indigenous peoples were styled after classical nudes, reappears in slightly different form as a literary topos that represents Brazilian national identity.[35]

The lukewarm critical reception Iracema received in Brazil might be attributed to a shift in style. Unlike O guarani, which appeared eight years earlier (and was made into an acclaimed opera by Antônio Carlos Gomes),[36] Iracema featured a plot and characters that were out of synch with a time when literary interest was shifting toward realism—a style more in line with the mission of the Geographic and Historic Institute—and newspapers and magazines had begun using Indians as caricatures for political ends. A good example is the Rio-based Semana ilustrada (Illustrated Weekly), whose symbol for the nation was the "hybrid" figure "Sr. Brasil" (Mr. Brazil), a semi-naked Indian who wore a feathered headdress.[37]

Although he was not especially popular for some of his opinions, the institute member and historian Francisco Adolfo de Varnhagen, author of História geral do Brasil (1854–1857), was disparaging of literary Indianism's attempts to create a national identity based on mythic interpretations of Brazil's indigenous past, and he proclaimed that the earliest inhabitants were little more than animals. (At the same time, he advocated the study of Tupi and indigenous ethnography.) The Minas Gerais poet and novelist Bernardo Guimarães is a good example of this transition from a romantic to a realist sensibility. A great admirer of Gonçalves Dias, whom he elegized in verse, Guimarães is widely known for his funny, albeit pornographic, satire of Dias's epic fragment, Os timbiras. Entitled Elixir do pajé (The Shaman's Elixir), Guimarães's poem focuses on the potency of the shaman's phallus after he ingests a special liquid that is a forerunner of Viagra. The work was

Early woodcut of native Brazilians (1505). Basel edition of *Mundus novus*. Spencer Collection, New York Public Library, Astor, Lenox and Tilden Foundations.

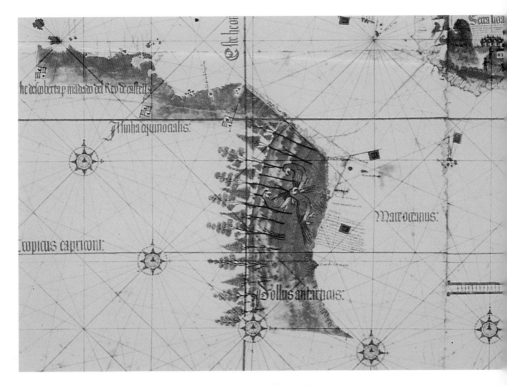

Brazil as parrots and trees on Cantino's world map (1502). Courtesy of the Lilly Library, Indiana University, Bloomington.

Nature and commerce on Lopo Homem-Reinel's map (1519). Courtesy of the Lilly Library, Indiana University, Bloomington.

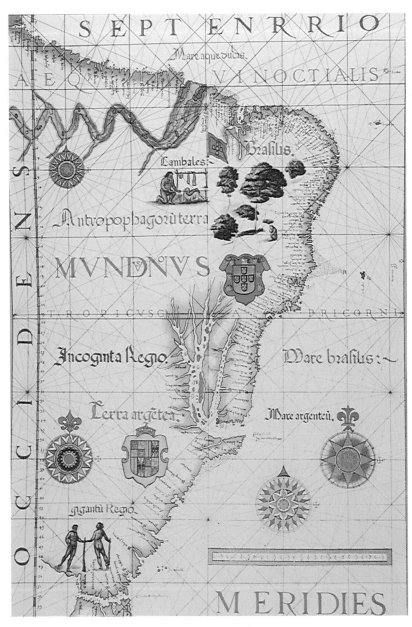

Land of cannibals, Diogo Homem (1568). Courtesy of the Lilly Library, Indiana University, Bloomington.

Adoração dos magos, by Grão Vasco (Vasco Fernandes), (circa 1505)

Plantation Scene, Frans Post (1655)

Tapuia man, by Eckhout (1643)

Tapuia woman, by Eckhout (1643)

Indian Hunter, by Manufacture des Gobelins (1692–1700)

Serro Frio, by Carlos Julião (circa 1780). Courtesy of the Lilly Library, Indiana University, Bloomington

A warrior, by Debret. Print Collection, Miriam and Ira D. Wallach Division of Art, Prints and Photographs, New York Public Library, Astor, Lenox and Tilden Foundations.

Execution of the Whipping, by Debret

Black woman with child, by Eckhout (1641)

A redenção de Cam, by Modesto Brocos (1895)

Facing page: The opera house in Manaus.
Permission, Latin American and Iberian Institute,
University of New Mexico.

A estudante, by Anita Malfatti (1915/1916)

Favela, by Laerte de Sousa (2007). Courtesy of Laerte de Sousa.

Suicides, by Vinicius Berton (2005).
Courtesy of Vinicius Berton.

immensely popular, circulating clandestinely in various editions prior to its official appearance in 1875. Guimarães also wrote Indianist works, including the novella *Jupira* (1872) and *O índio Afonso* (1873), both of which take place in the interior of Minas Gerais, where Guimarães was born and lived most of his life. In contrast to Dias and Alencar, he foregrounds the *mau sauvage*, whose maliciousness and cruelty recall descriptions of indigenous inhabitants from the late sixteenth century.[38] In *O índio Afonso*, he takes a somewhat different tack, creating a mixed-blood protagonist who is persecuted by "civilized" society for an act of vengeance that was partly justified. Ultimately, Guimarães's literary importance rests on his fictional works about the *sertão* and its residents, called *sertanejos*, who by the end of the romantic period gradually assumed a national status not unlike that of the Indian.

Regionalism

[I]t is not the cultured class that keeps Brazil united, but rather the common people.

AFONSO ARINOS, "A unidade da pátria," 1917

The usual color of the sertanejo is a dark brown; for even those who are born white, soon become as completely tanned as the dress which they wear, from exposure to the sun.

HENRY KOSTER, *Travels in Brazil*, 1816

Just as nineteenth-century foreign travelers and expeditions were illustrating and writing about little-known wilderness and frontier areas in Brazil, local authors began to think increasingly about the nation in terms of the majority of the population, who lived outside the cities in small towns and on farms in the *sertão* of Minas and the Northeast and on the grasslands in southern Rio Grande do Sul. No longer was the idea of the nation sufficiently conveyed by images of lush, verdant forests, noble Indians, and the colonial and precolonial past. It was becoming distinctly regional and contemporary in its manifestations—so much so that the image of the nation as a whole was often subsumed by different geographic areas and regional types.[39]

Beginning in the 1870s, efforts were made to study and record the oral literature of the interior—a practice regarded as fundamental to an understanding of who Brazilians really were. This practice was not unique to Brazil. Interest in oral literature was typical of the romantic period, as exemplified by Almeida Garrett's *Romanceiro* (1843, 1851), a three-volume collection of Portuguese ballads that was influential to the study and documentation of folk literature in Brazil. In 1873, Celso de Magalhães published a modest selection of popular verse in the Recife newspaper *O trabalho* (Work);[40] and a year later, Alencar published a commentary in the Rio daily *O globo* about "O nosso cancioneiro" (Our Songbook). Chief among scholars of popular literature at this time was Alexandre José de Melo Morais Filho, who wrote *Festas e tradições populares do Brasil* (Popular Brazilian Legends and Traditions), and literary critic Sílvio Romero, whose 1883 *Cantos populares do Brasil* (Popular Songs of Brazil) was followed in 1885 by *Contos populares do Brasil* (Popular Stories of Brazil), both of which appear in his three-volume *Folclore brasileiro* (1954).

Toward the end of the century, stories and novels began to appear about the *sertanejo* and the *sertão* of Minas Gerais, Mato Grosso, and Goiás as well as the large area known generically as the Northeast, which, according to novelist Franklin Távora, represented a purer Brazil because it was largely untouched by various European immigrant groups who were settling in the Central-South. Whether the Northeast was in fact ethnically "purer" is debatable, but figures for the period bear out Távora's point that the nation was undergoing a radical demographic change.[41] In her study of regionalism, Brazilian critic Lúcia Miguel-Pereira commented on the specific character of the new literature, stating that its "primary end was the fixing of types, customs and local languages, whose content would lose meaning without these exterior elements" (1973, 179). She also called attention to the commonality as well as opposition inherent in the novels and stories about the different provinces, observing that "they take place in environments where the habits and styles of life differ from those imposed by the *leveling* civilization" (ibid., emphasis mine).

What distinguishes Alencar, who wrote about the northeastern backlander in *O sertanejo* (1875), one of his last novels, and Bernardo Guimarães, author of *História e tradições da província de Minas Gerais* (History and Traditions of the Province of Minas Gerais), published in 1872, was proximity to and intimacy with the subject matter. Although both men were still under the influence of romanticism, Guimarães lived in the interior of Minas and had considerable knowledge of the people, language, and customs of the *sertão*. Alencar, who lived in Rio, constructed a backland community from distant memories of an early childhood spent in Ceará. Just as political independence had meant establishing an identity different from Portugal's, writers living outside the literary capital of Rio tried to establish regional identity and autonomy, which translated into writing about little-known geographies far removed from the coastal urban centers. The image of the *sertão* created by Guimarães, Távora, the Viscount Alfredo d'Escragnolle Taunay, and Afonso Arinos was as new and "exotic" to Brazilians in the capital cities as early descriptions of the country were to readers thousands of miles away in Europe. Regionalist literature expanded the concept of the nation, revealing it to be more complex than had ever been imagined.[42]

Books about the Northeast appeared at a time when the economy of the country was shifting more decisively to the Central-South. The images on the flag of independence of tobacco and coffee plants, which were mostly grown in the Central-South, but not sugar or cotton, crops associated with the Northeast, was a clear sign of that shift. In many ways, Franklin Távora's idea to found a "Northern Literature" was in response to the changes that were affecting the political power of the region. Such a literature would reaffirm the cultural and historical importance of the area, especially Pernambuco, which, Távora reminded readers, was once occupied by the Dutch and restored to the Brazilian nation by the patriotic people of the north. Among Távora's most memorable literary characters are his *cangaceiros* (bandits) based on actual outlaws from the *sertão;* and although his novels *O cabeleira* (1876) and *Lourenço* (1881) were criticized for being less than literary, they successfully documented *cangaço* (banditry) as a regional and social phenomenon, contributing to the mystique of what Eric Hobsbawm has called the "romantic robber" or "social bandit," whose adventures in Brazil were prominent in Northeastern popular literature and culture.

The backlands regionalism or *sertanismo* of late-nineteenth-century literature was, in the case of the viscount of Taunay, a direct result of his experiences in the interior as a military officer during the five-year war (1865–1870) that Brazil, Argentina, and Uruguay waged against Paraguay over borders and river domains. His best-selling novel, *Inocência* (1872), has a finely wrought introductory chapter whose sometimes lyric, sometimes realistic descriptions of the conjoined *sertão* of Mato Grosso, Minas Gerais, and São Paulo were no doubt of considerable inspiration to a later military officer and journalist, Euclides da Cunha. Da Cunha was the author of the famous 1902 backlands epic, *Os sertões* (*Rebellion in the Backlands,* 1944), which in turn was the source text for, among others, R. B. Cunningham's *A Brazilian Mystic* (1920) and Mario Vargas Llosa's 1981 *La guerra del fin del mundo* (The War of the End of the World).

It seems no coincidence that among Taunay's characters in *Inocência* is a German naturalist named Meyer, who bears a strong resemblance to the eccentric Austrian botanist Baron Georg Heinrich von Langsdorff, leader of a famous scientific expedition into Mato Grosso in the late 1820s that had included Taunay's uncle, the French painter Aimé-Adrien Taunay. In one unforgettable comic scene, Meyer becomes virtually orgasmic upon discovering a new species of butterfly, which he decides to name after Inocência, the daughter of his host, Pereira, who lives in the remote interior. *Inocência,* which Taunay described along the lines of a *roman à clef* in his memoir published posthumously in 1928, *Visões do sertão* (Visions of the Backlands), lampoons the foreign naturalist at every turn.[43] However, there is little question that, aside from its dramatic plot about a young couple who fall tragically in love, the novel's main interest is the region and its traditions. Taunay depicted the patriarchal and often violent land whose customs were ignored or reproved by outsiders, such as the bumbling, foolish, and ineffectual Meyer.

Taunay's insiders include the young protagonist Cirino, who travels the countryside and treats malaria victims, eventually meeting and falling in love with Inocência. Taunay deftly integrates the rules of backland comportment into the plot, showing how the uneducated Inocência is literally hidden away in the household until her marriage, which has been arranged by her father. Meyer is repugnant to Pereira because he repeatedly violates the code mandating that the strictest privacy and decorum be maintained to "protect" single and even married women from undesirable attentions. A guest in Pereira's house, Meyer happens across Inocência and praises her beauty to Pereira, who is insulted by the German's lack of discretion. At one point, Meyer even pontificates to his host in a somewhat stilted Portuguese about the backwardness of a tradition that keeps women locked up in the house: "Here in the *sertão* of Brazil is the bad custom of hiding women. Traveler does not know if they are pretty, or ugly, and those who can read can't count on books to know about them. But, word of honor, Mr. Pereira, if they all looked like your daughter, it's something very, very worthy to be seen and written about!" (1923, 21).

The botanist arrives with a letter of introduction from Pereira's brother, and although Pereira is exasperated with Meyer and sticks close to him throughout his stay, he cannot bring himself to breach the code of etiquette that requires him to treat his brother's acquaintance as a welcomed guest. Having grown up in the interior, both Inocência and Cirino are aware of the rules that govern their respective behaviors, and they painfully realize that a future together is impossible because of her arranged marriage to Manecão, whom Pereira already regards as a son. Knowing the importance of family ties, Cirino reasons that one way the arrangement might be dissolved is if Inocência's godfather, a person of standing in the family and someone whom Inocência trusts, were to convince her father that the marriage would not be in her best interests.

Cirino travels to plead their case to her godfather, Antônio Cesário. After some consideration, Antônio agrees to help Cirino, and he rides off to Pereira's farm. However, before Cirino can return, fate intervenes in the form of Manecão, who shoots and kills Cirino on the road. The novel ends three years later, in Austria, where Meyer is being honored for his expeditionary finds, the most sensational of which is the butterfly named after Inocência. A single sentence at the end informs the reader that two years have passed since Inocência was buried in the *sertão*.

The instant popularity of Taunay's work might be compared to that of Gonçalves Dias's "I-Juca-Pirama" or Alencar's *O guarani* in that each in its own way carved out a new image of the country for their readers, who saw in the heroism of the Indian and the youthful zeal of the backlander couple a will and determination that reflected their own sense or "instinct" of nationality. Patriotism went hand in hand with independence, but it had been fueled more recently by the long and bloody Paraguayan war in which thousands of Brazilians (including black slaves who were given their freedom for service to the cause) fought and died.[44] As Lúcia Miguel-Pereira has noted, the emphasis given to the *sertão* was a self-affirming movement by a literary generation eager to demonstrate to its largely European-based culture an ethnic identity that was genuinely national in origins (1973, 183).

A later surge of regionalist writing occurred at the turn of the twentieth century, following the proclamation of the Republic in 1889. Among the important figures of this generation was Minas Gerais writer Afonso Arinos, whose biography is interesting to consider in the light of discussions about Brazilian nationalism. Following a custom of the times, his father gave him and his siblings Indian names to add to the family name, Melo Franco; contrary to tradition, however, Afonso dropped the family name and kept his adopted Indian name, Arinos, which he used as an author for the rest of his life.

In his early years as a writer, Arinos wrote a number of essays about the nation, including an emotional piece about the attempted overthrow of the monarchy in Minas Gerais and the heroism of the leader Tiradentes from the interior whose rebel-comrades like Gonzaga received greater recognition because of their prominence in the intelligentsia. In his 1895 essay "O passado de Minas e a Inconfidência" (The Past of Minas and the Conspiracy), Arinos wrote: "Tiradentes is worth all of the other conspirators put together because he represents the candid and simple, generous and mild, fearless and brave soul of the *mineiro* in our people, of the uncultured people of this my land" (620). Two years later, after government troops killed the messianic leader Antônio Conselheiro and his followers and destroyed their vast settlement in the interior called Canudos, Arinos penned a strongly worded article in which he blamed the government for ignoring the interior and the problems that brought about the tragedy:

> Until now, Brazilians were considered only the inhabitants of the great cosmopolitan cities on the coast; until now, all the governments' attention and a large part of the public resources were used to support immigration or for foolishly imitating institutions or foreign customs. Central Brazil was ignored; in the backlands exists a population of which nothing is known, the Government doesn't address it. Behold, it rises up in a strange and tragic manifestation of energy, affirming its existence and carving out with its blood a vehement protest against the scorn or the neglect to which it had been relegated. Behold, an element that the architects of our laws and our organization did not count on and that issued forth, advocating its right to life.
>
> And this force that appeared had to be incorporated into our nationality and had to enter it as a perpetual affirmation of that very nationality. . . . Those who were killed or subdued by the nation's arms are part of the great group of people scattered throughout 8,300,000 surface square kilometers of our land, who live neglected and forgotten and do not speculate on the stock market or profit from smuggling; nor do they make deposits or rows, or lucrative contracts; nor do the civilizing actions of the Government reach them. . . . They received the splen-

did and mysterious baptism of blood and, clothed in this purple, they opened the door of Brazilian nationality for their fellow backlanders. (1969, 645–646)

At the same time that he was publishing these and other articles, Arinos was composing short stories about the interior for the *Revista brasileira* and the *Revista do Brasil*. In 1898, he also published a short-story collection, *Pelo sertão* (Through the Backland), as well as his only novel, *Os jagunços* (The People of Canudos),[45] which had been serialized the previous year and which predated Euclides da Cunha's account of Canudos in *Os sertões*. The importance of Arinos to the formation of a national literature directly relates to his portraits of different regional types and traditions in the *sertão*. One of his best-drawn characters is Manuel Alves, the boss of a group of *tropeiros* (muleteers), who is the protagonist of the short story "Assombramento" (Terror) in *Pelo sertão*. In the story, the muleteers come across a large, abandoned house in the *sertão* that, according to legend, is haunted and lethal to anyone who stays overnight in its ruins. Arinos ably captured both the bravado of Manuel, who decides to defy the legend and sleep in the ramshackle house, and the power of certain superstitions transmitted orally from one person to another that assume the status of religion or legend. Arinos's description of Manuel's night in the house is wonderfully drawn; the suspense slowly gives way to a series of dramatic scenes in which the muleteer, with a knife blade between his teeth and a gun in his hand, battles the diaphanous spirits that implode the house. But the true strength of the story lies in the small details that Arinos provides about the daily life of the backlanders, as demonstrated in the following brief passages:

> The muleteers, in their to-and-fro motion, stacked the cargo and panted from its weight. Contrary to custom, they neither proffered an oath nor shouted; just, at times, a hard slap on the rump of a stubborn mule. . . . The overloads and synched ropes, bridles, loads of horseshoes spread out in piles, the open tool bag with its hammer, file, and anvil; the dangling feedbags; the open saddlebags and kitchen utensils laid out on an animal hide; the row of saddle cloths set out to air at the edge of the building—all this meant to [Manuel] that the unloading had been completed in its customary orderly fashion. . . .
>
> The large kettle held in place by a strip of leather; the dried beef sizzling on the spit and the camaraderie, rounding the edge of the fire and glancing at the hogsheads with avid, anguished eyes in eager anticipation of dinner. One,

in passing, stoked the fire; another carried a barrel filled with fresh water. Still another ran to wash the tin plates while someone else asked anxiously if more wood were required.

There was a moment when the cook, needled by such attentions, raised his arm in a threatening gesture and shouted at his companions: "Dammit! There's plenty of time, folks! Looks like you'd never seen beans before. Mind your own chores, unless you want to be driven out of here under the power of a hot poker." (1969, 50–51)

Among the many other characters in Arinos's *sertão* is a young washerwoman, Ana Esteireira, whose jealousy drives her to murder her friend Candinha, a rival for the affections of her bandit-lover Filipinho. The story's conclusion is reminiscent of popular literature when the outlaw and Ana, now on the run, are trapped and killed by the police. The bandit-figure resurfaces in "Pedro Barqueiro," the story of a runaway-slave-turned-outlaw who is famous for eluding the local officials. One day, he is caught off guard and taken prisoner by a young man, Flor, whose youthful innocence belies a sagaciousness and temerity that characterize even the youngest backlanders. When Pedro later escapes from his police escort, he tracks down Flor and threatens to kill him unless he begs Pedro for forgiveness. When Flor remains mute, even after being dangled over a cliff, the bandit frees him, declaring that Flor is the only real man he has met in his life. The bravery and stoicism that distinguish Flor are also characteristic of still another young backlander-protagonist in the story "Joaquim Mironga." The difference is that Joaquim, who volunteers to try to save his boss from outlaws by riding incognito into their camp and gathering information, does not survive his proof of valor. Recognized by one of the gunmen, he is shot and mortally wounded but suffers his injury in silence until he manages to relay the information to his boss.

There is a timeless quality in the stories in *Pelo sertão*, although "O contratador de diamantes" (The Diamond Contractor) is specifically about the seventeenth-century rush for precious stones in Minas Gerais. The people and setting presented here are prosperous, and the conflict involves neither guns nor knives but a letter from the government in Portugal, which demands that the local contractor imprison certain individuals who have mined the land without royal authority or payment. One of those to be imprisoned is the love interest of the outspoken and patriotic daughter of the contractor. She protests the royal order, announcing: "One day, perhaps not too far into the future, the people of the Colony will have their own ministers and generals" (102)—a foretelling of the republic founded exactly one hundred years after the Minas Conspiracy.

The most unusual selection in the collection is not so much a story as a prose poem honoring a lone palm tree, "Buriti perdido," that symbolizes the still-unexplored interior of the nation. Arinos is eloquent in his characterization of the single surviving, ancient palm, which he likens to an "old petrified warrior in the midst of the battle" (70) and later addresses as "the silent singer of the virgin nature of the *sertão*" (71).[46] The palm represents the "nobility" that Rousseau attached to the natural world and its residents, and Arinos honors the tree as if it were the last vestige of the past. However, what Arinos actually commemorates here is the power of legends, stories, and traditions that, whether in written or oral form, serve the nation as a reminder of its origins and the people and events that constitute its history.

In 1917, a year after Arinos's death, his book *Lendas e tradições brasileiras* (Brazilian Legends and Traditions) was published with a preface by the country's then foremost poet, Olavo Bilac, who also wrote the lyrics to Brazil's "Hymn of the Flag." The preface is fascinating not only because Bilac was a gifted writer but also because he regarded Arinos as the embodiment of Brazil—this despite Arinos's decision late in life to move to Paris.[47] In the preface, Bilac recalled their wintertime visit to the cathedral in Chartres, where they talked about the history and art of Christianity:

> At the end of this long conversation . . . there was a moment when, I'm not sure through what vague association of ideas, Afonso started to tell me episodes from one of his recent hunts in the district of Diamantina [Minas Gerais], in the vicinity of the Serro. We were at the center of the cross made by the two main aisles between the chorus and the naves at the side. From the position where we were, our gaze encompassed a fantastic stretch of somber forest made of stone: the columns, in two rows, surrounded us like thin stipes of palm trees whose crowns mingled high up in the cupola, creating fans among the lianas, leaves and flowers, plants and vines, ivy and water lilies. . . . Afonso's voice gained momentum, rose up and shook the cathedral. He talked about the side trails, the steep slopes, the ramparts, the undergrowth, the whinnies of horses, the cracks made by gunshots, the joy of the hunters and the songs sung by comrades—and the Minas sun . . . And the gothic forest became a natural forest:

the black stone turned green, the cupola waved its fronds and whispered, the darkness was flooded with light and a Brazilian summer set fire to the European winter. We were no longer in Chartres: we were in Brazil. (1937, 6–7)

One of the salient figures in regionalist literature is the narrator or storyteller, who can be a character within the tale or simply an unnamed source who relates events. Among the most memorable storyteller-characters to emerge in the genre is the eighty-eight-year-old *gaúcho* Blau Nunes, the narrator of João Simões Lopes Neto's 1912 *Contos gauchescos* (Gaucho Stories), described as a *caboclo* (mixed-blood) cowboy "still with all of his own teeth" (1992, 12). The charm of these stories about Rio Grande do Sul state in southernmost Brazil owes a great deal to the homey voice of Blau and the idiomatic dialogue.[48] For example, in "Chasque do imperador" (The Emperor's Messenger), Blau recalls an amusing episode during his days as a soldier and escort to the emperor, who had come to the southern pampas during the Paraguayan war:

> In one town where we stayed, the Emperor was put up in a house of a certain fellow, a coarse but very *gaúcho* sort of guy. At lunchtime, there were sweets and more sweets on the table . . . and nothing else! The Emperor tasted a few out of politeness while his escorts weakened at the sight of those sugary mounds. When dinnertime came, the same thing: sweets and more sweets! . . . So as not to offend the fellow, the Emperor served himself, but very little. Night came and, once again, tea and sweets!
>
> The Emperor, in all his grand imperialness, was suffering mightily from hunger!
>
> The next morning, the host asked how his guest had fared the night, while in the fellow's hands was a breakfast tray with tea and . . . sweets . . . .
>
> Well, the Emperor couldn't stand it any longer . . . He was sick to his stomach!
>
> "My friend, the sweets are magnificent . . . but I would be very grateful to you if you could possibly arrange a few beans for me . . . with a slice of meat. . . ."
>
> The man looked serious and then he let out a huge laugh: "What's this! Your majesty eats meat!? They told me that royal people only ate little bird bites of things like sweets and pastries! Why didn't you say something before, sir? I'll be damned! How about that! Let's go right now for a *churrasco* . . . I can't stand this shit either!" (65–66)

Like his contemporary Arinos to the north, Simões Lopes Neto was fond of drawing portraits of different social types. Although Blau is his most engaging character, he offers a gallery of other backland figures, including a ninety-year-old smuggler Jango Jorge, who knows the pampas like the back of his hand; the roguish Black Bonifácio, who is a womanizer; old João Cardoso, who is famous for his *mates* and gift of gab; and the Indian Juca, now a pathetic figure whom Blau respects for having taught him to skin and dry hides and braid leather harnesses.

Lopes Neto's best-known story, "O negrinho do pastoreio" (The Little Black Boy of the Pasture), appears in *Lendas do sul* (Legends of the South), published in 1913.[49] The plot involves the mistreatment of a young black slave by his master, a rancher renowned for his mean and stingy ways. After losing a horse race and wager to a neighbor, the rancher takes his anger out on Negrinho, who was riding his master's bay horse in the race, making him sleep in the pasture to ensure the safety of his herd. Three times Negrinho falls asleep and loses the herd, and three times the master has him tied to a stake and whipped. The whipping is so fierce the third time that the little boy dies. The rancher throws his body on a large ant hill and sets out to find his bay and the herd. Unable to locate them, he returns later to the ant hill, where he anticipates finding a corpse stripped of its flesh. Instead, he discovers Negrinho alive, standing and smiling, without a trace of the beatings, brushing a few ants from his body. Standing behind Negrinho is his protectress, the Virgin Mary, and grazing nearby is the bay, which Negrinho mounts, as well as the herd, which he drives through the pampas. Legend has it that anyone who has lost something has only to light a candle and ask for Negrinho's help, and he will find and return it.

A number of regional works, including Lopes Neto's fiction and Arinos's *Os jagunços,* went largely unnoticed at the time because they were published by small local companies with modest print runs. It took nearly fifteen years before Lopes Neto would find a major publisher and gain (posthumously) a large readership for whom Negrinho would become as familiar a character as the impish Saci (a little *caboclo* boy with one leg) and the marauding *lobisomem* (werewolf), who are legendary in Northeastern lore. "O negrinho do pastoreio" is only one example of how regional literature continued to evoke, long after Brazil's "discovery," an image of the country that was both exotic and fantastic in its depictions of an otherworldly landscape and larger-than-life characters.

The African Slave

Don't scorn the little seed; one day it will become a giant palm tree.
AFRICAN PROVERB

You are the silver Caldas
I am the copper Caldas.
From a poem by DOMINGOS CALDAS BARBOSA to ANTÔNIO SOUSA CALDAS

It is significant that Simões Lopes Neto's story about a young black slave grew to be popular and generated compassion among its readers. Unlike some of the situations described in Lopes Neto's fiction, slavery was a historical reality and the brutalization of slaves almost commonplace. The same thing could be said about the Indian, who was enslaved but more commonly run off or killed and who, at the same time, became the foremost symbol of the nation. But the situation of the black slave community was very different from that of the Indians: unlike indigenous peoples, slaves could be seen everywhere in the cities and the countryside both before and after independence, and their presence did not diminish after the abolition of slavery in 1888. In fact, emancipation forced thousands of former slaves from rural sectors to seek work in the city, where they had to compete with newly arrived European immigrants for the most menial labor. Compassion for a fictional young slave in the remote southern plains of Brazil was one thing, but it was quite another for society to be moved by an emancipated people who were at the bottom of the social and economic rung and whose poverty, misery, and despair were everywhere evident. The emphasis on slavery's inhumanity in the nineteenth century did not change the fact that black Brazilians would never obtain the heroic and patriotic status given to the "noble savage" or the brave backlander.

The view of blacks as inferior was rarely challenged over the centuries, except perhaps in the work of the seventeenth-century Dutch artist Albert Eckhout, which includes a life-size portrait of a black warrior stunningly outfitted with weapons from both the indigenous and European cultures, and equally impressive paintings of a black woman with a basket of food and a child at her side and a man with a plumed hat. All these figures exude a pride and nobility of individuals who have somehow survived their circumstances. In his seminal book, *The Negro in Brazilian Literature* (1956), Raymond S. Sayers observed that there were few positive literary characterizations of blacks in the colonial period. Among the exceptions were the "Noble Negro" Quitubia, an African prince and protagonist of a short poem by Basílio da Gama (59), and Tomás António Gonzaga's portrait of slaves in *Cartas chilenas* (59–61).

One of the earliest romantic authors to write about the Brazilian slave was Gonçalves Dias. Although his poem "A escrava" (The Slave Girl) in no way rivals his Indian poems, it has a strong emotional appeal and a subject matter that is remarkably similar to his famous "Canção do exílio." Instead of a young Brazilian poet in Portugal who longs for his tropical homeland, the poem describes a Congolese slave in Brazil, Alsgá, who looks out over the ocean to Africa and recalls her life of freedom there. Just prior to the appearance of "A escrava" in *Primeiros cantos,* Dias was back in his home-town of Caxias, Maranhão, where he began composing a long prose work, *Meditação* (Meditation), most of which appeared in the Rio-based literary review *Guanabara.* This is one of the first strong denunciations of slavery in Brazilian literature, and its incisive, sometimes harsh, sometimes ironic descriptions of masters and slaves bear little resemblance to the more pastoral account written nearly a century later by Gilberto Freyre in *Casa grande e senzala* (published in translation as *The Masters and the Slaves*).[50]

In many ways, *Meditação* anticipates "O navio negreiro" (The Slave Ship), the great abolitionist poem by Castro Alves to be discussed later, not only in subject matter but also in technique. The perspective moves from a broad landscape to an increasingly detailed look at specific circumstances. The piece begins with a nameless old man placing his hands over the eyes of an unnamed youth and instructing him to describe what he sees. The youth remarks ecstatically on the vastness of the land, the dense foliage and trees, the fragrant flowers and singing birds, the serene and star-studded sky, all of which is reminiscent of the *ufanismo* in early writings about Brazil. As the youth's perspective narrows, he comments on the thousands of men of different shapes and colors. Looking more closely, he sees that these men are arranged in concentric circles similar to the circles created by pebbles tossed into a lake. Then he notices that all the men in the rings farthest from the centers of the circles are submissive, respectful, and black, while all those who stand in the center, which look "like a fist," are arrogant, over-bearing, and white. Suddenly, the youth becomes conscious of a long iron chain that binds the black men to one another "eternally, like a curse that passes from father to son!" (1846, 6).

4.2 Black warrior, by Eckhout (1641)

4.3 Black woman with child, by Eckhout (1641)

In the next part of *Meditação,* the youth describes the blacks' submission to beatings and returns to focus more closely on the shackled men: "And I saw these men trying to throw off their chains, and that blood ran from their purpled wrists to their shackles. And I saw that the iron resisted their attempts; but I also saw that their anger was frenetic and that the blood that emanated from their wounds engulfed the iron like burning brimstone" (7–8). Everywhere the youth looks, whether it be in cities, towns, or villages, on the docks, in doorways, or in small boats, the only people he sees are slaves: "That's why the foreigner who docks in the ports of this vast empire—rechecks his chart and looks attentively at the stars—because he thinks that an enemy wind has carried him to the coast of Africa. And he finally realizes that he is in Brazil—in the land of freedom, in the land adorned with perfections and a star-studded, magnificent sky!" But when the foreigner comes to realize that slavery is everywhere in this land of liberty, his smile becomes "ironic and scornful" (10–11).

In the remaining sections of *Meditação,* Gonçalves Dias evokes the original freedom of the indigenous inhabitants, the greed of the European slavers, and the patriotic expectations associated with Brazil's independence. But independence retains the "fist" of white men, who proclaim: "[Blacks] should serve because they are long used to servitude, and custom is law" (65). Dias brings to the fore not only the plight of slaves after independence but also the suffering of indigenous peoples and individuals of mixed race, who are neither masters nor slaves. They ask what their role should be, and their answer to their own question is chilling: "We will be happy because individuals will need our numbers to extract their vengeance, and politicians will need us for their revolutions. They will leave us without occupation because they will need us—and because our idleness will be necessary to them. And we will be happy" (67).

Dias's *Meditação* is an important reminder that slavery in Brazil was criticized and repudiated by outsiders, in particular by some of the English who, for moral as well as economic reasons, pressed the country to eliminate the centuries-old institution.[51] The *Tratado da abolição do tráfico de escravos entre . . . o príncipe regente de Portugal e el rey do Reino Unido da Grande Bretanha . . .* (1815) (Treaty for the Abolishment of Slave Trafficking Between the Prince Regent of Portugal and the King of the United Kingdom of Great Britain) is just one of various agreements to curtail trafficking. But the importation of slaves continued until 1850.[52] With the regional economic shifts created by the boom and bust typical of monocrop agriculture, a different kind of slave trafficking was instituted in which slaves were sold at premium prices and shipped internally by Northeastern sugarcane planters to coffee growers in the Central-South.

Among North American travelers who wrote about slavery in Brazil was Thomas Ewbank, who in 1845 decided to "hie away to the region of butterflies and flowers" (1971, vi). There he came across myriad illustrations by local artists of slaves and torture devices. He included several of these images in his book and wrote as follows:

> Among lithographic scenes of life in Rio, designed and published by native artists, those relating to the slaves are not the least conspicuous. There is no more fastidiousness, that I observed, about portraying them in shackles than in their labors and their pastimes. The one . . . represents common punishments: a negra [sic] in a mask, and a negro wearing the usual pronged collar, with a shackle round one ankle, and secured to a chair suspended from his waist.
>
> It is said that slaves in masks are not so often encountered in the streets as formerly, because of a growing public feeling against them. I met but three or four, and in each case the sufferer was a female. The mask is the reputed ordinary punishment and preventative of drunkenness. As the baril [sic] is often chained to the slave that bears it, to prevent him from selling it for rum, so the mask is to hinder him or her from conveying the liquor to the mouth, below which the metal is continued, and opposite to which there is no opening. (436–437)

If lithographs by Debret and Rugendas failed to capture the horrors of slavery, the same was not true of the poetry of the Bahian António de Castro Alves, whose recitation of "O navio negreiro" at an independence day celebration in Rio in 1868 received a standing ovation. By that time slave ships were mostly a thing of the past, and there was nothing especially radical about a poem against slave trafficking; no one prior to Castro Alves, however, had made the case against not only trafficking but also the institution of slavery seem such an urgent and patriotic cause. The emancipation of North American slaves by Abraham Lincoln in 1865 and the role of slaves turned soldiers in the Paraguayan war fueled the nation's growing intolerance toward slavery, and a movement that brought abolitionists together with the republican cause was on the rise.

Harriet Beecher Stowe's *Uncle Tom's Cabin* (1852) was immediately trans-

lated into Portuguese, and its huge success in Brazil inspired the abolitionist and feminist educator Nísia Floresta Brasileira Augusta to write in her
newspaper column in 1853: "We other Brazilians, who read this book, should
make our children memorize some of its most salient pages in the hope that
future generations will erase . . . the painful impression made by the crimes
committed by current generations against the suffering African race!" (in
W. Martins 1977, 2:461–462).[53] But the outrage and shame called forth in
"O navio negreiro" are unequaled by any other anti-slave work of its time,
and the poem remains one of the best-known works in Brazil literature.[54]

The cinematic technique used by Castro Alves in this poem resembles
Gonçalves Dias's gradual pinpointing of slavery in Meditação, except that
Alves's poet-narrator observes from afar a ship that is sailing on the high
seas. Although the ship's itinerary is unknown ("Where do you come from?
. . . Where are you going?"), the beauty, ecstasy, and freedom of a life at sea
seems almost beyond comprehension:

> Joyful is the one, there, who can at this hour
> Feel the majesty of this canvas! . . .
> Below—the sea . . . above—the firmament . . .
> And between sea and sky—the immensity! (1997, 277)

Wishing to accompany the ship, which curiously seems to be fleeing from
the poet, he calls to the "eagle of the ocean," the albatross, to loan him his
wings so that he might continue to hear the music and voices of the mari-
ners whose nationality he has yet to know.

> What does the vessel care about its origin,
> Whose child it is, or what it calls home? . . .
> It's in love with the cadence of the verse
> Taught to it by the ancient sea! (278)

A certain reverie comes over the poet as he conjures up images of sailors from different nations and legendary figures such as Ulysses and Nelson, and he urges the albatross to drop down closer to the ship. As with the
youth in Meditação, details of the picture come into greater focus, and the
narrator is gripped by "a vile and infamous scene" and by the "horror" of
"gruesome figures." He realizes that the music heard from afar is, in fact, a
"funeral dirge." (279).

The last half of the poem conjures up a nightmare image inspired by Dante's *Inferno*. Dark figures writhe and scream as they perform a forced dance whose rhythmic beat is maintained by the cracking of whips. The long chain that shackled the figures together in *Meditação* reemerges here as the "famished multitude staggers and reels / and weeps and dances / imprisoned by the links of a single chain" (280). Wondering why the sea has not washed the horror away, the poet asks his muse to identify these wretched people. The muse responds at length, contrasting their past lives as "children of the desert," "brave warriors" who lived freely in Sierra Leone and who now live as "miserable slaves / without air, without light, without reason," crowded into a deep dark hold and "not even free to . . . perish" (281–282).

The drama of the poem builds to the poet's final and most important question: "My God, my God! but what flag is this / That impudently dances on the mast?!" As he moves closer, he realizes in horror that it is the "green and yellow pendant of [his own] land" (283). Outraged by this discovery, he addresses the flag and curses it:

> You, who from freedom following the war
> were raised on the lance of heroes
> Would that they had destroyed you in battle
> rather than have you serve as a shroud for a people! (283)

The poem ends with the poet's appeal to Columbus and to Bonifácio de Andrada, the patriarch of Brazilian independence, to pull down the banner and to seal forever the entryway to the sea.[55]

Although Castro Alves's projected volume of abolitionist poems, *Os escravos* (The Slaves), did not appear until after his death at the age of twenty-four, several of his poems were published in newspapers and, like "O navio negreiro," were recited to cheering public audiences. The image of Brazil as a land of freedom is challenged again in his "Vozes d'África," in which the voices of Africa condemn a nation once symbolized by the free-soaring condor but now more like a "vulture, / Bird of slavery" (293).[56] Gonçalves Dias's patriotic "Canção do exílio" and his "A escrava" take on new meaning in Alves's "A canção do africano" (1863), in which a young black slave sings to her child of her African homeland:

> My country is over there, far away
> From the place where the sun rises;

This land is prettier,
But it's the other that I cherish . . .
There everyone lives happily,
Everyone dances in the square;
People there do not sell themselves
As they do here, just for money (220)

In his long poem "A cachoeira de Paulo Afonso" (The Waterfall of Paulo Afonso), a young slave couple in love prefers to leap into a gigantic waterfall than submit to the violence of the master. The poem brought to the fore, albeit in a romantic way, the frequent suicides of slaves to escape their incarceration.

Raymond S. Sayers has pointed out that "by 1870 there was hardly a poet who was not writing at least a few pieces about the life of the slave, and in the last decade of slavery the theme absorbed a large part of the space of the periodical press" (1956, 85). This was also true of fiction writers like Alencar, who had written about slavery much earlier in his plays O demônio familiar (The Family Demon) in 1857 and Mãe (Mother) in 1860. Joaquim Manuel de Macedo's little-known As vítimas-algozes (The Victims-Executioners) of 1869 took the position that emancipation was necessary to rid the plantation house of slaves who physically and morally corrupted whites.

One of the spectacular literary successes of this period was Bernardo Guimarães's A escrava Isaura (1875), about the travails of a light-skinned girl who is stalked by her master and rescued by the love of a young, idealistic (and white) suitor who marries her. Despite its condemnation of slavery, the book offered characterizations that became problematic with the passing of time. Isaura's beauty is constantly associated with her whiteness, and at one point she laments her situation as an attractive, literate slave, reasoning that her lot would have been much better had she been ignorant and deformed, like the most vile of black women. Nonetheless, poems and books such as Isaura were successful in appealing to the sympathies of readers, while the fiery oratory of abolitionists encouraged and sometimes instigated slave insurgency.

The life story of the Bahian poet Luís Gama reads as dramatically as any work of fiction. His mother was a freed slave who purportedly participated in the Sabinada, a protorepublican uprising in favor of federalism that took place in 1836 and 1837 in Bahia. His father, a once-well-to-do Portuguese gentleman, sold him into slavery when he was ten years old in order to pay off some debts. As a house slave, Gama managed to learn to read and, after fleeing captivity, spent nearly a decade struggling to prove that he was born a free man. Having made his case, he went on to become a soldier, then a government employee who in his spare time studied law. He helped other slaves prove their status as free people in the courts and later successfully defended hundreds who had been illegally enslaved. A leader in the abolition and republican movements, he wrote for newspapers and literary reviews but is best known for his satiric verses written under the pseudonym Getulino, which appears in his *Primeiras trovas burlescas* (First Burlesque Songs), published in 1859 and revised in 1861.

Gama's pleasure in wit and irony can be appreciated in the way he fashioned his poetry after the satires of Gregório de Matos, some of whose most vicious lyrics were directed toward mulattoes and blacks in seventeenth-century Bahia. Unlike his contemporaries, Gama refrained from writing sentimentally about slaves, preferring to poke fun at individuals of position and wealth who passed as white. Among his many amusing poems is a sonnet about a nobleman who insists that his ancestry is regal, only to be challenged by a bystander who states that one of his forebears is a mulatto. This challenge rings clear as Gama repeats the refrain: "And he can't deny being my relative."[57]

In a more caustic vein, Gama wrote "Quem sou eu?" (Who Am I?), a poem about the *bodarrada,* which is a neologism for a herd of *bodes* or "goats," but whose other, pejorative meaning refers to "persons of mixed race." Gama continued to satirize the citizenry by labeling everyone a "goat":

If I am black, or a goat,
Little does it matter. What can that do?
There are goats of every caste
For the species is very vast . . .
There are gray ones, there are striped ones,
Bays, white-faced ones and ones that are spotted,
Black goats, *white goats,*
And let's all be frank,
Some are common, others noble,

Rich goats, poor goats,
Wise and important goats,
And also a few rascally ones (112–113)

Nearly a century after this poem appeared, the Brazilian artist Angelo Coutinho drew an illustration, "A bodarrada," which appeared on the cover of the Rio-based magazine *Alvorada* (Dawn). The drawing shows goats of different shapes and hues standing on a rocky hillside. They have human heads and wear hats that represent different social types, such as a sea captain and a brigadier general, both of whom are mentioned in Gama's poem. The funniest goat has a modern-style brimmed hat, horn-rimmed glasses, and a pipe in his mouth and looks like a cross between a bird watcher and an academic. In his preface to the 1904 edition of *Trovas,* the writer Coelho Neto succinctly captures the playful but ultimately deadly nature of Gama's verses, which he describes as "light as an arrow that whistles, heads directly to the target's center, drives itself in, and keeps vibrating" (11).[58]

It is important to remember that even as the abolitionist movement was gaining momentum, there were blacks who owned black slaves, former slaves who were not abolitionists, and abolitionists who were not republicans. In the last group is the political firebrand Joaquim Nabuco, a fervent abolitionist whose life of privilege kept him committed to an imperial style of government. Nabuco's fundamental role as a lawyer, writer, and orator in the cause for emancipation has been widely discussed and documented; less discussed is the voice that he raised against the anti-Lusitanian sentiments of Ferdinand Denis and others for whom Brazil's rejection of Portuguese culture was deemed essential to the formation of a national literary identity. A great admirer of Camões, Nabuco made *Os lusíadas* the centerpiece of numerous essays and lectures, several of which he gave while on diplomatic duty in the United States; and he decried Brazilian writers' adulation of French works over the Portuguese epic masterpiece that was part of their nation's literary heritage (1949, 9:41–50).

That dedication to a European view of Brazilian literature came to the fore in 1875, when the young Nabuco wrote a review of the play *O jesuíta* by the popular Alencar. His review initiated a protracted newspaper exchange with Alencar that appeared almost daily over a two-month period. Their fiery, accusatory rhetoric thoroughly exhilarated readers.[59] In his responses, Alencar referred to Nabuco as a "pamphleteer" who wrote "indigestible prose" (Coutinho 1965, 115). He also vigorously challenged Nabuco's charges that he, Alencar, had built his theatrical success on less-than-felicitous representations of slaves and that he had done nothing to oppose or end slavery. Alencar's measured responses could sometimes turn personal and pointed:

> Slavery is a fact for which all Brazilians assume responsibility, for we are accomplices in it as citizens of the Empire . . . To reproach one's predecessors for a delay for which they bear no blame; to betray a past to aggrandize one's own person; to turn the memory of one's ancestors and the dignity of the nation into a trophy for grotesque idolatry is behavior that I hope to God will not have example in Brazil.
>
> Like the present generation, the pamphleteer was born in a country with slaves, and in the bosom of a respectable and illustrious family served by slaves. Those acidic lips that can no longer pronounce the word *moleque* [black boy] without becoming sickened perhaps suckled a slave's milk, as was the case, not with me, but with many others who exceed him with respect to human dignity. Those susceptible ears that can no longer suffer the word *iaiá* [missy], must have heard it constantly, or some other equivalent, during childhood. (In Coutinho 1965, 119)

But Nabuco had broken ties with the slaveholding aristocracy in which he was born to take up the cause of emancipation. In his last article in the polemic, Nabuco blamed Alencar for having a nationalistic imagination that alienated Brazilian literature and readers from their European roots:

> The imagination of Mr. J. de Alencar, serving him in literature only to conjoin words and discover the tonic accent of a phrase and the rhythm of a sentence, has exercised over his talent the most pernicious influence, which is reflected in our literature. His imagination destroyed the balance of his faculties, a balance that I only admit as an hypothesis. Taking measure of the extremely vast domain of the human spirit, Mr. J. de Alencar had no idea other than to occupy that domain completely, and he extended his little arms to embrace the sphere. From that came his extraordinary fecundity and also his imperfect production. (In Coutinho 1965, 210)

Alencar refrained from further comment. In a much later postscript to this debate, an older and wiser Nabuco wrote: "I locked horns with José de Alencar in a polemic in which I fear I treated the great writer with the presumption and injustice of youth. I say *I fear,* because I have not gone back to read those pamphlets and do not recall to what point my criticism offended that which is profound and national in Alencar: his *Brazilianness"* (in Coutinho 1965, 11).

The Writer as National Critic

The currently accepted critic does not excel in literary science; I even believe that one of the conditions for performing such a curious role is to relieve oneself of all concern for the questions that have to do with the domain of the imagination.

MACHADO DE ASSIS, "Ideal do crítico," 1865

One of Nabuco's most cherished correspondents, to whom he began writing when he was just fifteen years old, was the author and critic Machado de Assis. The occasion for his first letter (February 1, 1865) was to express appreciation for Machado's note in the *Diário do Rio de Janeiro* on some verses that he had written and which Machado described, albeit somewhat ambiguously, as having come from an "exuberant imagination" (in Graça Aranha 1949, 91).[60] Eight years later, Nabuco wrote Machado again, inviting him to attend his lecture on Camões and *Os lusíadas,* which would take place at the home of his father, Senator Nabuco, in the center of Rio. Their correspondence grew in the late 1890s: letters from Nabuco, who traveled widely and held government appointments in Paris, London, and the United States, and increasingly affectionate responses from Machado, who never left Rio. As time passed, they focused on the founding of a Brazilian Academy of Letters, which was finally established in 1897. Machado was its first president, and Nabuco gave the inaugural address. It was novelist Graça Aranha's later perception that the relationship between the two men, who were from vastly different backgrounds (Machado, a mulatto, was born into poverty in Rio), was based on their mutual appreciation of Camões, although he makes an important distinction between them. For Nabuco, he writes, Camões was a political force that fired his "social imagination," while Machado was attracted to Camões' discipline and classical-style perfection of form and tone (Graça Aranha 1949, 15).

Machado was also an admirer of the romantics, including Alencar, Gonçalves Dias, Castro Alves, and the Portuguese Almeida Garrett. Early in his career, Machado wrote his own version of "Americana" poetry in a volume in 1875 featuring Indianist verses and a poem about a pregnant slave called

Sabina that was perhaps the first book in Brazil to focus on the three races. But his later poems, published in 1880 under the evocative title *Ocidentais* (Occidentals), are considerably more in keeping with his classical sensibility and demonstrate in different ways his interest in humor, irony, and antithesis—all of which he applied with far broader and superior strokes in his fiction about the petit bourgeoisie in Rio.

There was nothing ethnically or racially distinctive about Machado's fictional creations, nor were they unusual or "exotic" in their speech and habits. Yet they created distinct urban types in mid- to late-nineteenth-century Brazil and are intriguing and memorable because of their sometimes whimsical, sometimes tragic-comic nature. Although Machado never explicitly talked about writing from the perspective of a person of color, his assessment of Cariocan (Rio) and, by extension, Brazilian society is a little like Luís Gama's *bodarrada* in the sense that the middle class shares if not a racial identity per se, then a set of psychological traits that include self-aggrandizement, greed, deceit, and a tendency to base judgments on material or empirical reality.

Machado's particular style of nationalism was not at all typical of the times. He has often been accused of being "un-Brazilian" because he preferred to write about the composition and foibles of a society in transition rather than about local color or racial and ethnic types. This does not mean that Machado never publicly commented on or reacted against an institution like slavery, only that he tended to be indirect and ironic in his observations. For example, in a review that appeared in 1859 in the Rio newspaper *O espelho* (The Mirror), Machado chides the author of the play *Escravo fiel* (Faithful Slave) for different problems that appear throughout the production. In discussing the character of the faithful slave, Lourenço, he criticizes his unrealistic language and concludes with the brief but deadly observation: "However, there is a very pretty line spoken by this black fellow. 'I am a black man but my intentions were white'" (1970b, 138–139). In "Gazeta de Holanda" (Holland Gazette), a chronicle written in verse and published nearly thirty years later, Machado satirizes the state of affairs, pointing out that while most of the country continued to argue for emancipation, the slave remained a victim:

A beating when I don't sell,
a beating that hurts, that burns;

If I sell what I am hawking,
Then I get a beating for getting back late.

Neither saint's day nor Sunday
Do I have. Food, very little:
A small plate of beans and a drop
Of coffee that barely wets the mouth.

For that reason, I say to the perfect
Institute, so grande and brave: *You speak* very well /
But you're free, and I'm still a slave. (1955, 392–393)

Machado was not the first person to write about the people and customs of Rio during the monarchy. Among his predecessors were Joaquim Manuel de Macedo, who wrote the highly popular *A moreninha* (The Little Brunette), a light, romantic novel published in 1844 about the trials and tribulations of two young people in love (and which changed the idea of aesthetic types from blonds to brunettes); and Manuel Antônio de Almeida, whose picaresque *Memórias de um sargento de milícias,* published in 1854–1855 (*Memoirs of a Military Sargeant,* 1999), is a running social commentary and critique of the capital city following the arrival of the Portuguese court. Almeida's novel anticipates the techniques of modernism, particularly in its ludic and formal experiments, which also can be found in Machado's fiction. Shortly after Machado's famous essay "Instinto da nacionalidade" appeared in 1873, Alencar published *Senhora* (1875), his last and best urban novel, about the psychological impact of arranged marriages and dowries on a capitalistic-minded Rio.

Even in Machado's earliest stories, most of which bear traces of romanticism, the relationship between cause and effect is not readily apparent or often exists only in the mind of the character, who is generally deluded. One of Machado's least studied stories of this period, "A parasita azul" (The Blue Parasite), published in 1872, is not as psychologically sharp as his later works but deserves attention for its own "national instinct." In the story, Machado creates a character who is the exact opposite of the Gonçalves Dias figure who lives abroad and pines away for Brazil. Machado's Camilo, a young man from a well-to-do family in the interior of Goiás, is sent abroad by his father, Seabra, to study in Paris under the watchful eye of his French godfather, a failed-poet-turned-naturalist who met Seabra and his family while on an expedition to Brazil in 1828.[61] The story begins with the title "Volta ao Brasil" (Return to Brazil) and describes Camilo's reaction upon arriving in Brazil after eight years in Europe:

> When it came time to disembark, he did it with the same joy with which a criminal crosses the threshold of a prison. The spectacle of the city [Rio], which he had not seen for such a long time, always seized his attention a little. But he did not feel the commotion inside him that Ulysses felt on seeing his country. He compared what he now saw with what he had been seeing for many years and felt the anguishing *saudade* burrowing more deeply into and squeezing his heart. (1970c, 10)

The reader learns that Camilo has managed to stay away from Brazil as long as he has by convincing his father of his need to further his studies, when in actuality he simply does not want to leave his friends and the Parisian good life that his father has bankrolled. Camilo is quite deft in his manipulation of his father, writing him poignant albeit deceptive letters, one of which declares that should his father absolutely insist upon his return, "[I] will not remain another second in [France], which has been like a second homeland, and which today (*alas!*) is but a land of exile" (13).

Machado also pokes fun at literary regionalism and its idyllic descriptions of life in the interior. Particularly amusing is the passage that describes Camilo's reaction to the music of the countryside as he travels on horseback to his home in the interior:

> One of the muleteers took out a little guitar and began to warble a ballad which would have enchanted any other person for the crude sincerity of its verses and its tune, but that simply made [Camilo] *prefer,* in sadness, the quick musical notes heard at the Opera. . . . The crickets, toads, and frogs formed a chorus in an opera of the *sertão,* which our hero certainly admired, but to which he undoubtedly preferred the comic opera (27).

Camilo is typical of the idle, educated, but unintellectual protagonist that Machado loved to spoof but also used to satirize populist literary conventions. Ironically, his primary concern as a writer and critic of Brazilian literature was to promote a very different idea of what the national meant. "A parasita azul" critiques the regionalist trend that was popular during his day while raising up for examination educated, middle-class types who, despite weaknesses in character and failed judgments, manage to delude themselves of the rightfulness of their thoughts and acts. Machado's "instinct of nationality" derived from a sense that the psychology of literary characters was more important than where they came from or what language or dialect they spoke. He wrote mainly about the bourgeoisie because it represented a relatively new class of individuals born of the industrial age whose main preoccupations concerned not the general welfare but rather the self, personal relationships, and social station.

Machado wanted Brazilian literature to take its place at the table of other great literatures, and that had little to do with republicanism, regionalism, the abolitionist movement, or the nation-state. He admired Balzac, Flaubert, Sterne, and Pascal, but he created his own gallery of unforgettable characters who live in Rio but whose disillusionments and conundrums are recognizable within and outside Brazil. His talent was to reveal through a highly personable yet subtly ironic narrator the sometimes banal and sometimes insidious nature of middle-class types who are hollow men without an inkling of their own hollowness.

One of his most celebrated stories, "Teoria do medalhão" (Theory of the Stuffed Shirt), published in 1882, consists of a late-night conversation between a father and son, the latter of whom is about to turn twenty-two at the stroke of midnight. On this important occasion, the father speaks to his son about his job prospects and the opportunities that will open to him in government, science, journalism, and so forth. He advises the young man to choose the profession that will bring him the most recognition but will also require the utmost dedication and ambition: the stuffed shirt. The story turns into a recipe of how to achieve this position, which basically demands that the son avoid any originality of thought and develop talents in mimicry, ingratiation, self-promotion, and empty rhetoric. The son is taken back by the many skills required of the position and tells his father that it appears "not at all easy" (1961, 121). The father's response is a good example of Machado's view of the middle-class preference for appearance over substance:

> "[The stuffed shirt profession] is difficult, it eats up time, a lot of time, it takes years, patience, work, and happy are those who manage to enter the promised land! Those that don't get in are swallowed up by obscurity. But those who triumph! And you will triumph, believe me. You will see the walls of Jericho and hear the sound of sacred trumpets and only then can you say that you have

made it. That day begins the phase of indispensable ornamentation, of the obliging figure, of the label on the bottle. Ended is the need to sniff out occasions, commissions, fraternities; they will come to you, with your solemn air of unmodified nouns, and you will be the adjective of those opaque sentences, the *scent-filled* of the flowers, the *dignified* of the citizenry, the *newsworthy* and *succulent* of the reports. And to be this is the main thing, because the adjective is the soul of the language, its idealistic and metaphysical essence. The noun is a naked and raw reality, it's the naturalism of our vocabulary. (122)

Machado also satirized official titles, which were handed out indiscriminately and sometimes in extraordinary numbers during the Empire. His "O espelho" (The Mirror) in 1882 is a *tour de force,* poking fun not only at pomp and ceremony but also at Comtean positivism promoted in Brazil by the military and political elite.[62] The story's subtitle, "Esboço de uma nova teoria da alma" (Outline of a New Theory of the Soul), satirizes Comte's various commentaries and treatises on the nature of humanity and demonstrates how a person becomes affected by and ultimately subservient to titles, clothing, and reputation. In this particular story, which is told in flashback, a young man who has been chosen for a lieutenancy in the National Guard acquires a title, a uniform, and the praise of his family and servants, the latter of whom now call him "lieutenant." His pride and sense of self grow, and a large mirror in his aunt's house, where he stays for a short period, enables him to confirm for himself what others see and admire. However, when an emergency requires his aunt to leave him for several days and when the house servants take advantage of their mistress's absence and flee, the young man begins to feel uneasy and despondent. Alone in the house, he rapidly loses the sense of self that others gave him; when he looks at himself in the mirror he is frightened by his image, which appears nebulous and distorted. In desperation, he decides to put on his uniform:

I was myself, the lieutenant, who finally found his exterior soul. With the departure of the lady of the house and the flight of the slaves, that absent soul had withdrawn there into the mirror. . . . I looked into the mirror, turned from side to side, stepped back, gesticulated, smiled, and the mirror expressed everything. . . . From that point on, I was the other. Every day, at a certain hour, I dressed myself as the lieutenant and sat in front of the mirror, reading, looking, meditating; at the end of two or three hours, I'd undress again. Following that regimen I was able to get through six days of solitude without a problem. (1961, 176)

Few of Machado's stories are as devastating a commentary on Brazilian positivism as his 1881 novella *O alienista* (The Alienist),[63] an allegory about the nineteenth-century vogue for "order and progress."[64] The story, the narrator tells us, is based on old village chronicles describing incidents involving a Dr. Simão Bacamarte.[65] Son of the nobility, a student of medicine at the universities of Coimbra and Pádua, and regarded as the greatest physician in Spain, Portugal, and Brazil, Bacamarte has returned to his native Brazil, where he sets up a practice in the village of Itaguaí. Soon thereafter, he marries a young widow, Dona Evarista, who is "neither pretty nor nice," but who, according to Bacamarte, "brought together physiological and anatomical characteristics of the first order, namely, she digested easily, she slept regularly, she had a good pulse and excellent vision" (1961, 51). "In this respect," he comments, "she was apt for bearing him robust, sound, and intelligent children" (ibid.).

In Itaguaí, Bacamarte studies the "health of the soul" and becomes the first specialist of "cerebral pathology" in the colony and the realm. He proposes the construction of an insane asylum where, like many an enlightened man of science who came to Brazil, he would collect, study, and classify different specimens. In just a few months the asylum, called the Green House, fills to capacity with the insane, and an annex is built to accommodate the overflow. With the passage of time, two things become evident: first, despite her excellent condition and his early, optimistic prognosis, Dona Evarista does not bear any children; second, Bacamarte discovers that insanity "was not an island lost in the ocean of reason, but rather a continent" (63), as he explains to the chemist, Mr. Soares: "Supposing the human spirit is like a gigantic seashell; my objective, Mr. Soares, is to see if I can extract the pearl, which is reason. Let us definitively demarcate the limits of reason and insanity through other means. Reason represents the perfect balance of all the faculties; beyond that, insanity, insanity, and only insanity" (65).

When Bacamarte reveals his theory to the town's vicar, religion, for the most part, keeps its counsel in the face of empirical science.[66] However, a hue and cry arises when Bacamarte commits one of the village's most prominent citizens, Costa, for having given away and without contract or interest the totality of his considerable inheritance from a deceased uncle. When Costa's cousin explains to Bacamarte that such generosity is the result of a curse placed on the miserly uncle's money, the doctor decides to commit her as well. Finally a committee led by the village barber, Porfírio, demands that local officials take action against "scientific despotism" (79). As the officials argue and hesitate over the issue, the committee of thirty grows into a movement of over three hundred, who demand the destruction of the Green House and the death of Bacamarte. When Royal Dragoons are sent to confront the outraged citizenry, Porfírio stands firm with his followers, and the soldiers back down. A coup d'etat ensues. Porfírio assumes the leadership of the government, and public expectations rise for the imminent demise of the asylum and the doctor.

As may be evident from this description, Machado's cynicism about order and progress in Brazil was not limited to "scientific despotism" but encompassed the political realm as well; in *O alienista* he delights in showing how local governments are easily deflected and dismantled, only to reconstitute and resurface as mirror images of their former selves. Machado also demonstrates how once-sacrosanct ideals are discarded when political power is gained. The barber cuts a deal with Bacamarte, who can continue to operate as long as he releases a few patients to pacify the citizenry and supports Porfírio's administration. After Bacamarte commits fifty more individuals, who have protested the new government, the people rise up again, this time under the leadership of the other town barber, João Pina, who overthrows Porfírio and takes control. This sudden change in government, which brings about no real change, simply fortifies Bacamarte's position, and he commits the former ruler, Porfírio. He even places his wife, Dona Evarista, in the Green House for her repeated indecisiveness about what style and color of clothes to wear—a mental deficiency that he attributes to her recent first visit to the capital city of Rio. After committing his beloved wife, no one in the village feels able to challenge the doctor's diagnoses or directives.

Machado's satire of empirical science and order and progress culminates in the final part of the novella. Bacamarte concludes that his theory about insanity must be in error because four-fifths of the village population now resides in the Green House. He informs the local officials that his initial theory is flawed and now proclaims that the opposite of this theory is true. According to his new theory, mental stability is the real pathology; and he immediately releases all his patients to the delight of families and friends, who commemorate the event with a village-wide celebration. However, when the celebrations are over and order is finally restored, the government officials begin to argue over which mentally balanced individuals should be exempt from the new theory's postulates and how long a period patients should be committed. Their public wrangles merely convince Bacamarte that they are all mentally unstable with the exception of one politician, whose voice of moderation and reason is deemed to be proof of his insanity. With his new theory in hand, Bacamarte also commits the vicar, the chemist's wife, and sixteen others, who are classified according to their different degrees of moral perfection, which include loyalty, truthfulness, sincerity, and the like. His cure involves introducing the opposite quality or sentiment into their personalities, and his treatment is so successful that by the end of five months, the Green House is completely vacated.

But instead of resting on his laurels, Bacamarte begins to wonder if he actually cured his patients and if there was something latent in their "insanity" that enabled them to cure themselves. He also wonders how any town can be without a single crazy person. After pondering these and other questions, the doctor calls a council of friends together to consult them about an anxiety that he begins to have about himself. As a result of this inquiry, he discovers to his dismay that they all consider his mental faculties to be balanced and without defect. The vicar slyly adds that Bacamarte's innate modesty is the reason he has been unable to detect his own superiority. Such assessments are more than sufficient to convince the doctor to commit himself, and he becomes the only resident in the Green House, where he dies trying to find a cure for his insanity. Subsequent to Bacamarte's death, a rumor circulates that he was the only insane person ever to reside in Itaguaí—a rumor attributed to the vicar, who, according to the village chronicles, presided over the burial service with "considerable pomp and a rare solemnity" (111)—a wry commentary on the resilient nature of Brazilian Catholicism, which, according to Sérgio Buarque de Holanda, has always been "more attentive to the outward pomp and splendor of the ceremonies than to their inner meaning" (1989, 108).

If the belief in reason and truth based on empirical evidence was important to Machado's human comedy of trial and error, his curmudgeonly Cariocan lawyer-protagonist Dom Casmurro was his greatest invention. Considered by many critics to be a masterpiece of Brazilian fiction, *Dom Casmurro* (1900) is the memoir of a man who suspects his deceased wife, Capitu, of having had an affair years earlier with their friend Ezequiel (who drowned at the seashore); he also suspects that his recently deceased son, Escobar, was the product of that illicit relationship. Now in late middle age,

Dom Casmurro decides to write a memoir to try to understand the past and to verify his convictions. The quantity of evidence raised by the lawyer throughout the memoir is substantial, but ultimately, Dom Casmurro's lengthy testimony about past events confirms what the aging lawyer indirectly acknowledges in the present, that is, that he will never know the truth.[67]

Although Capitu is probably the most famous of Machado's female fictional characters, others appear throughout his works who are similarly presented as objects of interest. Sensually aroused, Machado's predominantly male narrator-characters inevitably end up confused or frustrated by their inability to know what the opposite sex is thinking. This portrait of the sensuous yet sphinxlike woman appears alongside another, less obvious female character—the "dear reader" (or some variation thereof) in whom Machado's narrator often confides.

Of the many types caricatured in Machado's fiction, the female reader is perhaps the least discussed and appreciated. Far more studied are characters such as the sycophantic José Dias in *Dom Casmurro,* whose livelihood and social well-being depend on his ability to bow and scrape before his "betters," which he does expertly with his rhetoric filled with superlatives. Machado's anonymous female reader-character is undoubtedly based on the premise that the principal audience in the mid-to-late nineteenth century for fiction, and particularly the novel, was composed of middle- and upper-class women, who showed a special fondness for romances. The irony behind Machado's frequent reference to a "dear reader" in his later works is that while he wrote a great deal about relationships between men and women, his novels like *Dom Casmurro* are anything but sentimental narratives about amorous encounters and passion. Nonetheless, he addressed the "dear reader" as if his novels were of the very sort that were popular among women readers of the time. In this way, he commented ironically on both the literature of the period and an imagined female readership.

The same playfulness can be found in Machado's *A semana* (The Week), which consists of chronicles that he wrote over the years 1895 through 1900 for the Rio-based *Gazeta de notícias,* whose predominantly male readership was the focus of more than one of his columns. A particularly amusing caricature of these readers appears in the February 28, 1897, issue, in which Machado writes that he plans to stop penning chronicles, finding himself exhausted by "this tired century" that has exacted so much "hatred and applause": "Add to this the revolutions, the annexations, the dissolutions and inventions of every caste, political, philosophical, artistic, and literary, even acrobatic and pharmaceutical, and you will understand that it is a worn-out century" (255–256). This faux-homage to the century includes himself as writer and his reader, whom he parodies without respite:

> Farewell, reader. . . . There is nothing like talking to a person who never interrupts. One tells him everything that one wants, what is worthy and what is not, things and modes, phrases and ideas are repeated to him, opinions are contradicted, and the person who reads never interrupts. He can throw the paper to the side or end up sleeping. The person who writes never sees the gesture or the sleep, he just keeps on going until he is finished. Truth be told, just at this moment I am positing a guess about what you are thinking. You are thinking that the best way to withdraw from an obligation of this kind is not so different from leaving a dance, which is to go down to the cloak room, put on an overcoat and disappear into the carriage or the night. This business of plying so much discourse leads one to believe that, besides being outside the bounds of etiquette, *saudades* are presumed in the others. You are right, reader. And if there were time to rip up this page and write differently, believe me that I would do it. But it is late, very late . . . Farewell, friend, until we see one another. Or, if you prefer a way of speaking that is more ours, then, until some day. . . . Farewell!. (1970a, 428–429)

In true Machadian style, the author returned to writing chronicles, although more than three years had passed. His last piece, dated November 11, 1900, is ostensibly about his attempts to discover the origins and ownership of a sword that he saw at an auction and contains one of his typically informative but always amusing, if not sly, social commentaries. In this instance, the sword, like the pen, provides Machado with the means to comment on foreign immigration to Brazil at the turn of the century:

> I happened upon a statistic from São Paulo about last year's immigrants, and I found thousands of people had disembarked in Santos [São Paulo state] or had left here [Rio] by way of Central Station. Italian people were the most numerous. Then came the Spaniards, the English, the French, the Portuguese, the Germans, even the Turks, some forty-five Turks. Finally a Greek. My heart leapt, and I said to myself: the Greek is the one who hocked the sword.
>
> And here goes the reasons for my suspicion or discovery. First and foremost, I felt relieved because the Greek was not a Brazilian—or *national*, as per the

wording in police notices. Next, the Greek was only one, and I ran a lesser risk as opposed to suspecting someone from the other groups, who could gang up on me in defense of their compatriot. Third, the Greek is the poorest of the immigrants. Even in his homeland he is extremely poor. Fourth, perhaps he was also a poet, and might even have had a lyric ready with the refrain:

Eu cá sou grego [Here I am a Greek],
Levi a minha espada ao prego [I took my sword and hocked it].

Finally, it wouldn't have cost him anything to hock the sword since perhaps it was Turkish. . . .

Now that I'm about to finish this chronicle, it occurs to me that the sword might have been a theatrical prop pawned by the theater prompter because the company failed to pay him. The poor devil took this course of action just so he could eat lunch one day. If this were the case, make believe that I didn't write anything and take off for lunch as well. It's that time. (442–443)

Machado's reference to the numbers and nationalities of different immigrant groups parodies the data and other information being publicized nationwide about the large number of foreigners entering Brazil at the end of the nineteenth century. Machado's suspicion of an error in his original judgment of the sword and his equally humorous alternative proposition are the kinds of rhetorical "props" that he regularly used to satirize the foibles of his own social class.

CHAPTER 5

Modernist Brazil

Machado de Assis's ironic observations about a Greek bearing a sword do not obscure his point that a major demographic change was taking place in Brazil at the turn of the twentieth century. In 1870, the majority of the estimated 10 million Brazilians were of African descent; by 1900, more than 1 million immigrants from Europe had helped to raise the nation's population to approximately 17.5 million. An illustration from an 1876 issue of the *Revista ilustrada* shows immigrants drawn to Brazil by promises of a rich, fertile land, on the order of the sixteenth-century Edenic descriptions created to stimulate New World settlement. As historian Marshall C. Eakin and others have pointed out, this wave of European immigration, which began in the mid-nineteenth century, was looked upon favorably by certain members of the intelligentsia, who supported the idea of a whitening of Brazil's population and culture (Eakin 1997, 119).[1]

Although the early photographer Marc Ferrez regularly included black Brazilians in his works, images of the predominantly black Brazil like José Correa de Lima's *Intrépido marinheiro Simão* (Intrepid Sailor Simon), circa 1857, and the anonymous *Mulher da Bahia* (Woman from Bahia), circa 1850, were rare in paintings of the late nineteenth and early twentieth centuries. The predominant style was conservative, showing the continuing influence of the French Cultural Mission. Vítor Meirelles was among the best-known Brazilian painters of the mid- to late nineteenth century; in addition to his sweeping Cariocan landscapes, his most important works were paintings of key historical events, such as his *Primeira missa no Brasil* (First mass in Brazil)[2] and his equally renowned *Batalha de Guararapes* (Battle of Guararapes), which depicts the clash of forces between Brazilians and Dutch in the seventeenth century.[3] Like their French Cultural Mission predecessors, Meirelles and an even younger generation of artists including Augusto Rodrigues Duarte, José Maria de Medeiros, and Rodolfo Amoedo drew inspiration from romantic themes associated with Indianism. For example, Meirelles, Amoedo, and Duarte painted stunning portraits of Indians dramatically posed in death. Meirelles's *Moema* and Amoedo's *O último tamoio* (The Last Tamoio) portray solitary, heroic Amerindians whose bodies have washed up on shore,[4] while Duarte's *As exéquias de Atala* (The Funeral Rites of Atala) shows the Natchez warrior Chactas mourning the death of the European-ized Atala, who preferred suicide to marriage with a non-Christian. In both Amoedo's *O último tamoio* and Duarte's *Atala,* a priest attends the dead, and a crucifix appears in Atala's folded hands. In the spirit of Alencar, Christianity appears as a positive force in both paintings, its role in the Amerindians' subjugation and demise having been deftly sidestepped.

Amoedo's painting *Marabá* was likely influenced by Gonçalves Dias's famous poem by the same title that describes the suffering of a maiden-outcast of mixed Indian and European blood. With the possible exception of her dark hair, there is nothing in the portrait itself to identify her as an Indian. Her nude pose is in keeping with pseudo-classical eroticism of the time, and her skin appears alabaster against the painting's dark background. Medeiros's Alencar-inspired painting *Iracema* displays the melancholia associated with the "honey-lipped" maiden, who is darker in skin tone than the other indigenous figures just mentioned. Unlike the dramatic representations of many indigenous people of this period, she is portrayed as a living woman, although those familiar with Alencar's novel cannot help but associate Medeiros's solitary image at the water's edge with Iracema's fateful encounter with "civilization."

Meirelles did include a black figure in his *Batalha de Guararapes* (besides the heroic Henrique Dias), but the startled and bugged-eyed look of the

5.1 *Moema,* by Vítor Meirelles (1866)

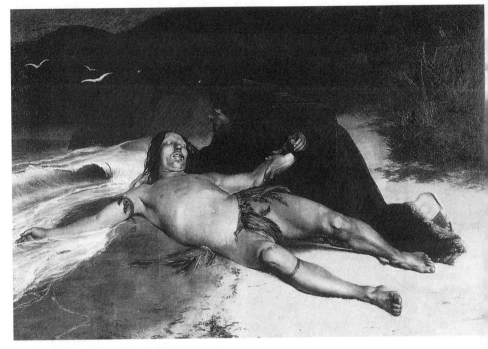

5.2 *O último tamoio,* by Rodolfo Amoedo (1883)

black soldier contrasts vividly with the more determined demeanor of the Dutch occupying forces and other local insurgents. A student of Meirelles, the Spanish painter Modesto Brocos, painted two important works that feature blacks in Republican Brazil. His *A redenção de Cam* (The Redemption of Ham) shows a black female servant with eyes raised to the heavens and hands lifted up in prayer as a light-skinned mother and father look adoringly at their even whiter son. This painting gained iconic status during the republic for its promotion of European immigration and the "whitening" process. Brocos's *Engenho de mandioca* (Manioc Mill) is a group portrait of black men and women sitting on the ground and working on a large pile of manioc roots. Brocos's pictures suggest that despite emancipation, little improvement had occurred in the lives of blacks.

As art historian Lourival Gomes Machado has noted, modernity, in the form of the advances in transportation, communication, and industrialization, was still not apparent in turn-of-the-century Brazilian art:

Each individual artist's history can be reduced to an identical basic graph: a youth of promising enthusiasm invariably ending up substituting national subjects for the so-called allegorical or mythological and becoming possessed by a mad desire to get to Europe to bring back something new. . . . [T]he price of these two liberties . . . is the submission of expression to a hard, formal discipline which produces artists who work within the same limitations, perfect the same techniques, and produce almost identical paintings. (In *Semana de 22* 1972, n.p.)

It was not until 1922 that the Brazilian intellectual and artistic community experienced the shock of the new. Paulo Mendes de Almeida has observed that the famous Modern Art Week held in February 1922 in the Municipal Theater in São Paulo was all the more astonishing because Brazilians had "never experienced Impressionism as a general, accepted fact" and had no way of understanding the transition to more experimental, vanguard forms of art (*Semana de 22* 1972, n.p.).[5] Nonetheless, the week achieved its primary goals, as set forth by one of its organizers, the poet Mário de Andrade: "The

5.3 *Iracema,* by José Maria de Medeiros (1884)

5.4 *A redenção de Cam,* by Modesto Brocos (1895)

permanent right to esthetic experimentation; actualization of the Brazilian artistic intelligence; establishment of a creative consciousness" (in *Semana de 22* 1972, n.p.).

Precursors of the artistic experiments featured in the Modern Art Week included Hélios Seelinger, whose Germanic-inspired mysticism caused many of those who saw his 1903 exhibit in the offices of the Rio publication *O malho* (The Mallet) to pronounce him insane. Ten years later, the Lithuanian immigrant Lasar Segall exhibited in São Paulo, where the public was introduced to an expressionistic style in which the human subject, unlike the portraiture art of bourgeois realism, was subordinate to a formal design. Few events could compare to the *succès du scandale* created by the 1917 exhibition by the young São Paulo artist Anita Malfatti,[6] whose colorfully expressionistic portraits, including *A mulher de cabelos verdes* (The Woman with Green Hair), *Uma estudante* (A Student), and *O homem amarelo* (The Yellow Man) raised public eyebrows. The popular but conservative writer Monteiro Lobato wrote a scathing review, "Paranóia ou mistificação" (Paranoia or Mystification), in the newspaper *O estado de São Paulo* denouncing her work as "decadent," "cross-eyed," and part of the "boils in the excess of culture" (in J. Leite 1994, 35). Among Malfatti's youthful defenders were poets Oswald de Andrade and Guilherme de Almeida and the artist Di Cavalcanti. Mário de Andrade made his own public statement of support when he later purchased Malfatti's *The Yellow Man* at the inauguration ceremonies for the Modern Art Week.[7]

5.5 *A estudante,* by Anita Malfatti (1915/1916)

Mário de Andrade once stated that he was not certain who proposed the idea of the Modern Art Week, but the event, which coincided with the centenary celebration of the nation's independence, prominently featured members of the older intelligentsia, including Graça Aranha, author of the acclaimed *Canaã* (1902), published in translation in 1920 as *Canaan,* a novel about German immigrants in the Brazilian South. Paulo Prado, who wrote *Retrato do Brasil* (Portrait of Brazil), a slim but provocative book about national identity, was the week's principal patron. Among the young literary Turks were Oswald de Andrade, Mário de Andrade, and Ronald de Carvalho, the last of whom already had collaborated with Portuguese modernist poets Fernando Pessoa and Mário de Sá-Carneiro on the transatlantic modernist review *Orpheu* (1915). The week also featured works by the renowned composer Heitor Villa-Lobos, the sculptor Victor Brecheret, and painters Malfatti, Di Cavalcanti (who designed the week's program cover), and Vicente Rego Monteiro.

According to a 1972 commentary by Yan de Almeida Prado, who illustrated the short-lived modernist review *Klaxon* (1922–1923) and was a friend of F. T. Marinetti, the works presented at the Modern Art Week would never have achieved canonical status had it not been for the efforts of Mário de Andrade and Oswald de Andrade, who kept the week "alive in the memory of the esteemed public" (in *Semana de 22* 1972, n.p.). Mário de Andrade's satiric ode to São Paulo, *Paulicéia desvairada* (1922; translated as *Hallucinated City,* 1968), and his folkloric "rhapsody" in the form of a novel, *Macunaíma* (1928; English translation 1984), whose black Indian "hero without any character" magically transforms into a blue-eyed white, were surreal and sensational, creating a vision of a fragmented yet racially fluid Brazil.[8]

Meanwhile, Oswald de Andrade repeatedly called for writers and artists to "ingest" European influences insofar as they could be "regurgitated" in the form of something new and Brazilian for export. In his poems, manifestos, novels, and literary reviews, we repeatedly encounter references to the emblematic brazilwood, Indians, and the practice of anthropophagy.[9] In his 2006 article "Poetry and Paradise in the Discovery of Brazil," critic K. David Jackson emphasizes the importance of early historiographies on Brazil for the modernists' rediscovery and reevaluation of the nation (45). As Jackson demonstrates, this was particularly true for Oswald de Andrade, who constructed his own pastiche-like version of the "history" of Brazil in his 1925 volume titled *Pau brasil* (Brazilwood).

To poet and essayist Afonso Celso, author of *Porque me ufano do meu país* (Why I Sing the Praises of My Country), published in 1901, Brazilian citizenship at the turn of the century required nationalistic pride expressed in the rhetoric of sixteenth-century *ufanistas*. Two generations later, following World War I, two unsuccessful military revolts by young officers in Rio and São Paulo, and Captain Luís Carlos Prestes's famous march with his column across Brazil to foment rebellion in the backlands against the oligarchy, Paulo Prado wrote about Brazil in a very different and highly contested way. In *Retrato do Brasil,* he called attention to a systemic "sadness" resulting from the country's unbridled greed and sensuality.[10] After a bloodless 1930 revolution that placed Getúlio Vargas in the presidency, the sensuality of which Prado wrote so despairingly became, in the writings of Gilberto Freyre, identified more explicitly with black Brazil. In his widely translated *Casa grande e senzala* (1933), Freyre wrote about miscegenation as the defining characteristic of the Brazilian people and emphasized the importance of the feudal agrarian system or "Big House" as the incubator for the "harmonious" mixing of the races. Freyre's evolving concept known as "Lusotropicalism" was deemed an innovative interpretation of race relations and hybridity, and it resulted in an image of Brazil as a racial democracy—an image that still exists. (In more recent years, Freyre's interpretation has been criticized as reactionary.) Freyre was also instrumental in reinvigorating a regionalist view that privileged the people and culture of the rural Northeast, along the lines of José Lins do Rego's "sugarcane" cycle of novels, in contrast to the cosmopolitan perspective of the Modern Art Week.

Architecture was part of Modern Art Week, but it was not until the appointment of architect Lúcio Costa to direct Rio's Escola Nacional de Belas Artes (National School of Fine Arts) in 1930 that a modernist initiative began to affect public spaces.[11] Throughout his presidency, which encompassed the Estado Novo (New State) dictatorship from 1937 to 1945, Getúlio Vargas was eager to bring modernism to the fore in the arts and architecture as a way of demonstrating the country's progress. (His strategy was similar to the one adopted by Mussolini in Italy.) As Daryle Williams observes in his study *Culture Wars in Brazil* (2001), Costa took advantage of the moment to invite the German painter Leo Putz, Brazilian sculptor Celson Antônio, Belgian architect Alexander Buddeus, and the Russian-born architect Gregori Warchavchik to join the faculty (56).[12]

Renowned for building the first modernist house and cubelike homes in São Paulo between 1927 and 1930, Warchavchik was an especially important addition to the school. He had been working in Brazil since 1923, and in 1925 he published a groundbreaking manifesto on modern architecture in the *Correio da manhã* newspaper. A short time later, he was appointed South America's representative to the prestigious Congrès Internationaux d'Architecture Moderne (Guillén 2004, 14–15). At the school, students were introduced to the works of Mies van der Rohe, Walter Gropius, and, most importantly, Le Corbusier. The last of these figures traveled to Brazil and lectured in São Paulo at the invitation of young architects who had won the commission to design a Ministry of Education and Public Health building, the first of several large projects planned by the Vargas government.[13] Abelardo de Souza recalls the difficulties that the younger architects faced in the 1930s:

> At that time to be an architect or "architect-engineer," which was the title on our diplomas, was to be regarded with skepticism by the larger public. Those who knew how to plan and construct . . . were the engineers and master workers. We architects, principally the "futurists," as we were called, encountered innumerable difficulties in convincing the people, through our projects, of the possibility that a new architecture was being born in Brazil. We wanted to show a new way of living, a new technique of construction. We wanted to show the "machine of living." (In Xavier 2003, 68)

The Ministry of Education and Public Health was a major architectural achievement that took seven years to build, but it retained the lines characteristic of European architecture. "Modern Brazilian architecture," Souza wrote, began with "the use of the curved line, and the light and sensual molding that only reinforced concrete could give, in the Conjunto de Pampulha [Pampulha Complex] by Oscar Niemeyer" (in Xavier 2003, 68).[14] Beginning in the early 1940s, and especially in the late 1950s and early 1960s, this curved line became as emblematic of modern Brazil as parrots and brazilwood were of its colonial past. In an interview at age ninety-two, Niemeyer stated that he preferred the curved shape because it was synonymous with the human form; but he also recalled that Le Corbusier once said to him: "When you design you have the mountains of Rio in your eyes" (Andreas and Flagge 2003, 21).

5.6 Saint Francis Church in Oscar Niemeyer's Conjunto de Pampulha. Permission, Latin American and Iberian Institute, University of New Mexico.

The years during World War II were pivotal in the development of architecture in Brazil. Among Nelson Rockefeller's "Good Neighbor" exchanges between Brazil and the United States was an architectural initiative in 1942 that involved Philip L. Goodwin, chairman of the Committee on Foreign Relations and the Architecture Committee of New York's Museum of Modern Art (MoMA), and architect G. E. Kidder Smith, both of whom traveled to Brazil to arrange a photographic exhibit for the Museum of Modern Art in New York. Three years earlier, in 1939, Lúcio Costa and Niemeyer designed the Brazilian Pavilion for the World's Fair held in New York. Architectural historian David Underwood emphasized the nationalistic character of that project:

> It is both ironic and appropriate that the first independent expression of Brazilian modernism emerged from a desire not to be overshadowed by the contribution of the French, who had dominated Brazilian art throughout the nineteenth century. . . . To minimize the inevitable comparison between the two, Costa and Niemeyer situated their pavilion as far as possible from the French building, and in doing so, made creative use of the curved extremity of the corner of the site; they also refused to compete with France's greater resources, choosing instead to emphasize lightness, airy grace, and formal simplicity to contrast with the bulkier French work. (1994, 48)

Although the pavilion with its sweeping entrance ramp was a success in the eyes of the U.S. visitors, what Goodwin and Kidder Smith encountered in their travels through Brazil was, in the words of architect Henrique Mindlin, equivalent to a "second discovery" of the country (Mindlin 1961, 27).[15] The result of their visit was a major photo exhibit at the MoMA that later went on the road and traveled to forty-eight cities in the United States. The exhibit was memorialized in a photographic book, *Brazil Builds: Architecture New and Old 1652–1942* (1943), in which the sweeping, futuristic curves of Niemeyer's Pampulha project and other modernist buildings are juxtaposed with some of Brazil's oldest and finest colonial architecture.[16] Published at the height of the Good Neighbor relations, the photographs show Brazil to be a country of amazing contrasts—not unlike the United States—but the illustrations also suggest that the older architecture, surrounded on all sides by modern structures, is gradually being squeezed out.

Twenty years after the Modern Art Week celebration, Mário de Andrade wrote an enthusiastic essay about *Brazil Builds* and the international recognition brought to Brazil by the book. Acclaim from the United States meant to Andrade, who was a mulatto, the affirmation of Brazil's limitless potential as a mixed-race society:

> I believe that [*Brazil Builds*] is one of the most fruitful gestures that the United States has ever shown in relation to Brazilians. Because it will regenerate, it has already regenerated, confidence in ourselves as it has diminished the disastrous

inferiority complex that we have as mestizos and that hurts us so much. . . . Only foreigners can give us this consciousness of our own human normality. Because we, as a result of this inferiority complex, react either by becoming a "why I praise myself" *ufanista* idiot or by adopting a conformist and putrified Jeca Tatuism. [17] No one can forget that it was an article by Henry Prundière that acknowledged Villa-Lobos's talent and opened the doors of one of the major journals of the country to modern music. No one can forget that it was a prize in the United States that recognized the genius of [artist] Portinari, in spite of the fact that a few Brazilians had already affirmed his genius.

We have to conform to our blood-based as well as intellectual-based miscegenation. We will never be Aryans, and perhaps we should thank God for that! . . . . The United States' gesture of discovering us in *Brazil Builds* should renew us . . . It isn't racial capability that we lack; this is ridiculous. What is it, then, that we lack? (In Xavier 2003, 180–181)[18]

Futurism on the Frontier

[I]f the beginning of the triumph over cultural dependence in architecture occurs in the 1940s, the actual triumph over cultural dependence takes place in 1960, in other words, with Brasília.

EDGAR GRAEFF, "The Triumph over Cultural Dependence," 1978

As if in response to Mário de Andrade's question above, Juscelino Kubitschek, who took office as president of the Republic in 1956, argued that Brazil lacked a capital city worthy of the nation's growing prosperity and modernity. The idea for the construction of a national capital in the interior can be traced back to the eighteenth century, but José Bonifácio de Andrada e Silva was the first to propose officially the building of the new city, to be called "Brasília" or "Petrópole," to the 1823 Constituent Assembly.[19] Francisco Adolfo Varnhagen, author of *A questão da capital: Marítima ou interior?* (The Question of the Capital: Coastal or Interior?) in 1877, had traveled to the Brazilian highlands and written favorably of the *planalto*, or plateau, as the site for such a city. This idea had significant economic and political implications: a city in the interior would attract people away from the more densely populated urban centers on the coast and serve notice that the future of the country lay to the west and the frontier. The first Republican Constitution of 1891 officially proposed the project and declared as state property more than five thousand square miles (later increased to nearly twenty thousand square miles) of highland territory in Goiás as the site of the new capital. In 1892, the Cruls Mission, a scientific expedition led by Belgian astronomer and geographer Luiz Cruls, studied the flora and fauna of the highlands and identified a specific location for the future capital in the hinterland.[20]

More studies and debates took place in the Brazilian Congress during the next fifty years, with each president urging the transference of the government seat from Rio to the heartland. But Kubitschek made the capital a central issue in his presidential campaign. As historian Norma Evenson observed, "Kubitschek seems to have sensed that the Brazilian people were ready for an adventure, and that popular imagination would respond to such a grand gesture more readily than to pedestrian and 'practical' enterprises" (in Underwood 1994, 99). Following his narrowly won election in 1955, the Congress authorized the establishment of the federally owned corporation NOVACAP (Urbanization Company of the New Capital), which set a March 11, 1957, deadline for submissions for a pilot-plan competition. Six days after the deadline, Lúcio Costa's entry was selected from more than forty others by a blue-ribbon committee; Kubitschek's "Fifty years of progress in five" initiative set a seemingly impossible deadline of April 1960 for Brasília's inauguration. The speed with which events transpired was reflected in Costa's pilot plan for the design of the city, which resembled for some an airplane and for others a bird. In either case, his design was minimalist and futuristic, representing both a streamlined velocity and a heavenly image of winged flight.

Architectural historian Lauro Cavalcanti has written that the plan's substitution of typical pedestrian-style streets for modern highways was central to Kubitschek's entrepreneurial drive to boost the automotive industry in Brazil (2002, 96). The conventional wisdom that questioned modernism's ability to project a sense of monumentality was overturned by Niemeyer, whose architectural wonder, the Palácio Alvorada (Dawn Palace), has an ethereal, free–floating quality created by the large, graceful, and tapering curves of its surrounding colonnade. That colonnade design became a signature motif in later Brazilian architecture and among the most recognizable symbols of the nation. The old and the new merge most vividly in Niemeyer's Catedral Metropolitana (Metropolitan Cathedral), with its sixteen modernist buttresses that resemble the wings design in the pilot plan. The broad, freestanding ramp, first made famous at the 1939 Brazilian Pavilion,

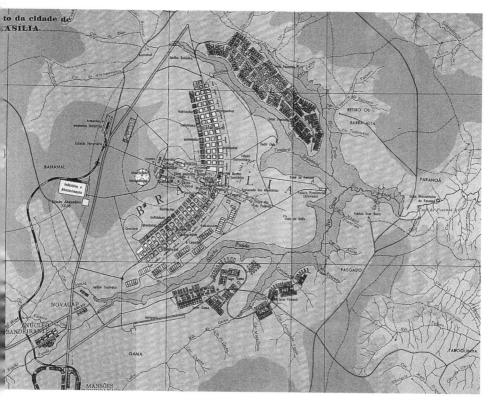

5.7 Blueprint for Brasília

forms the gateway to the National Congress complex, whose straight-line twin towers are complemented by the dome and open-bowl cupolas of the Senate and Chamber of Deputies that border it on either side. Like the colonnade, this complex of ingenuity, simplicity, and grace became a symbol of twentieth-century Brazil.[21]

The building of Brasília was a modern-day epic of conquest replete with charts, maps, blueprints, explorations, frontier settlements, and the arrival of peoples from different regions, countries, and social classes. The utopian city in the wilderness also reflected the Edenic motif that had been associated with the newly discovered Brazil. The once-leftist U.S. writer John Dos Passos traveled to Brazil in 1958 with the intent of examining "more carefully and more dispassionately than [the Communists] do the social structures we [the political right] have to deal with" (in Ludington 1980, 445).[22]

5.8 Senate and Chambers in Brasília. Permission, Latin American and Iberian Institute, University of New Mexico.

He toured Brasília with Israel Pinheiro, the city's enthusiastic mayor, and was overwhelmed by what he saw: "As Dr. Israel piloted us through the future city we had trouble distinguishing what was really there from what was going to be there. It was like visiting Pompeii or Monte Alban, but in reverse. Instead of imagining the life that was there two thousand years ago we found ourselves imagining the life that would be there ten years hence" (in Dos Passos 1963, 76).

In 1962, Dos Passos returned to Brasília, and although he was critical of Niemeyer's Congress building, which he regarded as the "faithful Communist's scorn for representative democracy," he was dazzled by the long, straight highways and the wide, open spaces between the low-rise buildings: "It's a city for the automotive age, for the age of jets and helicopters. Its vast spaces match the vast smooth arid ridges of the landscapes of the planalto" (130–131). Others who praised Brasília included Jean-Paul Sartre, who had traveled to Brazil with Simone de Beauvoir in 1960. Apparently de Beauvoir was less impressed with what she described as the capital's "elegant monotony."

For Lúcio Costa, Oscar Niemeyer, and landscape designer Roberto Burle-Marx, an essential requisite for the "city of the future" was architectural unity. Niemeyer conceived his *superquadras* (literally "superblocks," neighborhood units of 2,500 to 3,000 residents) as functional living spaces that would accommodate manual laborers, civil servants, and government officials alike. The *superquadras* were also self-contained: each had a cinema, shops, a church, a park, and a public school with a kindergarten. The buildings ranged from single-story residences for laborers to six-story buildings with housing for high-ranking public officials. In time, however, Niemeyer's attempt to design a standardized housing that would overcome social stratification was undermined by the logic of capitalism, which caused satellite cities to form and grow outside the city center.[23] Architectural historian Laurence Vale has observed that ultimately, "the distinction between privileged center and impoverished periphery that characterized other Brazilian cities was reinforced" (in Underwood 1994, 141). Unable to afford *superquadra* housing, which was sold on the open market in 1965, workers and lower-paid civil employees moved to the burgeoning satellite cities of Taguatinga, Planaltina, and Brazlândia, as well as to the newer satellites, Sobradinho and Gama, while the upper middle class purchased homes in the superblocks.[24] The wealthiest migrated to nearby Paranoá Lake, a huge artificial waterway twenty-four miles long and three miles wide in places, which was intended as a recreational and "green" space. There they built lakeside homes and mansions, some of which are replicas of famous neoclassical buildings, including the U.S. White House.

These and other changes in the pilot plan began to take hold in 1964, when a right-wing military overthrew the democratically elected government of President João Goulart and instituted a dictatorship that would last more than twenty years.[25] Niemeyer was frequently harassed by the government and was threatened twice with dismissal because of his left-wing politics. The regime's dismissal of "subversive" faculty from the Universidade de Brasília in 1965 finally resulted in Niemeyer's decision to move to Paris and later Algiers. There he witnessed from a distance the neglect of the pilot plan: "People transformed the whole thing into a mess. On Brasília's secondary streets the architecture is horrible. Times when the town had an architectural unity are long gone" (in Krohn 2003, 41).[26]

Although there was and continues to be debate over the habitability and function of Niemeyer's buildings, Brasília has remained one of the great visual achievements in modernist architecture. Early visitors like André Malraux, who coined the phrase "city of hope," were caught up in the energy and enthusiasm of the project, which created what seemed an overnight transformation of a wilderness into a sleek, futuristic metropolis. During this period a wealth of material including travelogues, memoirs, and letters was produced by foreign visitors who came to visit Brasília. One of the earliest responses to the capital, however, took the form of a movie released in 1964: Frenchman Phillipe de Broca's zany, award-winning *L'Homme de Rio* (*That Man from Rio*), a chase film starring Jean-Paul Belmondo. This film deserves more attention than it has received for its incisive commentaries about colonization, capitalism, modernity, and the arts.

Although the plot of the film has often been dismissed by critics as simply the means for Belmondo (described by *New York Times* critic Bosley Crowther as a "fast, fearless, modern-day Harold Lloyd") to race from Paris to Rio, Brasília, and finally the Amazon, it takes on special significance if we consider the film's setting in historical context. Belmondo's character, Adrien, a French major on a week's leave in Paris to see his girlfriend, Agnès (Françoise Dorléac), is loosely based on Ian Fleming's military man cum secret agent, James Bond, whose film popularity was already established when de Broca made his film.[27] The action is propelled by the theft of an ancient Maltec statue, indigenous to Brazil, from a Paris museum whose director is Professor Catalan (Jean Servais). It seems that Catalan, along with Agnès's deceased father and a man named Mário de Castro (Adolfo Celi), were members of an Amazon expedition that discovered three rare statues. Following the robbery, Agnès is kidnapped by the thieves (Milton Ribeiro and Sabu of Brazil) because she knows the whereabouts of the second statue that her father buried in Brazil just before his mysterious murder. (The third statue is in the hands of Castro, who now resides in Brasília.)

Adrien witnesses Agnès's kidnapping from a distance and chases her and her captors through Paris streets, around monuments and parks, into the airport, and finally across the ocean to Rio. In Rio, he rescues her, but only after her father's statue has been located and seized by the thieves. A second chase ensues that takes him, Agnès, and Catalan (who says he was kidnapped as well), to Brasília, where the three plan to warn Castro of the thieves' intentions. In Brasília, Catalan, who has secretly engineered the various thefts and kidnappings, murders Castro, steals his statue, kidnaps Agnès, and heads for the Amazon, where the statues were initially found.

Deep in the jungle, Catalan enters a cave, positions the statues as per written instructions hidden within them, and uncovers a buried treasure chest filled with diamonds. At this point, however, a series of explosions causes the cave to collapse on Catalan and the treasure. Adrien rescues Agnès from her captors once again, and he still has two days left on his leave, which they spend on holiday.

In addition to spoofing 1960s adventure-caper films, de Broca's movie takes a revisionist approach to the early history of Brazil. When Catalan explains to a Paris detective that the missing statue, like other indigenous treasures, was originally stolen by "barbarians" who killed off its rightful owners, the policeman asks who these barbarians were. Catalan's Montaignesque reply is explicitly ironic: "We are, the Europeans." This puzzles the policeman, who has difficulty comprehending how a conquered race has returned to life and made their way to the Trocadero to reclaim their statue. (The thieves are in fact Amazonians, but, as we later learn, they are allied with and in the pay of the French "barbarian," Catalan.)

As the plane bearing the kidnapped Agnès descends into Rio, de Broca provides the audience with the typical tourist shots of Copacabana Beach, Sugar Loaf, and Corcovado, whose large statue of Christ overlooks Guanabara Bay. But when Adrien searches for his girlfriend in Rio, he encounters places quite unlike the aerial postcard images. A disenchanted foreign traveler, he glumly proclaims, "Rio de Janeiro. You can keep it."[28] Shortly thereafter, he is befriended by a black shoeshine boy named Sir Winston (Ubiracy de Oliveira). Adrien uses Winston's shoe brush to polish a well-to-do Brazilian's shoes, which turn from gleaming white to shiny black. (The customer pays him without even noticing the change.) This amusing scene indirectly comments on race relations in Brazil, offering a symbolic reversal of the "whitening" process that Mário de Andrade satirized in *Macunaíma*. Later, after Agnès is rescued, de Broca alludes to the film *Black Orpheus* (1958) by his countryman Marcel Camus, in showing Agnès, like Eurídice of the earlier film, dancing a samba alongside residents of a *favela*.

The settings change dramatically when Adrien and Agnès encounter Professor Catalan and arrive in Brasília. The contrast between Rio, with its densely populated neighborhoods, broad sidewalks, beaches, and pedestrians, and Brasília, with its monumental architecture, superhighways, and topography of reddened earth, could not be more distinct. If we think about *That Man from Rio* in terms of the travelogue-like Bond films, which generally featured two or three major world cities, Brasília is the equivalent of the sometimes subterranean, other times aquatic, but always futuristic space where Bond confronts the villain. It is in Brasília that Catalan reveals his villainy when he dupes and strangles Castro and steals his statue. But Brasília is more than just a backdrop for melodrama; a closer look at this part of the film reveals a fairly nuanced commentary on the modernist capital and on "order and progress" in general.

The film introduces Brasília by focusing on the vast plains, the superhighways, and the much-photographed towers and cupolas of the National Congress complex. This magnificent and otherworldly setting is posed against an interior shot in which an immaculately groomed Castro tears up a blueprint as he descends a staircase in a building under construction. He angrily demands that more windows and better lighting be provided; waving his hands in the air, he calls for an interior design that resembles a "butterfly wing." The scene is amusing in itself, but it also subtly lampoons the architect Niemeyer, who wanted to draw tropical light into Brasília's buildings by using glass walls and windows, as well as designer Lúcio Costa, whose pilot plan envisioned a "winged" city.

An enthusiastic promoter of Brasília, Castro parodies the entrepreneurial spirit of both Kubitschek and Brasília's Mayor Pinheiro, who energetically promoted the city and attracted foreign attention and investment. In one sequence, Castro throws a huge outdoor party at his palatial residence, which is replete with cascading fountains and a bowling ally whose pins have been carved and painted in his image. The social equality for which Niemeyer strived in the *superquadras* is significantly absent from Castro's "hideaway," which he equates with Versailles. At the beginning of the party, we see men and women in formal cocktail attire step out of arriving helicopters wearing ridiculous football-like helmets over their coiffeurs. In the background, a lone black waiter, dressed in an eighteenth-century brocade jacket and white periwig, loudly sharpens a meat knife over the shoulder of an annoyed-looking Castro, who is trying to sweet-talk Agnès.

An elaborate chase scene like something out of Hitchcock begins when Catalan's two henchmen run after Adrien across the flat, red terrain of the broad *planalto*. The sequence also enables de Broca to show that behind the monuments and grandeur of the new capital are ramshackle scaffolds and half-constructed buildings filled with loose bricks, wobbly boards, and sacks of cement. Adrien throws building materials at his pursuers as he races up and down rickety stairways and across planks on rooftops. Like a silent-movie comic, he takes a dizzying high-wire ride in a small bucket attached to cables between two buildings. There is no sign of a pedestrian or worker during this long sequence, which can serve as a poignant reminder that Brasília was planned for automobiles and that economic problems often brought construction to a halt.

After Adrien runs past the beautiful Alvorada Palace, he arrives at Paranoá Lake, where Catalan is taking off in a small plane with Agnès. A moment before the acrobatic Adrien hops into a nearby plane to pursue them, de Broca provides a glimpse of rows of workers' wooden shacks on the shore of the lake. This fleeting image reveals the stark contrast between rich and poor in the capital; anyone who has visited Brasília in the past three decades knows that the only laborers who reside in the Lake Zone are in the

5.9 On the run in Brasília, in Phillipe de Broca's *That Man from Rio* (1964)

employ of the owners, who have the highest per capita income in all of Latin America.[29]

The ending of the movie is as ironic as its beginning: the explosions that cause Catalan's death in the cave are caused not by some ancient indigenous spell or curse over the treasure, but by dynamite that is being used nearby to fell trees for the construction of the Trans-Amazon Highway. In one of the last scenes, a happy Adrien and Agnès are standing in the back of a truck that is returning them to civilization. As they smile into the future, the truck whisks by an impoverished family of indigenous men, women, and children dressed in feathers and beads, who watch silently as they pass by. Beneath *That Man from Rio*'s slapstick exterior is a serious commentary about modern-day poverty and greed that savage capitalism breeds even in the "capital of hope."

Brasília appeared in several other movies made in Brazil in the 1960s and 1970s. Nelson Pereira dos Santos (who was teaching at the University of Brasília and resigned along with around two hundred other faculty members because of the military's dismissal of several colleagues) directed the 1966 documentary *Fala Brasília* (Speak Brasília), which shows the range of dialects spoken in the capital as a result of the migration of workers from around the country. In 1979, Carlos Diegues chose to end his popular comedy *Bye Bye Brasil* in the capital. The plot of the film revolves around a troupe of traveling circus performers who are losing the battle against modernization, in particular the proliferation of televisions in the Northeast interior, which is causing their kind of entertainment to become obsolete. When the troupe loses their caravan as a result of a wager, the young peasant couple Ciço (Fábio Júnior) and Dasdô (Zaira Zambelli), who joined the circus to escape the drought and accompany the acts with their Northeastern *forró* music, take a bus to Brasília, where they hope to begin a better life.

As the bus passes the giant government buildings and *superquadras*, which are beautifully landscaped, a social worker/tour guide informs them that there are more than one million people living in the city and that the future of the country is in the *planalto*. She also informs them that their particular future is not in the city center proper, at which point the film immediately cuts to a shot of a shantytown on a muddy road somewhere on the periphery. A subsequent shot shows the couple being dropped off in front of one of the wood and mortared homes. But Diegues's commentary on social stratification in Brasília quickly segues into a more positive image of the capital. Ciço and Dasdô, happy to have a place to live, turn to one another and contentedly pass through the rickety wooden fence that leads to their new home. The film fast-forwards into the future, showing the couple as successful *forró* musicians who perform live and on television for the Northeast immigrant community. In *Bye Bye Brasil,* even the periphery of Brasília is imagined as the capital of hope.

A more complex image of Brasília appears in Nelson Pereira dos Santos's 1994 *A terceira margem do rio* (The Third Bank of the River). The film concerns Liojorge (Ilya São Paulo), Alva (Sonjia Saurin), their young daughter (Bárbara Brandt), and her grandmother (Maria Ribeiro), who flee the *sertão* for the capital because of a band of sinister brothers, one of whom has designs on Alva.[30] Pereira dos Santos follows up an introductory aerial shot of Brasília with a scene reminiscent of Diegues's movie in which the backlander family silently gazes at the magnificent monuments as they travel by bus to their destination on the periphery. (In this case, the home belongs to Liojorge's sister, who left the *sertão* for Brasília some time before.) Pereira dos Santos gives even greater attention than Diegues to Brasília's futuristic architecture, his camera lingering on famous sites such as the Cathedral, the Palace, and the National Congress complex. Like de Broca, he emphasizes the futuristic otherworldliness of the capital, but he also realistically dramatizes the daily violence that pervades the frontier town, where men roam streets with guns and assassinations are carried out by hit men.

The Music of the "New Way"

The Brazilian modernist vogue was also characterized by new approaches to the popular samba that fused sounds as different as the orchestral modernism of Villa-Lobos with American jazz. By the end of the 1950s, what became known as *bossa nova* (new way) emerged in the bars and cafés in the fashionable Southern Zone in Rio, in particular the beachside communities of Copacabana and Ipanema. This music came to international attention as a result of *Black Orpheus* by Camus, which was based on the 1956 black musical-tragedy *Orfeu da Conceição* by poet-musician Vinícius de Moraes. Moraes's music for the play was the product of his collaboration as lyricist with the relatively unknown composer Antônio Carlos Jobim. Following the success of the play, Moraes and Jobim, along with guitarist Luiz Bonfá, composed new lyrics and a score for the movie, which won the grand prize at Cannes in 1958.

Bossa nova was born out of the hope and optimism associated with Kubitschek's forward-looking administration. As music historians Chris McGowan and Ricardo Pessanha have noted: "The term 'bossa nova' turned into an adjective for everything modern, surprising. There were bossa nova girls, a bossa nova president, and even bossa nova cars" (1998, 65). According to Ruy Castro, a 1958 reference to "uma turma bossa nova" (a new way group) was simply meant to introduce a "different kind of music" about to be played at a show in Rio. The musicians liked the expression and adopted it (2001, 58). Bossa nova also reflected the social stratification that Niemeyer tried but failed to neutralize with his *superquadras.* The unusual new sound was created by the middle class for the middle class.

Bahian guitarist João Gilberto's romantic vocals were hushed in comparison to the bold voices singing *samba-canção* compositions, and his trademark plucking of guitar strings (as opposed to the traditional strumming) generated unconventional yet melodic sounds and rhythms. According to McGowan and Pessanha, Gilberto's lyrics for the song "Desafinado" (Off-Key) were his "ironic reply to critics who mockingly said that bossa nova was 'music for off-key singers'" (55). Written by Antônio Carlos Jobim and Newton Mendonça, the lyrics of the song read almost like a manifesto that argues against the anti-musical charge levied against bossa nova and proclaims instead that the new sound is completely "natural."

Similar to the vanguard experimental poetry of the 1950s in Brazil, bossa nova lyrics often strung like-sounding words together—*é sol, é sal, é sul* (it's sun, it's salt, it's south); melodies were streamlined, and the language was kept simple. Poet and critic Augusto de Campos wrote: "It is like a simple way of talking that takes in aspects of everyday urban life, and the lyrics are filled with humor, irony, *blague,* sensuality, joy, naughtiness, and sometimes sadness (in Gomes 2002, 130). Although local critics were skeptical of the influence of American jazz on bossa nova, there was a renewed anthropophagic attitude expressed by the bossa nova musicians who proclaimed, like Oswald de Andrade in the 1920s, that foreign sources would be assimilated in a process from which new, local products would emerge for export. This was certainly the case with bossa nova, which was picked up by jazz guitarist Charlie Byrd while on a State Department goodwill tour of Brazil in 1961 and introduced by him to saxophonist Stan Getz. Their 1962 musical collaboration based on bossa nova hits by Gilberto, Bonfá, Jobim, and others brought the new Brazilian sound to the attention of millions in North America.

That same year, Getz and arranger-conductor Gary MacFarland released *Stan Getz: Big Band Bossa Nova*, which included Brazilian favorites such as Gilberto's "Bim Bom" and Jobim and Moraes's "Chega de Saudade" (Enough of Longing); and the following year, João Gilberto released his first LP in the United States, *The Boss of Bossa Nova*. In a 2002 essay on bossa nova, critic Renato Cordeio Gomes emphasizes the relationship between the old and new vanguards. He even includes illustrations that show how Gilberto's 1963 album cover design replicates Brazilian artist Tarsila Amaral's 1925 cover design for Oswald de Andrade's modernist publication *Pau brasil*. The only difference between the two illustrations is that the words "Pau Brasil," which Tarsila used in place of the national motto, "Order and Progress," in the central sphere have been substituted by a profile shot of Gilberto.

But it was the bilingual version of "The Girl from Ipanema" on the now-classic 1964 *Getz/Gilberto* album that catapulted bossa nova onto the charts in the United States—as well as the record's composer-pianist, Jobim, and the female vocalist, Astrud Gilberto, who was associated forever after with that song.[31] The image of Brazil became synonymous with the syncopated rhythms of a new, cool jazz, and dozens of musicians and vocalists in the United States began recording versions of their bossa nova favorites. A concert of bossa nova music at Carnegie Hall in 1962 brought Brazilian musicians, singers, and songwriters to the United States. Shortly thereafter, dance impresario Arthur Murray encouraged audiences to "do the Bossa Nova," while Eydie Gorme's "Blame It on the Bossa Nova" surged to number 7 on the top-40 hits charts in 1963.

One of the most surprising and creative U.S.-Brazil collaborations occurred in 1967, in the midst of the "British Invasion," when Frank Sinatra teamed with Antônio Carlos Jobim in New York City to record the album *Francis Albert Sinatra and Antônio Carlos Jobim*. Sinatra's vocals are subdued, tender, and yearning, similar to his sweetly melancholic voice on his 1958 album *Only the Lonely*. Jobim and Sinatra sing soft and sexy bilingual duos on two Brazilian compositions, and they pair together again on Cole Porter's "I Concentrate on You" and Wright and Forrest's "Baubles, Bangles, and Beads," which, along with Irving Berlin's "Change Partners," are completely transformed by the bossa nova beat. Another Brazilian artist making his way in the United States was Sérgio Mendes, who opened the famous concert held at Carnegie Hall.[32] After touring American university campuses and cutting an album in 1965, he and the members of his Sérgio Mendes & Brasil 65 climbed to the top of the pop charts with their *Brasil 66* album (McGowan and Pessanha 1998, 72).

Like literature, art, and architecture, bossa nova in Brazil experienced the impact of the military takeover in 1964, and artists began moving in different directions. Several, like songwriter Carlos Lyra, wrote protest lyrics to replace the traditional ones about girls, beaches, and love. Others were pulled toward the more diversified sounds of Brazilian popular music (MPB) of a newer generation of composers and musicians, which included Gilberto Gil and Caetano Veloso. A few, like Antônio Carlos Jobim, experimented with the bossa nova sound, fusing it with older forms and regional styles associated with folk. Still others, such as João Gilberto and Luiz Bonfá, left Brazil to live in the United States and Europe for long periods of time. The U.S. East and West Coasts benefited in particular from this musical exodus. Regardless of the location, however, jazz throughout the United States changed after the 1960s and would forever be indebted to the beat and scat of the "new way."

CHAPTER 6

Good Neighbor Brazil

I've never seen a Jaguar,
Nor yet an Armadill
O dilloing in his armour,
And I s'pose I never will,

Unless I go to Rio
These wonders to behold—
Roll down—roll down to Rio—
Roll really down to Rio!
Oh, I'd love to roll to Rio
Some day before I'm old!

RUDYARD KIPLING, "The Beginning
of the Armadillos," *Just So Stories,* 1902

In July 1934, Franklin D. Roosevelt became the first sitting president of the United States to visit South America. His trip to Cartagena, Colombia, was prompted by his determination to improve relations between the United States and Latin America through a policy of good neighborliness that would emphasize political and economic rapprochement and encourage cultural exchange. Following his reelection two years later, Roosevelt made a second trip to South America to attend a Pan-American conference in Buenos Aires that he himself had proposed. After the conference, he stopped briefly in Rio to visit Brazilian President Getúlio Vargas. The day that Roosevelt arrived was declared a Brazilian national holiday. He addressed a special joint session of the Brazilian Congress and Supreme Court, where he was acclaimed as "the *Man*—the fearless and generous man who is accomplishing and living the most thrilling political experience of modern times" (in Dozer 1959, 31).

The heady atmosphere of Pan-American cooperation continued through the 1930s, but late in the decade Latin America faced mounting economic pressures as a result of the escalating war and the loss of trade with Europe. In a June 15, 1940, communication to his Secretaries of State, Commerce,

Treasury, and Agriculture, Roosevelt advised that "emergency measures should be taken to absorb surplus agricultural and mineral products affecting the prosperity of the countries of the hemisphere" (in Dozer 1959, 72)—a move that was necessary to block trade negotiations between the Axis powers and South American nations. Two months later, Roosevelt reinforced his proposal by creating the Office for Coordination of Commercial and Cultural Relations Between the American Republics, which later became the Office of the Coordinator of Inter-American Affairs (CIAA); and he named Nelson A. Rockefeller to head the Washington-based organization.[1] At the time of his appointment, Rockefeller had investments in a Standard Oil subsidiary in Venezuela that led to his growing and sustained interest in Latin America. In the late 1930s, he was convinced that the United States would benefit from greater economic relations with Latin America, and he wrote a memorandum to Roosevelt advising greater cooperation among the Americas. The creation of the CIAA was Roosevelt's response to Rockefeller's proposal. The CIAA appointment was Rockefeller's first government job. In 1944, Roosevelt named him assistant secretary for Latin America.

In aid of the State Department, the CIAA was responsible for promoting hemispheric defense in matters pertaining to the economy and culture, and Rockefeller was provided with a $150 million budget. Historian David Jay Epstein gives a detailed view of some of Rockefeller's workings in the CIAA:

> To gain complete control over the media of Latin America, Rockefeller engineered a ruling from the United States Treasury which exempted from taxation the cost of advertisements placed by American corporations that were "cooperating" with Rockefeller in Latin America. This tax-exempt advertising eventually constituted more than 40 percent of all radio and television revenues in Latin America. By selectively directing this advertising toward newspapers and radio stations that accepted "guidance" from his office, he was effectively able to control the images that newspapers and radio stations of Latin America projected about America during World War II. By 1945, more than 75 percent of the news of the world that reached Latin America originated from Washington, where it was tightly controlled and shaped by Rockefeller's office. (1990, 36–37)

Dozer reports that Rockefeller launched an aggressive cultural campaign to bring the Americas closer together through "archaeological expeditions, art exhibitions, college glee clubs, a ballet caravan, and several outstanding movie stars." The CIAA also

> financed the publication of guide books to the Latin American countries and supplied [Latin America] with newsreels; it facilitated the exchange of "creative workers," medicine interns, and journalists; it brought the Chilean ski team to the United States; and it gathered fashion-promotion material for distribution to newspaper syndicates and magazines in an effort to stimulate the interest of Latin Americans in New York as a style center and the interest of New York fashion designers in Latin American motifs. (Dozer 1959, 81)

After the attack on Pearl Harbor on December 7, 1941, the CIAA launched other initiatives and invested even more heavily in programs to fortify the good neighbor relationship. In the United States, public schools and universities increased attention to studying Latin America, and scholarships for research and study abroad were made available. At this time, Alfred A. and (primarily) Blanche Knopf created the Borzoi book series featuring prominent Latin American writers. The Brazilianist Samuel Putnam translated several books for the series, including Gilberto Freyre's monumental *The Masters and the Slaves* (*Casa grande e senzala*) in 1946 and a year earlier, Jorge Amado's novel about nineteenth-century Bahian plantation society (*Terras do sem fim*), which Knopf titled *The Violent Land.*

Other books to appear in the series were Freyre's *Brazil: An Interpretation* (1945); L. C. Kaplan's translation, *Anguish* (1946), of Graciliano Ramos's *Angústia,* a complex psychological tale of obsessive love and revenge; and *The Green Continent: A Comprehensive View of Latin America by Its Leading Writers* (1944), edited by Germán Arcineigas. This last book contains selections from Graça Aranha's 1902 novel, *Canaã* (*Canaan*); *The History of the Reign of Dom Pedro* by Heitor Lyra; and an essay on Rio de Janeiro by the *gaúcho* writer Érico Veríssimo, who spent considerable time in the United States and published a history of Brazilian literature in English with the Macmillan Company in 1945.

Putnam translated Euclides da Cunha's epic *Os sertões* (as *Rebellion in the Backlands*) for the University of Chicago Press in 1944 (a selection of which appeared in *The Green Continent*), and four years later, Knopf published Putnam's *Marvelous Journey: A History of Four Centuries of Brazilian Writing.* In the foreword to his book, Putnam noted that despite cultural and historical similarities between the two nations, readers in the United States rarely demonstrated interest in Brazilian literature, and consequently, few works were translated: "a dozen novels of which eight have been done since 1943, two collections of short stories, and a couple of major sociological classics" (viii). He adds:

> This is not a great deal, certainly, and there would have been practically nothing at all to show if the exigencies of hemisphere defense in recent years had not caused us suddenly to become aware of our "good neighbors" and their culture as we had not before. Thanks to the war, many readers discovered to their surprise the existence in the Americas of a worth-while literature in Portuguese. Much of the credit must go to the Coordinator of Inter-American Affairs, Nelson Rockefeller . . . , but the American publisher also deserves to be commended for his co-operation during this period, not infrequently at a financial loss to himself. (viii)

The Good Neighbor policy and the CIAA helped to spawn other publications that had greater circulation. Published in 1944, *Our Latin American Neighbors* is a good example of the desire of high school educators to bridge the information gap in the United States with regard to the other Americas. In the preface to their textbook, Harriet McCune Brown and Helen Bailey Miller described some of the stereotypic notions that North and South Americans had of one other. They conclude:

> As you can see, there is a great deal of misunderstanding on both sides. . . . A citizen of Brazil is just as much an American as is a citizen of the United States. . . . It is very important for the United States and the Latin American countries to be on friendly terms. We need their trade and they need ours. We want to sell them manufactured goods and buy from them such products as coffee, tin, and rubber. We also need their co-operation in helping to maintain a world at peace. (1, 2)[2]

The map of Brazil that appears in *Our Latin American Neighbors* is remarkably similar to sixteenth-century maps of Brazil produced by navigators and others. The hardwoods that were so precious to Europeans in the colonial period continue to be represented here, although the iconography has moved farther inland as a result of centuries of timber removal in the coastal areas. The textbook map includes icons for numerous other products grown in the country, including coffee, cacao, and sugar. However, unlike early maps, this one has no graphic representation of any part of the population, whose identity is tucked away in the section "What Is a Brazilian?" in the last of three chapters on Brazil.

The authors' rhetoric in this textbook frequently reads like the *ufanista* prose style of the earliest writers who were fascinated by Brazil's size and resources. However, the sense of wonder and amazement in the textbook is counterbalanced by less buoyant observations about poverty and the need for better schools and transportation systems. One of Brown and Miller's most interesting commentaries is devoted to Vargas, whose Estado Novo dictatorship had suppressed all political parties, closed the Congress, and rigorously censored the media. Titled "The Iron Hand of Vargas Is Covered by a Velvet Glove," the section briefly describes reforms made by the New State while it acknowledges that freedom of speech and the press and the right to elections have been curtailed. But like the U.S. government, the authors ultimately endorse Vargas, remarking at one point that "he is no Hitler" and stating disingenuously that he "has never used the death penalty, but merely claps political prisoners into jail or sends them out of the country" (408). They conclude their commentary on Brazil by reminding readers that "under the leadership of President Vargas the Brazilians have once again allied themselves with the United States in the fight for freedom" (408).

Author Hubert Herring introduces his study, *Good Neighbors: Argentina, Brazil, Chile, and Seventeen Other Countries* (1941), with the following advisory: "It is high time the people of the United States discover the other Americans. Our world closes in upon us. American solidarity, once regarded as a pleasant elective, has become an imperious necessity. The United States needs Latin America for the goods she can sell, and as security against attack. The Latin Americans need the United States if their sovereignty is to be assured" (vi).

Herring devotes an entire chapter in the section on Brazil to "Germans," and it is quite likely that this chapter alone, with its references to Fifth Column activities, might have single-handedly boosted Washington's efforts on behalf of that nation. For example, Herring begins by describing the fascist activities of Germans in Rio de Janeiro, São Paulo, and Porto Alegre:

Wherever one turns, in coffee shop, bar, or hotel lobby, there will be two or three Germans at the next table, discussing the [war] news, making no effort to quiet their exultation. There is also a story (perhaps true) of a group of Brazilians on a Rio ferryboat, arguing the existence of the fifth column in Brazil. A German, listening to the talk, spoke up, 'We are *already* here.' They liquidated him—permanently. (152)

In a later chapter titled "1,600 Miles," he informs the reader about the short distance between the Brazilian coastal capital of Natal and the African city of Dakar and gives a possible scenario for the future: "Africa, unless Hitler's calculations go sadly awry, may become a German-Italian continent. Brazil would be within commuting distance of German bases" (158). He also cites the German military officer Hermann Rauschning's quote of Adolf Hitler on Brazil: 'We shall create a new Germany there . . . we shall find everything we need there. . . . The people will need us if they are going to make anything of their country'" (158).

Herring's 1941 argument is reiterated nearly word for word in a 1944 CIAA publication, *Brazil: Introduction to a Neighbor*:

Interest in Brazil is further heightened by its geographic situation. While most Americans have been vaguely aware that the coast of Brazil was nearer to Europe than to the United States, the present war has highlighted that point.

For months, while Dakar was held by Vichy, this strategic fact was a source of potential worry. Today the Brazilian bulge has become one of the most important spots in this hemisphere from an aggressive war standpoint.

The worry about Dakar was not entirely academic. Vichy collaborated with Hitler and it was he who told his one-time lieutenant Hermann Rauschning: "We shall create a new Germany in Brazil. We shall find everything we need here." (n.p.)

The pamphlet includes a full-page map with the title "Brazil . . . A Stepping Stone for Invasion . . . East or West," which further emphasizes the country's strategic position (while reinforcing a strained notion of its geographic vulnerability to Axis powers).[3] As in the history textbook, ample information is provided about Brazil's plentiful resources and the fact that Brazil is the chief buyer of U.S. goods in the hemisphere. A map of Brazil's commodities has even more product icons than the one in Brown and Miller. As for Vargas, the pamphlet sidesteps all references to the Estado Novo and describes "Vargas's 'New Deal'" administration as diligently at work on reforms.

In its continuing efforts to secure friendly relations with Brazil and the rest of Latin America, the CIAA increased the number of radio programs and movies that were exported south. A primary objective of Rockefeller's organization was the removal of demeaning characterizations of Latin Americans, who were frequently portrayed in movies as gangsters, villains, buffoons, or prostitutes.[4] To that end, in 1941 he established a Hollywood branch of the CIAA—the Motion Picture Society for the Americas—under the direction of John Hay (Jock) Whitney; among the agency's functions was supplying technical assistance.[5]

Hemispheric unity was not the only factor motivating Hollywood to produce movies about Latin America. In 1940, MGM's Arthur Freed frankly admitted that the recent craze for South American music and dances was the real reason for the swift rise in the number of these films: "Swing music which has held the center stage for five to six years is now passing out and the rhumba stuff is jumping into the number one position in the American taste" (in Woll 1974, 282). Critic Allen L. Woll adds that export markets were an even greater factor, and with the war raging in Europe in 1940, studio heads cast new eyes on the growing markets in Central and South America (1974, 282–283).

Hollywood's most visible response to that trend was the marketing of the "Brazilian Bombshell" Carmen Miranda, who became a major motion picture and recording star in the 1940s in the United States. At the same time, the CIAA invested a half-million dollars in Disney for research and production of animated movies and documentaries that would represent the Americas as partners (Dozer 1959, 132); Disney films at the time were distributed by an RKO studio partly controlled by Nelson Rockefeller. In 1942, as part of these efforts, Rockefeller invited Orson Welles, who was finishing *The Magnificent Ambersons* at RKO, to make a movie and to give talks in Latin America on behalf of the United States. A stockholder in RKO, Rockefeller gave RKO one million dollars to finance the film project. That invitation took Welles to Brazil, where he mapped out a very different kind of Latin American film, which he called *It's All True*. As two of Hollywood's chief goodwill ambassadors of the period—one who traveled to Brazil and the other who traveled to the United States—Welles and Miranda projected different images of Brazil to their largely North American audiences. But it was the culture industry that ultimately controlled the way Brazil was represented in the mass media, and both Welles and Miranda were affected by the images it wanted to convey.

Flying Down to Rio

C—coffee, cacao, cotton, cachaças, carioca, Copacabana, choro, casinos, Corcovado and Cabral, who first saw it.
"Brazilian Alphabet," 1942, ORSON WELLES archive, Lilly Library

On February 2, 1942, Orson Welles concluded his CBS radio show, which had just rebroadcast Norman Corwin's "Between Americans," by announcing that he and his Mercury Theater organization would be leaving the next day for South America:

> The reason, put more or less officially, is that I've been asked by the Office of the Coordinator for Inter-American Affairs to do a motion picture especially for Americans in all the Americas, a movie which, in its particular way, might strengthen the good relations now binding the continents of the Western Hemisphere. Put much less officially, the Mercury's going down there to get acquainted. We the people of these United Nations of America now stand together: We're going to have to know each other better than we do. My job—the Mercury's job—is to help with the introductions.[6]

There is considerable commentary and scholarship on *It's All True,* which Welles filmed during his eight-month residency in Latin America.[7] Had he been able to finish the movie, which contained interlocking segments about carnival in Rio and a much-publicized journey of 1,650 miles made by four Brazilian fishermen on a raft, it would have undoubtedly influenced the way North American audiences and moviegoers worldwide imagined Brazil. Indeed, it was because Welles was "introducing" North Americans to a racially integrated and largely poor, black, and mixed-race society that RKO studio executives finally cut off financial support for the project.[8] For Hollywood, Good Neighbor propaganda meant movies on the order of the mildly sexy musical comedies with newcomer Carmen Miranda, picturesque travelogues, and Disney's later animated films *Saludos amigos* (Greetings Friends) in 1943 and *The Three Caballeros* in 1945.[9] Studio executives did not want a film about dark-skinned Brazilians in carnival celebrations—no matter how famous the director was or how magnificent the footage might be. Vargas was also not pleased that Welles was making a film largely about poor and black Brazilians.

Despite the loss of the film, Welles remained an important radio star, and histories often overlook the fact that radio in the 1940s was a more in-

6.1 Orson Welles arrives in Brazil. Courtesy of the Lilly Library, Indiana University, Bloomington.

fluential mass medium than even the movies. One consequence of Welles's visit to Brazil was his live radio broadcast from Rio, which became the template for his Sunday radio show back in the United States titled *Hello Americans*. When Welles went on the air in Brazil in April 1942, there were between nine hundred thousand and one million radio sets in Brazil. Radio programs were carefully monitored by Vargas's Departamento de Imprensa e Propaganda (Department of Press and Propaganda), or DIP, which suppressed any material from the mass media (radio, movies, plays, and newspapers) that was deemed subversive or that created an unfavorable image of the country (Ortriwano 1985, 17–18).[10]

The most popular radio programs of this period featured the music of carnival, which was a central ingredient in the *chanchadas* (Brazilian musical comedies) such as *Alô, alô carnaval* (1936) featuring the singing duo Carmen and Aurora Miranda. In radio historian Mário Ferraz Sampaio's 1984 memoir, he recalled that among the best-loved radio songs were the "little marches and sambas that continue to be popular in dance clubs even today and during and even outside the carnival period . . . Despite the fact that today's youth never knew the majority of artists from that period, they still sing their compositions and dance orchestras play them by heart, without musical scores, in a crazy potpourri" (130). Carnival and other kinds of music, as well as series such as *O Sombra* (The Shadow), comedy sketches with *caipira* (hillbilly) duos Jararaca and Ratinho and Alvarenga and Ranchinho, and the news program *Repórter Esso* with Heron Domingues were among the options available to listeners.[11]

Broadcast on April 14, 1942, Welles's first radio show from Brazil was called "Pan-American Day" in honor of the Pan-American Conference being held in Rio. Welles began his program by posing the question to his radio listeners up north: "How does Brazil look to the average American?" His answer was that North Americans invariably associated Brazil with images of Rio, which of course was the setting of the conference. In later broadcasts, Welles delved into different aspects of Brazilian culture, while "Pan-American Day" was specifically about the war, although Welles carefully introduced the subject by first talking about the ties that bound the United States to Latin America. For example, he described Pan-American Day as the "Thanksgiving Day for all the Americas" and "a family celebration of the largest family on the globe, the family of the American nations." The war was the obvious subtext for these and other descriptions by Welles, who created a patriotic image of "a united Hemisphere" in which "nations of our two continents stand together."

His introduction to his guest Oswaldo Aranha, Brazil's foreign minister and the president of the Pan-American Conference, was long and effusive, and it bore the indelible imprint of Welles's dramatic and engaging style. Aranha was a "great American," "our oldest and best friend in South America," and "an honest man who looks like you could trust him"; he was renowned for his "distinguished career, patriotism, human heart, and adventurous mind—a real American, sharp without being slick." Welles also talked about Aranha's background as a *gaúcho,* which he said was like a "Texan" or Yankee," and he explained that the term denoted Aranha's origins in the southern state of Rio Grande do Sul.

In his comments to Welles, Aranha reinforced the strong relations between Brazil and the United States. He told Welles that "the heart of Brazil is in the United States" and "within the family of [American] nations, we are the closest." Aranha assured his North American radio audience of Brazil's intent to continue exporting goods north: "The products of our industry are yours in the fight against our common enemy."

At the end of his remarks, Aranha asked Welles if there was something special that Welles would like for him to say. Welles asked Aranha about the existence of a Fifth Column in Brazil—a sensitive topic that Welles said he had been told to avoid.[12] At this point, Brazil had not officially entered the war, so a question about pro-Axis sentiment in the country was legitimate and important. Moreover, although banned in 1938, the Brazilian Integralist Party (or Green Shirts) had been a strong political force for many years, and there were those who still adhered to its cause.[13] Aranha was skillful in his response to Welles, stating that the Fifth Column had been "reduced drastically," and he inquired whether Welles was aware of the "Sixth Column," Aranha's reference to anti–Fifth Column demonstrations held in Brazil. Welles asked Aranha if Brazil had lost confidence in the United States as a result of the destruction of Brazilian ships by Germans in the North Atlantic. Once again, Aranha affirmed the strong bond between Brazil and the United States and proclaimed that no confidence had been lost.

Four days after the "Pan-American Day" program, Welles aired a second, equally patriotic but more elaborate and upbeat show—aired on behalf of the Brazilian Red Cross—in honor of President Vargas's birthday.[14] Filming carnival in Rio had given Welles an enormous appreciation for Brazilian music, and the samba was the centerpiece of this program, which was broadcast live "throughout Brazil and to 100 radio stations in the United States" from the Grill Room at the Urca Casino. Welles began the show by praising Brazil as "the land of promise" and provided his listeners with a sense of the enormity of the country, stating at one point: "You could put the entire United States in the borders of Brazil and still have room for other Latin American countries." Welles talked respectfully about Vargas and hailed "the President of these United States of Brazil" for reforms carried out during his administration. But while positive, Welles's rhetoric here was less effusive than it was for Aranha, which may have been the result of Welles's more ambivalent attitude toward the "dictator of democracy."[15]

The music performed on the show included samba hits such as "Brasil" and "Tudo é Brasil" (Everything Is Brazil).[16] Welles was captivated by the samba, which he described as a "100 percent Brazilian institution," and he told his listeners, "If you scramble the two words 'music' and 'Brazil' together and then unscramble them again, you end up with the word 'samba.'" A little later he returned to this theme, remarking that "Brazilians love to dance" and "if you scramble a number of Brazilians together, you'll find they're dancing samba . . . dancing til dawn . . . then another [dawn] . . . then another."

For the most part, the show was about music, and among its performers were Brazilian composer Carlos Machado and Ray Ventura, a jazz band leader from Europe. Welles was an aficionado of jazz, and he talked about the relationship between the North American music and samba. Carlos Machado demonstrated how the same beat could totally transform the North American tune "Dolores," and Mexican singer Chu Chu Martínez gave his rendition of the Rio samba, "Amélia," one of the year's carnival hits. Another of Welles's featured performers was Urca Casino's samba star Linda Batista, and the conversation between Welles and Batista is delightful. Welles had cast Batista in the carnival episode of the film, along with the black cabaret performer Grande Otelo. In her limited English, Batista talked about Brazil as a "big country" and said things like "all Brazilians like Brazil very much!" (In a letter that Welles wrote to RKO executives, he stated that Batista was much better than Carmen Miranda, and he was euphoric about the talents of Grande Otelo, who went on to make numerous films in Brazil.) In a voice that resembles the delicate vocals of Edith Piaf, Batista sang the lyrics of the patriotic "Sabemos lutar" (We Know How to Fight),[17] which begin with the prophetic words, "If I have to fight in the war." Welles concluded the program by telling President Vargas that "this is a great day" as the orchestra played "Minha terra tem palmeiras" (My Land Has Palm Trees), based on the poem by the renowned nineteenth-century poet Gonçalves Dias.

There can be little doubt that Welles was changed by his experiences in Brazil. During his residence in the country he gathered a small storehouse of material that was provided to him by five full-time Brazilian researchers and English translators. Among the documents he amassed were studies on subjects such as "Brazil and Positivism," "How Coffee Came to Brazil," "Songs of the *Cangaceiros* (Bandits)," "Notes on the Amazon," "Holy Week in Ouro Preto," and "Drought in the Northeast." His researchers also churned out short histories of the different states in the nation as well as sketches of major historical and literary figures. Among the publications he collected was the booklet *Tipos e aspectos do Brasil* (Types and Aspects of Brazil) published by the Instituto Brasileiro de Geografia e Estatística in November 1940. In these pages Welles encountered the artwork of Peruvian-born Percy Lau, one of the most important illustrators in Brazil during the 1930s and 1940s. Although it is now commonplace to compare Welles's footage in *It's All True* with Sergei Eisenstein's epic images of 1930s Mexico in *¡Que viva México!,* there is a definite affinity between Lau's breathtaking black-and-white pointillist-style engravings of proud Northeasterners—in particular his illustration of *Jangadeiros* (Fishermen) and Welles's spectacular images of the four heroic fishermen from Ceará.

One of the longest and most complete studies prepared for Welles was Edmar Morel's "The Story of the *Jangada* in Brazil," which features black-

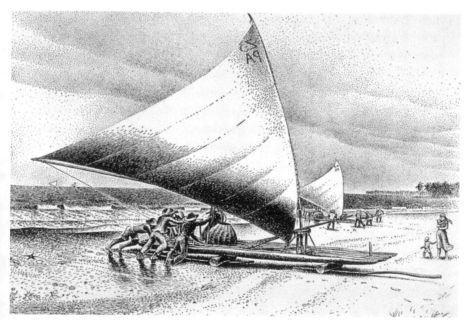

6.2 *Jangadeiros,* by Percy Lau

and-white photographs of *jangadas* (small raft-type boats) and the men who sailed them. Morel added to this illustrated narrative dozens of Brazilian newspaper clippings about the famous journey made the previous year by four fishermen who sailed south from Fortaleza, the state capital of Ceará, to Rio to present President Vargas with a list of requests on behalf of fishermen in the Northeast. Their feat is also featured in a March 5, 1942, clipping of Robert Ripley's "Believe It or Not" in which the drawing of a tiny raft is accompanied by the caption: "4 fishermen sailed 1650 miles in 61 days in 1941." This was the "true" story that had attracted Welles's attention as he made his way to Rio and that he reconstructed and filmed with the assistance of the original four raftsmen.

He also shot numerous reels of the carnival celebrations in Rio, a festivity that he described in *ufanista*-style letters to Hollywood executives as magnificent and impossible to imagine outside of Brazil. In this particular case, however, *ufanismo* failed to win over Hollywood's concerns about how a movie that featured a dark-skinned population would play to white audiences in the U.S. South.

It is difficult to know just how great an impact *It's All True* might have had on audiences had Welles been able to complete it. Brazil continued to figure prominently in the Good Neighbor policy; and Roosevelt made another journey to the country, this time to Natal, capital of the Northeastern state of Rio Grande do Norte, to discuss the war effort with Vargas. Back in the United States, Welles tried unsuccessfully to find money to finish *It's All True*. In an interview in the 1980s with Barbara Leaming, Welles talked about Rockefeller's refusal to grant RKO's request for funds so that he could finish the film. He also criticized Rockefeller's support of fellow filmmaker Walt Disney, whose *Saludos amigos* with its carnival footage was an especially painful reminder of his own incomplete project:

> Rockefeller was worried that he was being thought of as too much of an Eastern liberal and Disney was a sun-belt neo-Fascist. You see [Rockefeller] was already running for President. He wouldn't have *bothered* being Coordinator of Inter-American Affairs if he hadn't had that in mind. . . . Disney had such horrible taste and was so ineradicably pro-German that I just couldn't bear it. (In Leaming 1985, 271–272)

Nonetheless, Welles drew inspiration from his Latin American experience to launch his new CBS radio series, *Hello Americans*.

On November 15, 1942, Welles began *Hello Americans* with a program dedicated to Brazil. His initial comments continued in the spirit of Good Neighbor policy rhetoric, and he gave a dramatic introduction to the subject of the Americas: "the higher you stand, the better we can see a hemisphere—the two continents . . . the New World, whose tenants are Americans . . . Hello Americans. We ought to know each other better than we do . . . starting in Brazil." Welles's comments were followed by a (scripted) call from one of his listeners, who asked: "You mean you're broadcasting from Rio?" Although the program was aired from New York, Welles playfully responded by stating that the program was being broadcast by "dramatic license from Rio de Janeiro."

There are many similarities between the script for the "Brazil" program and the earlier Vargas birthday broadcast—especially Welles's emphasis on the samba. Welles clearly enjoyed introducing his audience to Portuguese words, and he attempted to explain terms such as *carioca* ("it's a word like 'Angelino,' 'Maverick,' or 'Hoosier'") and *samba* ("That's the Amazon and the Congo talking! Dig that rhythm, you cats!" or "It's the old two-step with a South American accent"). The show also featured Carmen Miranda, introduced by Welles as "North Americans' South American favorite," with whom he sang a short samba tune in Portuguese.

At this point, Welles launched into an "Anatomy of Samba" in which he and Miranda discussed the musical instruments used to play the music. Welles was at his best when he described not only the sound but also the shape of the different instruments, telling his listeners how the Brazilian *surdo* "looks like a drum, looks African" and that the *tamborim* in Brazil "is not a tambourine" as we know it, but rather is "square-shaped with a small hide" (which Miranda explained is a "cat's skin"). They also talked about the *pandeiro*, which Welles said "looks just like our own tambourine"; the *reco-reco*, or an instrument with wooden grooves and a stick; the *ganzá*, which is played just like a "bartender shaking a cocktail shaker"; and the *cuíca*, which "looks like a drum." Welles referred to samba as the "soul of Brazil," and he playfully described Brazilian babies who can "beat out a samba rhythm before they can talk, and dance to samba before they can walk."

Miranda told Welles that "Brazil is a big country," a statement that helped him segue into an unusual part of the script that involved a conversation with a "businessman," an "economist," a "mining engineer," a "sociologist," an "explorer," and a "naturalist." Similar to the way Brandônio's *ufanista* rhetoric appeared in Ambrósio Fernandes Brandão's seventeenth-century *Diálogos das grandezas do Brasil*, these various "Brazilian experts" proceeded to tout to Welles the riches and wonders of their country. For example, the economist states: "It seems simplest to say that Brazil could feed the world. Everything grows here—wheat, corn, tea, rice, sugar"—a reference to the fact that Brazilian ships were supplying the Allied war effort even before the country officially entered the war.[18] The mining engineer mentioned gold and diamonds, but he emphasized the importance of the country's manganese, which was used to make steel and was important to the war effort. The naturalist quoted Charles Darwin, who traveled to Brazil in 1831, and then said: "Brazilian scenery is nothing more or less than a view of the Arabian Nights, with the advantage of reality." His discourse is perhaps the most exaggerated, describing how five hundred different species of butterflies can be spotted in a single hour's walk around the northern city of Belém.

Other characters in the script were a honeymooning couple who talked about the colorful parrots and stunning baroque architecture and a writer who was fascinated by the juxtaposition of skyscrapers and jungle and by the idea that Brazilians had "a drop of all mankind's blood within them." Welles picked up on this last comment and talked about the need for tolerance—a remark that was likely directed not only at the general population but also at RKO, whose intolerance led to the jettisoning of *It's All True*. Welles ended the program by informing his audience that he was about to "fly" to the Andes for his next show ("The Christ of the Andes"), and he signed off with the phrase: "Good Night Americans."

The *Hello Americans* show was broadcast weekly for the next two and a half months and featured actors Edmund O'Brien, Agnes Moorehead, and Ray Collins from the Mercury Theater as well as other local and international celebrities such as Hans Conreid and the Mexican performer Tito Guízar. The shows touched on different parts of Latin America and the Caribbean, and two of the programs were dedicated to "Rhythms of the Americas," in which Brazil was featured prominently.

Brazil also appeared in the Christmas broadcast titled "The Bad-Will Ambassador," a loose adaptation of Charles Dickens's *A Christmas Carol*. In the role of the irascible Scrooge is "Bad-Will Ambassador" Martin Stone (Welles), a cynical and bigoted North American who works and travels for an export company. Stone narrates an account of a mysterious fellow who followed him as he stopped in one Latin American city after another on his way home to spend Christmas in New York. In the reenactment, Stone shows himself to be rigid in his thinking about Latin America and its people; and he expresses his opinion to a "smallish, but not too small, not young or old" man in the Buenos Aires airport after arriving late for the flight and refusing to give up his seat to a nine-year-old Brazilian boy whose family lives in Rio.

Shortly after arriving in the Rio airport, the man ("I still don't know his name") approaches Stone and tells him, "I have a surprise. We're guests at a Brazilian home." At this home, Stone is introduced to Christmas traditions such as the Missa do Galo (Midnight Mass), São Nicolau, and the *presépio* (miniature nativity). At the family's dinner table, Stone notices an empty chair, which he imagines is a place set in honor of someone deceased. The family tells him that the chair is normally occupied by their nine-year-old son, who was unable to get a seat on the only plane leaving from Buenos Aires. Stone's chagrin at being the guest in the home of the same boy from the airport is expressed in his comment "I never spent a longer night."

Stone's last stop is Mexico City, where he attends a Christmas play. The mysterious man appears again, this time in the role of the play's innkeeper, who denies Mary and Joseph a room at the inn. Stone is overwhelmed with guilt for denying the boy his seat and even more for having offered him money, which the child refused. He says: "Everything I do matters . . . I matter . . . Pan-American relations mean human relations, loving your fellow man . . . We're fighting [this war] for peace on earth. A lot of Americans are giving up their lives for other men." Like *A Christmas Carol,* the program ends with the transformation of the bad-tempered protagonist into a man of goodwill who is chastened by his experiences.

Welles aired five more programs in the *Hello Americans* series, which concluded on January 31, 1943, with a tribute to Pan-Americanism called "Bolivar's Idea." The following year, he wrote two editorials on Latin America for the New York–based monthly *Free World* in which he focused on the need to expand the Good Neighbor policy to encompass average Americans alongside presidential leaders and the importance of democracy in Latin America. At the same time, Hollywood was entering its peak phase in the production of Good Neighbor films that featured Latin stars such as Cesar Romero, Ricardo Montalban, Desi Arnaz, and most prominently, Carmen Miranda.

Top Banana

You know, bananas is my business.

CARMEN MIRANDA

Now they [the United States] needed us. They needed our film markets and our raw materials. And Carmen, Carmen Miranda was our raw material.

HELENA SOLBERG, director, *Carmen Miranda: Bananas Is My Business,* 1995

While Orson Welles was filming in Brazil, Carmen Miranda was on her way to becoming the most highly paid woman in the United States as lucrative recording contracts with RCA Victor and Decca augmented her growing pay as an actor. In addition to acting and singing in comedies on the order of *Down Argentine Way* (1940) and *That Night in Rio* (1941), she appeared on Broadway (*The Streets of Paris*) and made a "good neighbor" appearance at the Brazilian Pavilion during the 1939 World's Fair in New York City. When she returned briefly for a visit to Rio in 1940, she was greeted by thousands of her fans, who welcomed back the star of 1930s nightclubs, carnival films, and radio stations Educadora do Brasil and Mayrink Veiga, on which she was known as the *pequena notável,* or notable girl (Sampaio 1984, 123). But her visit was marred by a disastrous opening at the Urca Casino before an aloof and unappreciative café society that was unimpressed with her Americanized samba singing. After that short and unhappy visit, she returned to the United States, where she made thirteen movies in as many years.

In Hollywood, she morphed into an exaggerated version of a figure that she had invented in Brazil, modeled after Bahian female street vendors who carried baskets of fruits on their turbaned heads. Her signature sequined costumes, bare midriff, platform shoes, bracelets, bangles, and earrings were her own inventions that she combined with a fractured English that remained broken in performances long after her off-stage knowledge of the language was nearly perfected. She was one of the most colorful and imitated figures in Hollywood. In 1941, Mickey Rooney performed a lively impersonation of her in *Babes on Broadway* (which also starred Miranda), and countless male and female imitators followed. Jerry Lewis impersonated Miranda in the Martin and Lewis movie *Scared Stiff* (1953), which was the Brazilian star's last film. Others who performed Miranda impressions were Imogene Coco (the first to do it on stage, in 1939), Bob Hope, Milton Berle, Carol Burnett, and even Bugs Bunny. One of the most publicized Miranda impersonations occurred in the 1980s on NBC's *The Today Show,* when tall, stocky TV weatherman Willard Scott made a surprise appearance outfitted in full Carmen Miranda regalia. Her image had a special appeal to males, and, like Judy Garland and other divas, Miranda has been appropriated by a gay male culture. In Helena Solberg's 1995 documentary *Bananas Is My Business,* the Carmen Miranda impersonator is a male actor named Erick Barreto.

Miranda's 1943 film *The Gang's All Here* has gone down in movie history for her performance of "The Lady in the Tutti Frutti Hat" in Busby Berkeley's Freudian extravaganza in which she appeared with a gigantic crown of bananas on her head. In the 1940s, Miranda was the figure that North Americans popularly associated with Brazil and Latin America. For the most part, she played the petite, wise-cracking, "south-of-the-border" type who sang and swayed to a samba (and rhumba) beat while rolling her large, dark, flashing eyes. In her film roles, she was repeatedly cast as "Rosita"— a name that was neither Portuguese (which was her origin) nor Brazilian (which was her nationality), but Spanish.[19]

Prior to coming to the United States, Miranda had made her mark as a radio performer and singer in the popular *chanchadas Alô, alô Brasil* (1935) and *Alô, alô carnaval* (1936), in which she and her sister, Aurora, wore satiny tuxedo outfits and top hats. She worked with some of the major samba composers and musicians in Brazil, including Laurindo Almeida, Ary Barroso, and the Bando da Lua (Moon Gang); her popularity hit new heights when she teamed up with the young Bahian composer Dorival Caymi, who wrote the tune "O que é que a baiana tem?" (What Does the Bahian Girl Have?) for her 1939 movie *Banana da terra.* In the song, Miranda provided a litany of the accessories that a Bahian wears, including earrings, a turban, bracelets, and necklaces, and she adopted an elaborate faux-Bahian costume to go with the lyrics.

She also began performing her Urca Casino club act *à la baiana* to an appreciative and largely tourist audience. Her biographer Martha Gil-Montero states that at the carnival celebrations after the premiere of *Banana da terra,* "almost every man who participated in the parades along the streets of Rio wore a *baiana*—not quite the classic Bahian costume, but the new Miranda version. Even more striking was that the women, who generally kept away from the streets but participated in balls and contests, also had discovered the *baiana*" (1989, 58).

There is some debate about who from the United States "discovered" Miranda in Brazil, but her stage performance was so riveting that Broadway producer Lee Shubert, who was in Rio along with skating star Sonja Henie, offered her a contract in 1939. According to Gil-Montero, Shubert was concerned about Broadway profits that year because of the opening of the World's Fair in New York (62). Whether Miranda's decision to go to New York had anything to do with Good Neighbor relations is difficult to access, but she is quoted at the time as being committed to "chang[ing] the wrong ideas existing in the United States about our country" (Gil-Montero 1989, 67), which for Miranda meant singing in Portuguese and being accompanied by the Bando da Lua. But Good Neighbor relations were important to Vargas, who viewed Miranda as an ideal goodwill ambassador and a means to bolster coffee exports. Vargas was so committed to the idea of Miranda going to New York that the DIP covered the travel expenses of the six-member Bando da Lua (Gil-Montero 1989, 70–71)—a cultural initiative that predated the CIAA.

In 1942, following Miranda's success on Broadway and her first three feature films, Twentieth Century Fox released *Springtime in the Rockies,* a hit musical about quarreling Broadway show partners Dan Christy (John Payne) and Vicky Lane (Betty Grable). When Vicky discovers that Dan is still seeing other women, she breaks off their romance and ends their stage act. Unable to get work as a single performer, Dan goes on a drunken spree and hires an "Irish-Brazilian" secretary named Rosita Murphy (Carmen Miranda) and a valet, MacTavish (Edward Everett Horton).[20] Both accompany Dan to Lake Louise in the Canadian Rockies, where Vicky is performing with former partner Victor Prince (Cesar Romero), to whom she is now engaged. Dan hopes to convince Vicky to marry him and join his new show, whose financial backers insist that she be part of the act.

Upon recovering from his trip and hangover, Dan is surprised to learn that he has hired a valet. He remembers nothing about "Murphy," whom he contracted during a stopover in Detroit. Miranda's initial appearance in the movie is noteworthy: instead of her trademark *baiana* outfit, she enters Dan's hotel suite wearing a tailored black and white suit, a small black hat and veil, and black high heels. Following a conversation with MacTavish, she leaves and returns for her first day on the job. Her second entrance is startling if only because her first words to her new boss, "Here I am! Ready to go to work!" contrast with her outfit, which is no longer the tailored suit but rather a vibrantly colored costume with turban, puffy-sleeved midriff blouse, slim-fitting skirt, bracelets, and beads. When Dan turns around and sees her, the first words out of his mouth are "G-o-o-o-o-d Neighbors."

This playful reference to Roosevelt's policy was in keeping with the CIAA and Hollywood studios' desire to bring more positive images of Latin Americans to the screen. Carmen Miranda overturned earlier Hollywood stereotypes of Latin Americans by playing a charismatic, talented, and "good-willed" Latin who enchants everyone around her. However, by repeatedly playing that role, she became another kind of stereotype—a hybrid created by Hollywood of its image of Latin America on the order of the indigenous, exotic Other depicted in colonial texts.[21] Viewers seemed unconcerned that they were unable to understand her Portuguese lyrics. Like that of the Indians who appeared exotic to the European colonizers, Miranda's attraction was based not on what she said but on the spectacle of her persona, which, ironically, involved headdresses, beads, and a (partially) naked torso. To further dazzle the audience, Miranda's character (like some pop stars nowadays) underwent of necessity multiple costume changes in a single performance. To quote actor Rita Moreno from the biographical film *Bananas Is My Business,* like any Latin performer, Miranda "had to be a very exaggerated caricaturized person for the [North] American people to pay attention to [her]."

Much of the repartee between Rosita Murphy and other characters revolves around her clothing. When the startled Dan asks her, "Is that what a secretary wears in Brazil?" she quickly replies, "Why, don't you like my outfit? I think it's a knockdown." When Dan inquires, "What good is [the outfit] if there's not a Mardi Gras in town?" he literally opens the door to another surprise—he has also contracted "six more Murphys" (the members of the Bando da Lua), who appear with their musical instruments. After Murphy introduces each of her "brothers," she asks her boss, who has sat down on the couch in disbelief, if he likes Brazilian music. Dan replies in a beleaguered voice, "I love it," and she happily responds, "You got it!" The brothers perform a delicate prelude that segues into a lively, albeit bizarre, samba rendition of Harry Warren and Mark Gordon's 1941 hit tune "Chattanooga Choo-Choo." Murphy waves her hands and dances to the beat as she rolls her eyes and sings in Portuguese.[22] In the final moments of the song, Murphy's repetition of "Choo-Choo" becomes a locomotive-size sneeze that she accompanies with a resounding "ah-choo!"

6.3 Carmen Miranda and the Bando da Lua in *Springtime in the Rockies* (1942)

The success of *Springtime in the Rockies* was due in part to Miranda's show-stopping song and dance numbers but perhaps even more to her impeccable timing in scenes with veteran comedian Edward Everett Horton, who is a foil for further costume changes. In one of their scenes together, MacTavish opens the hotel door to find Murphy radiantly attired in an all-white sequined outfit replete with turban, midriff blouse, and long, tapered skirt. Murphy asks MacTavish what he thinks of the outfit Dan has bought for her to wear to a supper club that evening. MacTavish's tongue-tied reply is misconstrued by Murphy as a sign of his being less than impressed, and she looks him in the eye and says: "You're right. It needs some beads, some flowers, fruits, baubles, nuts, mix." Later, when Murphy and Dan enter the nightclub where Vicky and Victor are holding court, her all-white costume is practically unrecognizable as a result of the added decorations, which include a brilliant blue turban sash, a richly colored beaded top, bracelets, bangles, and a long multicolored belt. Dan dances a rhumba with Murphy, drawing her close to make Vicky jealous. An amused Murphy tells her boss that the rhumba should be danced farther apart, and she backs away and begins to instruct him with her trademark swaying of hips. But Dan pulls her to him again as he glances over at Vicky, saying he prefers to be cozy. Murphy merrily replies: "I've never danced cozy before."

Apparel is also the subject of Miranda and Grable's catty conversation in the nightclub restroom, where Vicky, dismayed by the apparent romance between Dan and his secretary, dangles Victor's diamond engagement ring in Murphy's face and asks: "Does the size of it startle you?" Murphy gives better than she gets in this scene, remarking: "Yes. In Brazil we throw that kind away." In a good-neighborly reminder of Brazil's prodigious natural wealth, Murphy subsequently balls her hand into a fist, waves it in Vicky's face, and boasts: "We pick them up this big." Later, Murphy dances and sings a lively "Tic Tic Toc, Meu Coração" (Tick Tick Tock, Goes My Heart) to the music of the Bando da Lua, which provides the nightclub audience (along with movie viewers) with another opportunity to enjoy the full spectacle of her over-the-top Brazilian character. The success of such routines in the United States cannot be exaggerated. In addition to soaring box office and record sales, Miranda's image was marketed in the form of coloring books and comic books. In 1942, the same year that *Springtime in the Rockies* was released, the Whitman Publishing Company in Wisconsin issued an exclusive paper doll collection that was "authorized" by Miranda and marketed her image as a fashion vogue. (Dover Publications reissued this collection in 1982.)

Springtime in the Rockies ends with the coming together of the different characters in a musical finale about the importance of hemispheric unity. A *Time* magazine critic wryly commented after the film's release: "[The movie] ends with a song called 'Pan Americana Jubilee' and attempts to be just that by whipping together (1) Latin America (Cesar Romero, Carmen Miranda and her band), (2) the United States (Betty Grable, John Payne, Harry James and his band), and (3) Canada (large Technicolor chunks of Lake Louise where the action takes place). Only the addition of an Eskimo and a penguin could have made the film more hemispheric in scope" (in Woll 1974, 286). What the *Time* critic overlooks is the hybrid nature of the spectacle: Betty Grable now dons a Carmen Miranda–style outfit, albeit a more discreet, single-colored version without the fruit and baubles, and she swing-dances and rhumbas with Cesar Romero. Edward Everett Horton looks more like an Italian gondolier with a flat hat, ribbon, and stripped jersey. Miranda appears in a winterized version of her trademark costume whose ruffled trim resembles a 1940s Sonja Henie skating costume. Good Neighbor unity is symbolized here as more than just friendship; it involves the fusion of an already constructed self with an Other imagined by Hollywood.[23]

The View from Below

Although cultural and economic initiatives toward hemispheric unity were generally welcomed, not everyone was pleased with the CIAA actions in Latin America. High-profile individuals including Chilean poet and Nobel Prize winner Gabriela Mistral and Brazilian newspaper magnate Francisco de Assis Chateaubriand were critical of the United States for attempting to purchase goodwill while force-feeding its culture and goods on Latin America.[24] With respect to Hollywood movies about Latin America, the results (as suggested above) were precarious and often disastrous. Three years after Argentina banned *Down Argentine Way,* the Argentine weekly *Sinfonía* described the United States' goodwill policy in terms of a "spiritual blitzkrieg prepared in the arsenals of Yankee advertising" (in Woll 1974, 289). The publication also complained that the local cinema industry was suffering because of the increase in Hollywood imports, which were especially popular with the public.[25]

In 1943, Getúlio Vargas placed a ban on MGM's *The Gang's All Here* despite Carmen Miranda's starring role in the film. Vargas was apparently uneasy with the gigantic phallic bananas wielded by dancers in Busby Berkeley's tribute to the "lady in the tutti-frutti hat."[26] In the documentary *Bananas Is My Business,* Brazilians reflect on Hollywood's Latin American films. Raul Smandek, a Brazilian cultural attaché in the 1950s in Los Angeles, remarked that "Hollywood created this image of Latin America. And there were a lot of mistakes made because it was Hollywood's *idea* of Latin America." Brazilian journalist Cassio Barsante recalled that the Brazilian Embassy cut problematic scenes from Miranda's second film, *That Night in Rio.* He also criticized Hollywood's treatment of Miranda: "Carmen was a cocktail of all of that and it was disagreeable for her. She became the object of derision in Brazil."

There were a few moments when Miranda was able to talk back to Hollywood. In a clip from one of the black-and-white propaganda films made in cooperation with the CIAA, Miranda appears joking with a stage announcer who pleads with her not to sing in Portuguese. She playfully insists, and after briefly bantering with the announcer, she begins to sing the popular wartime tune "Ka-ka-ka-ty" in Portuguese. In her Portuguese version she modifies the original lyrics, and a line in the second stanza, "I'll be waiting at the ki-ki-kit-chen door," becomes "sou brasileira, morena, faceira, não posso negar" (I am a Brazilian woman, brunette [dark-complexioned], and affected, I cannot deny"), which was Miranda's way of asserting her Brazilianness.

But even singing in Portuguese and proclaiming her Brazilian identity could not overcome the "cocktail" image of the myriad Technicolor films. In one of the few songs Miranda performed in English, she sang, "I make my money with bananas." Despite the song's jesting tone, this was how she was perceived and why she was criticized in Brazil. Later, as the widely recognized model for the Chiquita banana label, she became an icon not just of Brazil but also for the commodity that was her "business" and with which she made a lot of money for herself and Hollywood.

In concluding, it may be useful to say something about the different ways in which the image of Brazil was represented in the United States by Miranda and Welles. Welles was attempting, with the agreement of Rockefeller's agency, to emphasize the similarities between North Americans and Brazilians—he stressed that both countries were large, both had many resources, both were composed of different races and religions, and both aspired to democracy. Even when he spoke of samba and carnival, he linked them to New Orleans and jazz. His most elaborate expression of these themes, however, was a documentary film that Hollywood did not allow to screen. Miranda, on the other hand, was increasingly used by the U.S. culture industry as an image of exoticism and Brazilian "otherness"—a comic ethnicity associated with tropical agriculture that could be transformed into a charming and sexy stereotype. For various reasons, Welles was able to resist the sort of pure commodification that determined Miranda's star image, but by the end of the 1940s, he was an outcast from Hollywood. As with Miranda, his good-neighborliness had mixed success. The times and the political powers dictated only certain images and only an illusion of neighbors.

CHAPTER 7

From Revolutionary to Dystopian Brazil on Screen

In 1953, Carmen Miranda made her final big-screen appearance as a Cuban named Carmelita Castinha in Jerry Lewis and Dean Martin's comedy *Scared Stiff*.[1] Among the highlights of the movie are her performance of "Mamãe eu quero" (Mama I Want), her duets with Martin, and an over-the-top Miranda impersonation by Lewis, who dons Miranda's trademark bangles, fruit, and platform shoes. That same year, a very different image of Brazil was emerging at international film festivals. Director Lima Barreto's powerful western *O cangaceiro* (The Bandit) won prizes for best film at Edinburgh and best adventure movie at Cannes, and in retrospect it marks the beginning of an era in Brazil and the end of another. It was one of the last feature films produced by the Vera Cruz Film Company, a short-lived, Hollywood-style studio established in São Paulo in 1949 under the direction of Brazilian filmmaker Alberto Cavalcanti, who brought together directorial and technical talent from Brazil, the United States, and Europe to make popular, high-quality films that would compete with Hollywood. But after eighteen features that included melodramas, musicals, and comedies, Vera Cruz (unlike the vertically integrated Atlântida Productions, which produced the popular, low-budget *chanchadas*) was forced into bankruptcy. Ironically, this was just at the moment *O cangaceiro* secured international distribution—the first time ever for a Brazilian movie.[2] The first Brazilian western of its kind, it was followed by other films about outlaws and violence, particularly in the Northeast, where banditry figures prominently in folk literature and local history.[3]

Taking its cue from the highly popular and politicized Brazilian Northeastern novels of the 1930s and 1940s, which focused on the poverty and injustices suffered by the rural peasantry, *O cangaceiro* captured the imagination of its viewers with stunning scenes of vast, arid landscapes and dramatic close-ups of outlaws with bandoliers, rifles, and their signature hats studded with star emblems and gold and silver coins. Although the film's melodramatic plot (a love story that leads to rivalry and bloodshed in the bandit community) was predictable, the larger-than-life black-and-white images of bandits and backland terrain were fascinating. The film ran in Brazilian movie theaters long after its release—an uncommon occurrence for a local production—and it earned more at the box office than any other Brazilian film until quite recently (Silva Neto 2007, 153). It also played well in international art theaters and was reviewed in newspapers such as the *New York Times*, where an advertisement for the film showed a bandit figure based on a woodcut from Brazilian popular literature. The ad also featured a large-type phonetic spelling of *O cangaceiro*—"KAN-GA-SARO"—along with enthusiastic blurbs by critics from the *Mirror, Post, Herald Tribune,* and *World-Telegram.*

New York Times reviewer Bosley Crowther praised *O cangaceiro* in his column of September 3, 1954, comparing its "powerful pictorial framing" to that of Eisenstein's *¡Qué viva México!*. But Crowther's commentary also reveals how the cultural encounter (even in a movie theater) continued to generate images of Brazilians as savage others—even though outlaws and

7.1 *O cangaceiro*, Lima Barreto (1953)

violence were commonplace in Hollywood westerns at the time. Crowther's description of *O cangaceiro*'s "mood of savagery" even encompassed scenes in which no violence takes place: "when they [the bandits] gather for relaxation and the enjoyments of the dance, there is a passion and wildness in the rhythms that make the blood run cold rather than hot"—a statement not unlike sixteenth-century descriptions of Brazil's earliest inhabitants, whose customs both attracted and repelled European sensibility. It was exactly this kind of interpretation that later prompted the young Brazilian film director and critic Glauber Rocha to expose the image of Brazilian "primitivism" as a construction of technologically advanced nations. For Rocha, violence, whether on screen or in everyday life, was the direct result of Brazil's oppressed condition as an underdeveloped country and the poverty and hunger suffered by millions of its citizens.

The Violent Land

The most noble cultural manifestation of hunger is violence.
GLAUBER ROCHA, "Uma estética da fome," 1965

Rocha's "Uma estética da fome" (An Aesthetic of Hunger) is a key manifesto for what became known worldwide as Brazil's "Cinema Novo" (New Cinema). By the time it appeared in the *Revista civilização brasileira* (Brazilian Civilization Review), Rocha had already made two feature films: *Barravento* (The Turning Wind) in 1961 about a poor fishing community in Bahia and its struggle between religious acquiescence and social protest and *Deus e o diabo na terra do sol* (*Black God, White Devil*) in 1964 about a corrupt landowner and priest who contract a gunman, Antônio das Mortes, to kill a messianic leader (Sebastião) and a bandit (Corisco) who have rallied the poor during a drought in the *sertão*. The year prior to *Deus e o diabo na terra do sol*'s release, Nelson Pereira dos Santos filmed Graciliano Ramos's famous 1938 novel, *Vidas secas* (Barren Lives), which was grounded in new-realist images of the Northeast and offered a compelling portrait of a resilient migrant family.

These and earlier films such as Pereira dos Santos's neo-realist-inspired *Rio, 40 graus* (Rio, 100 Degrees) in 1955 and his urban drama of 1957, *Rio, Zona Norte* (Rio, Northern Zone), which anticipated Cinema Novo, stood in stark contrast not only to the popular *chanchadas* of the 1930s, 1940s, and 1950s but also to the image of modernity and prosperity constructed by

Kubitschek's administration in the late 1950s and early 1960s. At the same time, Cinema Novo was very much a product and reflection of the idealism of that period; indeed, the filmmakers' progressive, revolutionary spirit and hopes for a more just if not egalitarian society were not radically different from the utopian sentiments of the early planners and builders of Brasília. The discussion of agrarian land reform begun in the mid-1950s was pivotal to a growing national awareness of how unequal and divided the society was. Rocha, Pereira dos Santos, and other filmmakers seized the moment to bring that social reality to the screen in what Rocha described as "sad and ugly . . . screaming and desperate films."[4]

It is difficult to measure the popular impact of Cinema Novo in Brazil, but there is no question that productions on the order of *Vidas secas* and *Deus e o diabo na terra do sol* affected the way the nation was perceived both locally and abroad.[5] Brazil's image as a land of poverty, hunger, and violence steadily emerged in art cinemas with the release in 1961 of *Barravento* and Roberto Pires's *A grande feira* (The Great Marketplace), followed by Anselmo Duarte's *O pagador de promessas* (*Journey to Bahia*) and Ruy Guerra's *Os cafajestes* (The Scoundrels) in 1962, *Vidas secas* and Guerra's *Os fuzis* (The Guns) in 1963, and *Deus e o diabo na terra do sol* and Carlos Diegues's *Ganga zumba* a year later.

The idea of popular revolution was implicit if not explicit in both rural and urban dramas. For example, *A grande feira* focuses on the plight of small vendors in Bahia who are threatened with eviction. An adaptation of Alfredo Dias Gomes's play *O pagador de promessas* is about a peasant who carries a huge cross to a church in Salvador, Bahia, to fulfill a promise made to Saint Barbara, who is an African deity as well as a Catholic saint. His promise to carry the cross inside the church is thwarted by a Catholic priest, who refuses to accept his "sacrilegious" offering. Guerra's *Os fuzis* depicts the tensions between a starving population and soldiers who are ordered to keep them from invading a food storehouse. *Ganga zumba* is a portrait of the leader of Palmares, a republic in the interior composed of thousands of fugitive slaves, Indians, and whites that was destroyed by Portuguese troops in the seventeenth century.

In a 1964 roundtable discussion with Pereira dos Santos and director and film historian Alex Viany, Rocha emphasized that there was no unifying agenda for Cinema Novo and that the "Novo" label could be applied to films by directors outside the group, including the former Vera Cruz star

Anselmo Duarte's *O pagador de promessas* and Mozambican Ruy Guerra's *Os fuzis* ("Cinema Novo" 1965, 187–188). The three filmmakers also talked about different international movements and filmmakers who influenced Cinema Novo, among them Eisenstein, Italian neorealism, the French New Wave, and Hollywood *auteurs* such as John Ford and Orson Welles. Within Brazil, influences were culturally broader, encompassing the avant-garde filmmaker Mário Peixoto, who directed the 1930 film *Limite*; burlesque theater *(teatro de revista)*; and São Paulo's Teatro de Arena, a theater-in-the-round where Brazilian plays were performed about the poor and working class, including Gianfrancesco Guarnieri's *Eles não usam black-tie* (They Don't Wear Black Tie) in 1958, which was later adapted by New Cinema director Leon Hirszman. Rocha also mentioned the importance of certain newspapers that became more formally innovative and more political under Kubitschek, especially Rio's *Última hora* (Last Hour), *Diário carioca* (Rio Daily), and the *Jornal do Brasil* (Brazil's Newspaper).[6] He further commented on the contribution of the often-criticized *chanchada,* which nonetheless focused on *o povo* (the people) ("Cinema Novo" 1965, 192, 194).

From Viany's point of view, Cinema Novo also benefited from works by nineteenth-century playwright Martins Pena and novelist Manuel Antônio de Almeida, who made a "legitimate attempt to capture [social] types, the language of the people" (191). In addition he acknowledged the early-twentieth-century novelist Lima Barreto as "a notable chronicler of our people's behavior . . . in whose dialogue one can still sense the true speech of the people of that period" (191) and playwright Oduvaldo Viana, whose 1920s theater featured Brazilian rather than continental Portuguese. He added: "A realist, socially and politically motivated literature, a literature that depicts popular types and the way of speaking in Brazil is . . . something of our generation" (192). Although Viany did not mention any specific authors or works, left-wing novelists Graciliano Ramos and Jorge Amado were among the most influential of these—certainly for Pereira dos Santos, who successfully adapted both to the screen.[7]

One source that goes unmentioned here and that might be regarded as the structuring absence of several early Cinema Novo films is civil engineer and journalist Euclides da Cunha's 1902 *Os sertões* (*Rebellion in the Backlands*), often referred to as the "Bible of Brazilian nationality."[8] A 600-page chronicle about the land and people of the Northeast, *Os sertões* is best known for its detailed description of warfare between the followers of the messianic leader Antônio Conselheiro and government troops who were sent to destroy the religious community's stronghold of Canudos in the *sertão* of Bahia. In 1896 and 1897, troops were thwarted three separate times by the *canudenses* before they finally captured the town. All of Conselheiro's combatants were killed because they resisted to the last. In the end, the troops razed Canudos and beheaded Conselheiro's corpse.[9] The severed head was transported back to Rio, where scientists applied nineteenth-century theories to a study of the mystic's brain in an attempt to understand how a backlander was able to rise to such prominence and defy the nation's leadership.

Especially in its early phase, Cinema Novo presented a visual document of da Cunha's ethnographic description of the Northeast and the *sertanejo*. The elements of civil war in *Os sertões* provided Cinema Novo with images of a broader-based revolutionary warfare between the landless poor and the landed gentry. That warfare is expressed cinematically in different ways. In *Vidas secas,* the class struggle is internalized by the cowboy-protagonist, Fabiano (Átila Iório), who anguishes over the injustices meted out by his landowner-boss and the sadistic "yellow soldier" (local police).

Deus e o diabo na terra do sol resembles even more closely *Os sertões* in its portrayal of a peasantry that follows a mystic through the *sertão* in search of a better life. Unlike da Cunha, however, Rocha is critical of the ruling class. The *jagunço* (gunman) Antônio das Mortes (Maurício do Valle) is contracted by the rich landowner and local clergy to kill the "black god" Sebastião (Lidio Silva), whose following has depleted the local workforce and church congregation. Backland mysticism and *cangaço* (banditry) are viewed ambiguously in the movie as forces that serve but also harm the populace. Ultimately, the film's sympathy lies with the peasant population, symbolized by the cowhand Manuel (Geraldo del Rey) and his wife Rosa (Yoná Magalhães), who frantically race across the *sertão* to the sea after Antônio slays the "white devil" Corisco (Othon Bastos), whose bandit image also threatens the status quo. The couple's rush to the sea is taken straight from da Cunha, who described Antônio Conselheiro's millennial prediction that the sea would become the *sertão* and the *sertão* would become the sea.

Rocha's 1968 film *Dragão da maldade contra o santo guerreiro* (The Dragon of Evil Versus the Warrior Saint), better known as *Antônio das Mortes,* poses the question of what happens when those who serve the ruling class, as in the case of Antônio das Mortes (or the soldiers who were dispatched to Canudos), unite with the peasants in the struggle against the oligarchy.

7.2 *Deus e o diabo na terra do sol,* Glauber Rocha (1964)

Rocha explored this situation at the beginning of the most repressive years in Brazil's long military dictatorship. A highly stylized and allegorical film that apparently had no difficulty passing the censors, *Antônio das Mortes* is a revolutionary call to arms against those who consciously or unconsciously support the ruling class.

In the film, Antônio das Mortes (Maurício do Valle) is again contracted by the landowning elite to exterminate those who challenge its authority, including the white female "warrior saint" whose messianic visions are verbalized through oracles and the bandit Coriana, who is the last link to Brazil's legendary outlaw Lampião. After stabbing Coriana (Lourival Pariz), who dies slowly from his wound, Antônio das Mortes experiences a crisis of conscience and refuses to kill the saint (Rosa Maria Penna) and the *beato* (extremely devout) Black Antão (Mário Gusmão), who lead the peasant group. The blind landowner, Horácio (Jofre Soares), hires another *jagunço*, Mata Vaca (Cow Killer, played by Vinícius Salvatori), to carry out his orders. While mercenaries massacre the defenseless peasants in the town, Antônio das Mortes repents his actions in the wilderness. When Antônio learns of the massacre, he and the local schoolteacher (Othon Bastos), who criticizes but has also served the ruling class, take up arms and kill Mata Vaca and his gunmen in a shootout that parodies the Hollywood western.

In a scene at the beginning of the movie that resembles the triptych of Saint George slaying the dragon, Antão on horseback drives a lance into the body of Horácio—an action that is replayed two more times. Antão and the warrior saint survive to lead other popular movements, as Antônio walks down a highway to take on a more formidable enemy suggested by a Shell Oil sign in the distance.[10] The final images here and in *Deus e o diabo na terra do sol* and *Vidas secas*, the last of which ends with Fabiano and his family continuing their journey across the *sertão*, underscore the perseverance of individuals who, like the residents of Canudos, are oppressed. The

7.3 *Vidas secas,* Nelson Pereira dos Santos (1963)

difference is that New Cinema is more optimistic about the people's ability to survive and challenge the repressive forces that destroyed Canudos. In that sense alone, the people are victorious.

Cinema Novo and the European Imaginary

In terms of its critical and vital phase, Neo-realism was a movement about a revolution that was already over; the new Brazilian cinema is more important in the sense that it can provoke a revolution.

MARCO BELLOCHIO, in *Cahiers du Cinéma*, 1966

While the influence of French culture remained strong in Brazilian intellectual circles in the mid-twentieth century, the early productions by Pereira dos Santos and Rocha worked in an opposite direction, exciting film critics in France. The extent to which the French reception of these films defined what we now call Cinema Novo is suggested in Alexandre Figuerôa's 2004 study, *Cinema Novo: A onda do jovem cinema e sua recepção na França* (Cinema Novo: The Young Cinema Wave and Its Reception in France), which describes the early 1960s reviews and interviews of Brazilian cinema in *Cahiers du cinéma, Positif,* and other independent and cineclub publications. As Figueirôa notes, the appearance of films by Rocha and Pereira dos Santos in France occurred not long after the publication of Claude Lévi-Strauss's *Tristes tropiques* (1955), a seminal study of Brazil's indigenous peoples in little-known places in the interior like the Pantanal. The anthropological structuralism of Lévi-Strauss considerably influenced film writing in France and elsewhere during the period. In many ways, however, Lévi-Strauss's descriptions and photographs of tribal life and customs functioned culturally much like the illustrated narratives of earlier Frenchmen who traveled to the country and brought back "exotic" specimen-souvenirs including indigenous peoples. Struck by the images of the Northeast, a number of French film critics traveled to Brazil to learn more about the stark realities portrayed on-screen.

Among the earliest to travel to Brazil was the celebrated theorist André Bazin, who went to São Paulo shortly after the release of *O cangaceiro* in 1953 to visit Alberto Cavalcanti. Although Bazin died in 1958, prior to the reconfiguration of the bandit-character into a symbol of Cinema Novo,[11] he was greatly interested in the country as both a film critic and an unwitting practitioner of *dépaysement,* or the desire to create a sense of cognitive estrangement by visiting a non-European culture—a concept that will be developed later in this chapter. One of Bazin's most engaging pieces about Brazil, published in 1954 and reprinted in the January 1959 *Cahiers* homage to him, is titled "De le dificulté d'être Coco" (On the Difficulty of Being Coco") and describes, among other things, the numerous difficulties he encountered when trying to bring a parrot back to France (Figuerôa 2004, 76). He begins the short piece with an image that defines his idea of Brazil: "From the time I knew that I had been invited to the [film] festival in São Paulo, it seemed evident to me that I had to return with a parrot. There is between the idea of Brazil and that of the parrot a relationship that has been imposed on the spirit similar to the one that exists between the special lollipops or Calvados and Normandie" (Bazin 1959, 52). The amusing essay shows the degree to which the first iconographies of Brazil as the Land of Parrots continued to influence the foreign imaginary despite the passage of more than four hundred years.

Those French critics who traveled to Brazil after Bazin were attracted by the revolutionary aspects of New Cinema. As Figuerôa's bibliography of the French reception of Cinema Novo suggests, *Cahiers du cinéma* and *Positif* critics provided the kind of public discussion and international exposure that enabled a relatively loose coalition of young left-wing Brazilian directors to become a world-renowned cinema movement. To a certain extent the left-wing French critics constructed an image of Brazilian cinema that fit their own fascination with "anthropological" views of the Amazon and Northeast. Brazilian directors were committed to movies that exposed the injustices of colonialism and an age-old oligarchy, and that meant exploring topics beyond the Northeastern peasant. But the French image of Cinema Novo was so closely wedded to the early movies about the rural Northeast that when films about problems of the proletariat and the middle class appeared, the critical response was less enthusiastic, as Figuerôa observes:

> Certain [French] writers agreed that poverty should be denounced but were reticent about contradictions and existential conflicts within the Brazilian intellectual milieu. Even Glauber Rocha failed to overcome this attitude, as one can see in the qualified reception of his film, *Terra em transe* (Land in Anguish). The rejection of a cinema with an urban theme was, in certain cases, linked to the belief that in underdeveloped countries without a significant and mobilized industrial proletariat, the revolution would be made in the countryside, with

the peasant masses. Consequently, to depict urban alienation had no usefulness. (172)

Although not every French critic followed this political line, there was a clear preference for films that portrayed Brazil as a pre-industrial, agrarian society in which the peasant community, not unlike the earlier indigenous inhabitants, struggle against colonial forces. The French translation of Rocha's manifesto "An Aesthetic of Hunger" in *Cahiers du cinéma* sealed the association between Cinema Novo and peasant revolution, and Rocha's *Antônio das Mortes* became the exemplary film of the movement. Even the reluctant *Cahiers* critic Luc Mollet, a right-wing cinephile who disliked *Deus e o diabo na terra do sol,* was impressed by Rocha's new film. Writing for the French review *Cinéma,* Brazilian critic João Silvério Trevisan expressed reservations about the way the film was being received, arguing that the French praised *O cangaceiro* and *Antônio das Mortes* "with the same insatiable spirit for folklore and exoticism" without making any distinction between the two films. "Today," he wrote, "Brazil is of interest to the French because Revolution exists among us—a new exotic factor in our folklore" (in Figueirôa 2004, 182).

That statement has a ring of truth. Later films about the rural middle class, urban crime, racism, and the reactionary petit bourgeoisie—including Leon Hirszman's *São Bernardo* (1972), Pereira dos Santos's 1974 *O amuleto de Ogum* (The Amulet of Ogum), Jorge Brodansky and Orlando Senna's *Iracema* (1975), Carlos Diegues's *Xica da Silva* (1976), and Bruno Barreto's 1976 *Dona Flor e seus dois maridos* (Dona Flor and Her Two Husbands)—held little or no attraction for *Cahiers du cinéma,* whose focus by that time had shifted to film theory and social documentaries on the order of Fernando Solanas and Octavio Getino's 1968 *La hora de los hornos* (The Hour of the Furnaces) in Argentina and Patrício Guzmán's 1977 *La batalla de Chile* (The Battle of Chile), the last of which was smuggled out of Chile and actively promoted by the Chilean exile community in France.

Rocha's close relationship with leftist critics at *Positif* kept the idea of Cinema Novo alive for a while longer, but the term gradually disappeared from major film periodicals, only occasionally to appear in smaller publications like *Image et son* and *Cinéma,* which tended to comment on Rocha's older films such as *Barravento.* If film history regards Cinema Novo as a 1960s revolutionary movement, it is largely because the French defined it that way with Rocha's help. Once French critics turned their attention to other cinemas and subjects, Cinema Novo became merely historical, despite the continuing work of directors like Pereira dos Santos to make socially committed films. Like earlier productions, these films raise serious questions about the image and welfare of the nation—especially in the years following the military dictatorship's so-called "economic miracle."

The Revolution as Allegory

The dragon is first Antônio das Mortes, just as Saint George is the *cangaceiro*. Then the real dragon is the landowner, while the warrior saint becomes the teacher when he takes the weapons from the *cangaceiro* and Antônio das Mortes. In sum, I mean to say that those social roles are not eternal and fixed and that those stolidly conservative, or reactionary, or power-abetting components can change and contribute to change. Provided they know where the real dragon is.

GLAUBER ROCHA, "Antônio das Mortes," 1994

The military dictatorship posed serious problems and obstacles for left-wing filmmakers. This was especially true after 1968, when persecution, imprisonment, and torture were commonplace punishments for speaking out against the regime. Explicit films about class struggle were impossible to make under a government censorship that carefully scrutinized film and other forms of mass communication. The films made in Brazil during this period were a hodgepodge of low-level and soft-core (*pornochanchada*) comedies, *nordesterns,* carnival movies, melodramas, and low-budget, low-quality, Brazil-U.S. co-productions that in 1969 included the less than memorable *Tarzan e o grande rio* (Tarzan and the Great River), *Tarzan e o menino da selva* (Tarzan and the Jungle Boy), and *Fumanchu e o beijo da morte* (Fu Manchu and the Kiss of Death). Although some locally made films were profitable, especially the *pornochanchadas* (which later received government subsidies when other, serious films did not), very few movies from this period reached audiences outside Brazil. Glauber Rocha's *Antônio das Mortes* was a major exception. Its blend of folk narrative, non-representational performances, and modernist style may not have had wide appeal in Brazil, but it won accolades and major prizes from critics locally and in France, Belgium, and Spain. The war in Vietnam, racial turmoil, deep political divisions, and massive protest movements made films such as *Vidas secas,*

Deus e o diabo na terra do sol, and *Antônio das Mortes* even more popular with art cinema and university audiences in the United States who saw in the violence and poverty of Brazil a call for political action and social change.

As the military's grip tightened in Brazil, Cinema Novo films became more complex, wide-ranging in subject matter, and allegorical. For example, in *Der leone have sept cabeças* (The Lion Has Seven Heads) in 1970, Glauber Rocha shifts his focus to Africa and the history of colonialism there. Unlike *Deus e o diabo na terra do sol, Antônio das Mortes,* and Rocha's *Terra em transe* (1967) about power struggles amidst the instability or "trance" of a people living in the tropical Eldorado, *Der leone have sept cabeças* was Rocha's attempt to broaden the theme of oppression from Brazil and Latin America to the whole of the developing world. Although the film is similar in spirit and complexity to the Nietzchean, anarchistic, and lyrical *Terra em transe,* which Paris reviewer Jean-Louis Bory extolled in *Le nouvel observateur* as "a machine-gun opera" (in Rocha 1994, 59), the French expected a certain image of Brazil and were unimpressed with a Brazilian movie set in another country.

Two of the most popular films to appear at this time, Joaquim Pedro de Andrade's *Macunaíma* in 1969 and Nelson Pereira dos Santos's 1972 *Como era gostoso o meu francês* (How Tasty Was My Little Frenchman) were also allegories. Their critique of the situation in Brazil was couched in a language that combined elements of satire, parody, pastiche, and farce, which were mainstays of a left-wing movement in Brazilian culture known as Tropicália.[12] Both films were adapted from celebrated texts. *Macunaíma* was based on Mário de Andrade's novelistic "rhapsody" in the form of a modernist-style folktale about a "hero without any character" and his experiences as a Black Indian in the interior, his transformation into a blue-eyed white man who travels to São Paulo, and his ultimate metamorphosis into the constellation Ursa Major. *Como era gostoso o meu francês* was a different kind of adaptation, whose sources included a variety of sixteenth-century historical documents, prominent among them the German Hans Staden's eyewitness account of his captivity among the anthropophagic Tupinambá.

Both directors also were known for earlier adaptations. *Vidas secas* was Pereira dos Santos's homage to Graciliano Ramos and his celebrated novella about the Northeast, while Andrade's 1965 *O padre e a moça* (The Priest and the Girl) was loosely based on modernist Carlos Drummond de Andrade's poem "O padre, a moça," about an illicit love affair between a cleric and a girl in a small provincial town (Johnson 1984, 226n6). Film adaptations, especially adaptations of classics, tended to be ignored by the military regime, which regarded the process as simply the transposition of a literary work onto celluloid. (In fact, in order to increase its cultural capital, the government film agency Embrafilme later offered special subsidies for films based on Brazilian canonical works.) Andrade and Pereira dos Santos took advantage of the government's attitude and chose respected works from the past to comment on the present.

The theme of anthropophagy is central to both *Como era gostoso o meu francês* and *Macunaíma*, although its significance goes beyond the sixteenth-century debates about savage versus ritual acts, as well as the playful pronouncements by modernist Oswald de Andrade about the ingestion and transformation of the foreign. Joaquim Pedro de Andrade and Pereira dos Santos used the cannibalist motif to comment on the capitalism of the late 1960s and the devastation caused by largely unconscious consumption. Andrade's preface to the English version of the film emphasizes this use of metaphor: "*Macunaíma* is the story of a Brazilian devoured by Brazil." The focus on Brazil's indigenous past in Pereira dos Santos's film implies as much by showing that even acts of selected consumption bring about destruction—as noted by the film's final intertext about the genocide of the Tupiniquim by their former Portuguese allies.

I have commented elsewhere on the subtle ironies and cultural critique in *Como era gostoso o meu francês.*[13] The qualities that made the novel *Macunaíma* so unusual and rich are captured in the film: the representation of a modern colloquial Brazilian Portuguese; the use of stories and myths from Brazilian folklore; the focus on Brazil's multiracial society; and the appearance of fantasy characters and surreal events. But from the very beginning, Andrade sets a tone that is both parodic and grotesque. The book's initial description of Macunaíma's birth—"an Indian woman of the Tapanhuma tribe gave birth to an unlovely son" (Andrade 1984, 3)[14]—is portrayed as farce in a close-up of the black actor Grande Otelo as he drops in fetal position to the ground from the unseen heights of his "indigenous" mother's "bodily lower stratum," which is represented by two hairy, slightly bowed, and muscular legs. Macunaíma (played brilliantly by Grande Otelo) is born full-grown in the film, and his mother is played by the white actor Paulo José in drag. Andrade cast another white actor (Rodolfo Arena) to play Macunaíma's older brother, Maanape, who is black in the novel, while black

7.4 *Macunaíma*, Joaquim Pedro de Andrade (1969)

actor Milton Gonçalves plays the role of the brother Jiguê, whom Mário de Andrade described simply as "in his prime."

Viewers familiar with the novel may wonder if the film has not undercut the original text's emphasis on the importance of the Indian (who was sometimes described as "black" in colonial texts) to Brazilian culture in general.[15] In Chapter Five of the novel, Macunaíma takes a bath in a small pool of "magic" water that "wash[es] away all his blackness; there was nothing left to show in any way that he was a son of the black tribe of Tapanhumas" (1984, 31). Because the pool's water is decreased and darkened from Macunaíma's bathing, Jiguê jumps in and turns "the color of freshly minted bronze," while Maanape can "only wet the palms of his hands and the soles of his feet" (31).

The reader is told that the water is a relic from the time when Saint Thomas traveled around the country trying to convert the Indians; hence Macunaíma's transformation from black to white is a tongue-in-cheek commentary on Christian baptism or christening and the conversion of the "heathen" to a state of purity and grace in both body and spirit. But the novelist goes further: the blue-eyed, fair-haired Macunaíma comforts the bronzed-colored Jiguê, telling him that "at least the blackness has gone away. Half a loaf is better than no bread!" (31). The only consolation he offers to Maanape, who remains black except for his palms and soles, is: "don't let it get you down! Worse things happen at sea!" (33). What Mário de Andrade is presenting here is a faux-naif, folkloric-style tale of the three races that together would become the foundation for Brazilian identity: "The three brothers made a superb picture standing erect and naked on the rock in the sun; one fair, one red-skinned, one black. All the denizens of the forest looked at them in amazement" (33). At the same time, he implicitly endorses the hierarchy of race (skin color) in Brazil, making the novel's hero a white man who recognizes his color to be preferable to the bronze Jiguê and vastly superior to the black Maanape.

In the film, there is no reference to Christianity. The black Macunaíma, his black brother, Jiguê, and his white older brother, Maanape, come across a geyser instead of a pool of water. After Macunaíma's transformation into a white man (played by Paulo José, who also plays the mother), Jiguê rushes to the fountain; but it ceases to spew forth, and he disappointedly slaps the wet ground with his feet and his hands. When Maanape approaches, there is no water left. Filmmaker Andrade fashions his own ironic statement about racial hierarchy and skin color by having Macunaíma say to Maanape, "You're already white. What if you turn black?"

Earlier in the story, the young Macunaíma is accompanied into the forest by Sofará (Joana Fomm), the girlfriend of Jiguê. In the film, Sofará removes a magic cigarette from her genitals and gives it to Macunaíma, who smokes it and turns into a blond prince. In an early article on the film that appeared in *Jump Cut,* critic J. R. Molotnik refers to Macunaíma's metamorphosis into a "debonair Prince Charming" (1976, 4); two other critics comment on the "handsome white prince" (Johnson and Stam 1995, 185) and "comely prince" (B. Williams 1999, 335). Perhaps this is a matter of gender and perspective, but the prince on the screen seems neither handsome nor charming and debonair. He is definitely white and blond, but he looks more like a character out of Monty Python's *Spamalot* than a storybook figure. His anachronistic "courtly" attire, its tights, puffy sleeves, and shoes with turned-up toes, is ridiculous; and his manner is ingenuous and a bit dopey, which is not surprising since Macunaíma (like Tom Hanks in *Big*) is still a child.

Given Sofará's enthusiasm, there is no question that he is an able lover, and they replay their forest romp the following day only to be caught *in media res* by Jiguê, who beats Sofará and finds himself another girlfriend.

While the film emphasizes the endearing goofiness of the foppish prince, the novel is far more insistent upon his raging sexual appetite and acrobatic sexual foreplay to intercourse. The novel foregrounds the sexual implications of the folktale and fable; in later scenes, both the film and the novel emphasize the sexual act to the fullest and correlate the image of penetration with that of invasion, colonization, and consumption.

Among the most important characters in the novel and the film is Ci, who in the book is an Amazon called the "Mother of the Forest." The novel's still-black Macunaíma encounters her on his wilderness trek, and after months of exuberant lovemaking between the two, Ci bears a son who is "the color of blood." But the Black Serpent arrives in the night and sucks at Ci's breast, leaving venomous traces that fatally poison the suckling newborn. The grieving Ci gives Macunaíma an amulet, the *muiraquitã*, before dying and ascending to heaven, where she is transformed into a star. In the course of his mourning, Macunaíma loses the *muiraquitã*. From here on out, the book focuses on his journey to the city to recover the stone from the Peruvian river trader Venceslau Pietro Pietra (Jardel Filho), a giant and "Eater of Men" whose recent good fortune in São Paulo is attributed to the magical power of the amulet.

In the movie, the white Macunaíma meets the white, gun-toting revolutionary and bank robber Ci shortly after he and his brothers arrive in São Paulo.[16] Macunaíma takes up residence in Ci's loft-style apartment, where they make love in a vibrant red hammock that hangs above a conventional bed. This strange setup, which allows them to spill out of the hammock onto the mattress, comically melds rural and urban identities. After one particularly rigorous session in the hammock, Ci leans over Macunaíma, who is sprawled on the bed, and promises him the *muiratiquã* should she be killed. Stereotypic gender roles are reversed: she carries on urban warfare in the city while a laid-back, purple-robed Macunaíma stays at home and strums a guitar.

After a while, Ci gives birth to a son who is neither white nor blood-colored but black. The first shot of the newborn harks back to the film's comic opening: swaddled on Ci's lap and with a ruffled bonnet on his head is Grande Otelo, who innocently blinks his eyes as he sucks on a baby bottle. This riotous moment is followed by a bizarre scene that emphasizes Ci's continued dedication to the revolutionary cause. Using motherhood as a revolutionary guise, she tucks a time bomb into the bottom of the baby's carriage. Macunaíma places the "baby" in the stroller on top of the bomb, and Ci double-checks the time mechanism, although she is distracted by Macunaíma, whom she pets and fusses over prior to leaving with the child. Shortly after they depart, a loud explosion is heard offscreen. Their deaths leave Macunaíma alone and bereft—that is, until he happens to see a newspaper article about Venceslau Pietro Pietra and his discovery of the amulet. Apparently, the explosion launched Ci's *muiratiquã* into the water, where it was swallowed by a fish, which was subsequently caught and served to Venceslau, who bit down on the stone. As in the novel, the film's initial comic, picaresque narrative about a "hero without any character" segues into a spoof of the archetypal quest for a magical amulet or grail.

The climax of both the novel and the movie is a surrealistic *tour de force* in which Macunaíma confronts Venceslau (who looks like a darker version of Martin Short's Jiminy Glick) in his home.[17] The arrival of the irrepressible Macunaíma to Venceslau's house takes place during a wedding reception for one of his daughters. Dressed in a green jacket and yellow pants, the national colors of Brazil, Macunaíma is literally dragged by Venceslau into the festivities, which center around a huge swimming pool turned cooking pot filled with black beans for a *feijoada.* The large morsels afloat in this Olympic-size stew pot are neither beef nor pork but body parts of wedding guests who were pushed into the pool and partially consumed by piranhas. Venceslau forces Macunaíma onto a platform and then onto a trapeze-style swing that carries him out over the pool, and he tries to dislodge him in mid-air by shooting him with an arrow. Macunaíma manages to return safely to the platform, where he deftly slips the swing under the capitalist's large rump and strips the amulet from the giant's neck. He picks up a bow and arrow and shoots the ogre, whom he has pushed out over the disgusting mass. Struck in the back, Venceslau falls from his perch and screams, "It needs more salt!" A subsequent shot shows his bulky body bobbing facedown in the purplish-black muck. Macunaíma's skill with the bow and arrow is a subtle reminder of his indigenous roots. Indeed, in this sense he is far more successful than his ancestors, who were ultimately consumed by the colonization process. Here the tables are turned, and the capitalist-ogre is the one eaten as a result of his own aggressive consumption.

In the novel, the victorious Macunaíma and his brothers return to their home in the wilderness along with souvenirs of their urban adventure. Macunaíma continues to experience adventures and near-mishaps, including a near-death struggle with Uiara, a beautiful cannibal water siren from indigenous lore, to whom he loses his amulet. Left alone after his brothers' demise, he lacks the will to live. Tired and failing in health, he ascends into heaven, where he transforms into Ursa Major. The film takes a slightly different tack, emphasizing the theme of consumption. Laden with electrical goods and wearing a cowboy hat, boots, and a green-fringed western jacket, Macunaíma, along with his brothers, returns home. He has purchased a cartload of items that have no purpose in the wilds—a portable television, an electric coffee pot, and other commodities litter the ground like archaeological relics.

Macunaíma refuses to work for his survival in the wilderness, and his brothers leave him to waste away among his useless possessions. The film ends with Macunaíma's aquatic encounter with the seductive Uiara (Maria Lúcia Dahl). Still wearing the green jacket, Macunaíma removes the amulet from around his neck and dives into the lagoon—an action reminiscent of his youthful underwater sexual romps with Sofará. But here the outcome is different; this time he is the one who is the object of desire and consumption—as suggested by the final shot, which shows his green jacket rising to the surface in a cloud of blood.

In 1993, André Klotzel used a similar scene to end his movie *Capitalismo selvagem* (Savage Capitalism) about the struggle between conservation and Indian activists and an industrialist who, learning belatedly of his indigenous heritage, attempts to protect the culture endangered by his own capitalist enterprise. Some twenty years earlier, filmmaker Andrade suggested that the country as a whole was at risk as the green of Macunaíma's jacket is surrounded and darkened by blood. Desire, like free enterprise, must not be allowed to get out of hand. The consequence, as the final scene implies, is the demise of a nation and its people by its own consumptive drive gone amok.

On the Road

The arrival of modernity into the impoverished interior became a topos in films of the 1970s and 1980s, which literally took to the road to portray the impact of capitalist projects like the Plano de Integração Nacional (Plan for National Integration) implemented in 1970 to ensure Brazil's sovereignty over undeveloped and unoccupied lands to the north and west.[18] The road film introduced audiences to once-forested areas in and around the Amazon Basin where unchecked expansionism in the form of highways and *lati-fundismo* was especially evident. In a sense, socially committed filmmakers became modern-day chroniclers of this moment in the nation's history, except that instead of hailing the programs of exploration and colonization, they showed the programs' devastating effects on the people and the land.

The title of Jorge Brodansky and Orlando Senna's docudrama, *Iracema: Uma transa amazônica* (1975, released 1980), automatically conjures up novelist José de Alencar's "virgin of Tupã" with the "honey lips" (see Chapter Four).[19] In this case, the focus is on the contemporary encounter between Sebastião, or "Tião Grande Brasil" (Paulo César Peréio), a white trucker from Rio Grande do Sul, and a young, sweet-faced Indian girl, Iracema (Edna de Cássia), whose family resides on Marajó Island in northernmost Brazil. But unlike the romantic encounter in the novel, theirs is far from idealized, as suggested by the film's title—a play on words that couples the image of the Trans-Amazon Highway with that of the *transa,* or sexual transaction, that involves indigent women at the side of the road. Unlike the Portuguese colonizer Martim, the trucker is neither romantic nor heroic, but loud, foul-mouthed, and unsympathetic with the culture he encounters.[20]

The film's initial river scenes of Iracema and her family taking their harvest by boat to the warehouse outside the capital, Belém, emphasize Marajó Island's tranquil beauty and lush tropical forest. A diegetic announcer's voice coming from a radio onboard forms an anachronistic counterpart to the primeval setting. In a subsequent shot on the docks in Belém, Tião Grande Brasil talks to a local as workers load lumber onto his truck. Their dialogue replays sixteenth-century narratives about the wonders of Brazil. In this case, however, the *ufanista-nativista* message is of a different sort: the local man praises the area's beauty and natural resources, while Tião opines that Brazil's greatness is related to progress and the rapid development of those resources—thus his moniker, Grande Brasil, Great (Big) Brazil.

Iracema's troubles begin when she is separated from her family when they arrive in the city for a religious holiday's festivities. On her own, she marvels at the wares in the marketplace and enters a circus sideshow that features a woman "without a body" whose disguised torso turns her literally into a "talking head." As Iracema follows the example of other young Indian women who are prostitutes whom she meets in a bar, the significance becomes more evident. Like the bodiless circus freak, she is a commodity. Among those who pay for her is Tião, who takes her with him in his truck and later discards her at a bleak roadside stop in the middle of nowhere. Iracema's coarse language in this scene further dispels the romantic heroine myth, while her red-and-white short-shorts with their large Coca-Cola emblem reinforce her status as a (disposable) commodity. Later, she accompanies an older prostitute for a fly-in-and-out transaction with a North American who owns a large cattle ranch in a remote area of the Amazon Basin. Once there, they witness another kind of transaction whereby several from a group of itinerant laborers are picked out and sold to the ranch foreman by a coyote-type entrepreneur for burning and clearing the land. After a heated exchange with the foreman, the two women are forced into the back of a truck along with the rejected workers. Even before they reach their destination, Iracema is abandoned on a dirt road in the middle of a forested area and is forced to hitchhike back home.

Iracema prefers the road to the hand-to-mouth, sedentary existence for women on the island that requires that she learn needlework. Traveling is her destiny, she tells her older sister, and the film follows her rapid descent on the highway. In one chilling scene, she is beaten, dragged into a shack by a group of men, and raped. Later, she hitches a ride with a trucker to Altamira in the center-north of Pará state. There she sits at the side of a road with older, fat, and wasted prostitutes who are drinking and laughing. She is dirty and disheveled and has lost a tooth and a shoe; Tião, who happens by in his truck filled with cattle, seems not to recognize her, and when she asks him to take her with him to Acre on Brazil's westernmost frontier, he refuses her and her request for some money. "Great Brazil" departs with his cattle, which he says are more profitable than lumber, and Iracema is left standing alone in the middle of the road—a symbol of the displacement and degradation of a vulnerable population.

Co-produced by German television, *Iracema* did well on the international film circuit; but the regime's censors kept the movie from being locally exhibited until 1980, when the political opening and the film's success at a festival in Brasília prompted its general release. There is little doubt that the movie had a special resonance with local audiences, who could see in the pitiless descent of Iracema a harsher, more realistic version of her nineteenth-century predecessor. In Alencar's novel, Iracema slowly perishes as Martim roams the wilderness. Hers is a tragic but highly romanticized death with her newborn son and a pet bird by her side and majestic nature surrounding her. Filmed in cinéma verité style, the contemporary Iracema's

7.5 *Iracema: Uma transa amazônica,* Jorge Brodansky and Orlando Senna (1980)

encounters with outsiders are shown in all their dark violence and raw brutality. Although she is alive at the end, her destiny is etched on her dirty,
haggard face with its tooth-gaped grin—just as the once-lush forest's fate
is marked by razings and burnings that appear in the film's background.

This Iracema is also abandoned, but not by a distracted lover, nor does she produce an offspring; and she seems oblivious to nature (and its devastation) around her. Hers is an unsettling image of an individual and a race transformed and consumed by the forces of a "national greatness" beyond their control.[21]

One of the most popular films of this period is Carlos Diegues's *Bye Bye Brasil* (1979), a road movie *par excellence* that features thousands of miles of the country, from the Northeast to Belém and into the central plateau and Brasília. The troupe of the Caravana Rolidei (pronounced "holiday" in much of Brazil), comprised of the magician Lorde Cigano (Gypsy Lord, played by José Wilker), his companion and rhumba queen Salomé (Betty Faria), and strongman Andorinha (Príncipe Nabor), is more streetwise and sophisticated than their provincial audiences, who, like Brodansky and Senna's Iracema, are entertained by old-fashioned magic tricks, song and dance numbers, and mind-reading and iron bar-bending acts. The movie revolves around the sexual dynamics between Lord Cigano and Salomé and a young couple, Ciço (Fábio Júnior) and Dasdô (Zaira Zambelli), who join the caravan, and the troupe's increasing difficulty in finding paying audiences, which are becoming scarcer as a result of the arrival of television into the interior.

Diegues's treatment of the issue of the nation's rapid modernization is darkly ironic. In one scene, members of a poor indigenous family appear on the roadside with their meager possessions, a bottle of Coca Cola, a small transistor radio, a block of wood carved in the image of a television, and a monkey, all of which emphasize the increasingly anachronistic and surreal nature of their existence. The scene is initially humorous: a young Indian male dressed in a vibrant orange prison jumpsuit recommends a tribal remedy—fresh urine—for a painful stingray bite that Ciço gets on his first dip ever into the ocean; and Lorde Cigano delights in unzipping his trousers and threatening to pee on his young companion. But the portrait of the Indian family is an implicit commentary on hybridity and the ability of any culture to survive under capitalist siege. Salomé represents a certain kind of hybrid, not unlike Carmen Miranda, in the sense that although she is Brazilian, her commercial success depends on her adoption of an "exotic" Caribbean persona who wears outlandish costumes, speaks Spanish, and dances the rhumba.[22] Both Salomé and the indigenous family are spectacles, but Salomé is an ironic amalgamation constructed for entertainment and consumption purposes. In the case of the indigenous family, however, the transformation is anything but ironic and makes explicit the degree to which the indigenous culture is at risk.

Initially the Caravana truck, with its loudspeaker system and music, seems modern in the impoverished backlands contexts, but when parked along newer cars and semis at roadside truck stops, it appears increasingly antiquated. In a last-ditch effort to earn money for their expenses, Lorde Cigano bets the truck and its contents on Andorinha; the strongman's defeat by a confident younger arm wrestler signals the troupe's disempowerment. Lorde Cigano turns to Salomé, whose prostitution from that point on keeps them on the move. Despite Ciço's obsession with Salomé, the two couples finally split up, and each takes a different road. (Andorinha disappears without a word after his defeat.)

The Northeastern couple and their newborn daughter travel by bus to Brasília, whose highways and buildings epitomize the coming of modernity to the interior. Although they are provided with little more than a shack on the capital's periphery, they eventually prosper by performing tradition-al *forró* music on television and in dance halls for the large Northeastern migrant labor force. When they roll into Brasília a few years later, Lorde Cigano and Salomé are driving a large, neon-lit recreation vehicle replete

7.6 *Bye Bye Brasil,* Carlos Diegues (1979)

with a trio of singer-dancers dressed in tight-fitting sequined and satin outfits. The degree to which their caravan has been transformed by modernity is suggested by a large neon hand on the back of the RV that flashes the U.S. (as opposed to Brazilian) "fuck you" gesture. That neon hand and Frank Sinatra's swinging rendition of "Brazil," which blares over their loudspeaker system, signal the degree to which the culture in Brazil is changing as a result of U.S. capital. About the only vestige from their caravan days is the Spanish song "Para Vigo me voy" (I'm on My Way to Vigo), the title of which was Lorde Cigano's "abracadabra" expression used to impress his village audiences. Salomé now sings the song as she steers the RV toward Rondônia and migrant communities in the far-west frontier.

Migrant Mov(i)es

Migration is a prominent theme in early Cinema Novo features such as *Barravento, Deus e o diabo na terra do sol,* and *Vidas secas,* as well as in later movies including Nelson Pereira dos Santos's *O amuleto de Ogum,* Susana Amaral's 1985 *A hora da estrela* (The Hour of the Star), Walter Salles and Daniela Thomas's 1995 *Terra estrangeira* (Foreign Land), and Salles's 1998 *Central do Brasil* (Central Station). As critic Ismail Xavier points out, even *Macunaíma's* protagonists arrive in the city "as anonymous figures who add to the daily quota of expatriated poor, images common in Cinema Novo films" (1997, 136). Migration moves both to and from the urban centers: Macunaíma returns to the interior after his urban adventure; Tião Grande Brasil leaves Porto Alegre for more lucrative opportunities in the Amazon Basin; and Iracema moves from the Edenic Marajó Island to dismal outposts along the Trans-Amazon Highway. In *Bye Bye Brasil,* the young couple Ciço and Dasdô flee the all-too-familiar cycle of drought and poverty in the Northeast for a better future in the city, likewise the dream of Fabiano and Vitória in *Vidas secas* as they trek across the *sertão.*

To a certain extent, all of these films portray what the French surrealist André Breton called *dépaysement.* Breton used this word when writing in 1922 about the desirability of escaping the "bourgeois Europe" that had been responsible for World War I (Updike 2005, 4); there is also a relationship between the artist who seeks *dépaysement* and Baudelaire's *flâneur,* who was an important figure for the nineteenth-century Portuguese poet Cesário Verde. Verde's long poem "Sentimento de um occidental" (Feelings of an Occidental Man) describes the estranging and sinister sights and sounds of Lisbon's other/underworld of midnight streets, docks, and brothels, which were far from common fare in lyric poetry. I am not suggesting that Brazilian *retirantes* (migrants) are like the surrealists or the poet-*flâneur*, who voluntarily sought new worlds for their estranging effect. My point is that films about the Brazilian migrant use the theme of displacement and homelessness to induce a kind of *dépaysement* or estrangement of the familiar in the viewing audience. Susana Amaral's *A hora da estrela*, for example, estranges the modern city by viewing it through the experience of a young migrant woman from the Northeast.

In adapting Clarice Lispector's 1977 novella to the screen, Amaral dispensed with the book's first-person narrator, Rodrigo S. M., an alienated intellectual, to focus on the central character, Macabéa. Shortly after arriving in São Paulo, Macabéa (Marcélia Cartaxo) finds a low-paying job and a room, which she shares with three other women, to whom she announces: "I'm a typist and a virgin and I like Coca Cola." Unlike her native Northeast (and Rio, where the novella takes place), São Paulo is cloud-covered and bleak. The gray, dystopian atmosphere of the film is enhanced by locales such as a vacant underground metro stop, a highway underpass, and a fenced-in pedestrian overpass, as well as the dilapidated boarding house where Macabéa sleeps and the dark office where she works. A barely educated orphan raised by a prudish aunt, Macabéa is ill-equipped for life; her typing is excruciatingly bad, her diet consists largely of hot dogs and Coca-Cola, her hygiene and dress are slovenly, and she is painfully shy. She is in awe of her co-worker Glória (Tamara Taxman), a working-class Cariocan who uses cosmetics and decolletage to manipulate the males around her. Macabéa also looks up to Olímpico (José Dumont), a fellow Northeasterner whose boastfulness conceals the fact that he ekes out a living as a day laborer.

A hora da estrela focuses on Macabéa's daily struggle to adapt to her new surroundings, which leads her to imitate her officemate and follow examples given by the media. Like Glória, she lies to her boss to get time off; and she listens and copies down things she hears on the radio and unsuccessfully asks Olímpico to interpret them. She watches *telenovelas* and pastes fashion ads from magazines on the wall above her bed. She buys nail polish and lipstick even though she is not particularly adept in their application. She attempts to sing like Caruso on the radio, and she mimics the pose of department store mannequins dressed in bridal gowns.

A close-up shot of her transistor radio and a Coca-Cola bottle is met-onymic of everything that Macabéa associates with the city. Her room-mates, who own very little, note her poverty, but Macabéa says with convic-tion, "I have a job and I'm going to buy things." Because she earns less than minimum wage, she is unable to afford much beyond her room, her daily diet of hot dogs and Coca-Cola, and her occasional ticket to the public zoo or a ride on the metro. To lessen Olímpico's painful rejection and her con-stant alienation, she borrows aspirins from Gloria, which she vigorously chews as if they were food. Ultimately Macabéa turns to a huckster–for-tune teller (Fernanda Montenegro) who predicts Macabéa's encounter with a wealthy and handsome foreigner—a prediction that thrills Macabéa but seems as unlikely as her succeeding in her job or surviving the city. Ironically, the encounter does occur, although not in the manner foretold. Stepping off a street corner, she becomes the victim of a hit-and-run by a foreigner in a Mercedes with a star emblem on its hood. Even in the death throes, Macabéa fails to comprehend her circumstances; and in her final at-tempt to find happiness and success, her thoughts take the form of a once-famous Clairol commercial in which she now stars along with the foreigner and toward whose embrace she runs.

Actor José Dumont, who plays Olímpico in *A hora da estrela*, had already played a similar role in João Batista de Andrade's 1980 *O homem que virou suco* (The Man Who Turned into Juice), about a migrant storyteller-poet, Deraldo, who tries to make a living in São Paulo by selling his *literatura de cordel*, or chapbooks, about famous Northeastern characters. Deraldo wants to succeed in the city but is forced to work as a day laborer. He is constantly reminded by his various employers that he needs to reform and cast off his "easygoing-ness" (a stereotype of Northeastern life) and adopt a "must-work-hard" attitude. One of the film's most powerful scenes takes place in a classroom where Deraldo and other migrants watch an indoctrination-style cartoon created by a subway construction company for their new migrant employees. The cartoon slide display uses a hard-drinking, knife-wielding *cangaceiro* (bandit) to represent the migrant who loses his city job because of his failure to adapt. The humiliation, anger, and indignity of the work-ers are tangible, although they swallow their pride in order to keep their newfound employment. (That night Deraldo has a dream in which, dressed as a *cangaceiro*, he stands on a street corner and challenges passersby, who point and laugh at him.) After leaving the classroom, Deraldo finds himself walking behind a wooden fence that resembles a cattle chute. The scene is particularly poignant: as he moves through the chute, he stops from time to time to utter a plaintive "moo"—a sound associated with his rural homeland as well as a consciousness of being gradually led toward the slaughter.

Like the subway contractor, his other employers are insensitive and inhumane. They include a neurotic construction boss (who chases Deraldo in a scene with an elevator that rivals the manic antics of Buster Keaton) and a suburban housewife who scolds him after he dances at a pool party with her teenage daughter and her friends. Prior to quitting this job, he pitches a prize piece of Northeastern pottery, a gift from a visiting Northeastern "colonel" friend, into the pool. That pottery and the cattle horns that hang on the woman's living room wall indicate that a certain Northeastern artisan culture has found a commercial niche in the city. But Deraldo has yet to find his place as a balladeer; his verses are rejected by one bookstore manager as being "too regional."

In fact, his chapbooks and most of his possessions have been confiscated by the police as the result of the murder of an American CEO by a migrant laborer-turned-informer by the name of José Severino da Silva (a common name, similar to John Smith; played by Denoy de Oliveira) who looks exactly like Deraldo and has the same last name. The doppelganger intrigue provides the suspense for the film as the "good" Deraldo protests his innocence in the face of the "bad" José's action. Escaping the policemen who arrive late one night at his shack in a *favela,* he sees fellow migrants momentarily illuminated by the headlights of passing cars. Andrade's image of the shantytown and its migrant population is all the more powerful because the solemn faces of men, women, and children disappear as quickly as they appear, as if swallowed up by the menacing urban landscape. After numerous humiliations and frustrations as a fugitive and day laborer, Deraldo tracks down José, who is living in a shantytown on the outskirts. He writes José's tale of migration and disaster into verse, and he uses modern printing techniques to publish his booklet. One of the final scenes shows Deraldo's successful transition to the city as passersby stop to look and purchase his chapbook.

Andrade is careful to show that not every migrant is like the educated and self-assured Deraldo and that hardships and alienation are the norm. The film emphasizes the "barren lives" that most Northeastern migrants experience in the city—as represented by José, who becomes distraught, estranged from his family, and so deranged by his circumstances that he commits murder and is finally taken away in an ambulance. Andrade concludes the film with a series of aerial shots of São Paulo, whose immense landscape of shantytowns, factory buildings, and modern skyscrapers elicit and register that mixture of fascination and foreboding of a place that for thousands of migrants can be a dream come true or a nightmare in the making.

The theme of migration also creates a sense of *dépaysement* in Tizuka Yamasaki's 1988 period film *Gaijin: Caminhos da liberdade* (Stranger: Roads to Freedom) about the arrival of Japanese farmers to Brazil in the early twentieth century. Among the hundreds to arrive in the port city of Santos in 1908 is Titoe (Kyoko Tsukamoto) and her new husband (Jiro Karawasaki). Because they do not speak Portuguese, they fail to understand that they are being transported to Santa Rosa, a coffee plantation whose reputation for worker abuse is the worst in the area. An excellent example of montage that produces the feeling of *dépaysement* appears early in the film when the newcomers' initial wonder at their surroundings in Santos is followed by shock and disbelief at Santa Rosa's crumbling housing and then followed by flashback images of their poor but tidy homesteads in rural Japan.

Unlike the "fractured" migration of many Brazilians who have come to the United States, Titoe and her family and the other Japanese workers remain together and hold fast to their language and traditions. They steadfastly avoid complaints and walkouts organized by the Italian immigrant worker Enrico (Gianfrancesco Guarnieri), who is fired for "sedition." Early on in the movie, an unidentified British man of means in Santos complains that Brazilians are always praising Europe and Europeans but only want to hire Japanese for their plantations—the suggestion being that European laborers of the period, especially those who participated in strikes and revolution, could be problematic—a suggestion that the character Enrico confirms. (Later, a British entrepreneur tells Santa Rosa's owner: "Agitation is bad. Kill it before it takes root—call in the police.")

At the same time, Yamasaki shows the steady yet difficult compliance of the Japanese to the demands of their Brazilian boss and how they try to deal honorably with Santa Rosa's corrupt accounts and balances system. Not every Japanese remains in the inner colony: Titoe's brother is attracted to a young Italian girl, and he finally runs off; and an older woman who is both a wife and mother dresses in her best Japanese traditional clothing be-

7.7 *Gaijin,* Tizuka Yamasaki (1980)

fore hanging herself after months of pining for her homeland. After Titoe's husband dies from lack of medical attention, she escapes with her newborn daughter and a few others, and together, like *retirantes,* they make their way to the city. (The husband's last words to Titoe are: "Go back to Japan. Look for a father for our daughter.") A fast-forward in time shows a more prosperous Titoe who is now a factory worker with her own domestic help. But when she suggests to her daughter that they return to Japan, the young girl is reluctant. Her response, "Mother, you go and then come back," shows that despite being Japanese, she regards her mother's country as a foreign land.

Yamasaki's 2005 *Gaijin 2: Ama-me como sou* (Stranger 2: Love Me As I Am) takes up the story of Titoe (Aya Ono) in the 1940s after her move to southern Paraná state, where being a Japanese during World War II was easier than in São Paulo. The film is an epic tale that encompasses three generations of Titoe's family; the more contemporary plot describes the impact of President Collor's 1990 austerity program on her granddaughter, Maria (Tamlyn Tomita), and her husband, Gabriel (Jorge Perrugoria), who temporarily move in with Titoe after his company goes bankrupt. The turn-of-the-century image of Brazil as a mecca for migrants from abroad changes drastically because of the country's economic instability, and Gabriel leaves his homeland to become a *dekassegui*, or temporary worker, in Japan's booming economy. News in Brazil of a major earthquake in Hyogo, where Gabriel is employed, force Maria and her daughter to go in search of him in Japan. Their wonder at an entire population who looks just like them is tempered greatly by the prejudice of the Japanese, whose language and culture are markedly different from their own.

In the tradition of early Cinema Novo, *Gaijin 2* emphasizes the resilience of the migrant, although it only scratches the surface of the question posed more directly at the conclusion of *Vidas secas*: what will the future be like for children who migrate to a foreign land? In the case of *Vidas secas*, we can see the myriad problems that the family faces even in their briefest encounters with the tiny town and "civilization." The children's demonstrated precociousness and inquisitive nature suggest their potential for a successful transition to a better life in the city that their parents talk about at the end of the film; and the fact that they all speak Portuguese—even if only rudimentarily—is important. What Yamasaki's film leaves unresolved is the situation of the children of the *dekassegui*, who are forced to travel back and forth between Brazil and Japan and whose slim hold on the different linguistic and cultural codes inhibits development.[23] That situation is a more recent one, although its potential for transforming the Japanese culture in Brazil is real and imminent.

The Road Home

It is important to note that Titoe never returns to Japan and the younger generations make the journey that she had imagined. But while she had long desired to return to her homeland, Gabriel and his family have no sentimental attachment to Japan, and their forced migration is far from pleasurable. Directors Walter Salles and Daniela Thomas already had explored a similar situation in their 1995 film *Terra estrangeira*. An older Basque immigrant and seamstress (Laura Cardoso) who lives modestly in São Paulo with her Brazilian-born son, Paco (Fernando Alves Pinto), banks her hard-earned monies to pay for a trip back home. As in *Gaijin 2*, Collor's economic plan has drastic consequences: after learning that Collor has frozen all bank accounts, she suffers a heart attack and dies. Up to this point, Paco, a dreamy student with pretensions for a theatrical career, has given little heed to his mother's talk about returning home, but in his grieving, he uncovers picture postcards of her beloved San Sebastián and becomes more desperate. Needing money to survive, he agrees to deliver a package to Lisbon for an antiques dealer named Igor (Luís Melo) whom he meets in a bar. He is pleased with the assignment, since he will earn considerable money for his courier job, and he will be able to fulfill his mother's dream of seeing her birthplace.

Shot in black and white, *Terra estrangeira* has a noir-like plot and atmosphere, especially evident in the second half of the film when Igor and his international gangster buddies attempt to recover the package, which *is* "the stuff that dreams are made of" because it contains diamonds hidden in a violin case. The plot twists and turns: Paco is robbed of the package and feverishly tracks down Alex, the girlfriend of his murdered contact in Lisbon, whom he believes has the violin case. Igor and company give chase through Lisbon's dark, winding streets and pursue the couple north toward San Sebastián, where Paco decides they should hide out. Gravely wounded in a shootout with the villains at a restaurant just before the Spanish border, Paco will probably not live to see his mother's homeland. The film has an ironic ending similar to John Huston's *Treasure of the Sierra Madre*: the violin is in the hands of a blind man, who performs for change in Lisbon's underground and has no knowledge of the hidden diamonds. A close-up shows the gems spilling onto the floor as he plays in a darkened corner of the metro. The tiny stones scatter and disappear like bits of gravel under the feet of passengers, who like Paco and Alex up north, rush toward their destinations.

Terra estrangeira takes up the migratory issues made popular by Cinema Novo, except that now the migration pattern is away from Brazil's metropolitan areas to the former colonial power Portugal, whose economic buildup since 1986 (as a result of its membership in the European Union) has attracted thousands of Brazilians in search of a better life.[24] Alex's job in a dismal Lisbon tavern shows that speaking Portuguese does not guarantee a successful transition to an otherwise foreign land. The film also has scenes between Paco and a group of Angolans who have fled their country because of the protracted civil war. Social and racial prejudices within this complex Lusophone world form the backdrop for a film that is darker than *Gaijin 2* and points to the various obstacles facing a younger and more educated Brazilian migrant population.

Salles's *Central do Brasil* is closer to early Cinema Novo productions. The movie begins with the arrival of Ana (Soia Lira) and her son, Josué (Vinícius de Oliveira), in Rio and their attempt to locate his father, who migrated there some time earlier and seems to have vanished. In the large, bustling bus station, they encounter Dora (Fernanda Montenegro), a middle-aged former teacher who earns money by writing and posting letters for illiterate migrants. (She actually stashes the letters at home in order to pocket the postage.) That single, brief encounter forever changes the lives of Ana, Josué, and Dora. After Dora writes a letter for them, Ana and her son leave the station filled with hope; but, like Macabéa's, Ana's contentment is cut short; she is run over by a bus outside the station.

Without family or money, Josué lives and sleeps in the terminal. After a couple of days, an uneasy Dora takes Josué home and perks up considerably after striking a deal with a private adoption firm that gives her a finder's fee. She later retrieves Josué after a friend shames her by pointing out that such agencies are warehouses for buying and selling children for people in need of organ transplants. Dora decides to help Josué find his father, and they travel to the Northeast—a journey that is as much a voyage out of Rio as a psychological voyage inward for the embittered ex-teacher, whose charge is a sweet but precocious pupil.

7.8 *Terra estrangeira,* Walter Salles and Daniela Thomas (1995)

7.9 *Central do Brasil,* Walter Salles (1998)

Salles's film suggests that you can go home again. Josué locates his absent father (who is traveling when they finally reach his new address in the Northeast) as well as two adult brothers who know nothing of Ana's and Josué's existence but embrace their half-brother and take him in as their own. In an essay on Brazilian films of the 1990s, Ismail Xavier points out that the theme of reverse migration places *Central do Brasil* in direct dialogue with Cinema Novo (2003, 61); the entire film is built around issues that Cinema Novo brought to public attention, in particular Northeastern migration to the city, poverty, and corruption. (Dora initially swindles her poor clients, just like the landowner cheats Fabiano in *Vidas secas.*[25] The bogus adoption ring is a new addition to the various criminal acts perpetrated on Brazil's youth and most vulnerable citizens.) Following a long and eventful trip that binds the woman and boy together in friendship and affection, Dora leaves Josué with his family and returns home. In an interesting variation on Cinema Novo productions, Salles portrays the Northeast not as an impoverished region but as a rural community whose communal way of life appears superior to that of the city.

Mean Streets

In recent years, images of poor and abandoned children have moved from the periphery to center stage in news reports on Brazil. One of the earliest films to focus on this subject was Pereira dos Santos's *Rio, 40 graus*. In capturing the struggles and resilience of shantytown children in Rio, Pereira dos Santos followed the cinematic lead of Luis Buñuel, whose 1950 classic, *Los olvidados* (*The Young and the Damned*), examined youth and crime in Mexico City. In many ways, Argentine-born Hector Babenco's 1980 *Pixote: A lei do fraco* (Pixote: The Law of the Weak, based on journalist José Louzeiro's 1977 novel, *Infância dos mortos* (Childhood of the Dead), is a contemporary version of these two important films. Like *Los olvidados*, it is relentless in exposing the dark world that children experience and to which they sometimes contribute; but like *Rio, 40 graus*, it is also sympathetic toward its young protagonists (a sentiment that Buñuel avoided altogether), especially the freckle-faced Pixote (Fernando Ramos da Silva), whose image became synonymous with the plight of Brazil's "young and damned."[26]

In registering the struggle of poor children in the city, *Central do Brasil* and *Pixote* follow the model of *Rio, 40 graus*, but they also differ from their predecessor and each other in interesting ways. The tranquil, golden landscape in which Paco's tight-knit, Northeastern family lives is utopian in comparison to the brutal Northeast of early Cinema Novo productions; moreover, *Central do Brasil* subverts the idealized notion of the big city as the migrant's promised land by focusing on swindles and other unsavory enterprises.

In *Pixote*, the blood ties that provide children with some measure of love and a much-needed safety net in Cinema Novo films as diverse as *Rio, 40 graus*, *Vidas secas*, *Bye Bye Brasil*, and even *Macunaíma* are entirely absent. In one of the most moving moments in the film, a traumatized Pixote suckles at the breast of the prostitute Sueli (Marília Pera), who has recently aborted a fetus in her bathroom. Sueli becomes upset by her maternal feelings and pulls Pixote away from her breast, ordering him to leave. Babenco is forceful in his denunciation of Brazilian society's failure toward children who are mistreated and even murdered by the very agencies created to protect and rehabilitate them. Because of systemic failures and the difficulty of the few individuals (the reformatory's doctor, for example) to counter

7.10 *Pixote,* Hector Babenco (1980)

abuses, the children go from victims to perpetrators of violence and often die young.[27]

In *Vidas secas,* the young boys' view of the *sertão* that lies ahead (the commanding shot that ends and brings the movie full circle) includes the figures of their parents, who have been talking about a better life and whom they follow into the future—whatever it may hold. By contrast, Pixote has nothing secure or even reassuring in his sights as he walks down railroad tracks into the unknown. The film suggests that the future of this child, who has already killed and now carries a gun, is frightening; and although Pixote has demonstrated remarkable resilience in his various run-ins with characters from the reformatory and the city outside, his survival will be difficult at best.[28]

Babenco's utter despair over the condition of children in poverty, which was not typical of Cinema Novo in the 1960s, is what makes *Pixote* so difficult to watch and in many ways more disturbing than more recent but also downbeat films such as Fernando Meirelles and Kátia Lund's 2001 *Cidade de Deus* (City of God) and José Padilha's 2003 *Ônibus 174* (Bus 174).

The relationship between the blockbuster hit *Cidade de Deus,* the critically acclaimed documentary *Ônibus 174,* and earlier movies about children and poverty is interesting to contemplate. More in synch with *Pixote* and Cinema Novo social realist films, *Ônibus 174* is a cinematic call to action that does not completely despair of a better future for children raised in poverty—this despite the new levels of violence in Brazil that have made headlines both locally and abroad. The film documents an incident that occurred on June 12, 2000, when an attempted robbery on a bus in Rio turned into a hijacking that was televised live across the nation, transfixing an entire population with images of the hijacker, his victims, and the police. The ordeal, which lasted for several hours, culminated with the deaths of two young people: the black hijacker, Sandro do Nascimento, who died at the hands of poorly equipped, undertrained, and frustrated police, and a white female hostage whom Sandro accidentally shot.

Padilha juxtaposes TV footage of the hijacking with commentaries by a range of individuals including former hostages who address various concerns such as the incompetence of the police and city officials who mishandled the hijacking and the pervasive discrimination against poor, black youths like Sandro. We learn that, like many children on the streets, Sandro was traumatized by a violent act (his mother's murder) and grew up to a life of petty thievery and detentions. On this particular day, Sandro, a survivor of the 1993 Candelária massacre (when vigilante police fired machine guns at street children sleeping on the steps of a church, killing eight youths and wounding many others) bungled a robbery of passengers on a bus in Rio, defied the police, and ended up handcuffed and finally suffocated in the backseat of a police car.

Different from other street crimes, however, this specific attempted robbery turned into a televised event that catapulted Sandro's image and story into the homes of millions of television viewers. He became a symbol of Brazil's failure to address the problem of street children and the violence by and against them. Similar to *Ônibus 174, Cidade de Deus* also focuses on street children and violence, but unlike films in the Cinema Novo tradition, which include Babenco's *Pixote* and his 2003 prison movie, *Carandiru,* it is not a protest film. Adapted from an autobiographical novel by Paulo Lins, *Cidade de Deus* is an exposé of violence perpetrated by and against children in the City of God slum on the periphery in Rio. But in glamorizing acts of violence by gangs as well as the police, it undermines any sense of moral outrage, social indignation, or national urgency.

Still another way to think about *Ônibus 174* and *Cidade de Deus* is their different approaches to stories about two black youths from the shantytowns. Rocket (Alexandre Rodrigues), the protagonist in *Cidade de Deus,* narrates his own childhood journey from the streets of City of God to the city, where he moves up the ladder from newspaper delivery boy to a fledgling photojournalist. Despite various experiments with camera angles, color, music, and time, *Cidade de Deus* is basically modeled after the *Bildungsroman,* a nineteenth-century linear narrative that follows a protagonist's journey through trials and tribulations to a realization of some truth that brings happiness and success—which, in the case of Rocket, is his move toward middle-class status. It also has something in common with the Horatio Alger "rise-to-success" narratives that were once popular in Hollywood. By contrast, in *Ônibus 174* there is no linear development of the protagonist's character; we are simply given a montage of television footage and pieces of information that provide a sociological idea of who he was and why he did what he did. Moreover, *Ônibus 174* is never technically slick; the grainy television footage recalls the "imperfect" cinema of the 1960s, which, born out of economic constraints, created an urgent, on-the-spot style.

Ultimately, both *Cidade de Deus* and *Ônibus 174* are films about sensationalized violence in the media. In the former film, Rocket's budding talents with the camera—a gift to him from a charismatic drug dealer (Bené Phelipe Haagensen)—are called upon by a gang chief (Leandro Firmino), who strikes a menacing pose with gang members holding machine guns. That dramatic photograph serendipitously finds its way to the front page of the newspaper where Rocket works and literally "rockets" him into a career as a photojournalist. The movie makes no commentary about the newspaper's reportage or methods; it makes clear that violence sells newspapers, but it seems unconcerned about the success of Rocket, who proceeds to "shoot" his community for the media and for his own personal gain. *Ônibus 174* takes a more critical approach to the media, showing how the daylong coverage of the hijacking resulted in nothing beyond shocking images of violence and death. A self-reflexive narrative, *Ônibus 174* desensationalizes the television footage by dissecting and juxtaposing it with interviews and other material that form a different narrative about crime and violence.

7.11 *Cidade de Deus,* Fernando Meirelles (2001)

7.12 *Ônibus 174,* José Padilha (2003)

Cidade de Deus has a happy ending for Rocket, but there seems little hope for the many other children who appear in the movie. The reality of that hopelessness is suggested by a final scene in which the gang chief, who commits mass murder as a child, is murdered himself by a gang of young street children. The tragic implication of that act is left hanging as the enterprising Rocket, like the chicken that expertly weaves and bobs at the beginning and end of the movie, miraculously elides the various obstacles in his way and not only survives but thrives.

In his fifteen minutes of fame, the real-life Sandro of *Ônibus 174* became part of the dystopian reality that films like *Cidade de Deus* have chosen to portray. But as Padilha's film shows, it was Sandro who broke through the hypnotic nature of the media coverage by shouting recriminations against those who had carried out the Candelária massacre. Just as his own invisibility transforms to material form on the television, the massacre, which had made headlines years earlier but went unresolved and disappeared from newspaper and television coverage, returned as a specter of those wounded and dead children who were mercilessly gunned down. Padilha does not excuse or condone Sandro's actions, but he does show how Sandro became the voice for those children who were left for dead and about whom the nation seemed to care only as long as the media took up their plight. Sandro's raging voice on the bus could have been stopped, but it was the specter of that massacre, along with the city administrators' fear of a potential political backlash for killing him live on TV, that made a televised shooting by police undesirable. Ultimately Sandro was captured and hustled into a police car, where his anger was finally silenced.

Land of the Future

Brazil's emergence as a global economic power alongside China, Russia, and India seems in contradiction with its daily media coverage of unprecedented levels of government corruption, rampant poverty, and widespread violence. Rio de Janeiro in particular has sustained several body blows to its reputation as Brazil's premier tourist mecca, and its beachfront communities now look askance at hillside slums whose dimensions defy the imagination. By contrast, the Northeast has become a popular tourist destination, and its once-tranquil coastal capitals are now bustling urban centers. In Recife, for example, tourists and locals dance to *forró* and high-volume *axé* music from the *trios elétricos* (trucks with loudspeakers) that cruise up and down trendy Boa Viagem in a simulacrum of carnival celebration; poverty is no less dire in Recife than in Rio, but the lack of hillsides makes it less visible.

In the Brazilian cinema, uplifting, rags-to-riches films like Breno Silveira's 2005 major hit, *Os dois filhos de Francisco* (The Two Sons of Francisco), about the rise of a young country-singing duo appear alongside Sérgio Machado's 2005 *Baixa Cidade* (Lower City) about prostitution in Bahia and Nelson Pereira dos Santos's 2006 *Brasília 18%*, a film noir about political intrigue and murder that is perhaps too close to the national reality to be regarded as "entertainment." Detective fiction and other literature by popular authors such as Jô Soares, Ruben Fonseca, Paulo Lins, and Chico Buarque de Holanda explore the desperate, seamy side of everyday life, while the mega-best-selling novels of New Age writer Paulo Coelho offer solace and encouragement in the form of biblical-style parables and individual spiritual journeys in which faith and perseverance overcome adversity.

The extremes of Brazilian popular culture, which oscillates between carnival and dystopia, make it difficult for anyone to assess the national mood of the nascent twenty-first century. Given the inherently speculative nature of any writing about the future of Brazilian identity, I have constructed this epilogue more along the lines of a collage of iconographic images similar to the ones found on early maps. My aim here is to suggest the complexity and diversity of the contemporary Brazilian imaginary and to provide a tentative mapping of new trends and recurrent concerns, drawn mostly from journalism and television.

The Amazon, Ecology, and the Land(less)

Covering approximately 60 percent of the country, the Amazon River Basin historically has held a special place in the way Brazil has been imagined. Once described as "the Sweet Sea" and "Empress and Queen of all Floods,"[1] the river itself has been the subject of wonder and fantasy since the arrival of the Europeans in 1500. A 1558 map of the region represents it as a long, green serpent whose tapered head juts out at Belém and looks eastward, as if watching for oceanic prey. In 1500, the Spaniard Vicente Yáñez Pizón wrote of an Amazonian *animal monstruoso*, which turned out to be an opossum—supposedly the first indigenous South American animal ever captured and recorded by a European (in Papavero et al. 2000, 1). Later, in the 1540s, Spanish friar Gaspar de Carvajal wrote about a Brazilian race of fierce women called the Amazons, thus reviving the ancient Greek myth about a female warrior tribe.[2] In later years, especially in the eighteenth and nineteenth centuries, the Amazon region attracted myriad local and foreign scientific expeditions that produced thousands of colorful illustrations of unknown flora and fauna as well as detailed ethnographies of the various indigenous peoples.

The discovery of rubber in the Amazon in the early nineteenth century was followed by a boom period that financed the construction of the jungle capital Manaus, replete with riverfront buildings and docks, electric trolley cars, and the Teatro Amazonas, a world-renowned domed opera house whose image appeared on early Brazilian postcards. A postcard dated 1906 shows a frontal view of the opera house, a huge structure that easily dwarfed adjacent riverfront buildings. In another postcard panorama taken from the rear, the Teatro's multicolored dome is shown rising above the nearby jungle as if it were the eighth wonder of the world. The "golden era" and gradual internationalization of the Amazon region are suggested by still another postcard image of the Belém water tower that was built in 1912. Constructed from elaborate ironwork imported from France, it resembles a smaller version of the Eiffel Tower in Paris or the Santa Justa Elevator in Lisbon.

E.1 The opera house in Manaus. Permission, Latin American and Iberian Institute, University of New Mexico.

Other images associated with the Amazonian industrial "golden age" are more disturbing. These include photographs of displaced Indians, devastated forest areas, and the Madeira-Marmoré or "Mad Maria" railway folly, which later became the subject of Márcio de Souza's ironic novella *Mad Maria* (1980) and a 2005 TV Globo miniseries of the same title. In 1914, one year after the collapse of the rubber market that had prompted the construction of this useless rail line, Brazilian newspapers ran front-page stories with pictures of former U.S. president Teddy Roosevelt wearing a pith helmet and proudly displaying his animal trophies. Roosevelt had barely survived a "scientific" expedition into the Rio da Dúvida (River of Doubt) tributary to the Amazon. In fact, the name of the River of Doubt that nearly took his life was officially changed to Roosevelt River, and visitors to the area nowadays can stay at the Roosevelt River Lodge.

The media continue to shape the image of the Amazon today; indeed the news coverage of preservation and ecological issues, together with reports on macro- and micro-economic debates, have kept the rainforest in the forefront of the local and global conscience. Among the most powerful contemporary emblems of the Amazon are Sebastião Salgado's black-and-white photographs from the 1980s of gold miners scaling the muddy slopes of the Serra Pelada (Bald Mountain) with sacks of dirt lashed onto their backs. These and other dramatic portraits reveal the exploitative, hellish labor conditions that accompanied the euphoric reports in 1980 of a gold strike. Later reports of gold discovered in the Serra Parima, a mountainous region inhabited by the Yanomami tribe, drove thousands of prospectors even deeper into the Amazon. Their beehive population centers and tent encampments were captured by photographers as emergency-action reports on the Yanomami's displacement and decimation from disease transmitted by outsiders were released in the press.

In the 1980s, debates and protests over mining, logging, and the proliferation of agribusinesses and cattle ranches that claimed thousands of acres of rainforest terrain found a leader in Chico Mendes, a *seringueiro* (rubber tapper) who gained worldwide attention and became a popular hero.[3] His assassination by a disgruntled rancher in 1988 turned him into a martyr and gave further impetus to the rainforest conservation movement. More recently, the U.S.-born nun Dorothy Stang, who lived in the Amazon for more than twenty years, was killed after accusing loggers and ranchers of threatening peasant farmers. The flurry of media coverage over her death in February 2005 took place as loggers and their families conducted mass protests against a government decision that had halted logging in the Amazon the previous year. Those protests resulted in an about-face by officials, who reinstated logger permits. Newspaper images and reports of the murdered nun, who was a Brazilian citizen, appeared at the same time as images and reports of buses captured and burned by the pro-logging protestors who had blocked all transport on the BR-163 highway. A photograph of a bus's charred, skeletal remains was a symbolic reminder of the wartorn area's land feuds, outlaw capitalism, and internecine warfare.

Ever since the formation of the *capitanias,* whose names and boundaries were fixed on sixteenth-century maps, land distribution has been and continues to be a factor in the welfare of the people and the nation. Reports estimate that two-thirds of the nation's arable land is in the hands of 3 percent of the population. The internationalization of the Amazon was effected by large-scale occupation of public lands by corporations, smaller companies, and wealthy landowners, among others, who subdivided their holdings and sold off sections for profit. Some of the areas to which companies laid claim are the size of small nations, and, as Brodansky and Senna's film *Iracema* documents, the razing of forests for ranching has had major consequences for the local cultures and ecosystems.

At the same time, the reality of the hundreds of thousands of Brazilians without land has come to greater national and international attention through protests organized by the Movimento dos Trabalhadores Rurais Sem Terra (Movement of Landless Rural Workers), popularly known as the MST, which is the largest social movement in Latin America. Allied for years with the Workers Party, the movement has its own history and martyrs, as illustrated by Tetê Moraes's 1987 documentary *Terra para Rose* (Land for Rose). The expectations of the MST skyrocketed following President Luiz Inácio Lula da Silva's election to the presidency in 2000, but despite the government's distribution of some lands to peasant farmers, as of this writing the MST is disenchanted with Lula's slow response to the problem. Reports of plots being sold to locals by peasants who gained title to unused land through government intervention have added to the disillusionment of the larger population.

Meanwhile there has been positive news about the Amazon. The year 2004 marked the discovery of some 20,000 new species in the area, including insects, fish, and mammals, and the results for the future look equally promising if not more so. A British TV series called *Amazon Abyss* asked viewers to vote on proposed names for new species as a way of involving the public more directly in ecological matters (McKie and Thorpe 2005). The extent to which the Amazon and conservation are in the forefront of the Brazilian consciousness is suggested by an unpublished survey study titled "Quem é o brasileiro?" (Who Is the Brazilian?) by Universidade de São Paulo Professor Antônio Ribeiro de Almeida, who interviewed 1,610 people from the states of São Paulo and Minas Gerais. Asked to consider a list of nearly one hundred traits, the majority of participants in the survey rated "respeita e preserva a natureza" (respects and preserves nature) as the most important attribute of an *ideal* Brazilian. What is noteworthy is the priority given to this attribute (23.4 percent) over the next-highest ideal traits—that an ideal Brazilian is "honest" (20.1 percent), "work-oriented" (19.9 percent), and "well-educated" (15.8 percent). Although there is always a gap between perceptions of the real and ideal, it seems significant that preservation was nowhere near the top of those characteristics that the respondents attributed to typical citizens of the country.[4]

The extreme economic contrasts in the Amazon region, as shown in movies like *Iracema* and *Bye Bye Brasil,* are not all that different from those that exist today, but the growth of global capital has resulted in some unusual sights. The selling of Avon products by women who travel by boat for their "door-to-door" business is one example of recent trends in local entrepreneurship. In 2003, the governor of Amazonas created floating governmental offices in the form of multidecker riverboats that provide citizens with access to health care and other social programs. High-technology surveillance systems have also been constructed to monitor drug trafficking in two million square miles of the Amazon, and there are plans to build special airplanes with sensors and radar to evaluate pollution levels and illegal mining. In space, satellites assess deforestation and provide advance alerts for flooding or fire. Eco- and other kinds of tourism on the Amazon River have grown substantially, and the desire for ecologically friendly housing in forested regions of the Amazon Basin and nationwide has seen a move in architectural design to embrace the out-of-doors rather than raze forests.[5]

Brazilian *telenovelas* have produced some of the most influential images of the Amazon in recent years. Between 2005 and 2007, three *telenovelas* were centered on the region, two of which—*Amazônia: De Galvez a Chico Mendes* (Amazonia: From Galvez to Chico Mendes) in 2007 and the aforementioned *Mad Maria*—were major prime-time TV Globo productions. By far the most unusual of the three was *Mãe do Rio* (River Mother) in 2006, an Amazonia-based TV Tucuju production conceived and written by Gilvam Borges, a senator from the state of Amapá, along with local artists and series director Ângela Nunes. Unlike *Mad Maria* and *Amazônia, Mãe do Rio* focuses on *caboclo* culture and the appeal and power of local myths such as the legend of the *boto* (dolphin) that transforms itself at nighttime into a seductive man who impregnates young, unmarried women. Although a modest production by Brazilian *telenovela* standards, *Mãe do Rio* was promoted to local audiences and on the Internet as a unique and authentic "view from within" of the Amazon as opposed to "outsider" images by Hollywood and Brazil's major television networks.

TV Tujucu's critique probably had an influence on TV Globo's production of *Amazônia,* which seems partly based on the 1976 best-seller *Galvez, o imperador do Acre (The Emperor of the Amazon,* 1980) by Amazonian novelist Mário Souza. The Globo production focuses on two distinct historical periods: the rubber-boom era of the late nineteenth century and the more recent age of environmental protest, which the series frames with the rise and death of Chico Mendes. Unlike Manchete network's earlier *Amazônia* series, in which the region was largely used as exotic backdrop, Globo's 2007 version has been promoted by Globo as a means to raise the public's awareness of the rainforest's continuing decimation. The relationship between fiction and reality, entertainment and social consciousness grew closer when members of the Globo *Amazônia* cast published an online open letter to the public in the form of a manifesto-petition. In it, they denounced the devastation wrought by deforestation and encouraged viewers to act by signing the petition. More than 200,000 signatures were collected shortly after the petition went online. The actor-activists' ultimate target for the petition was 1 million signatures, following the receipt of which they planned to send the document to President Lula.

Favela Sprawl

The conflicting images of Brazil as the utopian "land of the future" where "God is Brazilian" and as a dystopia of burgeoning crime and poverty have grown more extreme and yet are melding into one another in ways never before imagined, especially in the relationship between landscape and architecture.[6] In the past, the relative costs to market Copacabana and Ipanema as tourist havens were not anywhere near the $18 million spent in 2002, because the *favelas,* although visible on the hillsides, were smaller and more removed from luxury hotels and condominiums. As the hillside communities grew and spread, newer, upscale neighborhoods were constructed farther south along the coast. Real estate companies for upscale and gated housing in Barra da Tijuca (a beach area less accessible by public bus service than crowded Copacabana and Ipanema) regularly advertise secure onsite shopping, restaurants, and movie theaters in an effort to make potential residents and tourists feel more insulated from the rising crime in the *favelas.*

But the haves and have-nots live in increasingly close proximity, so much so that iron bars on windows, iron fencing, alarms, not to mention the twenty-four-hour *porteiros,* or doormen, are standard for most middle-class housing, while pricey resorts and residential developments are marketed as gated and guarded communities.[7] Despite the various security measures taken by the middle and upper classes in Rio, hillside shantytowns abut expensive beachfront properties in Ipanema and São Conrado as well as in Santa Teresa near downtown. Newspaper articles and news photographs focus on this topographic melding of wealth and abject poverty. For example, once highly desirable São Conrado highrise apartments that were built facing the hillsides are being sold by owners who fear *balas perdidas* (stray bullets) from the massive and encroaching Rocinha *favela*. The value of these residences has plummeted some 20 percent, in contrast to condominiums in the same building that face the sea.

Lifestyles Brazil Digest, a magazine published in Rio for the "expat and visitor community in Brazil," explicitly states the now well-known fact: "What lies outside the windows of a given apartment in Rio will often carry greater importance than what is inside." Of the various problem vistas, which include noisy bus routes or back alleyways, the editors remark: "perhaps worst of all in the mind of the market [is] a view of one of Rio's favelas" (2005, 38). The terrestrial constellation of lights from the *favelas* at nighttime is denser and remains one of the scenic wonders of the city, although that glittering sight has now merged in the minds of many with the sparks produced by gunfire.

E.2 Early *favela* sprawl. Permission, Latin American and Iberian Institute, University of New Mexico.

With newspaper coverage of the growing *favelas* in Rio and São Paulo (two cities that once rivaled one another as "best" places to live in Brazil and are now described as the "worst"), hot market properties promoted by *Lifestyles* and other real estate magazines are in remote areas such as seaside Búzios (made famous by Brigitte Bardot's repeat visits in the 1950s) and small coastal towns in the Northeast. *Lifestyles'* brightly colored illustrations of these towns show none of the *favela* sprawl (at least for the present) that appears even in the environmentally protected enclaves of the Costa Verde (Green Coast). Situated some seventy miles outside Rio, the sprawl in the Costa Verde is a relatively recent phenomenon that shows that the poor will migrate to even more remote regions to work and live.

Rio's Tribunal Auditing Office reported that the number of *favelados,* favela residents, in the Costa Verde town of Angra dos Reis rose 419 percent from 1991 to 2000 (Engelbrecht 2005). The 20,000 additional people were drawn by global capital in the form of new luxury hotels and resorts, as well as the construction of the BR-101 highway that now links the Costa Verde to Rio and São Paulo. One of Brazil's most prized ecological South-Central retreats, advertised as having as many islands as there are days in the year, the Costa Verde and Angra in particular have undergone drastic change as slums overtake once-preserved "green" areas.

Prominent local businesses and multinational corporations in the industrial capital of São Paulo seem less timid about the *favela* and in the spirit of entrepreneurial enterprise have moved into areas adjacent to or within *favelas.* This is the case of Daslu, the 183,000-square-foot elite "shopping bunker" (Benson 2005), whose *palazzo*-inspired architecture contrasts sharply with the *favela.* The construction of this high-end shoppers' paradise peaked the ire of some socially conscious *paulistas,* who waged protests outside the store and cajoled well-heeled citizens who rushed through Daslu's heavily guarded doors.[8] Some of the country's most acclaimed hotel chains have built highrise structures side by side with poor São Paulo neighborhoods, and *favelados* are feeling the pinch. In an ironic twist, a trendy bar in Vila Olímpia, a poor area that now sports a five-star Blue Tree chain hotel, is called Bar Favela.

Brooklin Novo is another area in São Paulo where the very poor and the very wealthy co-exist, although in this instance, corporate Brazil razed most of the original slum to construct highrise buildings. Still, the *favela* survives, and corporations employ security guards to patrol and greet visitors to expensive enclaves. Even the Canadian consulate's office in Brooklin Novo can view a *favela* in the distance. Of course in São Paulo, the poor do not live eye-to-eye with highrise occupants. In the case of Brooklin Novo, the remaining *favela*, which extends considerably, looks small from the thirtieth floor of a highrise office building and is completely overshadowed by the panorama of the downtown skyline. The broad windows of one corporation's "stress-free" room for employees has a *favela* view. Whether or not employees think about the less fortunate or the possibility of stray bullets there is difficult to say. The room's dim lighting, comfortable sofas, and soothing sound track may help ease or eliminate any troubled sensibility.

One of the chief ironies of the current scene is that although Brazil's tourist engine and travel sections for newspapers like *The New York Times* continue to promote postcard images of Rio's Pão de Açúcar (Sugar Loaf) and its beaches from Copacabana to Barra, the *favela* has also become a commodity. In addition to prepaid guided tours of certain *favela* neighborhoods, tourists and others can purchase *favela* artwork of various kinds at local art fairs. The least expensive purchases include small, hand-carved wooden blocks, each of which represents the exterior of a shack. Buy four or five of these different-sized pieces, and you can design your own miniature hillside *favela* and display it on a wall as picturesque folk art. There are also *favelas* carved into larger pieces of the local brazilwood, whose rich red color, textured grain, and polished surface makes poverty look opulent. The most expensive works are oil paintings that range from abstract *morro* (hillside) reproductions in muted red and brown hues to more detailed, although far from realistic, representations of brightly colored, tightly knit dwellings. Some of the canvases are small, while others are quite large. Generally speaking, the larger the image of poverty, the more money it costs the buyer.

Among Brazil's best-selling books in the 1960s was a diary written by Carolina Maria de Jesus, whose 1960 *Quarto do despejo* (*Child of the Dark*, 1962) described her rugged life as a single mother in a São Paulo slum. Brazilian readers were moved by her daily accounts of collecting paper and aluminum for resale, carrying water in cans, and fighting hunger and disease while putting up with noisy and nosey neighbors. Newspapers and magazines chronicled her rags-to-(comparative)-riches story, and she was photographed with political and literary celebrities. Ironically, her second book, *Casa de alvenaria: Diário de uma ex-favelada* (Block House: Diary of

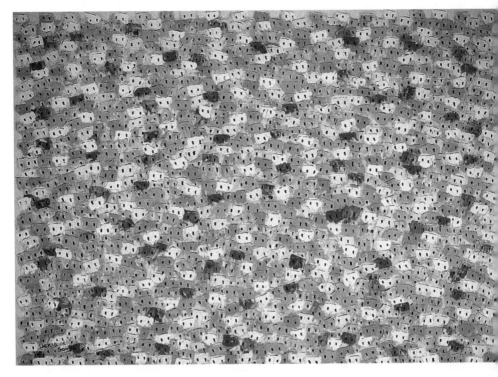

E.3 *Favela,* by Laerte de Sousa (2007). Courtesy of Laerte de Sousa.

an Ex-Favela Resident), published in 1961 and translated in 1997 as *I Want To Have a Little House: The Second Diary of Carolina Maria de Jesus,* which focused on her celebrity and purchase of a modest, cement-block house in a working-class neighborhood, failed to attract a large readership. Perhaps this was because the portrait of an *ex-favelada* did not offer the same kind of sensational effects as reading about the forbidden and "exotic" world of the slum.[9]

The *favela* of Carolina Maria de Jesus had none of the topographic presence of today's poor communities, which are massive in size and densely populated. The 1958 film *Black Orpheus* by Marcel Camus provided viewers with a charmingly colorful Rio *favela* where a mostly black population sang, danced, and made love—a utopian image that contrasted sharply with Cinema Novo and later filmmakers' attempts to represent the spread of poverty.

Today's shantytowns are pervaded with drugs and guns, and wars between local and federal police and drug traffickers—not to mention between rival gangs and traffickers themselves—have become part of everyday life. They are the stuff of newspaper headlines and articles, radio and television programs, Internet sites, and fiction and nonfiction books and movies. *Ônibus 174* showed that the consequences of poverty are no longer confined to the *favela*.[10] The artwork of São Paulo artist Vinicius Berton provides a more ironic commentary on the nation's social ills that is nonetheless poignant. People tend to become inured to daily violence on television newscasts and in the newspapers and to reports of corruption, both of which have reached epidemic proportions.

E.4 *Suicides,* by Vinicius Berton (2005). Courtesy of Vinicius Berton.

Political Corruption and Sex Tourism

Headlines about large-scale corruption involving millions of dollars and officials at the highest level of the government has transformed Brazilians' optimism about the country's present and future into widespread disenchantment. The degree of frustration was captured in a photograph on the front page of the Rio daily *O globo* of November 30, 2005, that showed a well-dressed, elderly man striking former Chief of Staff José Dirceu de Oliveira e Silva with his cane. Charged with *mensalão* (vote buying) and other fiscal crimes in the summer of 2005, Dirceu finally resigned his position as chief of staff but held onto his congressional seat until December 2005, when he was found guilty by a majority of the Congress of "breaching parliamentary decorum." (The punishment for his crime was a ten-year embargo on his running for any elected office.) Although Dirceu is just one of many Partido dos Trabalhadores (PT), or Workers Party, officials who have been charged with or found guilty of corruption, he was President Lula's "team captain"—a Karl Rove and Donald Rumsfeld (although of a different political persuasion) rolled into one, who had masterminded Lula's rise to presidential power. The image of Dirceu's "caning" was viewed with both glee and dismay: glee because finally someone had stepped forward to mete out a punishment that the public felt was long overdue; dismay because Dirceu had been instrumental in raising the hope for a better future that the PT and Lula had long promised.

The level of political corruption reported in 2005 and 2006 exceeded even the scandalous financial dealings that led to former President Fernando Collor's impeachment and the death of his financial advisor, P. C. Farias, who had both hands in the till. It is instructive to note how foreign publications represented this crisis for their readers. In July 16, 2004, the London *Times Literary Supplement* carried John Ryle's review of Peter Robb's *A Death in Brazil*, whose account of Farias's rise and fall is couched in a travelogue that surveys violence in Brazilian history and literature while emphasizing the importance of food and sex. The sensationalism of Robb's account was rivaled only by the *Times Literary Supplement*'s cover image. Occupying the magazine's entire front page is a photograph of a young black woman on the beach in a white bikini-thong with the accompanying caption: "Brazil Now."

Unfortunately for Brazil, the foreign fascination with dark-skinned women, which dates back to colonial accounts of "lascivious" indigenous females (accounts that were instrumental in the creation of the hypersexual image of *mulatas* in particular) has propelled a sex industry second only to that of Thailand. Advertised in magazines and on the Internet, sex-tour packages attract mostly working-class males from Europe and the United States. The *Times Literary Supplement* cover image could easily be mistaken for a promotional ad for one of these packages, which include round-trip airfare with lodging and meals in three-, four-, and even five-star hotels. According to police in Recife's beachfront Boa Viagem district, hotels lodge these tourists in special areas complete with restaurants that are separated from the general clientele.[11]

Among the violent incidents reported to police stations in Northeastern tourist towns like Recife are sex crimes by foreigners who mistreat women and even children, who are increasingly brokered for sex. The Internet has given new momentum to an industry that operates behind closed doors despite recent laws enacted to thwart and punish facilitators or traffickers. Child prostitution has reached alarming proportions in the Northeast—so much so that one town mayor took it upon himself to distribute leaflets during the carnival high season to warn tourists about laws against sex with minors. The spread of global capital also has moved the sex industry into more remote places such as the Amazon. As Brodansky and Senna's *Iracema* showed three decades ago, foreign and local exploitation of the rainforest has led to an abuse of the indigenous population not so different from that of the earliest colonial times. The difference today is that the focus of the sexual industry and encounters is increasingly turned toward the country's children.

Black Brazil

The recognition and celebration of African heritage is a recent phenomenon in Brazil. The National Day of Black Consciousness (November 30) established in January 2003 celebrates this heritage, while recent affirmative-action legislation has encouraged Brazilians' self-identification as black. In a 2000 census, 44.7 percent of the population classified themselves as black or mulatto. Former President Fernando Henrique Cardoso's appointment of soccer hero Pelé as Minister of Sports and President Lula's more recent appointment of Gilberto Gil as Minister of Culture were seen as a recognition of blacks; and whether in terms of culture or politics, Brazil's African roots and a new sense of Africanness have become part of the national conscience.

That recognition has yet to translate into a better life for Brazilian blacks. In a United Nations survey of human development, Brazil ranked 73rd out of 173 countries worldwide. However, a separate study showed that if white Brazilians and Brazilians of color were separately categorized, "White Brazil" would rank 44th, while "Black Brazil" would rank 105th. According to a 2003 study of 500 of the country's major companies by the Ethos Institute, only 1.8 percent of high-level executive jobs were held by blacks, who also occupy only 23.4 percent of the lowest-level professional jobs. These figures are reflected in the low percentage of blacks enrolled in the university, which was 2.5 percent in 2000.[12]

While in the United States the Confederate flag has been removed from most public buildings in the South, the words on the flag of the historic mining town Ouro Preto in Minas Gerais have been changed from the 1931 *proetiosum tamen nigrum* (precious although black) to *proetisoum aurum nigrum* (precious black gold). The initial wording referred to the dark, oxidized gold found in the region and was inspired by the eighteenth-century motto *libertas quae sera tamen* (liberty although late) of the Minas rebels who tried to overthrow the monarchy. But with a 70 percent black and mixed-race citizenry, Ouro Preto residents were eager to eliminate the racist implications of the original wording, and a new flag was raised on National Day of Black Consciousness.

National consciousness is political and cultural. In 2001, one of Brazil's most famous samba schools, Beija Flor (Hummingbird), selected the story of an enslaved West African queen as the basis for its songs, dances, floats, and costumes. According to one report, for the first time nearly all of the Beija Flor participants were black or mulatto, including the "queen of the drums," who is generally a "white young starlet with blonde hair" (P. Jones, 2001). A beauty pageant held at the site of the Carandiru prison in São Paulo was another indication of a change in the racial atmosphere. Although the pageant was criticized by some as a state-sponsored glorification of women jailed for crimes against society (Prada 2005), prison officials believed the contest was good for the women's morale. Of the ten finalists, four of whom were white and five of whom were mixed-race or mulatta, the judges selected the dark-skinned Angolan Angélica Nsanguas as the winner. Perhaps this was not the most positive representation for the black community, but the idea of a dark black woman participating in a beauty contest was never popular in Brazil; in the 1940s, when the Teatro Experimental do Negro (Black Experimental Theater) sponsored a black beauty contest in Rio, the event was treated as a scandal.

The recently opened Museu AfroBrasil's images of the poor and enslaved alongside images of important writers and statesmen has elevated black consciousness in original and significant ways. The main exhibits chronicle the history of blacks over the centuries, and one features a large replica of a slave ship accompanied by a sound track composed of cries and whispers. Here Marc Ferrez's nineteenth-century photographs of *baianas* appear alongside Madalena Schwartz's contemporary portraits of famous black figures such as actor Ruth de Souza and *mãe de santo* (priestess) Olga do Aleketo. The collection contains rare items such as a 1865 slave receipt and *cartões de visita* (visiting cards) with photographs of black wet nurses and their small white wards.[13] A particularly shocking photograph from 1899, enlarged to life size, shows a black nurse on her hands and knees and a white child sitting astride her back as if she were a horse. Victor Fond's 1850s lithographs record the backbreaking toil of fieldworkers alongside myriad photographs of *candomblé* rituals and *irmandades* (religious fraternal societies) that were sometimes secret. Housing more than 11,000 works of sculpture, painting, and folk art, the museum is a reaffirmation of an image of Brazil that has been ignored if not suppressed because of a long-held belief of Brazil as a racial democracy.

Blame It on the Simpsons

In April 2002, Fox television's *The Simpsons* aired a segment called "Blame It on Lisa," a tongue-in-cheek reference to Stanley Donen's 1984 film *Blame It on Rio*, which concerns an affair between an older man (Michael Caine) and his best friend's troubled teenage daughter (Michelle Johnson) while the two families vacation in Rio.[14] Although minimally clad women and sexual adventures on the beach are regular fare in Hollywood films about Rio, *The Simpsons* episode, which showed those and a variety of other images and was seen by more than 11 million viewers in the United States, touched a nerve when it was broadcast in Brazil. It spoofed major problems in the country, focusing in particular on daylight robbery, kidnappings,

E.5 "Wet Nurse Playing with Child in Petrópolis," by J. H. Papf (1899)

and abandoned children—topics that U.S. television, newspapers, and the film *Cidade de Deus* have reinforced to U.S. audiences.

In the episode, the Simpsons' young daughter Lisa has "adopted" a Brazilian child named Ronaldo, whom she sponsors through a charitable agency. However, the child mysteriously disappears from the orphanage, and the Simpson family travels to Brazil to find him. (He reappears riding on a carnival float at the end of the program.) Shortly after their arrival in Rio, Homer and Bart are robbed by street children, and Homer is captured at gunpoint on a city street and held for ransom by two thieves. The segment fuels the typical conceptions that North Americans have about "the Marvelous City": in this case Brazilians speak Spanish and there are daily carnivals with people singing and dancing in the streets. Much like early foreign representations of Brazil as an exotic Wild Kingdom sort of place, the TV cartoon depicts Rio as a metropolis overrun with monkeys and poisonous, man-eating snakes.

The Simpsons episode provoked a general ire among television viewers in Brazil and the threat of a lawsuit by Riotur, a government agency that claimed its $18 million campaign to promote Rio as a tourist haven had been irreparably damaged by the cartoon. Fernando Henrique Cardoso, who was president at the time, issued a statement criticizing the distortions in the show. The tourist secretary in Rio launched an attack against the Fox channel, stating that if the company were so deeply concerned about orphaned children like Ronaldo, then it should donate all income from the episode to social programs in Brazil. Ultimately, Fox issued a condescending apology of sorts, adding that if the tepid apology was not sufficient, then Bart would agree to fight Henrique Cardoso in a televised match on the network's "Celebrity Boxing" show.

What Brazilians were reacting against was not simply the cartoon's image of Brazilian poverty and violence, but the extent to which, since the early twentieth century and especially since World War II, Brazil's culture has become increasingly influenced and shaped by the United States. It is one thing to saturate Brazil with Hollywood movies or television programs like *Desperate Housewives* or *CSI*; it is quite another to broadcast a show that treats Brazil's social problems as a running joke. *The Simpsons* imagines Brazil as a primitive jungle filled with monkeys and snakes, where semi-nude locals perform for outsiders like Bart, who happily "go native." In the London *Guardian* of April 9, 2002, critic Alex Bellos wrote about other inaccuracies in the program:

> Part of the anger in Brazil about *The Simpsons* is that, as well as the stereotypes, there are many inaccuracies—Marge, the mother, finds that the local mode of transport is the "conga," which is a Caribbean dance. (She takes a conga to the hotel.) Also, the family visits a samba school to learn the *macarena*—a Latin dance not performed in Brazil. There is also the *penetrada,* a fictitious and lascivious dance shown them by the teacher.

One might recall that Orson Welles emphasized the importance of dancing to Brazilians in his 1940s radio program *Hello Americans,* but his was an informed, good-neighbor commentary on the samba. In more typical Hollywood fashion, creators of *The Simpsons* mixed together a miscellany of inaccurate and fictional dances to create an image of "Brazilianness" that is not only exotic and sexually explicit but also ludicrous.

Urban and Rural *Telenovelas*

A 1998 study cited in *Zona latina* (1999) indicated that 73 percent of Brazil's TV audience watched *telenovelas*, far more than other major *telenovela*-producing nations, including Colombia (43 percent) Venezuela (52 percent), and Mexico (34 percent). That percentage helps to explain the impact of the five-nights-a-week stories on Brazilian identity. In an article on the *telenovela* and national identity in Brazil, media analyst Mauro Porto adopts Benedict Anderson's concept of "massive ceremonies" to describe ways in which programs constitute "material for conversations and everyday gossip, as well as a forum for the discussion of not only stories and characters, but also national problems" (Porto 2000).[15]

The greater realism of the Brazilian *telenovelas* (as opposed to the high melodrama of their Mexican counterparts) tends to strengthen their influence on everyday life. The genre's traditional emphasis on politics and the nation, including such contemporary topics as government corruption, the landless movement, the environment, and the pattern of immigration to the United States, provides audiences with an image of Brazil that it sometimes satirizes. A few *telenovelas* have been known to turn news items appearing one day into material for the next day's fictional episode, while daily news often comments on *telenovela* stars and plots. In the case of the real-life murder of one soap star by another, who was her onscreen lover, the *telenovela* became the focus of headlines and news stories that ran for months. The fascination with the *telenovela* in Brazil cannot be understated, and daily rewrites are often influenced by surveys that analyze viewer reaction to plots and characters. Most *telenovelas* focus on the white middle class; when the poor and black appear, they are usually marginal characters. (As I write, there are plans for a new Fox channel in the United States that will provide viewers with *telenovela*-style programming on the order of Brazil's. Costs for such programs are far less than other U.S. series, and they attract viewers for the long term, on the order of reality TV.)

Competition between the different networks sometimes results in new and popular trends. While the dictatorship favored soaps that focused on the urban middle class, a different image, closer to early Edenic representations, appeared after the *abertura*, the political opening of the 1980s. The best example is a frontier soap, *Pantanal*, a TV Manchete production televised in 1990 that, according to media critic Esther Hamburger, was about "the Brazil that Brazil doesn't know" (2005, 124).[16] Filmed on location in the interior of Mato Grosso, *Pantanal's* popularity with audiences caught the leading network, TV Globo, by complete surprise. (It was rebroadcast in 1991 and again in 1998.) Long takes of the little-known Pantanal, with its alluvial plains, winding rivers, herons, and old-style plantation life provided a sense of well-being for viewers who were weary of behind-the-doors family dramas and urban blight and unrest. The plot of this advertised "rediscovery of America after 500 years" (in Hamburger 2005, 124) was partly influenced by folkloric beliefs and legends. One of its central female characters has the ability to turn into a leopard. Like early explorers from other worlds, viewers were captivated not only by the natural beauty of the Pantanal but also the nudity of its inhabitants. (The introductory scene shows a leopard changing into a woman who dives into a crystal-clear lake and embraces what seems to be a naked man.)[17]

Ads for the soap called attention to the benign innocence and exoticism of the inhabitants: "People who speak the language of plants and animals, people who know the byways of the waters, land and the sky" (in Hamburger 2005, 124). As Hamburger notes, *Pantanal* opened the door to a new genre of *telenovelas* focused on the "other Brazil," which, just a few years later, would become a favorite destination of ecotourists (127). In contrast to the prevailing "developmental" view of urban soaps, *Pantanal* and later *telenovelas* about the hinterland like *Renascer* (Rebirth) in 1993 about cacao plantation society in Bahia and *O rei do gado* (Cattle King) in 1996 about cattle farms in the western part of São Paulo state shared a "tone of regret for the negligence toward nature, the native populations . . . and wilderness" (125).

A more recent vogue in the *telenovela* industry is the depiction of North America, which became an increasingly popular tourist destination beginning in 1994 after the introduction of the Plano Real, which initially raised the value of the Brazilian *real* currency above the U.S. dollar. As growth in the U.S. Brazilian immigrant population surpasses that of Spanish-speaking immigrants, Brazilian migration to the United States has changed the way the United States is imagined in Brazil. Capitalizing on the public's interest in immigration to the north, TV Globo launched *América* in 2005 about illegal immigration from Brazil and the struggle for survival in the United States. Apparently the producers initially wanted to show Brazilians crossing the Rio Grande from Mexico, a port of entry that was being used by thousands when the soap was broadcast. The scene was also to include a Texas farmer who shoots at the immigrants. After protests lodged by American embassy personnel, who believed the soap would encourage more Brazilians to enter through Mexico, the venue was changed to Miami, whose sunshine, palm trees, and beaches make it hard to distinguish from Rio, where some scenes were filmed.

The *Favela* and the Small Screen

Although the production values of most *telenovelas* are quite good, the more expensive TV miniseries have better writing and acting, along with more elaborate sets and interesting locations. Over the years, several series have been based on literary works. For example, to celebrate the country's 500th anniversary in 2000, TV Globo adapted Dinah Silveira de Queiroz's 1954 novel about the colonial past, *A muralha* (The Wall), published in translation as *The City of Women.* The nine episodes focused on the *bandeirantes'* expeditions into the interior of São Paulo and the bloody battles between indigenous inhabitants and frontiersmen. Publicity for the DVD version of the miniseries emphasizes the epic nature of Brazil's frontier past:

> Duels on muddy streets: *bandeirantes,* outlaws, and renegade mestizos all bearing arms. Hidden treasures, blood oaths, gold, and evildoing—yes, friends, Brazil had its Far West! Long before and with far more action than in the United States. What Brazil never had was an industry like Hollywood to produce myths based on its own history. But you now have in your hands . . . *A muralha* . . . a fine mix of action, reflection, and entertainment.

Unlike the *telenovela,* which leans toward contemporary stories, the miniseries are most comfortable with epic views of the past. Hence they have something in common with the British adaptations that appear in the United States on PBS's *Masterpiece Theater.* We can see this in adaptations of Eça de Queiroz's *Os maias,* a novel about the moral decay of nineteenth-century Lisbon, and Rachel de Queiroz's *Memorial de Maria Moura,* about romantic, religious, and social struggles in the backlands of nineteenth-century Brazil. The highly successful 1986 *Anos dourados* (Golden Years) is about 1950s Brazil and the customs and mores of the middle class, whose conservative foundations were shaken by a sexual awakening brought about by rock and roll. The series was followed six years later by a sequel of sorts called *Anos rebeldes* (Rebellious Years), about the 1960s and protests against the military dictatorship. Ironically, this look back at a time of intense political unrest was broadcast at the height of protests against the administration of Fernando Collor (the first elected president since the 1964 coup) and his subsequent impeachment.

If *A muralha* provided lessons about the nation that, according to its publicists, "were never told [to Brazilians] in school," the series *Cidade dos homens* (City of Men) about black youths in the *favela* offers a view of Brazil usually neglected by soaps and miniseries in general. Following the success of the movie *Cidade de Deus,* Fernando Meirelles, Kátia Lund, and other directors collaborated on fourteen episodes that take place between 2002 and 2005 in a hillside *favela* in Rio. There is a tendency to equate the series with the earlier film because of the directors, the camera style, and the appearance of several actors in both vehicles; but *Cidade dos homens* is more realistic, less glamorized, and consequently more powerful to watch. It includes scenes of drug trafficking and violence but is chiefly concerned with the lives and adventures of two boys and their interactions with family, friends, and others in the *favela.*

There is humor and charm in the way the boys banter with one another as they negotiate life in the slum. But we also see their fear of other, hardened *favela* youths and their attempts to avoid gun-toting drug dealers and police raids. Perhaps the most powerful image is the *favela* that the boys traverse. The dark and narrow passageways, winding stairs, shacks of various shapes and sizes, not to mention the detritus that draws rats and other vermin, constitute the boys' playground, which they only occasionally leave. One of the most compelling scenes in the 2002 four-part series occurs outside the *favela.* One of the boys stops and looks through the iron bars of a security fence in front of an apartment building. As he pushes close to the bars, he makes faces and sticks his tongue out at a security camera whose televised image is being watched by a doorman in the lobby. Although luxurious compared to a shack, the apartment house has a coldness, sterility, and prisonlike atmosphere that is as depressing in its own way as the *favela.* The menacing security devices are used to deter crime and violence from without, but the boy pokes fun at them and enjoys being seen on TV. The scene is more bitter than sweet: it represents the disparity, fears, and barriers constructed between the haves and have-nots that in this case is the difference between being white and being black in Brazil.

E.6 *Cidade dos homens,* Fernando Meirelles (2002)

Back to the Future

Poverty, corruption, and violence are exacting their toll on a nation that at the same time has taken the lead in the fight against HIV and AIDS and is a model of treatment, prevention, and control of the disease worldwide. While the United States and other countries are feeling the economic pinch caused by rising gasoline prices, Brazil has gained a certain level of self-sufficiency through decades-long experiments with the production of sugarcane-based ethanol, which fuels some cars and trucks. Although successful AIDS prevention plans or alternative fuel programs will probably never substitute for beaches, carnival, or soccer in the foreign imaginary, these are efforts that have already benefited Brazil and will have even greater benefits in the future. Lula's $10 million payment in 2005 to allow a Brazilian astronaut to ride a Russian spacecraft did not meet with widespread public approval, but the idea of going into space is another aspect of a nation whose struggles against various kinds of colonialism are counterbalanced by a deep-rooted resiliency and spirit of moving *para frente* (ahead)—and not only into space but cyberspace as well. The initially by-invitation-only U.S. website and chatroom known as Orkut has been taken over by Brazilians on the Internet, and its popularity is such that the term "Orkut" has now become part of the daily vocabulary.[18] Cyberspace commentators speculate that the success of the site partly has to with an "outgoingness," which is perhaps just another way of saying *para frente.*

The Internet has also given some Brazilians a chance to assert their identity in the face of powerful ideological forces. For example, Pope Benedict XVI made a much-publicized trip to Brazil in May 2007, a trip reminiscent of the early proselytization efforts of the Church in the New World. The press coverage of the event was enormous not only in Brazil but also worldwide. In the past, and as a cardinal, the pope had spoken out against the evils of liberation theology; his new enemy is Pentecostalism, whose self-help advocacy has found fertile ground among Brazilians. During his visit he also preached against homosexuality, birth control, sexual union not sanctioned by marriage or for purposes other than reproduction, and abortion. Unlike the amenable indigenous groups that welcomed the first Jesuits, many Brazilians were unhappy with the media blitz surrounding the pope's preachings, and they took to the Internet to form coalitions in opposition to the old image of a nation of pagans being chastised and shown the light. Indian rights groups protested the pope's claims that pre-Columbian indigenous peoples were silently longing for Christ. A virtual coalition generated a "message to the Pope" that appeared not only on the Web but also in hard-copy form in various cities around the nation: "Catholics practice sex for pleasure, they use condoms, they support sexual diversity, and they don't condemn women who have abortions. When is the church hierarchy going to change?"

Statements such as these provide evidence that the nation is no longer awed by the coming of European leaders and no longer automatically swayed by their messages. In the nineteenth century, Machado de Assis introduced the famous European alienist Simão Bacamarte to an awed and largely complacent Brazilian society only to demonstrate the nonsense of Bacamarte's pronouncements. Brazilians today have greater opportunity to express a native skepticism in ways that might have delighted Machado. In the process, the idea of Brazilianness will continue to evolve, and perhaps new communities will be formed across national divides.

NOTES

Chapter One

1. Spices were especially desirable because they were used to preserve meats and other foods as well as to make perfumes. William Brooks Greenlee mentions the importance of a trade in drugs as well (1938, xxxii).

2. Prior to Cabral's voyage, the Venetians completely dominated the spice trade with the East. The sea route to India gave the Portuguese unrestricted access to the spice market there, and within a few years they were the main exporter for the rest of Europe. See Greenlee 1938 (xxxii nn1–2).

3. See Câmara Cascudo's essay "Intencionalidade no descobrimento do Brasil" in *Dois ensaios de história* (1965). This is a revised version of an article he wrote in 1933 based on his doctoral dissertation.

4. Various reasons could explain why Cabral selected the name Vera Cruz (True Cross) for the new land. It is a reference to the May 3 religious holiday known as the Invention of the Cross, which celebrates the discovery of the true cross in Jerusalem by Saint Helena in 326 (Greenlee 1938, 6n7). Cabral was a knight of the Order of the Cross, and his ship bore the flag with the red cross on white background that was the insignia of that order. The crew also erected a cross on the coast and held a mass there on May 1 to commemorate the Easter holidays and bless the expedition.

5. For more discussion of these two terms see Cortesão 1967 (261–275).

6. In his *Portuguese Voyages to America in the Fifteenth Century* (1965), Samuel Eliot Morison states that in 1486, Dom João II gave letters patent of donation to Fernão Dulmo of Terceira in the Azores "to find and seek a great island or islands or *terra firme* in the Atlantic" (44). See also Greenlee 1938 (xlvi–lxvii).

The question of the "discovery" was an important issue debated by nineteenth-century writers, among them Joaquim Norberto de Sousa e Silva and Gonçalves Dias, whose arguments appeared in the *Revista do Instituto Histórico e Geográfico Brasileiro* in 1852 and 1855, respectively. Historians Francisco Adolfo de Varnhagen and Capistrano de Abreu also hypothesized about the issue in their works—Varnhagen in *Descobrimento do Brasil: Crônica do fim do décimo-quinto século* (Discovery of Brazil: Chronicle of the End of the Fifteenth Century), published in 1840, and Abreu in *O descobrimento do Brasil pelos portugueses* (The Discovery of Brazil by the Portuguese), published in 1900. See Morettin 2000.

7. The quote is from folio 1, verso. All citations from Caminha's letter are from the facsimile folios in J. Cortesão 1967. Unless otherwise noted, translations from Portuguese texts are my own. For a brief overview of the history of the publication of the letter see Morettin 2000 (6).

8. There is no mention here or elsewhere of the nature of Osório's crime, but exile was used as both short-term and long-term punishment for various misdeeds.

9. According to Louis-André Vigneras (1976, 40), the first maps to refer to an island called Brazil were by Angelino Dalorro (1325 or 1330) and Angelino Dulcerto (1339). A third, anonymous map, thought to have been drawn prior to 1324, is housed in the British Museum in London.

10. Cabral named the new territory the "Land of Vera Cruz," but Caminha signed his letter to the king "From your island of Vera Cruz." This difference in perception suggests that Cabral knew that he had discovered a continent; on the other hand, Caminha's wording seems to coincide with the considerable literature about legendary island utopias in the Atlantic.

11. Laura de Mello e Souza's "The New World Between God and the Devil" (2003) provides information on this and other ideas associated with the encounter with the New World. Also, there is a significant literature that discusses the myths and lore of imaginary Atlantic islands that were believed to be terrestrial versions of paradise. In *Utopia* (1516), Sir Thomas More describes an imaginary island nation based on New World explorations by the Portuguese.

12. For a postcolonial reading of the letter see Silviano Santiago's "Destinations of a Letter, Predestinations of a Country" (2000). Also see his "Why and for What Purpose Does the European Travel?" (2001) for commentary on the indigenous Other.

13. There is some disagreement by historians about this issue. Emert wrote that Cabral did not send any brazilwood back and that the Spanish navigator Pinzón was actually the first to do so (1944, 18).

14. More than four hundred years after the voyage of Cabral in 1500, Brazilian filmmaker Humberto Mauro made *O descobrimento do Brasil* (1937), a Hollywood-style adaptation based on Caminha's account; the film appeared at the beginning of the right-wing dictatorship of Getúlio Vargas (1937–1945) known as the Estado Novo (New State). Here the spirit of *ufanismo* is also in evidence, but with an ironic twist: emphasis in the film is on the Portuguese captain and crew, who are portrayed as thoughtful, kindly, and even benevolent toward the native Brazilians, who are played by white actors in "redface" and seem more "primitive" than "Edenic." Although Mauro was a highly regarded filmmaker, the film received mixed reviews, with Vargas apparently among those pleased with the production. Perhaps both critics and Vargas saw the film in more contemporary terms as an allegory in celebration of a newly established authority (in this case the Estado Novo) over a populace that showed little or no resistance. See Morettin 2000 for a detailed analysis of the film.

15. In the fourteenth, fifteenth, and early sixteenth centuries, Portugal was far more

interested in developing the art of navigation and claiming new lands than with colonization per se. As demonstrated on both the east and west coasts of Africa, the Portuguese built forts to protect their sovereignty and trading posts to facilitate commerce. But there was no real attempt by the monarchy to encourage migration to Brazil until its sovereignty there was challenged by the French in the early sixteenth century.

16. One must add the Southern Cross to the various implications of the name Vera Cruz.

17. The Portuguese armada carried sailors from Florence and Venice who were eager to share information with Vespucci when they met him in Cape Verde. Also, one of the armada's ships was partly financed by the Florentine banker Bartolomeo Marchionni, who, along with other Italian residents in Portugal, quickly wrote back to their country's officials about the commercial success of the voyage.

Dom Manuel was concerned for political reasons that Spain learn directly from him about the founding of land on the Portuguese side of the line of demarcation. My colleague Heitor Martins suggests that the appearance of the name Santa Cruz in Manuel's letter to the Spanish Catholic royals most likely stemmed from his desire to shift the emphasis from the "true" or actual cross itself to the religion of the holy cross. Others speculate that Cabral's letter to Manuel, which no longer exists, referred to the country as Santa Cruz. The name Brazil was adopted shortly thereafter: Dom Manuel referred to "Brasil" in a letter written in 1513 to Fernando de Aragão; and the German pamphlet *Newen Zeytung auss Presilg Landt* (Newspaper from Presilg Land), published around the same time, contains the first printed reference to a Portuguese voyage to Brazil. Religious leaders, distressed by the name change, often continued to refer to the country as Santa Cruz.

18. Vespucci had good relations with both Portugal and Spain, and he was considered ideal for clarifying the papal bull's territorial line and the respective holdings of the two countries. For further information on Vespucci's commissions by both Spain and Portugal see Pohl 1966.

19. Vespucci gained much information from Italian sailors aboard one of Cabral's ships, but his primary informant was a well-traveled Jewish refugee named Guaspare (Pohl 1966, 106–107).

20. For a detailed study of Vespucci and others as official messengers or "representational go-betweens" consult Alida C. Metcalf's *Go-Betweens and the Colonization of Brazil: 1500–1600* (2005).

21. The image of an earthly paradise was repeated in sixteenth-century writings on Brazil such as *A nova gazeta alemã [da terra do Brasil]* (The New German Gazette [About the Land of Brazil]) and Frenchman Jean de Léry's 1578 *Histoire d'un voyage fait en la terre du Bresil autrement dite Amerique* (*History of a Voyage Made to the Land of Brazil Otherwise Called America*, 1990).

22. Vespucci makes a particularly fascinating if not ironic observation when he confesses that he cannot understand why the local populations declare war on one

another—especially given the fact "that they held no private property or sovereignty of empire or kingdoms and did not know any such thing as lust for possession, that is, pillaging or a desire to rule, which appear to me to be the causes of war and of every disorderly act" (in Pohl 1966, 134). He also remarks on the good health and longevity of the people, one of whom he estimates to be 132 years old. Vespucci ends his letter by commenting on the natural wealth of the new land, especially the dyewood, and the possibility of precious stones and metals in the region.

23. Barros seemed to ignore the association between Brazil and the mythic islands of the Atlantic. His contemporary chronicler Pero de Magalhães Gândavo not only agreed with Barros's argument but also prioritized the name in his *História da Província Santa Cruz,* while relegating the term "Brazil"—a name he said came from the wood's coloring like a *brasa,* an ember—to the book's subtitle, *a que vulgarmente chamamos Brasil* (Amado and Figueiredo 2001, 511n37). According to Emert (1944, 10), the French navigator Binot Paulmier de Gonneville used the name Brazil as early as 1503 in his *Relation authentique du voyage du capitaine de Gonneville ès nouvelles terres des Indes.* Emert states that he and other Frenchmen used the name because they were aware of the Portuguese designation of Santa Cruz.

24. For more information on the commerce of brazilwood by the Portuguese and French see Metcalf 2005 (59–62).

25. See these and other maps in Jaime Cortesão's *História* (1957) and Armando Cortesão and A. Teixeira da Mota's *Portugaliae* (1960–1962).

26. According to Marchant (1942, 73) and others, African slaves were few in number in Brazil prior to 1549.

27. Scholar and bibliophile José E. Mindlin regards the Frankfurt edition as a possible "pirate copy" whose illustrations were taken from a 1548 book about the Middle East by Ludovico Varthema. See Mindlin's "Viajantes" (1991).

28. The Brazilianist Ferdinand Denis uncovered this manuscript and wrote about it in *Fête* (*Uma festa brasileira,* 1944).

29. Here we see that Brazil continues to be considered an island.

30. As will be discussed, the Indians also adopted European approaches to such practices as torture and killing.

31. This contrasts sharply with Vespucci's account, in which he talks about the libidinousness of the indigenous women.

32. See Ana Miranda's novel *Desmundo* (1996) about the Church's practice of sending Portuguese Christian female orphans to Brazil to keep Portuguese settlers from marrying indigenous females.

33. For more discussion of this work see Cohen 1998 (19–32).

34. In 1955, French anthropologist Claude Lévi-Strauss, who sailed by the island in Guanabara Bay once occupied by Huguenots, wrote in *Tristes tropiques* (1973) that the events surrounding the rise and fall of the Villegaignon enterprise would make a wonderful movie. In 1972, Nelson Pereira dos Santos did just that when he made

his celebrated *Como era gostoso o meu francês* (How Tasty Was My Little Frenchman). Pereira dos Santos combined the Villegaignon episode with the plot of Hans Staden's captive-witness tale in a wonderfully tongue-in-cheek movie about colonial and post-colonial Brazil. For a discussion of the film see Sadlier 2003 (58–74).

35. Villegaignon's comment is a good example of what Hayden White calls the "technique of ostensive self-definition by negation." According to White, "When men were uncertain as to the precise quality of their sensed humanity, they appealed to the concept of wildness to denigrate an area of subhumanity that was characterized by everything they hoped they were not" (1978, 152).

36. In his later *La cosmographie universelle*, Thevet retracted his commentary on the Amazons, stating that they did not exist.

37. Léry's preface includes a transcription of Villegaignon's letter to Calvin in which he requests the help of missionaries. It is important to note that Léry was not alone in his dislike of Villegaignon. There is a fascinating engraving of Villegaignon as the *Cyclops Polyphemus* in Sérgio Millet's Portuguese translation of Léry's *Histoire*. A caption states that the image appears in the allegory *Apologie* by Pierre Aicher.

In *Villegagnon e a França Antártica* (2005), Vasco Mariz and Lucien Provençal offer a reevaluation of the period and contend that Léry wrongly accused the French admiral of treacheries that he did not commit.

38. Léry stated in a letter that he had not read Staden until 1586, when a friend lent him the book in German and another person translated parts of it for him. Léry praised the book, commenting that he and Staden were in total agreement on interpretations of indigenous life. He used Staden as a weapon against Thevet, saying that Staden's book confirmed his stand that Thevet (in his *La cosmographie*) was a liar (Léry 1990, 52n67).

39. Nóbrega early on experienced difficulties in ministering to the Portuguese colonists, who were reluctant to give up their sexual indulgences with many indigenous women and not at all interested in religious or moral lessons or going to confession. For more on the Jesuit mission in Brazil see Cohen 1998.

40. For more information on the plays of Anchieta and Jesuit literature in general see Bosi 1992 and Moreau 2003.

41. This phrase appears in the Italian Cretino's letter of June 27, 1501. Parrots are also a central image in Waldseemüller's 1516 map.

42. In his *Crônica*, Góis embellished upon a fantastic tale told by João de Barros in *Décadas* (recounted in 1561 by Bartolome de las Casas in his *História de las Indias*) about a fish of gigantic proportions: "While the armada was [in Porto Seguro], the sea tossed upon the beach a fish that was thicker than a large cask and as long as two large casks. The head and eyes resembled those of a pig without teeth, the ears were like those of an elephant, its tail was as long and wide as an eel, its skin was like that of a pig and thick as a finger" (Góis 1926, 1:119).

43. See Metcalf's lengthy and detailed discussion (2005, 175–193).

Chapter Two

1. These and other maps can be found in *Frontières entre le Brésil et la Guyane Française* (1899).

2. For a detailed history of this period see Boxer 1973.

3. Historian Maria Beatriz Nizza da Silva writes that in 1572, the ratio of African to indigenous slaves on Mem de Sá's plantations was 20 to 132 at Sergipe and 9 to 123 at Santa Ana (1999, 15).

4. Stuart B. Schwartz charts the mortality rate of slaves in his *Sugar Plantations* (1985, 366).

5. Simão de Vasconcelos's 1668 study, *Notícias curiosas e necessárias das coisas do Brasil* (Curious and Necessary News of Things from Brazil), is filled with anecdotes about Amazons and other unusual beings. He commented on the existence of "monstrous" nations composed of dwarves, people born with feet turned backwards, and giants. Of the Amazons he wrote:

> Finally there is the other nation of women who are also monstrous in their way of life (they are those that today we call the Amazons, similar to those of antiquity, and who are named after the river) because they are women warriors who live on their own without the commerce of men. Huge communities live in a Province in the interior, where they cultivate the lands and support themselves with their own labors. They live between the great mountains and are women of known valor, who have always maintained themselves without the customary marriage with men. (2002, 55)

For additional reading about fantastic creatures in the literature on Brazil consult Alfredo d'Escragnolle Taunay's 1937 publication, *Monstros e monstrengos* (1998).

6. Drawings of headless men, or *blemee,* appeared in the Middle Ages. One can be found on the Hereford World Map (1300). In *Marvels of the East,* an eleventh-century manuscript, Cotton Tiberius wrote about headless men with "eyes and a mouth in their chest. They are eight feet tall and in similar manner eight feet wide" and were thought to reside on an island south of Brixton (in Mittman 2003, 7).

7. In many ways, Jonghe's iconography anticipates the fanfare surrounding Prince Maurits's 1644 departure from Brazil, as described by Boxer: "When [Maurits] finally reached the shore, a mob of Brazilian Indians pushed all the white men aside, and carried him shoulder-high through the surf to the waiting boat" (1973, 156–157).

8. To shore up its colony and the workforce there, the government sanctioned and sometimes underwrote raids by settlers (known as *bandeirantes,* or flag bearers) in the São Paulo region into the interior to capture Indians for use as slave labor on plantations and farms. Enslaved Indians often participated in the raids, preferring servitude to the Crown over a life of backbreaking toil in the cane, wheat, and tobacco fields. These raids were highly successful ventures and at the same time fueled conflict between colonists and Jesuits, the latter of whom, having lost thousands of converts/laborers to *bandeirante* actions, continued to complain to the monarchy about the

criminality and avarice of the settlers. The Jesuit Fernão Cardim was among those who wrote to the king to bring an end to the *bandeirantes'* illegal seizure and enslavement of Indians in the interior (Cardim 1993, 65).

In 1653, in one of his famous Sunday sermons to the populace, Jesuit priest Antônio Vieira attempted to negotiate a middle ground that would divide Indian labor between plantations and Jesuit villages. According to Vieira's finely argued proposal in "Sermão da primeira dominga da Quaresma" (Sermon of the First Sunday in Lent), by serving the spiritual needs of native inhabitants, most of whom had been unjustly enslaved, the Portuguese would not only reap greater profits from their labors but also be spiritually redeemed (Vieira 2001, 2:451–466). Because of his passion for keeping the Indians in the Jesuit fold, Vieira had no objection to the African slave trade, and he even rationalized the *doce inferno* (sweet hell) of working in a sugar mill. In his fourteenth sermon in the series *Sermões do Rosário,* he equated labor in the fiery and dangerous mills to Christ's work and suffering, promising the slaves in his audience that those who turned to Christ would, like him, be resurrected and enter everlasting glory (2001, 312).

9. For more information see Schwartz's "Sugar in Dutch Brazil" (2004, 166–172).

10. Despite Vieira's dubious notions about the redeeming aspects of the "sweet hell" of the sugar mills, he was very articulate about what he had seen in them:

And truly, whoever were to see those tremendous furnaces in the dark of the night; the flames gushing from each of them through the two mouths, or nostrils through which they breathe the fire; the Ethiopians, or Cyclops, bathed in sweat and so black as robust as they supply the thick and hard material to the flame, and the pitchforks with which they stir and poke it; the cauldrons or boiling lakes with waterfalls always beaten and beaten back, then vomiting foam, exhaling clouds of steam, more from the heat than from vapor, and the turning back into rain to exhale them once again; the noise of the wheels, the chains, the people the color of the very night, working lively and moaning at the same time, without a moment of respite or rest; whoever, then, were to see all the confusing and thunderous machinery and apparatus of that Babylonia will never be able to doubt, even though they may have seen Etna and Vesuvius, that it is a picture of hell. (2001, 312)

11. At one point, Brandônio says to Alviano: "I shall endeavor to prove that taking nothing more than sugar out of Brazil is a greater thing, and brings in more profit to His Majesty's Treasury, than all those East Indies" (1986, 132).

12. A major exhibit of Eckhout's Brazilian work took place at the Mauitshuis in the Hague from March to June 2004. Benjamin Moser wrote a long review in the *New York Review of Books,* "Dutch Treat" (2004), on the exhibit and the catalogue edited by Quentin Buvelot, *Albert Eckhout: A Dutch Artist in Brazil.*

13. For this passage and the complete text in Portuguese see the Universidade de São Paulo virtual library at www.bibvirt.futuro.usp.br.

14. Here Matos may be repeating the stereotypical treatment of the Moor that was common in Spanish satirical literature.

15. Apparently a government official and friend of Matos deemed that deportation was a better option than imprisonment in a local jail.

16. Like Matos, Vieira had his share of problems with the authorities—in particular officials of the Inquisition who were less than happy with his commercially driven pro-Judaic stance and his messianic pronouncements about Portugal as a Fifth Empire or spiritual world leader.

17. According to Boxer, the Paulistas who made up the *bandeirantes* were quite willing to follow directives from the Crown. In the late seventeenth century, he says, the monarchy authorized the governor of Rio de Janeiro to encourage the Paulistas to engage in mining activities by promising them royal titles and knighthoods (1969, 34–35). John J. Monteiro's 1994 *Negros da terra* (Blacks of the Land) is an important revisionist study that emphasizes the brutality of the *bandeirante* in the capture and transportation of Indians and "blacks of the land"—that is, slaves—back to São Paulo.

18. The treaty stated that England would purchase agricultural products from Portugal, principally wine and cork, while Portugal was obligated to purchase textiles and other manufactured goods from Britain. Not surprisingly, the monies spent on imports by Portugal far exceeded the revenues from its exports to England. In a letter dated 1810, Thomas Jefferson accurately described England's commercial and political advantage in the relationship: "To Portugal alone she has steadily adhered, because, by her Methuin [sic] treaty she has made it a colony, and one of the most valuable to her." For more information on this topic see Virgílio Noya Pinto's 1979 study, *O ouro brasileiro e o comércio anglo-português* (Brazilian Gold and Anglo-Portuguese Commerce).

19. A. J. R. Russell-Wood cites a later study by Michel Morineau of untapped sources such as Dutch gazettes and the *Gazeta de Notícias* (News Gazette) for additional data on the commerce of precious metals. Russell-Wood's point is that the estimate of gold extracted was undoubtedly greater than one thousand tons—a figure traditionally cited and based on Virgílio Pinto's seminal work (Russell-Wood 2000, 861).

20. This long poem is filled with nativist imagery. Lisboa celebrates Brazil's myriad delicious fruits, such as the *jaboticaba, sapucaia,* and *mandapuçá,* whose Indian names give the poem its grace and musicality. Another part of the poem reads like an homage to Brazilian foods and the daily cuisine:

> Our lands are sated
> With palm leaves, coconut trees,
> Scented caroa palms, primrose,
> And balls of manioc flour.

> These little balls, Marília,
> Are regularly used by those people,
> To make a pap with eggs
> Nearly every morning. (In H. Martins 1982, 164)

Lisboa states in the introduction to his 1804 book, *Descrição curiosa das principais produções, rios e animais do Brasil* (Curious Description of the Principal Productions, Rivers, and Animals of Brazil), that his objective was to inform his friends in Portugal of the abundance and variety of products in Brazil and the various terms and unknown vocabulary used to describe foods unknown outside the country.

21. Jefferson quoted Maia's letter in correspondence to John Jay the following year. All citations from Jefferson's correspondence are from the Library of Congress website, http://international.loc.gov/intldl/brhtml/br-1/br-1-4-8.html. Excerpts can be found also at the website of the School of Cooperative Individualism, www.cooperativeindividualism.org.

22. In later correspondence with government officials, Jefferson referred to Brazil and the treasures it offered to outsiders. In 1810, he wrote to Governor John Langdon about his fear that Napoleon might try to cross the Atlantic: "But will he attack us first, from whom he will get but hard knocks and no money? Or will he first lay hold of the gold and silver of Mexico and Peru, and the diamonds of Brazil?"

23. In her 1953 *Romanceiro da Inconfidência* (Ballad of the Conspiracy), Brazilian poet Cecília Meireles paints an emotional picture of the doomed soldier-martyr and portrays Queen Maria I, who sentenced Tiradentes to his horrific fate, as a ruthless monarch whose deed ultimately drove her into madness.

24. The request was made by Martinho de Melo e Castro in his *Instruções para o cumprimento do alvará que proíbe as manufaturas no Brasil* (Instructions for Complying with the Royal Order that Prohibits Manufacturing in Brazil), dated 1785.

25. For more on this subject see Belluzzo 2000 (2:64–73).

Chapter Three

1. Kirsten Schultz refers to an even earlier proposal to move the court in the 1580s by a counselor of the Prior do Crato, the Portuguese challenger to the throne who was defeated by the claim of Felipe II, king of Spain (2001, 16).

2. In Carla Camurati's 1994 satirical film, *Carlota Joaquina,* about the arrival of the Portuguese court in Brazil, there is a tongue-in-cheek scene in which members of the royal court, still in Lisbon, leaf through pictures that depict Brazil as the home of wild and fearsome beasts. As a result, they foresee nothing good, let alone civilized, awaiting them should they be forced to flee to Brazil.

3. John Luccock's travelogue, *Notes on Rio de Janeiro and the Southern Parts of Brazil* (1820), gives a good idea of the lack of hygiene that characterized Brazilian society when he arrived in Rio in 1808. He also described the many advances that took place in the urban areas within the next ten years, largely because of the opening of the ports, the influx of travelers and news from abroad, and the greater access to and affordability of commodities.

4. Wied-Neuwied is best known for his study of the Botocudo Indians. According to Luis da Câmara Cascudo, the prince had amassed a huge collection of Brasiliana for

his private museum that included 400 species of mammals, 1,600 birds, 400 reptiles and amphibians, and 500 fishes (Cascudo 1977, 95). Wied published the first of many of his findings, along with observations by earlier naturalists, in *Reis Nach Brasilien in Den Jahren 1815 Bis 1817*. Other volumes would follow.

5. John Mawe's description of Rio de Janeiro included more general observations about this "opulent" yet "unhealthful" city. He was impressed by the capital's beautiful buildings and by the hills, villas, and gardens that "have a rich and magnificent appearance" (1816, 104, 105). And like early chroniclers, he praised the variety of fruits and the "abundance of very fine prawns" (106). But he was dismayed by the "general filthiness of the streets," filled with pools of stagnant water (106), and the scarcity of adequate accommodations, which, even when available, were extremely uncomfortable and yet as pricey as those in London (105). He discovered that wood was also "unaccountably scarce, considering the amount that grows in almost every part of Brazil; even firewood [was] dear" (105).

6. According to literary historian Wilson Martins, the *Correio braziliense* circulated in Brazil and was even indirectly protected by Dom João. Citing historian Francisco Adolfo de Varnhagen, Martins writes that the prince regent read the newspaper to keep himself apprised of the opposition's commentary and to seek better counsel from his advisors about issues addressed by its editor (1977, 2:32).

7. There was some early effort to reform Portuguese opinion about the so-called inferiority of New World inhabitants. Schultz quotes the Portuguese diplomat Luiz da Cunha on the "many and good Portuguese" who settled Brazil and the indigenous inhabitants who "differed only in color from the rustic people" in Portugal's provinces (2001, 58n2).

8. Initially, the title was Imperial Academy of Fine Arts, which was changed to National School of Fine Arts after 1889 and the establishment of the republic.

9. Debret makes this point later in volume 2 when he discusses the importation of African slaves to replace indigenous slave labor.

10. Graham reported on being struck by the size of the black population in Pernambuco, which constituted more than two-thirds of the state's 70,000 inhabitants. She was also quite frank about the discrimination that existed between Europeans and Brazilians: "European Portuguese are extremely anxious to avoid intermarriage with born Brazilians, and prefer giving their daughters to the meanest clerk of European birth, rather than to the richest and most meritorious Brazilian" (1824, 126). Her observation echoes the racial condescension and scorn described by Aluísio Azevedo in his novel *O mulato* (1881) and by Hipólito da Costa in the *Correio braziliense*.

11. Nature scenes were the most popular images on early postcards in Brazil. The Royal Botanical Gardens postcard captured the magnificence of the royal palms that tower over the tiny figure of a man with an umbrella and his dog. The image of the palms on either side of a boulevard-style path suggested that, at least in this instance,

nature had been harnessed and now served the pleasure of the citizens of Rio. See Vasquez 2002 (100).

12. Von Martius's first impressions of Rio contrasted the "civilization" brought to the capital by Europeans with the "savage" and "disagreeable" nature of its black population:

> Language, customs, architecture, and the influx of industrial products from all parts of the world give the main square in Rio a European look. Nevertheless, what reminds the traveler that he is in a strange part of the world is especially the mob of blacks and mulattoes, the working class which he runs across as soon as he sets foot on land. This particular aspect was more surprising than pleasing to us. The inferior, brute nature of these importune, semi-naked men wounds the sensibility of the European who ends up abandoning the refined customs and obsequious rules of his country. (In Oliveira 2002, 7–8).

13. For extensive discussion of Humboldt's influence on the creation of a tropical imaginary see Driver and Martins 2005. Although Graham and Ewbank were basically writers, they, too, illustrated their books.

14. Debret's was the quintessential pictorial that included historical paintings (long considered the supreme genre in art), individual portraits, city and country scenes, landscapes, and still lifes. Watercolor and oil paintings of serene landscapes were one of Ender's great strengths as an artist; wilderness landscapes were drawn expertly and quite intricately by his scientist-colleague Martius. Spix's watercolors of different animal species have a beauty and delicacy that rival the illustrations of Audubon.

Chapter Four

1. Prince Maximilian von Wied-Neuwied, members of the French Cultural Mission and the Austrian Mission, the Baron of Langsdorff, Gilbert Farquhar Matheson, and Prince Adalbert of Prussia are a few of the many who studied and produced materials on the Indian.

2. Cláudio Manuel da Costa's poem "Vila Rica" (1773) describes the indigenous culture, but it is always subordinate to the European presence. In Santa Rita Durão's epic poem *Caramuru* (1781), indigenous inhabitants are secondary to the story of the historical figure Diogo Álvares Correia, who lived with the Indians and was rewarded by the monarchy for his assistance to the colonial cause. Basílio da Gama wrote his epic *O uraguai* (1769) to curry favor with the Portuguese minister at the time, the marquis of Pombal, who had expelled the Jesuits from the Portuguese empire. The poem narrates the struggle between the Portuguese and Spanish against the Jesuits, who enlisted the help of the indigenous community in the struggle over the missions of Uruguay. Although Gama creates a sympathy between the reader and the brave Cacambo and his wife, Lindóia, who dies by snakebite after learning of Cacambo's death, the hero of the poem is the leader of the expedition, the Portuguese Gomes Freire de Andrade.

3. Cruz e Silva was a major writer, but his work has been neglected, probably because he was the judge in the Inconfidência Mineira trial in which fellow poets like Cláudio Manuel da Costa were found guilty of treason.

4. These citations are from the sonnets "A um célebre mulato Joaquim Manuel, grande tocador de viola e improvisador de modinhas" (To a Celebrated Mulatto Joaquim Manuel, Great Viola Player and Improviser of Modinhas) and "Ao mesmo" (To the Same), in Bocage (1875).

5. Writing about his visit to Brazil from 1824 to 1826, Carl Schlichthorst observed: "During my various years of residency, perhaps I never would have had the occasion to see a savage if the Government, from time to time, had not persuaded small groups of these wandering dwellers from the north of the Fluminense Province to stop on the outskirts of the capital, primarily to satisfy the Europeans' curiosity more than for a loftier end" (Schlichthorst n.d., 142).

6. Wilson Martins states that the little-known poet João Cardoso de Meneses e Sousa was a forerunner of the "Indianist" writers of the mid-nineteenth century and that his historical importance has largely been ignored (1977, 2:403). Antônio Cândido considers the poem "Nênia" (1837) by Firmino Rodrigues Silva to be the beginning of a Brazilian nationalist or Indianist literature (1971, 1:312). Others who wrote early on about the Indian were Macedo, Bernardo Guimarães, and Martins Pena.

7. Unlike the American and French Revolutions, there was no significant change in leadership in Brazil following its independence.

8. Boris Fausto notes that John Buckle's and Joseph Gobineau's racist theories were important to the imperial rulers (1999, 117), but they appeared after the classification system that Debret cites in his work. During his stay in Rio, Schlichthorst observed that the Portuguese often changed the first verse of the national hymn from *brava gente do Brasil* (brave people of Brazil) to *cabra gente do Brasil*—goat (black) people of Brazil (n.d., 80n27).

9. Literary critic Flora Süssekind discusses the stage curtain in her book *O Brasil não é longe daqui* (1990, 38), as does Ricardo Salles in his *Nostalgia imperial* (1996, 98–99). Although José Bonifácio was uneasy with the "savage" implication of palm trees painted on a stage curtain, he nevertheless titled his newspaper *O tamoio*. Cândido reminds us that Indian names were often used for their symbolic significance. He writes that members of secret societies often adopted indigenous names to signify their resistance to the colonizing forces and that Dom Pedro I was known as "Guatimozim," a creative counterpart to the regal Aztecan Montezuma (1971, 2:18–19).

10. Pedro I returned to Portugal to fight his younger brother, Miguel, who had used the regency of Pedro's young daughter, Maria, to rule the country and to reinstate an absolutist reign there. Pedro was ultimately victorious in what became known as the War of the Brothers (1831–1834), and his daughter assumed the throne. He became the duke of Bragança and died shortly thereafter.

11. Garrett's critique is not entirely correct, since Gonzaga did depict Brazilian

scenes—as did other neoclassical poets of the time, including Cláudio Manuel da Costa and Silva Alvarenga.

12. According to the translator's note in the Portuguese edition, the engraving was made by Gianni in 1825 and was reproduced in volume 25 of the *Publicações do Arquivo Nacional* as well as in Schlichthorst's book. Of the barely clothed figure Schlichthorst noted: "I do not dare to affirm that [the beautiful viscountess] posed for the painter in the same clothes with which she is presented in the engraving" (n.d., 55).

13. The marquis of Pombal disliked the autonomy exercised by the Jesuits, who had built up veritable strongholds throughout Brazil. His concern was to assert absolute sovereignty over the region, and this meant that all properties held by the Jesuits, including their schools, would be seized and dismantled.

14. In his 1835 *Bosquejo histórico, político e literário do Brasil* (Historical, Political, and Literary Outline of Brazil), General José Inácio Abreu e Lima stated that with the exception of a few important works, there was no literature in Brazil. A monarchist, Abreu e Lima was writing in opposition to a proposal by Senator Antônio Ferreira França, who wanted to revoke monarchical rule in Brazil. Abreu e Lima based his objections on his perception that Brazilians had dismal intellectual capabilities and that they were unable to produce major works in the various disciplines. For those reasons, he warned that they were incapable of self-government. Seven years later, in the first volume (November 1843) of the literary review *Minerva brasiliense*, Santiago Nunes Ribeiro challenged Abreu e Lima's thesis in his essay "Da nacionalidade da literatura brasileira" (On the Nationality of Brazilian Literature). I am grateful to Heitor Martins for providing me with this information from *Cadernos do Centro de Pesquisas Literárias* 5, no. 2 (August 1999), at www.pucrs.br/letras/pos/historiadaliteratura/textosraros/nossoestadointelectual.htm.

Writing in 1829, Schlichthorst remarked that "Brazil could very well boast today about its great number of good writers if their works had not been lost or hidden away in the Torre de Tombo, the archive of the Portuguese State, seeing as the tyranny of the Metropole always made an effort to destroy or hide that which threatened to spread light on its interesting colony" (n.d., 152). In a footnote (152n3), the Brazilian translators of Schlichthorst's work remind the reader that no presses or newspapers were allowed in Brazil prior to the arrival of Dom João VI.

15. Magalhães is regarded as the most important poet of the early romantic period, and he devoted himself to the cultivation of a Brazilian national literature. The epigraph in *Niterói*, "Everything in the Name of Brazil, Everything for Brazil," gives an indication of his dedication to the cause. In 1836, he also published a volume of poetry, *Suspiros poéticos e saudades* (Poetic Sighs and Longings), that exemplified his ideas of what the new literature should be. Sérgio Buarque de Holanda has said that the appearance of these two publications was comparable to the "preface by Cromwell and the cry of Ipiranga (Brazilian independence) in verse" (in S. Castro 1999, 2:35n12).

16. This poem has an epigraph from Goethe's poem "Mignon" that foregrounds

this nativist motif: "Do you know the country, where the lemons bloom, / Where the golden oranges glow in the dark, / Do you know it well?—Over there, over there! / I would like . . . to go over there" (Gonçalves Dias 1942, 22).

17. In an autobiography that Dias wrote at the urging of Ferdinand Denis, he stated:

> Some time passed without anyone commenting on this volume [*Primeiros cantos*], which, despite all its defects, was going to bring about a kind of revolution in our national poetry. Then everyone awoke to the volume at the same time, and the author of the first songs saw himself praised far beyond his due. The most revered of Portuguese writers—Alexandre Herculano—wrote flattering words about this volume, and his article had an impact in Portugal and Brazil.
>
> The people adopted the poet, repeating and singing [his verses] in every corner of Brazil. (In Cândido 1971, 2:82–83)

The poem also was admired by French traveler Adèle Toussaint-Samson and included along with a French translation in the appendix to her 1883 book, *Une parisienne au Brésil* (*A Parisian in Brazil*, 2001). Her note on the poem is significant in terms of its widespread acclaim: "This Brazilian poetry of Gonçalves Dias, which has been set to music by M. Amat, accompanied by a guitar, has an exquisite grace and the perfume of the country. I have had the pleasure of having it heard at my home sometimes, and, thanks to the composer, it always was the success of the evening" (2001, 105). The subject and fame of the poem also resulted in a number of parodies written by Portuguese poets.

18. Early nativist writers likewise challenged the unflattering stereotype to some extent by praising fruits and other commodities from Brazil. Domingos Caldas Barbosa does so as well. But these various authors were writing as citizens of Portugal, while Dias was making comparisons as a citizen of Brazil.

19. In 1849, Nísia Floresta Brasileira Augusta published a long poem titled "A lágrima de um caeté (The Tear of a Caeté), which, like the "songs" of Gonçalves Dias, focused on the plight of the Indian at the hands of the colonizer.

20. A fourth Indianist poem, "Deprecação" (Deprecation), appears a bit later in "Poesias americanas." It describes the European rush for gold and the subsequent dislocation of the Indian, who becomes a wanderer in his own country. The poem ends with the speaker asking the god Tupã to seek vengeance against the intruders.

21. Alexandre Herculano was especially enthusiastic about "Poesias americanas," which he hoped would "occupy greater space" in the poet's future work (in W. Martins 1977, 2:355).

22. The first document published in the *Revista* (in 1839) was "História dos índios cavalheiros ou da nação guaycurú" (History of the Noble Indians or of the Guaycurú Nation), written by Francisco Rodrigues Prado in 1795.

23. In his study of the poems, the Brazilian poet Cassiano Ricardo emphasizes the "authenticity" of Gonçalves Dias's Indianism based on three points: Dias himself was

the offspring of a mother who was Indian and black and a father who was Portuguese; he had direct contact with indigenous inhabitants in Caxias, Maranhão, where he was born and lived as a child; and he studied indigenous culture and authored two books on the subject (Ricardo 1964, 26). Those works are *O Brasil e oceânia* (1851), which he wrote for the Instituto Histórico and which literary critic Cláudia Neiva de Matos considers the first work of Brazilian ethnography (1988, 3–4), and his *Dicionário da língua tupi* (1858).

24. Antônio Cândido describes Dias as a medievalist who greatly appreciated Portuguese literature. This is evidenced by Dias's Portuguese-inspired works such as the play *Leonor de Mendonça* in 1846 and the book of verse *Sextilhas de Frei Antão* (Friar Antão's Sextets) in 1848. During his career, Dias wrote other Indian poems that appeared in his second and third volumes, *Segundos cantos* (Second Songs) in 1848 and *Últimos cantos* (Last Songs) in 1861, as well as his long poem *Os timbiras*, of which four *cantos* survived.

25. In the May 4, 1862, issue of the magazine *Charivari*, there is an unsigned caricature of Dom Pedro II in which he is shown balancing on one leg atop a donkey that, in turn, is balancing on an Egyptian pyramid positioned on top of Pão de Açucar (Sugar Loaf, the prominent rock formation of Rio-postcard fame). The monarch, whose head has been replaced by a cashew nut, holds a page of Magalhães's book in his right hand and a bunch of bananas in his left hand. The caption reads: "Goodness gracious! . . . At least no one can say that I never wrote for the press; I'm wise and I'm also a journalist! It's general opinion that my analysis of the *Confederação dos tamoios* was a veritable *chef-d'oeuvre* . . . I even came out well in Greek . . . I'm decidedly going to arrive at the Capitol" (in H. Lima 1963, 98).

26. Although he was not specifically talking about Debret, the romantic author Manuel de Araújo Porto Alegre condemned the inaccuracies portrayed by foreign visitors—especially the French:

> The carelessness of the majority of French travelers and the superficiality with which they look upon things that they find in our country, together with an insatiable desire to take back novelties to their country, has been the cause of these great depositories of lies that are found spread throughout many books of these people who, the majority of times, sacrifice the truth to witticisms of the spirit and the faithful picture of practices and customs of a nation to the fantastic portrait of their ardent imagination, which is freely aided by a lack of knowledge of the language and by the belief that everything which is not France is on the last rung of humanity. (In Süssekind 1990, 51)

27. Debret was likely influenced by his compatriot Chateaubriand's popular Indian novels *Atala* (1801) and *René* (1802), and there is no question that Dias was familiar with both *Atala*, which he quotes in *Primeiros cantos,* and Basílio da Gama's *O uraguai*.

28. In his memoirs, *Reminiscências* (1908), Alfredo Taunay recalled the excitement—especially among women readers—that *O guarani* produced. He also described the public's enthusiasm whenever a new chapter of the novel appeared:

When the mail arrived in São Paulo . . . many students met in a fraternity where there was a happy subscriber to the *Diário do Rio* in order to hear, absorbed and shaken from time to time by an electric thrill, the reading by those among them who had the strongest voices. And the newspaper was then fought over impatiently, and in the streets groups formed around the smoking lights of the public illumination system of that time—and listeners, avid, would surround them like an improvised audience of readers.

On a comparably larger scale . . . the same thing happened in Paris when the first fascicles of *Les miserables* appeared. (In Proença 1966, 18–19)

The Parisian Adèle Toussaint-Samson, who was living in Rio, wrote enthusiastically about *O guarani*: "One of their best novels has for its title *Le guarany*, by Alaincar [*sic*], and of which I propose to offer a translation one of these days to the Parisian public. It is a faithful portrait of the Indian, which is at the same time poetical and true" (2001, 94–95).

29. Gonçalves Dias's tragic figure in his poem "Marabá" (a word that means offspring of an Indian and a white) is a forerunner of the beautiful dark-haired Isabel, whose mixed-blood heritage is a forecast of her suffering and eventual doom. Heitor Martins reminded me in a conversation in July 2006 that Ceci and Isabel are based on the blond (innocent) and brunette (passionate) characters of the gothic novels that Alencar read as a child.

30. In his opera based on the novel and performed at La Scala in Milan, Carlos Gomes changed the villain from the Italian Loredano to a Spaniard called González.

31. There was considerable criticism about Alencar's use of a poeticized Portuguese for the Indians' speech. Alencar recalled in his 1873 memoir-essay "Como e porque sou romancista" (How and Why I Am a Novelist) that he had to pay out of pocket to publish *Iracema* in book form and that fortunately the edition sold out in two years (120).

32. Renata R. Mautner Wasserman calls attention to these interesting details provided by Plínio Doyle and Manuel Cavalcanti Proença, respectively, in her study "The 'Indian' Novels of José de Alencar" (1983). She cites, among others, names such as "Ingeborg Iracema Rann" and "Iracema Müller."

33. In the early 1970s, filmmaker Nelson Pereira dos Santos reintroduced the plot of *Iracema* in his movie *Como era gostoso o meu francês*. But instead of leaving the community, bearing an offspring, and dying for the love of the European, his Indian character, Sepiobebe, ensures that the Frenchman Jean remains a captive (she shoots him with an arrow when he tries to escape), and although they live as man and wife, she looks forward to his execution, when he will be ingested and thus literally become part of the community. The film ends with a close-up that shows her contentedly gnawing on a piece of flesh, supposedly the neck that she covets.

34. Alencar wrote: "In *O guarani*, the savage is an ideal that the writer attempted to poeticize, stripping him of the rough crust in which the chronicles wrapped him, and tearing him away from the ridiculous person that the brutish remains of the almost extinct race project on him" (1965, 117).

35. For studies in English on Brazilian nationalism and Alencar's Indianist novels see Doris Sommer 1991 and Renata Wasserman 1983, 1984.

36. Gomes was the most important Brazilian conductor-composer in the nineteenth century, and he was internationally acclaimed for his third opera, *O guarani,* which opened at La Scala on March 19, 1870. The opera debuted in Rio in December that same year and was later performed in all the European capitals between Lisbon and Moscow (Vainfas 2002, 123).

37. In his study of caricature in Brazil, Herman Lima quotes Josué Montelo about the political take on caricature during the empire: "Caricature experienced a golden age in the rowdy press of the Empire. . . . The freedom then granted the press created the necessary groundwork for the development of the art. . . . Freedom of the press had come to the First Empire and had grown in the Second, thanks to the parliamentary government and the liberal spirit of the monarchy" (1963, 95).

38. Varnhagen wrote unsympathetically about Indians in his *História geral do Brasil* and even postulated that their demise was self-inflicted. The literary historian José Veríssimo specifically commented on Varnhagen's attitude: "Varnhagen is perhaps the only one who, besides not being an Indianist, that is, showing no sympathy for the Indian as a factor in our population, on the contrary scorns and disparages him and even applauds his destruction" (154). Capistrano de Abreu's *O descobrimento do Brasil: Povoamento do solo—evolução social. Memória* (The Discovery of Brazil: Peopling of the Land—Social Evolution. Memoir), published in 1900, dialogues with Varnhagen's text yet is more balanced in its interpretation of the Indian and rituals such as anthropophagy.

39. José Maurício Gomes de Almeida distinguishes the two principal ideas behind the genre of literature that became known as "regionalism." He says that, in its strictest sense, regionalist literature seeks to emphasize the different elements that characterize a region in contrast to the rest or the national totality; in its more latent sense, however, he states that the works express an affirmation of the national through types that are regionally configured (in *Biblos* 2001, 4:666).

It is interesting to consider late-nineteenth-century Brazilian regionalism in light of Benedict Anderson's discussions of the nation as an imagined community. Perhaps the concept of regional literature, which focuses on a specific area and community, was a way for writers to circumvent the vastness and variety that make knowing or representing Brazil as a whole implausible.

40. This may be what critic José Veríssimo was thinking when he wrote that 1873 was the year "Brazilian mentality . . . completely abandon[ed] the 'Indianist cult'" (in Miguel-Pereira 1973, 32n22).

41. Emília Viotti da Costa writes that in 1872, nearly one-third of the population of Rio de Janeiro was foreign-born, and immigrants comprised 12 percent of the populations of the southern towns of Curitiba and Porto Alegre (2000, 191).

42. Even today, people from the Central-South look to the Northeast and the *sertão*

as a more "authentic" or "pure" Brazil, perhaps an indication of the influence these writings had long after their initial publication. I heard this characterization on different occasions when I was living in Recife. Individuals who had never visited or resided in the Northeast were fascinated by the idea of the region and talked about it in enthusiastic terms as something akin to an ur-Brazil. At the same time, people I knew in Recife often felt dismayed by that very "purity" or "provincialism" that was associated with the Northeast.

43. In his introduction to the Heath 1923 edition of *Inocência* (xxii), Maro Beath Jones attributes the Meyer-Langsdorff analogy to Alfredo de Carvalho and his 1908 book, *Três naturalistas* (Three Naturalists). In *Visões do sertão*, Taunay describes a trip into the interior, where he met a Senhor Manoel Coelho, "a father with daughters whose beauty merited notice, and which was the reason for the zealous head of the family's not small concern, even though he was less cross and mistrustful a man than one generally finds in the interior" (1928, 40). He adds that Coelho "contributed to the physiognomy of Inocência's father" (40). In an earlier passage, he attributes the character Tico to a "small, mute but delightful dwarf with agile movements" whom he met as he crossed the Sucuriú River (35).

44. Fausto estimates that between 135,000 and 200,000 men from a total male population of 4.9 million had been mobilized for the war effort (1999, 124).

45. The word *jagunço* has different interpretations, but in this case it is used to refer to the peasants led by Antônio Conselheiro. In its broader usage, the term refers to a hired gun who works as a bodyguard for a boss and protects his property.

46. The *buriti* is also one of the most important and symbolic trees in the works of Guimarães Rosa.

47. Arinos was a staunch monarchist and contended that any other form of government for Brazil would be disastrous. According to João Cruz Costa (1964), prior to 1889, even liberals expressed a desire to retain the monarchy in fear that a republic would bring about the disintegration of the country. Arinos's critique of the government's handling of Canudos is an expression of his unhappiness with and distrust of the republican government.

48. At the beginning of the book, Blau is introduced by a nameless character who directly addresses the interlocutor as an old friend and vouches for and praises his longtime cowboy acquaintance: "Now an aging but hardy *vaqueiro,* [Blau Nunes] is a genuine type—a Rio Grande creole . . . loyal and ingenuous, impulsively joyful and derring-do, cautious, perspicacious, somber, and untiring; blessed with a memory of rare clarity that shines through an imaginative and enchanting loquaciousness, which is aided and adorned by a lively and picturesque gaucho dialect" (12).

49. Lopes Neto dedicated the story to the much-admired regionalist writer Coelho Neto in 1907. In a letter to Lopes Neto, Coelho Neto lauds the *gaúcho* author's faithfulness to the language of storytelling: "Many writers believe that they should correct the fable-telling and the form, taking away the ingenuous quality of such old tales . . . But

my friend cannot be blamed for having done that. . . . Reading ["O negrinho"], I had the impression of hearing it told, in a slow tempo, by one of those little old women who are the meticulous guardians of popular [p]oetry, which is so rich in our country and yet so undervalued" (in Lopes Neto 1991, 67).

50. I want to acknowledge Heitor Martins for conversations about *Meditação* and for pointing out that when Gonçalves Dias returned to Brazil after years in Portugal, he briefly stopped writing about noble savages and began writing about slavery, which was everywhere around him in Maranhão. But he abandoned the topic shortly thereafter and resumed writing poems on the Indian and the ethnographic study on Amerindian nations commissioned by the emperor—a course of action that may have been more politically prudent for the up-and-coming poet.

51. After abolishing its own slave trafficking in 1807, Britain encouraged its ally Portugal to follow suit. Even after 1850, there were violations of the treaty. For example, a coastal area in Pernambuco served as an entryway for slaves who were secretly brought into the Northeast. The area was called Porto das Galinhas—Port of the Chickens, as "chickens" was a code word for "African slaves."

52. The playwright Martins Pena's one-act play of 1845, *Os dous ou o inglês maquinista* (The Two or the English Machinist), satirizes the greedy slave trafficker as well as the English entrepreneur who condemns slavery while profiting from the loss of slave labor in Brazil's economy.

53. Brasileira Augusta repeatedly criticized the institution of slavery in her *Opúsculo humanitário* (1853). Wilson Martins expressed doubts about the accepted notion that Stowe's novel had a decisive impact on the abolition of slavery in Brazil. He comments: "We should not extrapolate from its tremendous *literary* success [in Brazil] an effective interference in the change of social and economic structures (suffice it to note that, in the United States, the system of slavery needed a war to become extinct *fourteen* years later); in Brazil, the sentimental impact of abolitionist literature, including *Uncle Tom's Cabin,* failed, and abolition would only occur thirty-seven years later" (1977, 2:461).

54. In a chapter on Castro Alves in his book *Three Sad Races* (1983), David Haberly speculates about why the poet decided to write abolitionist verse. One of his hypotheses is that the writer equated his own sense of personal entrapment with the lack of freedom of the slaves: "This basic fact—that Castro Alves was writing not about the slaves but himself—explains the nature of his abolitionism" (62). Haberly acknowledges that, regardless of the reasons that propelled him, Castro Alves produced some extraordinarily powerful poetry and became famous as "the Bard of the Slaves" (56).

55. Critic José Guilherme Merquior has pointed out that Castro Alves's poems such as "O navio negreiro" excited audiences because of their tremendous orality. Merquior also observes that Castro Alves was in synch with European authors of the time and in particular with Victor Hugo, whose public declamations engaged social issues of international concern (Merquior 1977, 91–92).

56. Fagundes Varela, a fellow poet and a classmate of Castro Alves, published two

volumes of poetry—*O estandarte auriverde* (The Green and Yellow Standard) in 1863 and *Vozes d'América* (American Voices) in 1864—whose titles and themes resonate in Castro Alves's poems.

57. A similar note is struck in Aluísio Azevedo's 1881 novel, *O mulato* (*The Mulatto*, 1941), in which gossip mongers whisper to one another about the protagonist: "I hear said that he's a mulatto!" (116). Another character in the novel is far more direct in her disdainful assessment and refers to him as a *cabra,* or "goat" (126).

58. For a concise commentary on Gama see Heitor Martins 1996.

59. See Vera Follain de Figueiredo 2004 for her examination of this polemic.

60. The reference to Nabuco's poetry appears in Machado's chronicle "Ao acaso" (To Chance), which appeared on January 31, 1865.

61. Machado's ironic characterization of the foreign naturalist is similar to Taunay's treatment of Meyer, except that Machado prefers not to give his character a name and simply refers to him as "the godfather" or with tongue in cheek as "the former poet of 1810." We learn that Camilo is named after the protagonist of his godfather's only moderately successful poem, which, the narrator tells us, "time—eternity's old trapdoor—carried off to the infinite warehouse of useless things" (1961, 11).

62. The first Positivist Association of Brazil was established in 1876 (Costa 1964, 99), although positivism had been introduced to Brazil much earlier, in the 1850s. One of the first Brazilians to embrace positivist doctrine was Nísia Floresta Brasileira Augusta, who was living in Paris in 1851 and came to know and admire Auguste Comte. There she introduced visiting compatriots to the philosopher, whom she considered "the most extraordinary man of the century" (in Lins 1964, 22).

63. In his *A History of Ideas in Brazil* (1964), João Cruz Costa comments on the nature and possible implications of positivism in Brazil:

> Although the other doctrines imported after the first half of the nineteenth century seem to me mere intellectual games—typical of erudite elites, no more than embellishments for curious intellects—about Positivism, I nevertheless have the impression (paradoxical, to be sure) that some deeper relationship exists between the nature of this doctrine and the nexus of contradictory factors which gave rise to our national life and which still govern it. Although Positivism, like the other doctrines, is an importation, it contains elements that reveal its compatibility with our formative influences and the most profound verities of our spirit. (182)

64. Following the establishment of the republic in 1889, a new flag was adopted with the positivist motto, "Order and Progress."

65. "Bacamarte" translates as "blunderbuss" in English, or in more colloquial terms, "worthless fellow." As we shall see, both meanings aptly describe the doctor.

66. João Cruz Costa summarizes the relationship between religion and science in Brazil as if he were talking about the relationship between the vicar and Bacamarte: "Relations between the Church and the 'skeptical and rationalist' ruling classes of the Second Empire were not exactly happy. . . . Nevertheless, more from habit and tra-

dition than from conviction, the intellectual elite continued to respect Catholicism, which was the state religion" (1964, 56).

67. More than one literary critic who read *Dom Casmurro* was convinced beyond a reasonable doubt of Capitu's infidelity. Others took umbrage at this verdict and protested her innocence. Critic Doris J. Turner (1976) presented the case that both sides missed the point if only because nearly everything to which Dom Casmurro attests in the novel is carefully couched in the language of contradiction or conjecture. The critical literature on Machado's fiction is immense. Among important books in English are Helen Caldwell, *The Brazilian Othello of Machado de Assis* (1960); Earl E. Fitz, *Machado de Assis* (1989); John Gledson, *The Deceptive Realism of Machado de Assis* (1984); Richard Graham, *Machado de Assis* (1999); and Roberto Schwarz, *A Master on the Periphery of Capitalism* (2001).

Chapter Five

1. Immigrants from Germany, Portugal, Italy, Spain, and other European countries were desirable among those who advocated whitening the population. The Brazilian government was less enthusiastic about Japanese immigrants, a quarter-million of whom arrived in the early twentieth century; however, their conscientious work ethic made them an exception to the whitening initiative. Tizuka Yamasaki's 1980 film *Gaijin: Os caminhos da liberdade* (Stranger: The Roads to Freedom) portrays the arrival of early Japanese immigrants in São Paulo and the harsh working conditions they encountered on coffee plantations there. For a concise study of immigration to Brazil see Oliveira's *O Brasil dos imigrantes* (2002).

The Memorial do Imigrante in São Paulo has preserved the tram that carried immigrants from the port city of Santos to São Paulo. The building houses a museum with photographs and other items associated with the different people who came to Brazil—as well as simulacra of dental and medical services that were offered to the newly arrived immigrant.

2. In his article, Eduardo Morettin discusses *First Mass in Brazil*, which was a touchstone for the republican government and became inextricably associated with the idea of the nation (2000, 21–23). He comments on turn-of-the-century textbooks, many of which were heavily illustrated with paintings like the one by Meirelles and employed didactic methods including sets of questions that required students to write specifically about the meaning of the images. According to historian Circe Bittencourt (ibid.), the most reproduced images in these textbooks were Meirelles's *First Mass* and Pedro Américo's representation of Brazilian independence, *7 de setembro de 1822* (September 7, 1822).

3. The famous *Batalha de Guararapes* hangs prominently in the Museu de Belas Artes in Rio, but the epic work was initially criticized for being too static in its representation of war.

4. Moema was a young Indian woman who fell in love with the Portuguese castaway

Diogo Álvares Correa, more famously known as Caramuru. When he returned to Portugal with another Amerindian woman, Moema purportedly swam after his ship and drowned.

5. Elyseo Visconti, who incorporated impressionist tendencies into his works, would be an important exception to this generalized assessment.

6. Malfatti's first exhibition was in 1914, and, as she later stated, it provided the "seed" for her celebrated 1917 exposition (in Aracy Amaral 1970, 75).

7. In many ways, Malfatti's *Tropical* was the most extraordinary of her works in this period. In the painting, a young black woman in contemporary dress gazes off to the side as she holds a bowl of fruit in her hands. Large palm fronds appear to her left and right in the background. The composition has both cubist and expressionistic elements, yet it is Malfatti's subject of the underrepresented African Brazilian as neither slave nor servant that is as remarkable as her innovative style. She anticipates Brazilian social realism's epic-heroic treatment of the African Brazilian by some fifteen years.

8. There is a wealth of material in Portuguese and English on the vanguard literature and personalities associated with the Modern Art Week. For sources in English see, for example, Jackson 1987, W. Martins 1970, Nist 1967, Reis 1992, and Santiago 2001.

9. Tarsila do Amaral's cover for Oswald de Andrade's book *Pau brasil* (1925) shows the Brazilian flag with the nation's motto "Order and Progress" replaced by the word "Brazilwood."

10. In 1915, the novelist Lima Barreto lampooned the nationalistic fervor of the early part of the century in his novel *Triste fim de Policarpo Quaresma* (The Sad End of Policarpo Quaresma), whose *ufanista-nativista* protagonist demonstrates his patriotism by studying Tupi. Barreto's comic-satiric approach was appropriated by early modernists who introduced the *poema-piada* (joke-poem). A good example is Manuel Bandeira's "Os sapos" (The Frogs), which pokes fun at frog-poets whose style is modeled on art for art's sake:

> Says the tree frog,
> a frustrated bard,
> "To produce songs
> I work very hard.
>
> Note with what ease
> I take up the spaces.
> Pure art! Never rhyme
> Cognate phrases" (in *Semana de 22* 1972, n.p.)

11. The Spanish Antonio Moya and the Polish Georg Przyrembel presented neoclassical designs during the Modern Art Week. According to Aracy Amaral, Vicente Licínio Cardoso gave a lecture in Brazil in 1916 on the "new" wave of architectural design and skyscrapers in the United States (1970, 149), but he was not a participant in the week.

12. See also H. Mindlin 1961 (29). For more details on Warchavchik and the dialogue between literary modernism and modernist architecture in Brazil at this time see Philippou 2005.

13. Philippou writes that "Le Corbusier's admiration for the creativity of popular architecture [hillside shanties] found him in agreement with the pioneer artists of Brazilian Modernism as well as with those young Brazilian intellectuals who were in the process of defining the identity of an imaginary Brazilian national community" (2005, 246).

14. The buildings at Pampulha were built in the early 1940s at the invitation of Juscelino Kubitschek, who was then mayor of Belo Horizonte, the capital of Minas Gerais state. The project consisted of a church, a casino, a club, and a dance hall/restaurant that were constructed on an artificial lake in the suburbs of Belo Horizonte. Lauro Cavalcanti has observed that "Pampulha was thirty years ahead of the end of rational functionalism, and it pointed the way for alternatives to aesthetic bureaucracy that threatened the architecture of the 1940s. . . . The Church of Saint Francis is the birthplace of proper Brazilian architecture. With its self-supporting vaulting of various dimensions, it makes use of the structural potential of concrete, which is used to form a waved roof on an almost nonexistent wall tiled with azulejos" (2003, 34). Early on, the Pampulhas Complex was not fully utilized for various reasons, including the presence of parasites in the lake and the community's rejection of the modernist-style church for their religious services. Problems continue to plague the complex to this day.

15. For a detailed discussion of Brazil's Pavilion as "tropical modernism" see D. Williams 2001 (203–215).

16. Goodwin's preface to the book is an indication of how the United States' national and cultural interests in Brazil merged during the war years. He states: "The Museum of Modern Art, New York, and the American Institute of Architects in the spring of 1942 were both anxious to have closer relations with Brazil, a country which was to be our future ally" (Goodwin 1943, 7). The censorship arm of the Vargas government, the Departamento de Imprensa e Propaganda (DIP, Department of the Press and Propaganda), and Nelson Rockefeller's Office of Inter-American Affairs are both acknowledged for their support of the project.

17. "Jeca Tatuism" is a reference to Afonso Celso's book and is based on Monteiro Lobato's popular hillbilly protagonist from his 1919 novel, *Idéias de Jeca Tatu* (Ideas of Jeca Tatu).

18. Daryle Williams comments on the reluctance of Brazil to export art about Afro-Brazilian culture to the United States as well as the divided critical reception received by Portinari's one-man show at the Museum of Modern Art (2001, 218–221).

19. The idea of a new capital dates back to 1789, when the Minas Gerais conspirators promoted the cause of transferring the capital to the interior. Later, in 1809, Hipólito da Costa, the editor of *Correio braziliense,* wrote of moving the capital inland, arguing

that "Rio de Janeiro did not possess any of the qualities required for a city that was to be the capital of the empire" (in Gicovate 1959, 27).

20. Highlands travel was extremely difficult and dangerous. In 1914, Theodore Roosevelt led a zoologic and geographic expedition to the central highlands and the Amazon and nearly died on the trip. See his *Through the Brazilian Wilderness,* revised edition 1994.

21. An image of this complex appears on a 1972 stamp issued by Lebanon in celebration of Brazil's fifty years of independence.

22. Unlike Dos Passos, who became a conservative in his later years, Niemeyer never changed his political stance and has been a longstanding member of the Communist Party.

In addition to Dos Passos, Brasília attracted artists and celebrities from different political persuasions, including Aldous Huxley, André Malraux, Frank Capra, Le Corbusier, and the Russian astronaut Yuri Gagarin, who is quoted as saying upon his arrival, "I feel I have just disembarked upon another planet, not earth" (in Shoumatoff 1980, 53).

23. Workers lived in a shantytown called Cidade Livre (Free City) while building the capital. It was also known as Provisional City because it was initially believed that it would disappear once Brasília was built. The first satellite city, Taguatinga, was created in 1958. By 1980, three-quarters of the population of the Federal District lived on the periphery (Holston 1989, 28).

24. On his return trip to Brasília in 1962, Dos Passos criticized the low-income units: "The rows of identical concrete hutches for low income renters express, even more perfectly than some federal housing in the United States, the twentieth century bureaucrat's disdain of the faceless multitudes to whose interests he is supposed to be devoted and whose exploitation furnishes his keep. The worst shack in the adjacent shanty town of Cidade Livre or Taguatinga would be a better place to live" (1963, 130).

25. The building of Brasília put considerable pressure on the nation's economy, and construction often came to a halt for lack of resources. A portion of the citizenry also criticized the massive expenditures required by the building of the capital when hunger, poverty, and a weak infrastructure were more pressing national needs. There is little doubt that Brasília was a factor in the instability that led up to the military overthrow of the government. But even greater factors were Goulart's left-wing politics and his support of agrarian reform.

26. In a 2002 essay, Lauro Cavalcanti offered a far more devastating commentary on Brasília: "The level of architecture produced in the last ten years is the very worst, cheap copies of a Miami postmodernism" (102).

27. In his June 1964 review of the film for the *Motion Picture Herald,* Richard Gertner wrote: "In all the history of the movies, and that includes the days of *The Perils of Pauline*—no character could possibly have undergone so many narrow escapes from danger and death as the hero of *That Man from Rio.* Jean-Paul Belmondo portrays this

plucky and indefatigable fellow, who is really a combination of Tarzan, Houdini and Superman" (75).

28. It should be noted that Adrien's attitude here is radically different from that of foreign companies and multinationals that were beginning to heavily invest in the former capital and elsewhere in Brazil in the 1960s.

29. In the 1960s and 1970s, various educational films in English appeared on the construction of Brasília, and an undated pamphlet titled *Brasília* was issued by the Brazilian Government Trade Bureau in New York and provided to tourists on their way to Brazil. The booklet informed the reader that "everything in Brasília is a tourist attraction" (40), including the Free City, which is described as "a log-cabin village in Far West fashion, housing the famous 'candangos,' the workers who have built Brasília." It further observes that Free City "offers a unique contrast to the 'Capital of the Century'" (42). Although the lakeside settlement that de Broca filmed is not Cidade Livre, it does serve to emphasize the "contrast" pointed out by the promotional literature, although not quite in the way that the booklet intended.

30. For a discussion of this film within the context of dos Santos's work see Sadlier 2003 (110–114).

31. Ruy Castro observes that bossa nova slightly improved the imbalance in commercial relations between Brazil and the United States. But he points out that, unlike producers of some other exports, bossa nova musicians back in Brazil realized little profit (2000, 101, 116).

32. See R. Castro 2000 for a description of the complex preparations for that concert, which garnered recording contracts and singing engagements for Jobim, Gilberto, and Mendes, among others.

Chapter Six

1. For more information on Rockefeller's interests in Latin America see Darlene Rivas 2002 and Martha Gil-Montero 1989.

2. Perhaps the authors were unaware of how debilitating this kind of trade was to less industrially advanced nations. As history has shown, Portugal and later Brazil were dependent on manufactured goods from England, and they retained a one-crop approach to agriculture that (as the textbook authors noted in a later section of their book) experienced booms but also busts.

3. In an address to the nation on May 27, 1941, Roosevelt stated:

[The Nazis] have the armed power at any moment to occupy Spain and Portugal, and that threat extends not only to French North Africa and the western end of the Mediterranean Sea, [but] it extends also to the Atlantic fortress of Dakar, and to the island outposts of the New World––the Azores and Cape Verde Islands. Yes, [these] Cape Verde Islands are only seven hours distance from Brazil by bomber or troop-carrying planes. They dominate shipping routes to and from the South Atlantic." (At http://ibiblio.org/pha/timeline/410527bwp.html)

One might understand such concern in 1941, when Roosevelt gave his speech and when Herring's book was published, but by the time the CIAA booklet appeared three years later, the possibility of an Axis invasion of Brazil from Africa was highly remote.

4. The Production Code Administration also was concerned with the image of Latin Americans in films and appointed Addison Durland to oversee this aspect of film production in order to assure hemispheric unity (Woll 1974, 280).

5. Motion Picture Society of the Americas members were individuals from various organizations, including the CIAA and the Hollywood Academy of Motion Pictures Arts and Sciences. They regularly reported to Rockefeller about projects relating to Latin America. Martha Gil-Montero states that among the organization's most important achievements of the time was convincing Twentieth Century Fox to spend $40,000 for reshooting certain scenes from its 1940 movie *Down Argentine Way,* which had been banned in Argentina (1989, 117). A June 4, 1941, article in *Variety* cited some of the problems, which Allen L. Woll summarizes in the following way: "Why was Carmen Miranda portraying an Argentine when she was obviously Brazilian? Why were Argentines depicted as the owners of a crooked race track and the Americans once again as the good guys?" (1974, 288–289). New footage was shot on location in Buenos Aires, and the edited movie, which now had "Brazilian" music in the sound track, was finally released in Argentina (Gil-Montero 1989, 118).

6. Except as otherwise noted, Welles quotes are from scripts, recordings, and other materials in the Orson Welles archive at the Lilly Library, Indiana University, Bloomington.

7. See, for example, Benamou 2007 and Stam 1997. In 1985, a segment of what had long been considered Welles's "lost" film was discovered in the Paramount vaults. Richard Wilson, Welles's assistant on the project, produced an excellent short documentary, *Four Men on a Raft,* based on the recovered footage. His work was followed in 1993 by a feature-length reconstruction of *It's All True.*

8. In *The Magic World of Orson Welles,* James Naremore describes RKO's change of attitude toward Welles and his Brazilian project: "Meanwhile the new [RKO] management began circulating rumors that Welles's Rio footage was chaotic and extravagant. With *It's All True* nearly complete, Welles was ordered home; RKO collected its guaranteed money from the government, printed about 13,000 feet of Welles's work (which was never shown), and supposedly destroyed the rest" (1989, 85).

9. Both Disney films feature footage shot in Brazil and the cigar-smoking Brazilian parrot and cartoon character Zé Carioca. Among the celebrities who appear in *The Three Caballeros* is Carmen Miranda's sister, Aurora.

10. In 1936, Rio's Rádio Nacional went on the air with the announcer Celso Guimarães, who always started his program with the popular greeting "Alô, alô Brasil!" Four years later, Vargas transformed Rádio Nacional into an "instrument of affirmation for his regime" (Ortriwano 1985, 18), an instrument that used the newspaper *A*

noite (The Night) as well. Among the documents in the Lilly Library's Welles archive are numerous photographs of Welles with Lourival Fontes, who was head of the DIP.

11. The *caipira* skits often poked fun at the government. Jararaca and Ratinho had serious problems with the censors, while Alvarenga and Ranchinho managed to survive the Estado Novo.

12. It is most certain that Welles had DIP clearance for his radio show and that his question to Aranha about a Fifth Column was not improvised.

13. Two Brazilians accused of collaborating with Germany were the poet Geraldo de Mello Mourão and an air force officer, Oceano Araújo de Sá, who later adopted the name Yokaanam and became the leader of the religious sect Fraternidade Eclética Espiritualista Universal, which is still active today in an area near Brasília called Cidade Eclética.

14. According to Welles in his and Bogdanovich's book, *This Is Orson Welles,* both the "Pan-American Day" and "President Vargas's Birthday" programs were sponsored by NBC–Blue Network (1998, 370).

15. "Dictator of democracy" was the image generated by the United States to make Vargas acceptable at a time when the United States was fighting other fascist regimes. Vargas had styled his dictatorship after Salazar's Estado Novo in Portugal—which the United States also tolerated and described as a "benevolent dictatorship." This enabled the United States to gain Salazar's support during the war for the construction of strategic mid-Atlantic air bases in the Azores.

16. Filmmaker Rogério Sganzerla used the title *Tudo é Brasil* for his 1997 documentary about Welles in Brazil.

17. Nássara, the composer of "Sabemos lutar," dedicated the song to Oswaldo Aranha. The sheet music (a copy of which is in the Lilly Library Welles archive) with its cover image of a Brazilian soldier was used as a recruitment poster for the military reserves. Brazil was the only nation in South America to send troops to fight in World War II.

18. Brazil declared war on August 22, 1942, after its merchant ships were repeatedly torpedoed by German submarines.

19. For a study of Miranda and ethnicity see Ana M. López 1993.

20. Aside from her last name, there is nothing "Irish" about the character played by Miranda, who explains this by telling MacTavish that her Irish father left her mother, who was Brazilian, and that she was raised in Brazil. For a detailed discussion of ethnicity, performance, and female spectatorship see Shari Roberts 1993.

21. In her description of Miranda's role in *Down Argentine Way,* Gil-Montero emphasizes the hybridity of her character: "Carmen Miranda, a *Brazilian* star, sings in *Portuguese* a *Tin Pan Alley rhumba* which speaks of *tangos* and rhumbas being played beneath a *pampa* moon" (1989, 97).

22. Ruy Castro comments on how Brazilians lyricists were often liberal in their translations of English into Portuguese. "Chattanooga Choo-Choo" was a good ex-

ample. Aloysio de Oliveira, Miranda's accompanist and romantic partner, wrote the Portuguese lyrics:

> Vou explicar o que é
> O Chattanooga choo-choo
> Choo-choo é um trem
>
> Que vai me levar perto de alguém . . .
> Você pega o trem na Pennsylvania Station
> As três horas e tal
> Pouco a pouco vai saindo da capital
> Toma um cafezinho, tira uma pestana
> E come ham and eggs lá em Carolaina . . .
>
> Vou encontrar com certo alguém
> I used to call funny face
> Porque tem cara de Spencer Tracy
>
> [Translated literally: I'm going to explain what is the
> Chattanooga choo-choo
> Choo-choo's a train
> That's going to take me close to someone . . .
>
> You take the train at Pennsylvania Station
> At three o'clock or thereabouts
> Little by little, you leave the capital
> You drink an espresso, take a nap,
> And eat ham and eggs there in Carolaina . . .
>
> I'm going to meet with a certain someone
> Who's awaiting me at the station
> A certain someone
> I used to call funny face
> Because he looks just like Spencer Tracy] (In Castro 2001, 125)

23. Ruy Castro comments on Hollywood's approach to Brazilian music of the period and the commodification of Latin America:

> On the way from Rio to Hollywood, some American erred and sambas, *choros* and *baiões* would be transformed into congas, *beguines* and rhumbas to go along with scenery that included mustachioed men in sombreros, women dressed in bibs, and everyone moaning "ay, ay." It would take a while for Buenos Aires to stop being the capital of Brazil.
>
> What Americans were buying was not exactly the music, but a "climate," a "tropical," folkloric spirit that evoked beaches, cocoanut and banana trees, sacks of coffee and boys dressed in striped shirts and straw hats who would go well with the necklaces and fruited headdresses of Carmen Miranda. (2001, 108)

24. Dozer quotes from an article titled "El grito" (The Cry) in which Mistral urged Chilean manufacturers to "help us conquer or at least restrain the deadly invasion

. . . from blond America, which wishes to monopolize our markets and to overwhelm our farms and cities with its machinery and textiles" (in Dozer 1959, 130). Her words were undoubtedly linked to the Anaconda Copper Company and its revenues from the extraction of copper from mines purchased in Chile. Dozer also quotes Assis Chateaubriand, who remarked in Rio's *O jornal* that "though unexcelled in commercial propaganda . . . Americans are mediocre in intellectual or political propaganda" (133).

25. John King notes that the United States ultimately punished Argentina for its less-than-neighborly political stance during the war by starving it of raw film stock and supporting greater film production in Mexico (1990, 36).

26. The episode is chronicled in *The Busby Berkeley Book* by Thomas and Terry with Berkeley (1973, 152–154) and by Woll (1974, 292). The likelihood is that the censors restricted the film to viewers over eighteen years of age and did not impose a total ban of the movie in Brazil.

Chapter Seven

1. Miranda died two years later, just hours after performing a dance routine on Jimmy Durante's television program.

2. One of the reasons for Vera Cruz's demise was its decision to give film distribution rights to Columbia Pictures, which prioritized distribution of its own movies over those of the Brazilian company. For a discussion of Vera Cruz see Maria Rita Galvão 1995.

3. For instance, *O primo do cangaceiro* (The Bandit's Cousin) appeared in 1955, followed by *A lei do sertão* (The Law of the Backland) the next year. The latter featured Milton Ribeiro, who had won numerous best-actor awards for his riveting portrayal of the bandit Captain Galindo in *O cangaceiro*. A remake of *O cangaceiro* was released in 1997.

4. Rocha is quoted in an interview with him and fellow filmmakers Pereira dos Santos and Alex Viany; see "Cinema Novo" 1965. There is a significant body of literature in Portuguese, English, and French on the history of Cinema Novo and specific directors and films. Important sources in English include Armes 1987, Burton 1986, Johnson 1984, Johnson and Stam 1995, King 1990, Sadlier 1993, Stam 1997, and I. Xavier 1997. The journals *Cineaste* and *Jump Cut* have published considerable material on Brazilian New Cinema and Latin American films in general.

5. For various reasons, most prominently the absence of limits placed on films imported from the United States and Europe, Brazilian production continued to be small in the postwar years and consisted mainly of low-budget *chanchadas,* occasional adaptations, and other kinds of movies, some of which attempted to be socially or politically relevant. To give an idea of the postwar industry, an article in the July 25, 1955, issue of *Cine repórter* stated that close to 200 million movie tickets were purchased in Brazil in 1950, but only 28 films of the 599 exhibited that year were Brazilian (393 were imported from the United States, a trend that continues to this day). Of the 809

films exhibited in 1955, only 24 were Brazilian (Farias 1960, 21). In 1960, just one year prior to the release of *Barravento*, only 30 Brazilian features were made. These included *chanchadas* with actors Oscarito and Dercy Gonçalves and a *caipira* film with the talented Amácio Mazzaropi—all of which drew substantial audiences. Among other films that year were the lackluster comedy *Pequeno por fora* (Small on the Outside) by Aloísio T. de Carvalho; Carlos Manga's *Cacareco vem aí* (Cacareco Come Here), a comedy superior to most but which was accused of being a knock-off of Byron Haskins's 1947 film *I Walk Alone* (Silva Neto 2002, 141); Lima Barreto's disappointing melodrama *A primeira missa* (The First Mass), which was his last film; Nelson Pereira dos Santos's western *Mandacaru vermelho* (Red Cactus), the most notable feature of which is its black-and-white footage of the *sertão*; and Roberto Farias's edgy urban drama *Cidade ameaçada* (Threatened City), which anticipates the urban dramas of Cinema Novo.

In 1960, French director Marcel Camus reappeared with *Os Bandeirantes* (The Flag-Bearers), an adventure film about vengeance and redemption in the Brazilian interior. This movie was far less successful than his *Black Orpheus* (1958) despite (or perhaps because of) the latter's stereotypic view of Brazilians as a poor but happy people.

6. I asked Heitor Martins, who was poetry editor for the *Suplemento dominical do Jornal do Brasil* in the 1950s, if he could explain what Rocha meant by his reference to these particular newspapers. He replied in an e-mail dated November 4, 2004:

> I do not recall what happened with the *Diário Carioca*. *Última Hora* started using the color blue on its title page, and I believe in some headlines. It was a new newspaper and some of its features remind me of *USA Today*. It also had some very popular sections, like the revived "folhetim" (serial) section that featured [playwright] Nelson Rodrigues (*Asfalto Selvagem* [Wild Asphalt]). It was created to support Vargas, and was very populist.
>
> *Jornal do Brasil* was the most traditional of the three. This newspaper was very bad, yet it did very good business by featuring classifieds on the front page. People would buy it just to look for jobs or sell or rent merchandise. Suddenly it came out with a literary supplement (the SDJB—*Suplemento Dominical do Jornal do Brasil*) that started filling the blank spaces with graphic compositions. Its language, starting with the use of the acronym, was very modern, very much against the language of the so-called "Geração de 45" (Generation of '45). (Up to that moment, the major literary supplement in Brazil had been the *Letras e Artes,* the voice of the "Geração de 45" which was published by the [newspaper] *A Manhã.*) SDJB was influenced by advances in graphic design and it really revolutionized the way newspaper printing was done. I do not remember any pictures or drawings being used, only large letters and blank spaces. Reynaldo Jardim (the SDJB's editor), Ferreira Gullar and Oliveira Bastos were mainly responsible for it. At the same time, Mário Faustino started writing poetry criticism following "new criticism" practices. (Of course, Afrânio Coutinho had written about it [new criticism] before, but his influence was much less evident.) And Assis Brasil, J. J. Veiga and O. G. Rego de Carvalho instituted new forms of prose, primarily influenced by Faulkner. The São Paulo

"concretistas" started to write for it as well, and it was the first time they reached a national audience. Today I would consider it the first document of a move from French to American influence in Brazilian art. It was the most influential publication in the contemporary "avant garde" in Brazil, perhaps in the Portuguese language. To tell you the truth, I do not see how the SDJB could influence Glauber—it was a very international publication. It coincided with the Teatro de Arena in its desire to look for new FORMS of presentation as opposed to content. Probably *Última Hora*, a left-leaning publication, was more in line with Glauber's position.

7. Consciousness-raising about socioeconomic and political injustices was as much a trope and objective of Brazilian literature in the 1930s and 1940s as it was for other world literatures, including works produced in the United States. Some of Brazil's most celebrated writings emerged in this period and were translated into English and other languages for a broader, international audience. As we have seen, before and during World War II, the Good Neighbor policy encouraged greater cultural exchange in the Americas, and organizations such as the União Cultural Brasil–Estados Unidos were active in promoting Brazilian literature in the United States. Brazilian literature received special attention by way both of Brazilians who were invited to the United States and of North Americans who were interested in Brazil, the most prominent among the latter being the essayist and editor Samuel Putnam. During the war, Putnam wrote extensively on Brazilian literature for the *Books Abroad* publication series. His 1945 translation of Jorge Amado's *Terras do sem fim* opened the way for numerous translations of Amado that appeared in subsequent years, which resulted in the Bahian author's becoming the best-known Latin American writer in the United States. Putnam's selection of *Terras do sem fim* for translation was a politically judicious one. A historical novel about the exploitation of cacao plantation workers by land barons in nineteenth-century Bahia, the book passed inspection by the DIP censors in Brazil who had suppressed (and even burned) some of Amado's earlier works as well as books by other left-wing writers. Ultimately there was little difference between the Bahian plantation society of the nineteenth century and its contemporary counterpart, and no writer exposed the similarities more adroitly than Amado.

   The years following the war and throughout the 1950s and tumultuous 1960s saw translations of older Brazilian works about the Northeast and interior alongside more contemporary writings both with and without political overtones. In the former group were Graciliano Ramos's 1938 *Vidas secas* (translated as *Barren Lives*, 1965) and Rachel de Queiroz's 1939 *As três Marias* (*The Three Marias*, 1963) about young women struggling against the patriarchal values of Northeastern life. Among the latter group were Alfredo Dias Gomes's 1959 *O pagador de promessas* (*Journey to Bahia*, 1964); João Guimarães Rosa's epic 1956 adventure about good and evil in the interior of Minas Gerais, *Grande sertão: Veredas* (*The Devil to Pay in the Backlands*, 1963), and his short-story collections *Sagarana* in 1946 (*Sagarana*, 1963) and *Primeiras estórias* in 1962 (*Third Bank of the River*, 1968), which continued to focus on the Brazilian interior. The first English translation of Clarice Lispector also appeared at this time; unlike much of her fiction, which focuses on young middle-class women and existential crisis in the city, *A maçã no escuro* in 1961 (*The Apple in the Dark*, 1967) is about an angst-ridden man's self-exile in the interior.

8. A survey of fifteen Brazilian intellectuals who were asked to list the twenty most influential works in any area of Brazilian culture resulted in the unanimous selection of *Os sertões* as number 1. See Rinaldo Gama 1994.

9. President Prudente de Morais believed that Canudos was pro-monarchical and a threat to the government. When the people of the town refused to pay taxes to the government, he launched the military campaign that ultimately destroyed the community. Robert Levine's documentary *Canudos Revisited* (1986) also points to the government's concern that Canudos was attracting the peasant labor force that normally worked the plantations of the Northeast.

10. In his essay on the film, Terry Carlson views Antão's action as symbolic of a black political awakening with origins in colonial black rebellion and the Palmares *quilombo*, a slave settlement in Northeastern Brazil.

11. In his study of the French reception of Cinema Novo, Figuerôa comments that film magazines and journals regularly used images of the Brazilian bandit to accompany their articles about Cinema Novo and that the figure assumed an iconic status. He also describes an interview in which Rocha was asked if the bandit had any relevance to present-day Brazil. Not surprisingly, Rocha counteracted any notion that the bandit was a relic or simply a myth and talked about the reported recent appearance of a *cangaceiro* who was being pursued in Pernambuco by an Antônio das Mortes–style *jagunço* (2004, 147).

12. Tropicalism was an artistic movement that emerged during the most repressive period of the dictatorship. Its most renowned figures were singer-musicians Gilberto Gil and Caetano Veloso, who were harassed and arrested for their songs. To escape further persecution, both artists went into exile for several years. There has been a recent surge of books and articles on this movement; in October 2005, the Museum of Contemporary Art in Chicago held the premiere exhibit of "Tropicália: A Brazilian Revolution: 1967–1972," which included Hélio Oiticica's environmental installation "Tropicália," considered to be the inspiration for Caetano Veloso's song by the same name; the sensory-oriented art of Lygia Clark; and the three-dimensional works by the Neoconcrete poet Ferreira Gullar. For more information see the 2005 catalog *Tropicália*, edited by Carlos Basualdo.

13. See "Cannibalism and Culture" in Sadlier 2003, *Nelson Pereira dos Santos*.

14. All *Macuníma* quotes are from the 1984 English translation of the novel.

15. For a detailed study of the film adaptation see Johnson 1982. A more recent commentary appears in Stam 2005.

16. There is an implied reference to Ci's revolutionary leanings in the book. After the birth of her son, the Amazon is given a red bow for her hair ("the color of calam-

ity") and becomes the leader of the "Red Circle" in all the Pastoral plays (1984, 19). In the movie, Ci represents the activist movement that uses violent measures to defy the military dictatorship.

17. This is not Macunaíma's first visit to the capitalist's house. In fact, two of the funniest scenes in the movie focus on his escapades in the villain's mansion while he searches for the amulet. In the first episode, Macunaíma, disguised as a Frenchwoman, tries to trick the unsuspecting Venceslau into giving him the stone. However, his identity is finally revealed after a trouserless Venceslau, whose sexual appetite has been whetted by Macunaíma's ridiculous, genteel disguise, offers the stone in exchange for a striptease. A second attempt is foiled when Macunaíma is caught by Venceslau's wife and two daughters, who toss him into a large cooking pot and seem prepared to eat him alive. The younger daughter, whose appetite is more carnal than carnivorous, helps Macunaíma to escape, although her expectations for a romp in a jacuzzi-style bathtub in her bedroom are dashed when he jumps out a nearby window. In this scene, the large, sunken tub effectively replaces the cooking pot as a receptacle—albeit for a different kind of eating. In the climactic confrontation between Macunaíma and Venceslau, director Andrade creates a more daring and grotesque image to emphasize the anthropophagic theme.

18. According to economist Thayer Watkins, the plan, which likely came about because of a major drought in 1970 and the need to provide government assistance in the Northeast, involved five initiatives:

1. The construction of roads to link the various regions of Brazil.
2. Moving the surplus population from the Northeast and the shantytowns of the Southeastern cities in the unsettled areas of the west, in particular the states of Rondônia and Acre. The slogan for this program was "Unite men without land and land without men."
3. Create settlements of small farmsteads in the areas along the national roads and in the settlement areas in the west.
4. Subsidize cattle ranching to produce food for the coastal cities and for export.
5. Develop Brazil's national resources such as the newly discovered mineral deposits in the Carajás Region. (Watkins n.d., n.p.)

19. In *Nelson Pereira dos Santos* (2003), I discuss the implicit and ironic treatment of the Iracema tale in *Como era gostoso o meu francês.*

20. In the movie, the trucker, played by Paulo Cesar Peréio, occasionally interacts with "real" people in restaurants and the out-of-doors. These improvised moments are what give the film its cinema verité style.

21. In 1913, the poet Augusto dos Anjos presented a similar portrait of the Indian, and he mentioned Iracema. Several excellent commentaries exist on Brodansky and Senna's film. For more reading consult Pick 1993, Stam 1997, I. Xavier 1999, and B. Williams 1999.

22. Salomé is reminiscent of the *rumberas* of 1950s Mexican movies who were played by actors such as Ninón Sevilla.

23. I am indebted to my former students Masako Hasikawa and Aiko Kitagawa for bringing issues concerning Japanese-Brazilian migrant children's experiences in Japan to my attention. Because the *dekassegui* is a fairly recent phenomenon in Japan, there are few safety nets for Brazilian-born Japanese children.

24. European countries decided to bestow citizenship on children of emigrants. As a result, many Brazilians today (along with people of other nationalities) carry dual citizenship.

25. Dora herself is victimized by a system that fails to provide for its teachers, and she passes on her victimization to others. One aspect of her character that is troubling is the suggestion that Dora's single status may be the real reason for her cranky disposition and that a husband and child would have "naturally" made her a happier and better person.

26. For a more extensive comparison of Buñuel and Pereira dos Santos's films see my *Nelson Pereira dos Santos* (2003).

27. To ensure that this point was not lost, Babenco shot a prologue in the form of a documentary that addresses the issue of children on the streets. In the background is Fernando Ramos, the young actor who plays Pixote, standing next to his mother in the shantytown where they live.

28. Brazilian viewers and those knowledgeable about the country could easily infer that Babenco's sympathetic characterizations, especially Pixote, were his way of representing the thousands of abandoned children who are increasingly classified as "a menace to society"—especially in high-tourist areas like Rio. As most viewers know, Fernando Ramos, who was a child of the slums, was killed by police several years after the film was made. His death sent a shock wave through the country, and a documentary about his troubling death, *Quem matou Pixote?* (Who Killed Pixote?), appeared a few years later.

Epilogue

1. These two references appear in John Day's "A Publication of Guiana's Plantation" (1632), which recounts the efforts of British and Irish attempts at colonization (Day 2000, 125).

2. Candace Slater writes about women warriors and other Amazonian topics in *Entangled Edens* (2002).

3. For a discussion of the Amazon and Chico Mendes see Kenneth Maxwell's *Naked Tropics* (2003).

4. In his 1963 study, *Aspirações nacionais: Interpretação histórico-política* (*The Brazilians: Their Characters and Aspirations*, 1967), José Honório Rodrigues offered his own summation of desirable and undesirable character traits of Brazilians. He listed na-

tionalist pride and optimism as the most positive characteristics and procrastination as the leading negative trait (1967, 60–65).

5. The Vila Barulho d'Água (Sound of Water Villa) project in the historic coastal town Paraty in Rio de Janeiro state is an example of this trend. Homes are built low to the ground but otherwise look like ultramodern treehouses that comfortably merge with the wooded setting.

6. Austrian writer Stefan Zweig described Brazil as "the land of the future" in the title of his 1941 book about the country. Zweig was overwhelmed by what he saw in Brazil, and he wrote that "one of the greatest hopes for future civilization and peace . . . rests on the existence of Brazil, whose desires are aimed exclusively at pacific development (13). "God is Brazilian" is a popular phrase that Carlos Diegues adopted for his 2003 film, *Deus é brasileiro*, about the Brazilian God who takes human form and searches the country for a substitute so he can take a long-overdue rest.

7. For a discussion of São Paulo gated communities see Teresa Caldeira 2000.

8. To call attention to the proximity of these economic extremes, 250 students from the Universidade de São Paulo marched from the nearby *favela* to Daslu's entrance, where they begged arriving shoppers for alms (Benton 2005).

9. Despite the different setting of her second diary, the publishers of the English translation opted to market the book as if the author were still writing about life in the slums. Instead of her "little house," the book's cover shows Carolina in her former wooden shack. The translation's title conveys that she still lives in the slum, and the subtitle removes the reference to her status as a "former slum dweller."

10. A similar but even more deadly episode involving a petty criminal and a bus full of passengers in Rio captured headlines and public attention in early December 2005, although the absence of a live telecast made the tragedy less immediate and intimate for news consumers than the ordeal with Sandro.

11. This information is from a personal interview conducted with police at the Boa Viagem police station in November 1994.

12. The statistics appear in Takahashi 2005.

13. For additional commentary on the representation of slaves in Brazilian visiting cards see Azevedo and Lisovsky 1987 and Levine and Crocitti 1990.

14. *Blame It on Rio* may be an allusion to the 1948 movie *Melody Time*, which featured a segment made during World War II by Walt Disney called "Blame It on the Samba." But it is more likely a reference to the popular tune "Blame It on the Bossa Nova."

15. Anderson uses this concept to describe the consumption of the first newspapers by individuals who, in turn, envisioned themselves as part of a larger readership sharing a language-field. He refers to these readers as the "embryo of the nationally imagined community" (1991, 44).

16. *Saramandaia* was an earlier and extremely successful soap that used surreal imagery to convey the "otherness" of life in a small Northeastern town.

17. Apparently in order to better compete with *Pantanal*, other networks began to show more nudity in their soaps.

18. When I mentioned Orkut in a class, Brazilian-born students and U.S. students who had lived in Brazil became excited, while other students from the United States had no idea what I was talking about. In a matter of a week or so, many of those who knew nothing about the site had been invited to join Orkut and were happily engaged in conversing with Brazilians and others in their respective groups.

BIBLIOGRAPHY

Abreu, João Capistrano de. 1999. *O descobrimento do Brasil pelos portugueses.* São Paulo: Martins Fontes. Originally published in 1900.

Alencar, José de. 1865. *Iracema: Lenda do Ceará.* Rio de Janeiro: Instituto Nacional do Livro.

———. 1965. *Ficção completa.* Vol. 1. Rio de Janeiro: Companhia Aguilar Editora.

Alexander, Michael, ed. 1976. *Discovering the New World: Based on the Works of Theodore de Bry.* New York: Harper and Row.

Almeida, Antônio Ribeiro de. N.d. "Quem é o brasileiro?: Um estudo de sua imagem social nos anos 80 do século XX." Unpublished manuscript.

Almeida, Manuel Antônio de. 1969. *Memórias de um sargento de milícias.* Rio de Janeiro: Instituto Nacional do Livro.

Almeida Garrett, João Baptista da Silva Leitão. 1826. "Bosquejo da história da poesia e língua portugueza." Introduction to *Parnaso lusitano; ou, poesias selectas dos auctores portuguezes antigos e modernos.* 6 vols. Paris: J. P. Aillaud.

———. 1843, 1851. *Romanceiro.* 3 vols. Lisbon: Imprensa Nacional.

Amado, Janaína, and Luiz Carlos Figueiredo, eds. 2001. *Brasil 1500: Quarenta documentos.* Brasília: Editora UnB.

Amado, Jorge. 1945. *Capitães da areia.* São Paulo: Livraria Martins.

———. 1995. *Jubiabá.* Rio de Janeiro: Record.

Amaral, Aracy A. 1970. *Artes plásticas na semana de 22.* São Paulo: Editora Perspectiva.

Anchieta, José de. 1988. *Cartas: Informações, fragmentos históricos e sermões.* Belo Horizonte/São Paulo: Itatiaia/Universidade de São Paulo (USP). Originally published in 1582.

Anderson, Benedict. 1991. *Imagined Communities: Reflections on the Origin and Spread of Nationalism.* Rev. ed. London: Verso.

Andrade, António Alberto Banha de. 1972. *Mundos novos do mundo: Panorama da difusão, pela Europa, de notícias dos descobrimentos geográficos portugueses.* 2 vols. Lisbon: Justiça de Investigações do Ultramar.

Andrade, Mário de. 1976. "Paulicéia desvairada." In *Letras floridas,* ed. Amadeu Amaral. São Paulo: HUCITEC. Originally published in 1920.

———. 1984. *Macunaíma.* Trans. E. A. Goodland. New York: Random House.

———. 2003. "Brazil Builds." In *Depoimento de uma geração: Arquitetura moderna brasileira,* ed. Alberto Xavier, 177–180. Rev. ed. São Paulo: Cosac and Naify.

Andrade, Oswald de. 1972. *Do pau-brasil à antropofagia e às utopias.* Rio de Janeiro: Civilização Brasileira.

Andreas, Paul, and Ingeborg Flagge, eds. 2003. *Oscar Niemeyer: Eine Legende der Moderne/A Legend of Modernism.* Frankfurt, Germany/Basel, Switzerland: Deutsches Architektur Museum/Birkhäuser.

Antonil, João André (pseudonym). 1955. *Cultura e opulência do Brasil.* Salvador: Livraria Progresso Editora. Originally published in 1711.

Arciniegas, Germán, ed. 1944. *The Green Continent: A Comprehensive View of Latin America by Its Leading Writers.* New York: Alfred A. Knopf.

Arinos, Afonso. 1937. *Lendas e tradições brasileiras.* 2d ed. Introduction by Olavo Bilac. Rio de Janeiro: F. Briguiet. Originally published in 1917.

————. 1969. *Obra completa.* Rio de Janeiro: Instituto Nacional do Livro.

Armes, Roy. 1987. *Third World Film Making and the West.* Berkeley: University of California Press.

Arroyo, Leonardo. 1976. *A carta de Pero Vaz de Caminha.* 2d ed. São Paulo: Edições Melhoramentos/Instituto Nacional do Livro.

Assis, Joaquim Maria Machado de. 1900. *Dom Casmurro.* Rio de Janeiro: Instituto Nacional do Livro.

————. 1955. *Crônicas.* In *Obras completas de Machado de Assis.* Rio de Janeiro: W. M. Jackson.

————. 1961. *Seus 30 melhores contos.* Rio de Janeiro: José Aguilar.

————. 1970a. *A semana: Crítica literária.* In vol. 4 of *Obras completas de Machado de Assis.* Rio de Janeiro: W. M. Jackson.

————. 1970b. *Crítica teatral.* In vol. 10 of *Obras completas de Machado de Assis.* Rio de Janeiro: W. M. Jackson.

————. 1970c. *Várias histórias.* Vol. 8 of *Obras completas de Machado de Assis.* Rio de Janeiro: W. M. Jackson.

Augusta, Nísia Floresta Brasileira. 1997. *A lágrima de um caeté.* 4th ed. Natal, Brazil: Fundação José Augusto.

Avellar, José Carlos, ed. 1994. *Glauber Rocha: Um leão ao meio-dia.* Rio de Janeiro: Centro Cultural Banco do Brasil.

Azevedo, Aluísio. 1937–1944. *Obras completas.* 14 vols. Rio de Janeiro: F. Briguiet.

Azevedo, Paulo César de, and Maurício Lisovsky, eds. 1987. *Escravos brasileiros do século XIX na fotografia de Christiano Jr.* São Paulo: Ex Libris.

Baerle, Caspar van. 1647. *Rerum per Octennium in Brasilia.* Amsterdam: Blaev.

Barbosa, Januário da Cunha. 1906. *Revista do Instituto Histórico e Geográfico Brasileiro.* Rio de Janeiro: Imprensa Nacional.

Barman, Roderick. 1988. *Brazil: The Forging of a Nation, 1578–1852.* Stanford, CA: Stanford University Press.

Barreiro, José Carlos. 2002. *Imaginário e viajantes no Brasil do século XIX: Cultura e co-*

tidiano, tradição e resistência. São Paulo: Editora da Universidade Estadual de São Paulo (UNESP).

Barros, João de. 1945. *Décadas da Ásia*. 4 vols. Lisbon: Livraria Sá da Costa. Originally published in 1552.

Basualdo, Carlos, ed. 2005. *Tropicália*. Trans. Christopher J. Dunn, Aaron Lorenz, and Renata Nascimento. São Paulo: Cosac Naify.

Bazin, André. 1959. "De la difficulté d'être Coco." *Cahiers du Cinéma* 16, no. 91 (January): 52–57.

Bellos, Alex. 2002. "Doh! Rio Blames It on the Simpsons." *Guardian* (London), April 9.

Belluzzo, Ana Maria de Moraes, ed. 2000. *O Brasil dos viajantes*. 3 vols., 3d ed. São Paulo: Metalivros; Rio de Janeiro: Editora Objetiva.

Benamou, Catherine L. 2007. *It's All True: Orson Welles's Pan-American Odyssey*. Berkeley: University of California Press.

Benson, Todd. 2005. "An Oasis of Indulgence Amid Brazil's Poverty." *New York Times*, July 16.

Bethell, Leslie, ed. 1987. *Colonial Brazil*. New York: Cambridge University Press.

Biblos: Enciclopédia verbo das literaturas de língua portuguesa. 1995–2005. 5 vols. Lisbon: Verbo.

Bienal Brasil século XX. 1994. São Paulo: Fundação Bienal de São Paulo.

Bilac, Olavo. 1937. Introduction to *Lendas e tradições brasileiras*, by Afonso Arinos. 2d ed. Rio de Janeiro: F. Briguiet. Originally published in 1917.

Bittencourt, Gean Maria. 1967. *A missão artística francesa de 1816*. Petrópolis, Brazil: Museu de Armas Ferreira da Cunha.

Bocage, Manuel Maria Barbosa du. 1875. *Obras poéticas de Bocage*. Vol. 1, *Sonetos*. Oporto, Portugal: Imprensa Portuguesa Editora.

Bogdanovich, Peter, and Orson Welles. 1992. *This Is Orson Welles*. New York: HarperCollins.

Boorstin, Daniel J. 1983. *The Discoverers*. New York: Random House.

Bosi, Alfredo. 1992. *Dialética da colonização*. São Paulo: Companhia das Letras.

———. 1997. *História concisa da literatura brasileira*. 3d ed. São Paulo: Cultrix.

Boucher, Philip P. 1992. *Cannibal Encounters: Europeans and Island Caribs, 1492–1763*. Baltimore, MD: Johns Hopkins University Press.

Boxer, Charles R. 1969. *The Golden Age of Brazil 1695–1750*. Berkeley and Los Angeles: University of California Press.

———. 1973. *The Dutch in Brazil 1624–1654*. Hamden, CT: Archon Books.

Brandão, Ambrósio Fernandes. 1986. *Dialogues of the Great Things of Brazil*. Trans. Frederick Holden Hall. Albuquerque: University of New Mexico Press.

Brasília. Pamphlet. New York: Brazilian Government Trade Bureau, n.d.

Brazil from Discovery to Independence: An Exhibition Commemorating the 150th Anniversa-

ry of the Declaration of Brazilian Independence on September 7, 1822. 1972. Introduction by Heitor Martins. Bloomington, IN: Lilly Library.

Brazil: Introduction to a Neighbor. Washington, D.C.: Office of the Coordinator of Inter-American Affairs (CIAA), 1944.

Brelin, Johan. 1955. De passagem pelo Brasil e Portugal em 1756. Trans. Carlos de Almeida. Lisbon: Casa Portuguesa.

Brown, Harriet McCune, and Helen Miller Bailey. 1944. Our Latin American Neighbors. Boston: Houghton Mifflin.

Bruyas, Jean-Paul. 1979. Introduction to Os maxacalis, by Ferdinand Denis, ix–cxcv. São Paulo: Conselho Estadual de Artes e Ciências Humanas.

Buarque de Holanda, Sérgio. 1959. Visão do paraíso. (Os motivos edênicos no descobrimento e colonização do Brasil). Rio de Janeiro: José Olympio.

———, ed. 1979. Antologia dos poetas brasileiros da fase colonial. São Paulo: Editora Perspectiva.

———. 1989. Raízes do Brasil. Rio de Janeiro: José Olympio. Originally published in 1936.

Bucher, Bernadette. 1981. Icon and Conquest: A Structural Analysis of the Illustrations of de Bry's "Great Voyages". Trans. Basia Miller Gulati. Chicago: University of Chicago Press.

Bueno, Eduardo, ed. 2003. Brasil, uma história: A incrível saga de um país. 2d ed. São Paulo: Editora Ática.

Burton, Julianne, ed. 1986. Cinema and Social Change in Latin America: Conversations with Filmmakers. Austin: University of Texas Press.

Caldas, António Pereira de Souza. 1821. Poesias sacras e profanas. Paris: P. N. R. Rougeron.

Caldeira, Teresa Pires do Rio. 2000. City of Walls: Crime, Segregation, and Citizenship in São Paulo. Berkeley: University of California Press.

Caldwell, Helen. 1960. The Brazilian Othello of Machado de Assis. Berkeley: University of California Press.

Campofiorito, Quirino. 1983. História da pintura brasileira no século XIX. Rio de Janeiro: Edições Pinakotheke.

———. 2003. "As artes plásticas na arquitetura moderna brasileira." In Depoimento de uma geração, ed. Xavier, 322–330.

Cândido, Antônio. 1971. Formação da literatura brasileira. 2 vols. São Paulo: Martins.

Cândido, Antônio, and J. Alderaldo Castello, eds. 1968. Presença da literatura brasileira. 3 vols., 3d ed. São Paulo: Difusão São Paulo.

Cardim, Fernão. 1980. Tratados da terra e gente do Brasil. Belo Horizonte, Brazil: Editora Itatiaia.

———. 1993. "Artigos referentes ao dever da majestade de el-rei nosso senhor e ao bem comum de todo o estado do Brasil." In Documentos do Brasil, ed. Inês da Conceição Inácio and Tania Regina de Luca, 63–66. São Paulo: Editora Ática.

Carlson, Terry. 1995. "Antônio das Mortes." In *Brazilian Cinema,* ed. Randal Johnson and Robert Stam, 169–177. Rev. ed., New York: Columbia University Press.

Cascudo, Luís da Câmara. 1965. *Dois ensaios de história.* Natal, Brazil: Edições da Imprensa Universitária.

———. 1977. *O príncipe Maximiliano de Wied-Neuwied no Brasil, 1815/1817.* Rio de Janeiro: Livraria Kosmos Editora.

Castro, Ruy. 2000. *Bossa Nova: The Story of the Brazilian Music That Seduced the World.* Trans. Lysa Salsbury. Chicago: A Capella.

———. 2001. *A onda que se ergueu no mar: Novos mergulhos na bossa nova.* São Paulo: Companhia das Letras.

Castro, Sílvio. 1985. *A carta de Pero Vaz de Caminha (A descoberta do Brasil).* Porto Alegre, Brazil: L&PM Editores.

———. 1999. *História da literatura brasileira.* 3 vols. Lisbon: Editora Alfa.

Castro Alves, Antônio de. 1997. *Obra completa.* 2d ed. Rio de Janeiro: Editora Nova Aguilar.

Catalogue of the Greenlee Collection, the Newberry Library, Chicago. 1970. 2 vols. Boston: G. K. Hall.

Cavalcanti, Lauro. 2002. "Brasília: A construção de um exemplo." In *Anos JK,* ed. Wander Melo Miranda, 91–106. São Paulo/Rio de Janeiro: Imprensa Oficial/Casa de Lúcio Costa.

———. 2003. "Oscar Niemeyer and Brazilian Modernism." In *Oscar Niemeyer,* ed. Andreas and Flagge, 27–36.

"Cinema Novo: Origens, ambições, perspectivas." 1965. Interview of Nelson Pereira dos Santos, Glauber Rocha, and Alex Viany. *Revista civilização brasileira* 1 (March): 185–196.

Coelho Neto, Henrique M. 1904. "Duas palavras sobre Luiz Gama." *Primeiras trovas burlescas,* by Luiz Gama. 3d ed. São Paulo: Typografia Bentley Junior.

Cohen, Thomas M. 1998. *Fire of Tongues: Antônio Vieira and the Missionary Church in Brazil and Portugal.* Stanford, CA: Stanford University Press.

Conisbee, Philip. 1981. *Painting in Eighteenth-Century France.* Ithaca, NY: Cornell University Press.

Cortesão, Armando, and A. Teixeira da Mota, eds. 1960–1962. *Portugaliae monumenta cartographica.* 6 vols. Lisbon: Comissão Executiva das Comemorações do Quinto Centenário da Morte do Infante D. Henrique.

Cortesão, Jaime. 1957. *História do Brasil nos velhos mapas.* Vol. 1. Rio de Janeiro: Instituto Rio Branco.

———. 1967. *A carta de Pero Vaz de Caminha.* Lisbon: Portugália Editora.

Costa, Emília Viotti da. 2000. *The Brazilian Empire: Myths and Histories.* Rev. ed. Chapel Hill: University of North Carolina Press.

Costa, João Cruz. 1964. *A History of Ideas in Brazil: The Development of Philosophy in*

Brazil and the Evolution of National History. Trans. Suzette Macedo. Berkeley: University of California Press.

Costa, Lúcio. 1986. *Razones de la nueva arquitectura, 1934 y otros ensayos.* Lima: Embajada del Brasil.

Coutinho, Afrânio, ed. 1955. *A literatura no Brasil.* 3 vols. Rio de Janeiro: Editorial Sul Americana.

———. 1965. *A polêmica Alencar-Nabuco.* Rio de Janeiro: Edições Tempo Brasileiro.

———. 1990. *Machado de Assis na literatura brasileira.* Rio de Janeiro: Coleção Afrânio Peixoto da Academia Brasileira de Letras.

Day, John. 2000. "A Publication of Guiana's Plantation." In *O novo Éden: A fauna da Amazônia brasileira nos relatos de viajantes e cronistas desde a descoberta do Rio Amazonas por Pinzón (1500) até o Tratado de Santo Ildefonso (1777),* ed. Nelson Papavero, Dante Martins, William Leslie Overal, and José Roberto Pujol-Luz, 124–133. Belém, Brazil: Museu Paraense Emílio Goeldi.

Debret, Jean Baptiste. 1954. *Viagem pitoresca e histórica ao Brasil (1834–1839).* 3 vols., 3d ed. São Paulo: Livraria Martins Editora. Originally published 1834–1839 as *Voyage pitoresque et historique au Brésil.*

Denis, Ferdinand. 1824. *Scènes de la nature sous les tropiques.* Paris: Janet.

———. 1944. *Uma festa brasileira.* Trans. Cândido Juca. Rio de Janeiro: EPASA. Originally published 1850 as *Une fête brésilienne à Rouen en 1550.*

———. 1968. *Resumo da história literária do Brasil.* Trad. Guilhermo César. Porto Alegre: Livraria Lima.

———. 1979. *Os maxacalis.* Introduction by Jean Paul-Bruyas, trans. Maria Cecília Moraes Pinto. São Paulo: Secretaria da Cultura, Ciência, e Tecnologia.

Dicionário prático ilustrado. 1979. Oporto, Portugal: Lello e Irmão Editores.

Dos Passos, John. 1963. *Brazil on the Move.* New York: Doubleday.

Dozer, Donald Marquand. 1959. *Are We Good Neighbors?: Three Decades of Inter-American Relations.* Gainesville: University of Florida Press.

Driver, David Miller. 1942. *The Indian in Brazilian Literature.* New York: Hispanic Institute in the United States.

Driver, Felix, and Luciana Martins, eds. 2005. *Tropical Visions in an Age of Empire.* Chicago: University of Chicago Press.

Eakin, Marshall C. 1997. *Brazil: The Once and Future Country.* New York: St. Martin's Press.

Eames, Wilberforce. 1922. "Description of a Wood Engraving Illustrating the South American Indian (1505)." *Bulletin of the New York Public Library* 26, no. 9:755–760.

Emert, Martine. 1944. *European Voyages to Brazil Before 1532: A Chapter in International Rivalry in America.* Ph.D. diss., University of California.

Engelbrecht, Daniel. 2005. "Barracos na Costa Verde." *O globo* (Rio de Janeiro), November 12.

Epstein, Edward Jay. 1990. *Agency of Fear: Opiates and Political Power in America*. Rev. ed. London: Verso.

Ewbank, Thomas. 1971. *Life in Brazil: A Journal of a Visit to the Land of the Cocoa and the Palm*. Detroit: Blaine Ethridge Books. Originally published in 1856.

Fabris, Anateresa. 1994. "Modernism: Nationalism and Engagement." In *Bienal Brasil século XX*, 72–83. São Paulo: Fundação Bienal de São Paulo.

Farias, Marcos de. 1960. "Situação do cinema brasileiro." *Cine clube* 1, no. 1 (Spring): 19–37.

Fausto, Boris. 1999. *A Concise History of Brazil*. Trans. Arthur Brakel. Cambridge, England: Cambridge University Press.

Figueiredo, Vera Follain de. 2004. "Creating the National Imaginary." In *Literary Cultures of Latin America: A Comparative History*, vol. 3, ed. Mario Valdés and Djelal Kadir, 100–111. Oxford, England: Oxford University Press.

Figuerôa, Alexandre. 2004. *Cinema Novo: A onda do jovem cinema e sua recepção na França*. Campinas: Papirus Editora.

Fitz, Earl E. 1989. *Machado de Assis*. Boston: Twayne.

Formisano, Luciano, ed. 1992. *Letters from a New World: Amerigo Vespucci's Discovery of America*. Trans. David Jacobson. New York: Marsilio.

Freyre, Gilberto. 1964. *Casa grande e senzala*. 2 vols. Rio de Janeiro: José Olympio.

Frontières entre le Brésil et la Guyane Française: Atlas contenant un choix de cartes anterieures au traité conclu a utrecht le 11 avril 1713 entre le Portugal et la France. 1899. Paris: A. Laheure Imprimeur Editeur.

Gallagher, Tom. 1983. *Portugal: A Twentieth-Century Interpretation*. Manchester, England: Manchester University Press.

Galvão, Maria Rita. 1995. "Vera Cruz: A Brazilian Hollywood." In *Brazilian Cinema*, ed. Randal Johnson and Robert Stam, 270–280. Rev. ed. New York: Columbia University Press.

Gama, José Basílio da. 1941. *O uraguai*. Rio de Janeiro: Publicações da Academia Brasileira.

Gama, Luiz (Luís). 1904. *Primeiras trovas burlescas*. 3d ed. São Paulo: Typografia Bentley Junior.

Gama, Rinaldo. 1994. "Biblioteca nacional." *Veja*, November 23, 108–112.

Gândavo, Pero de Magalhães. 1995. *Tratado da terra do Brasil*, 5th ed., and *História da Província Santa Cruz a que vulgarmente chamamos Brasil 1576*, 12th ed., in 1 vol. Recife: Fundação Joaquim Nabuco/Editora Massangana.

Gertner, Richard. 1964. "That Man from Rio." *Motion Picture Herald* 231, no. 13 (June): 75.

Gheerbrant, Alain. 1992. *The Amazons: Past, Present, and Future*. Trans. I. Mark Paris. New York: Harry N. Abrams.

Gicovate, Moisés. 1959. *Brasília: Uma realização em marcha*. São Paulo: Edições Melhoramentos.

Gil-Montero, Martha. 1989. *Brazilian Bombshell: The Biography of Carmen Miranda.* New York: Donald I. Fine.

Gledson, John. 1984. *The Deceptive Realism of Machado de Assis: A Dissenting Interpretation of "Dom Casmurro".* Liverpool: Francis Cairns.

Góis, Damião de. 1926. *Crónica do felicíssimo rei D. Manuel.* 4 vols. Coimbra, Portugal: Imprensa da Universidade.

Gomes, Renato Cordeiro. 2002. "Bossa-Nova: Uma nova afinação." In *Anos JK,* ed. Miranda, 119–130.

Gonçalves Dias, António. 1846. *Meditação.* In *Obras póstumas de A. Gonçalves Dias,* ed. Antônio Leal. Rio de Janeiro: H. Garnier.

———. 1942. *Obras completas.* São Paulo: Edições Cultura.

Goodwin, Philip L. 1943. Preface to *Brazil Builds: Architecture New and Old 1652–1942.* New York: Museum of Modern Art.

Graça Aranha, Jose Pereira da, ed. 1942. *Correspondência entre Machado de Assis e Joaquim Nabuco.* 2d ed. Rio de Janeiro: F. Briguiet.

Graeff, Edgar. 1978. "The Triumph over Cultural Dependence." In *Depoimento de uma geração,* ed. Xavier, 277–279.

Graham, Maria. 1824. *Journal of a Voyage to Brazil, and Residence There, During Part of the Years 1821, 1822, 1823.* London: Longman, Hurst, Rees, Orme, Brown, and Green.

Graham, Richard, ed. 1999. *Machado de Assis: Reflections on a Brazilian Master Writer.* Austin: University of Texas Press.

Greenlee, William Brooks. 1938. *The Voyage of Pedro Álvares Cabral to Brazil and India, from Contemporary Documents and Narratives,* trans. with introduction and notes by Greenlee. 2d series, part 1, no. 81. London: Hakluyt Society.

Guillén, Mauro F. 2004. "Modernism Without Modernity: The Rise of Modernist Architecture in Mexico, Brazil, and Argentina, 1890–1940." *Latin American Research Review* 39, no. 2:6–34.

Guimarães, Bernardo. 1976. *História e tradições da Província de Minas Gerais.* Rio de Janeiro: Civilização Brasileira.

Guimarães Rosa, João. 1956. *Grande sertão: Veredas.* Rio de Janeiro: Livraria José Olympio Editora.

———. 1963. *The Devil to Pay in the Backlands.* Trans. James L. Taylor and Harriet de Onis. New York: Knopf.

Haberly, David. 1983. *Three Sad Races: Racial Identity and National Consciousness in Brazilian Literature.* New York: Cambridge University Press.

Hamburger, Esther. 2005. *O Brasil atenado: A sociedade da novela.* Rio de Janeiro: Jorge Zahar Editor.

Hartmann, Thelka. 1975. *A contribuição da iconografia para o conhecimento de índios brasileiros do século XIX.* Coleção Museu Paulista, Ethnology Series, vol. 1. São Paulo: Edição do Fundo de Pesquisas do Museu Paulista da Universidade de São Paulo.

Hemming, John. 1978. *Red Gold: The Conquest of the Brazilian Indians.* Cambridge: Harvard University Press.

Herkenhoff, Paulo, ed. 1999. *O Brasil e os holandeses: 1630–1654.* Rio de Janeiro: Sextante Artes.

Herring, Hubert. 1941. *Good Neighbors: Argentina, Brazil, Chile, and Seventeen Other Countries.* New Haven, CT: Yale University Press.

Holston, James. 1989. *The Modernist City: An Anthropological Critique of Brasília.* Chicago: University of Chicago Press.

Horch, Rosemarie Erika, ed. 1977. *Cartas dos compadres de Belém e Lisboa.* São Paulo: Revista de História.

Humboldt, Alexander von, and Aimé Bonpland. 1821. *Personal Narrative of Travels to the Equinoctial Regions of the New Continent During the Years 1799–1804.* 6 vols. Trans. Helen Maria Williams. London: Longman, Hurst, Rees, Orme, Brown and Green. Originally published in 1814 as *Relacion historic du voyage aux régions équinoxiales du nouveau continent.*

Huxley, Aldous. 1960. *On Art and Artists.* New York: Harper.

Inácio, Inês da Conceição, and Tania Regina de Luca, eds. 1993. *Documentos do Brasil colonial.* São Paulo: Editora Ática.

Jackson, K. David. 1987. *Transformation of Literary Language in Latin American Literature: From Machado de Assis to the Vanguard.* Austin: Abaporu Press.

———. 2006. "Poetry and Paradise in the Discovery of America." In *Studies in Honor of Heitor Martins,* ed. Darlene J. Sadlier, Zak K. Montgomery, and Renato Alvim, 43–62. Luso-Brazilian Literary Studies 3. Bloomington: Department of Spanish and Portuguese.

Jesus, Carolina Maria de. 1960. *Quarto de despejo.* São Paulo: Livraria Francisco Alves.

———. 1961. *Casa de alvenaria: Diário de uma ex-favelada.* Rio de Janeiro: Editora P. de Azevedo.

———. 1962. *Child of the Dark.* Trans. David St. Clair. New York: New American Library.

———. 1997. *I'm Going To Have a Little House: The Second Diary of Carolina Maria de Jesus.* Trans. Melvin S. Arlington Jr. and Robert M. Levine. Lincoln: University of Nebraska Press.

Johnson, Randal. 1982. *Literatura e cinema: Macunaíma, do modernismo ao Cinema Novo.* São Paulo: T. A. Queiroz.

———. 1984. *Cinema Novo x 5: Masters of Contemporary Brazilian Film.* Austin: University of Texas Press.

Johnson, Randal, and Robert Stam, eds. 1995. *Brazilian Cinema.* Rev. ed. New York: Columbia University Press.

Jones, Maro Beath. 1923. Introduction to *Innocencia,* by Alfredo d'Escragnolle Taunay. Boston: D. C. Heath.

Jones, Patrice. 2001. "Race Issues in Brazil Join Spectacle of Carnival." *Chicago Tribune,* February 24.

Karasch, Mary. 1987. *Slave Life in Rio de Janeiro, 1808–1850.* Princeton, NJ: Princeton University Press.

King, John. 1990. *Magical Reels: A History of Cinema in Latin America.* London: Verso.

Koster, Henry. 1966. *Travels in Brazil.* Carbondale: Southern Illinois University Press. Originally published in 1816.

Krohn, Carsten. 2003. "Order and Progress: Oscar Niemeyer, Urbanist." In *Oscar Niemeyer,* ed. Andreas and Flagge, 37–44.

Leaming, Barbara. 1985. *Orson Welles.* New York: Viking.

Leite, Ilka Bonaventura. 1996. *Antropologia da viagem: Escravos e libertos em Minas Gerais no século XIX.* Belo Horizonte: Editora Universidade Federal de Minas Gerais (UFMG).

Leite, José Roberto Teixeira. 1994. "Brazilian Painting From 1900 to 1922." In *Bienal Brasil século XX,* 24–37.

Léry, Jean de. 1980. *Viagem à terra do Brasil.* Belo Horizonte: Itatiaia and Editora da Universidade de São Paulo (EDUSP).

———. 1990. *History of a Voyage to the Land of Brazil Otherwise Called America.* Trans. Janet Whatley. Berkeley: University of California Press. Originally published in 1578 as *Histoire d'un voyage fait en la terre du Bresil autrement dite Amerique.*

Lestringant, Frank. 1997. *Cannibals: The Discovery and Representation of the Cannibal from Columbus to Jules Verne.* Trans. Rosemary Morris. Berkeley: University of California Press.

Lévi-Strauss, Claude. 1973. *Tristes tropiques.* London: Cape. Originally published in 1955.

Levine, Robert M., and John J. Crocitti. 1990. "Faces of Brazilian Slavery: The *Cartes de Visite* of Christiano Júnior." *Americas* 47, no. 2:127–159.

———, eds. 1999. *The Brazil Reader: History, Culture, Politics.* Durham: Duke University Press.

Lifestyles Brazil Digest. 2005. Vol. 1, November. Rio de Janeiro: Editora Prometheus.

Lima, Hernan. 1963. *História da caricatura no Brasil.* Vol. 1. Rio de Janeiro: Livraria José Olympio Editora.

Lima, José Inácio Abreu e. 1835. *Bosquejo histórico, político e literário do Brasil.* Niterói, Brazil: Tipografia Niterói do Rego.

Lima, Oliveira. 1945. *Dom João VI no Brasil: 1808–1821.* Rio de Janeiro: José Olympio.

———. 1997. *Formação histórica da nacionalidade brasileira.* Rio de Janeiro: Topbooks. Originally published in 1944.

Lins, Ivan. 1964. *História do positivismo no Brasil.* São Paulo: Companhia Editora Nacional.

Lisboa, Joaquim José. 2002. *Descrição curiosa das principais produções, rios e animais do*

Brasil. Belo Horizonte: Fundação João Pinheiro, Centro de Estudos Históricos e Culturais. Originally published in 1804.

Lopes Neto, J. Simões. 1991. *Lendas do sul.* Porto Alegre, Brazil: Martins Livreiro-Editor.

———. 1992. *Contos gauchescos.* Porto Alegre: Martins Livreiro-Editor. Originally published in 1912.

López, Ana M. 1993. "Are All Latins from Manhattan?" In *Mediating Two Worlds: Cinematic Encounters in the Americas,* ed. John King, Ana M. López, and Manuel Alvarado, 67–80. London: BFI.

Luccock, John. 1820. *Notes on Rio de Janeiro and the Southern Part of Brazil; Taken During a Residence of Ten Years in That Country, from 1808 to 1818.* London: Samuel Leigh.

Ludington, Townsend. 1980. *John Dos Passos: A Twentieth Century Odyssey.* New York: E. P. Dutton.

Macaulay, Neill. 1986. *Dom Pedro: The Struggle for Liberty in Brazil and Portugal, 1798–1834.* Durham, NC: Duke University Press.

Machado de Assis. See Assis.

Marchant. Alexander. 1942. *From Barter to Slavery: The Economic Relations of Portuguese and Indians in the Settlement of Brazil: 1500–1580.* Baltimore, MD: Johns Hopkins Press.

———. 1945. "The Discovery of Brazil." *Geographical Review* 35, no. 2:296–300.

Mariz, Vasco, and Lucien Provençal. 2005. *Villegagnon e a França Antártica: Uma reavaliação.* 2d ed. São Paulo: Nova Fronteira.

Marrocos, Luiz Joaquim dos Santos. 1939. *Cartas de Luiz Joaquim dos Santos Marrocos.* Rio de Janeiro: Biblioteca Nacional and Ministério de Educação e Saúde.

Martín-Barbero, Jésus. 2001. "The Processes: From Nationalisms to Transnationals." In *Media and Cultural Studies: Keyworks,* ed. Meenakshi Gigi Durham and Douglas Kellner, 351–381. Oxford, England: Blackwell.

Martins, Heitor, ed. 1982. *Neoclassicismo: Uma visão temática.* Brasília: Academia Brasiliense de Letras.

———. 1983. *Do barroco a Guimarães Rosa.* Belo Horizonte: Itatiaia.

———. 1996. "Luís Gama e a consciência negra na literatura brasileira." *Afro-Ásia* 17:87–97.

Martins, Luciana de Lima. 2001. *O Rio de Janeiro dos viajantes: O olhar britânico (1800–1850).* Rio de Janeiro: Jorge Zahar.

Martins, Wilson. 1970. *The Modernist Idea.* New York: New York University Press.

———. 1977. *História da inteligência brasileira.* 6 vols. São Paulo: Editora Cultrix.

Matheson, Gilbert Farquhar. 1825. *Narrative of a Visit to Brazil, Chile, Peru, and the Sandwich Islands During the Years 1821 and 1822.* London: C. Knight.

Matos, Cláudia Neiva de. 1988. *Gentis guerreiros: O indianismo de Gonçalves Dias.* São Paulo: Atual Editora.

Matos, Gregório de. 1976. *Poemas escolhidos*. São Paulo: Editora Cultrix.

Mawe, John. 1816. *Travels in the Interior of Brazil*. Philadephia: M. Carey; Boston: Wells and Lilly.

Maxwell, Kenneth. 2003. *Naked Tropics: Essays on Empire and Other Rogues*. New York: Routledge.

McGowan, Chris, and Ricardo Pessanha. 1998. *The Brazilian Sound: Samba, Bossa Nova, and the Popular Music of Brazil*. Philadelphia, PA: Temple University Press.

McKie, Robin, and Vanessa Thorpe. 2005. "Amazon Gives Up Deepest Secrets." *Observer*, April 3.

Meireles, Cecília. 1953. *Romanceiro da Inconfidência*. Rio de Janeiro: Livros de Portugal.

Mello e Souza, Laura de. 2003. *The Devil and the Land of the Holy Cross: Witchcraft, Slavery, and Popular Religion*. Trans. Diane Grosklaus Whitty. Austin: University of Texas Press. Originally published in 1986 as *O diabo e a terra de Santa Cruz*.

Meneses, Djacir, ed. 1957. *O Brasil no pensamento brasileiro*. Rio de Janeiro: Ministério de Educação e Cultura (MEC).

Menezes, Philadelpho. 1994. *Poetics and Visuality: A Trajectory of Contemporary Brazilian Poetry*. Trans. Harry Polkinhorn. San Diego, CA: San Diego State University Press.

Merquior, José Guilherme. 1977. *De Anchieta a Euclides—I: Breve história da literatura brasileira*. Rio de Janeiro: Livraria José Olympio Editora.

Metcalf, Alida C. 2005. *Go-Betweens and the Colonization of Brazil: 1500–1600*. Austin: University of Texas Press.

Miguel-Pereira, Lúcia. 1973. *História da literatura brasileira: Prosa de ficção de 1870 a 1920*. 3d ed. Rio de Janeiro: José Olympio Editora.

Milliet, Maria Alice. 1994. "The Abstractions." *Bienal Brasil século XX*, 184–197.

Mindlin, Henrique E. 1961. *Brazilian Architecture*. London: Royal College of Art.

Mindlin, José E. 1991. "Viajantes no Brasil: Viagem em torno de meus livros." *Estudos Históricos* 4, no. 7:35–54.

Miranda, Ana. 1996. *Desmundo*. São Paulo: Companhia das Letras.

Miranda, Wander Melo, ed. 2002. *Anos JK*. São Paulo: Imprensa Oficial; Rio de Janeiro: Casa de Lúcio Costa.

Mittman, Asa Simon. 2003. "Headless Men and Hungry Monsters." Sarum Seminar, Stanford University Alumni Center, Stanford, CA, March. At hpl.hp.com/personal/John_Wilkes/Sarum/2003-03-Mittman-Headless-Men-and-Hungry-Monsters.pdf.

Moerbeeck, Jan Andries. 1626. *Spaenschen Raedt*. Graven-Haghe, Netherlands: Nae't Brabandsche exemplaer by Aert Meuris.

———. 1942. *Motivos porque a Companhia das Índias Ocidentais deve tentar tirar ao rei da Espanha a terra do Brasil, e quanto antes*. Trans. Agostinho Keijzers and José Honório Rodrigues. Rio de Janeiro: Gráfica Rio-Arte.

Moisés, Massaud. 1976. *A literatura brasileira através dos textos*. São Paulo: Editora Cultrix.

Molotnik, J. R. 1976. "*Macunaíma*: Revenge of the Jungle Freaks." *Jump Cut: A Review of Contemporary Media* 12/13:22–24. At ejumpcut.org/archive/onlinessays/jc12-13folder/macunaima.html.

Montaigne, Michel de. 1927. *The Essays of Montaigne*. 2 vols. Trans. E. J. Trechmann. London: Oxford University Press.

Monteiro, John J. 1994. *Negros da terra*. São Paulo: Companhia das Letras.

Moreau, Filipe Eduardo. 2003. *Os índios nas cartas de Nóbrega e Anchieta*. São Paulo: Annablume.

Morettin, Eduardo Victorio. 2000. "Produção e formas de circulação do tema do descobrimento do Brasil: Uma análise de seu percurso e do filme *Descobrimento do Brasil* (1937), de Humberto Mauro." *Revista brasileira de história* 20, no. 39:135–165. At www.scielo.br.

Morison, Samuel Eliot. 1965. *Portuguese Voyages to America in the Fifteenth Century*. New York: Octagon Books.

Moser, Benjamin. 2004. "Dutch Treat." *New York Review of Books*, August 12, 8–11.

Mourineau, Michel. 1985. *Incroyables gazettes et fabuleaux métaux: Les retours des trésors américans d'áprès les gazettes holandaises*. Cambridge, England: Cambridge University Press; Paris: Maison des Sciences de l'Homme.

Mullaney, Steven. 1988. "Strange Things, Gross Terms, Curious Customs: The Rehearsal of Cultures in the Late Renaissance." In *Representing the English Renaissance*, ed. Stephen Greenblatt, 65–92. Berkeley: University of California Press.

Nabuco, Joaquim. 1949. *Obras completas de Joaquim Nabuco*. 14 vols. São Paulo: Instituto Progresso Editorial.

Nagrib, Lúcia, ed. 2003. *The New Brazilian Cinema*. London: I. B. Tauris.

Naremore, James. 1989. *The Magic World of Orson Welles*. Rev. ed. Dallas, TX: Southern Methodist University Press.

Nascimento, Abdias. 1968. "O mito da democracia racial." *Cadernos brasileiros* 10, no. 47 (May-June): 3–7.

———. 1978. *O genicídio do negro brasileiro: Processo de um racismo mascarado*. Rio de Janeiro: Paz e Terra.

Navarro, João de Azpilcueta. 1988. *Cartas jesuíticas 2. Cartas avulsas (1550–1568)*. Belo Horizonte: Editora Itatiaia.

Needell, Jeffrey D. 1987. *A Tropical Belle Epoque: Elite Culture and Society in Turn-of-the-Century Rio de Janeiro*. New York: Cambridge University Press.

Nguyen, Kristina Hartzer. 1992. *The Made Landscape: City and Country in Seventeenth-Century Dutch Prints*. Cambridge, MA: Harvard University Art Museums.

Niemeyer, Oscar. 1961. *Minha experiência em Brasília*. Rio de Janeiro: Vitória.

Nieuhof, Johannes. 1703. *Voyages and Travels into Brasil, and the East-Indies*. London: A. and J. Churchill.

Nist, John A. 1967. *The Modernist Movement in Brazil.* Austin: University of Texas Press.

Nóbrega, Manoel da. 1988. *Cartas do Brasil.* Belo Horizonte, Brazil: Itatiaia.

Oliveira, Lúcia Lippi. 2002. *O Brasil dos imigrantes.* 2d ed. Rio de Janeiro: Jorge Zahar Editor.

Ortriwano, Gisela Swetlana. 1985. *A informação no rádio: Os grupos de poder e a determinação dos conteúdos.* São Paulo: Summus Editorial.

Papavero, Nelson, Dante Martins, William Leslie Overal, and José Roberto Pujol-Luz. 2000. *O novo Éden: A fauna da Amazônia brasileira nos relatos de viajantes e cronistas desde a descoberta do Rio Amazonas por Pinzón (1500) até o Tratado de Santo Ildefonso (1777).* Belém, Brazil: Museu Paraense Emílio Goeldi.

Peixoto, Afrânio. 1940. *Panorama da literatura brasileira.* São Paulo: Companhia Editora Nacional.

Pena, Martins. N.d. *Comédias de Martins Pena.* Rio de Janeiro: Edições de Ouro.

Pereira, Moacyr Soares. 1984. *A navegação de 1501 ao Brasil de Américo Vespúcio.* Rio de Janeiro: ASA.

Perrone, Charles A. 1996. *Seven Faces: Brazilian Poetry Since Modernism.* Durham, NC: Duke University Press.

Philippou, Styliane. 2005. "Modernism and National Identity in Brazil, or How to Brew a Brazilian Stew." *National Identities* 7, no. 3 (September): 245–264.

Pick, Zuzana. 1993. *The New Latin American Cinema: A Continental Project.* Austin: University of Texas Press.

Pinto, Estevão, trans. 1944. Introduction to *Singularidades da França antártica, a que outros chamam de América,* by André Thevet, 7–30. São Paulo: Companhia Editora Nacional.

Pinto, Virgílio Noya. 1979. *O ouro brasileiro e o comércio português.* São Paulo: Companhia Editora Nacional/MEC.

Piso, Willem, Georf Marggraf, and Joannes de Laet. 1648. *Historia naturalis brasiliae.* Lugdunum Batavorum, Netherlands: F. Hackius.

Pita, Sebastião da Rocha. 1880. *História da América portuguesa desde o ano de 1500 até o ano de 1724.* 2d ed. Lisbon: Livraria Guimarães.

Pohl, Frederick J. 1966. *Amerigo Vespucci: Pilot Major.* New York: Octagon Books.

Poppino, Rolli. 1968. *Brazil: The Land and the People.* New York: Oxford University Press.

Porto, Mauro P. 2000. "Telenovelas, política e identidad nacional en Brasil." *Ecuador debate* no. 49 (April). At www.dlh.lahora.com.ec/paginas/debate/paginas/debate44.htm.

Prada, Paula. 2005. "Felons All, But Free to Try Being Beauty Queen for a Day." *New York Times,* December 1.

Prado, Maria Lígia. 1999. "Lendo novelas no Brasil Joanino." *América Latina no século*

XIX: Tramas, telas e textos. São Paulo: Editora da Universidade do Sagrado Coração (EDUSC) and EDUSP.

Prado, Paulo. 1928. *Retrato do Brasil*. 2d ed. São Paulo: Duprat-Mayença.

Pratt, Mary Louise. 1992. *Imperial Eyes: Travel Writing and Transculturation*. New York: Routledge.

Proença, M. Cavalcanti. 1966. *José de Alencar na literatura brasileira*. Rio de Janeiro: Civilização Brasileira.

Putnam, Samuel. 1948. *Marvelous Journey: A Survey of Four Centuries of Brazilian Writing*. New York: Alfred A. Knopf.

Queiroz, Rachel de. 1948. *Três romances: O quinze, João Miguel e Caminho de pedras*. Rio de Janeiro: José Olympio.

Rabassa. Gregory. 1965. *O negro na ficção brasileira*. Rio de Janeiro: Tempo Brasileiro.

Raminelli, Ronald. 1996. *Imagens da colonização: A imagem do índio de Caminha a Vieira*. São Paulo: EDUSP.

Ramos, Graciliano. 1953. *Vidas secas*. Rio de Janeiro: José Olympio.

Reis, Roberto. 1992. *The Pearl Necklace: Toward an Archeology of Brazilian Transition Discourse*. Trans. Aparecida Godoy Johnson. Gainesville: University Press of Florida.

Revista do Instituto Histórico e Geográfico Brasileiro. 1839–present. Rio de Janeiro: Tipografia Universal de Laemmert.

Ribeiro, Darcy. 1995. *A formação e o sentido do Brasil*. São Paulo: Companhia das Letras.

Ricardo, Cassiano. 1964. *O indianismo de Gonçalves Dias*. São Paulo: Conselho Estadual de Cultura.

Rivas, Darlene. 2002. *Missionary Capitalist: Nelson Rockefeller in Venezuela*. Chapel Hill: University of North Carolina Press.

Robb, Peter. 2004. *A Death in Brazil*. New York: Henry Holt.

Roberts, Shari. 1993. "'The Lady in the Tutti-Frutti Hat': Carmen Miranda, a Spectacle of Ethnicity." *Cinema Journal* 32, no. 3 (Spring): 3–23.

Rocha, Glauber. 1965. "Uma estética da fome." *Revista civilização brasileira* 3 (July): 165–170.

———. 1994. "Antônio das mortes." In *Glauber Rocha: Um leão ao meio-dia*, ed. José Carlos Avellar. Rio de Janeiro: Centro Cultural Banco do Brasil.

Rodrigues, José Honório. 1967. *The Brazilians: Their Character and Aspirations*. Trans. Ralph Edward Dimmick. Austin: University of Texas Press.

Roosevelt, Theodore. 1994. *Through the Brazilian Wilderness*. Rev. ed. Mechanicsburg, PA: Stackpole Books. Originally published in 1914.

Rousseau, Jean-Jacques. 1950. *The Social Contract and Discourses*. Trans. G. D. H. Cole. New York: E. P. Dutton.

Rugendas, Johann Moritz. 1989. *Viagem pitoresca através do Brasil*. São Paulo: Editora Itatiaia/EDUSP. Originally published in 1835 as *Malerische reise in Brasilien* and as *Voyage pitoresque dans le Brésil*.

Russell-Wood, A. J. R. 2000. "Holy and Unholy Alliances: Clerical Participation in the Flow of Bullion from Brazil to Portugal in the Reign of Dom João VI (1704–1750). *Hispanic American Historical Review* 80, no. 4 (November): 815–837.

Ryle, John. 2004. "Live Fast, Die Young." (London) *Times Literary Supplement*, July 16, 3–4.

Sadlier, Darlene J. 2003. *Nelson Pereira dos Santos.* Urbana: University of Illinois Press.

Salles, Ricardo. 1996. *Nostalgia imperial: A formação da identidade nacional no Brasil do segundo reino.* Rio de Janeiro: Topbooks.

Salvador, Vicente do. 1965. *História do Brasil: 1500–1627.* São Paulo: Edições Melhoramentos. Originally published in 1627.

Sampaio, Mário Ferraz. 1984. *História do rádio e da televisão no Brasil e no mundo.* Rio de Janeiro: Achiamé.

Sanchéz, Alex, and Annie Hamel. 2006. "Gradual Resurgence of France as a Strategic Presence in Latin America." Press release, May 3. Council on Hemispheric Affairs. At www.coha.org/2006/05/03/gradual-resurgence-of-france-as-a-strategic-presence-in-latin-america-and-the-caribbean.

Santiago, Silviano. 2000. "Destinations of a Letter, Predestinations of a Country." *Interventions: International Journal of Postcolonial Studies* 2, no. 3:330–342.

———. 2001. "Why and For What Purpose Does the European Travel?" In *The Space In-Between: Essays on Latin American Culture*, ed. Ana Lúcia Gazzola and trans. Tom Burns, Ana Lúcia Gazzola, and Gareth Williams, 9–24. Durham, NC: Duke University Press.

Sayers, Raymond S. 1956. *The Negro in Brazilian Literature.* New York: Hispanic Institute in the United States.

Schlichthorst, Carl. 1943. *O Rio de Janeiro como é: 1824–1826.* Trans. Emmy Dodt and Gustavo Barroso. Rio de Janeiro: Editora Getúlio Costa. Originally published in 1829 as *Rio de Janeiro wie es ist.*

Schultz, Kirsten. 2001. *Tropical Versailles: Empire, Monarchy, and the Portuguese Royal Court in Rio de Janeiro, 1808–1821.* New York: Routledge.

Schwartz, Stuart B. 1985. *Sugar Plantations in the Formation of Brazilian Society: Bahia 1550–1835.* Cambridge, England: Cambridge University Press.

———. 2004. *Tropical Babylons: Sugar and the Making of the Atlantic World 1450–1680.* Chapel Hill: University of North Carolina Press.

Schwarz, Roberto. 2001. *A Master on the Periphery of Capitalism: Machado de Assis.* Trans. John Gledson. Durham, NC: Duke University Press.

Semana de 22: Antecedents and Consequences. 1972. Trans. Edwina Jackson. São Paulo: Museu de Arte de São Paulo.

Seoane, Carmen Sylvia Sicoli. 1990. "Aquarelas do Brasil: Estudo iconográfico e textual da natureza do índio em Debret e Rugendas (1816–1831)." Master's thesis, Universidade Federal Fluminense, Rio de Janeiro.

Shoumatoff, Alex. 1980. *The Capital of Hope*. New York: Coward, McCann and Geoghegan.

Silva, J. Romão. 1981. *Luís Gama e suas poesias satíricas*. Rio de Janeiro: Cátedra/Instituto Nacional do Livro.

Silva, Maria Beatriz Nizza da. 1999. *História da colonização portuguesa no Brasil*. Lisbon: Colibri.

Silva Neto, Antônio Leão da, ed. 2002. *Dicionário de filmes brasileiros*. São Paulo: A. L. Silva Neto.

Skidmore, Thomas E. 1988. *The Politics of Military Rule in Brazil, 1964–85*. New York: Oxford University Press.

Slater, Candace. 2002. *Entangled Edens: Visions of the Amazon*. Berkeley: University of California Press.

Smith, Robert C. 1938. "The Brazilian Landscapes of Frans Post." *Art Quarterly* 1, no. 4 (Autumn): 239–266.

Sodré, Nelson Werneck. 1943. *Síntese do desenvolvimento literário no Brasil*. São Paulo: Livraria Martins Editora.

Sommer, Doris. 1991. *Foundational Fictions: The National Romances of Latin America*. Berkeley: University of California Press.

Sousa, Gabriel Soares de. 1971. *Tratado descritivo do Brasil em 1587*. São Paulo: Companhia Editora Nacional.

Sousa-Leão, Joaquim de. 1973. *Frans Post: 1612–1680*. Amsterdam: A. L. Gendt.

Spix, Johann Baptist von, and Karl von Fredrich Phillip von Martius. 1823–1831. *Reis in Brasilien*. Munich, Germany: M. Lindauer.

———. 1938. *Viagem pelo Brasil*. Trans. Lúcia Furquim Lahmeyer. Rio de Janeiro: Imprensa Nacional.

Southey, Robert. 1810–1819. *History of Brazil*. 3 vols. London: Longman, Hurst, Rees, and Orme.

Staden, Hans. 1988. *Viagem ao Brasil*. Rio de Janeiro: Coleção Afrânio Peixoto, Academia Brasileira de Letras. Originally published in 1557 as *Warhaftig Historia und beschreibung eyner Landtschafft der wilden, nacken, grimmigen Menschenfresser Leuthen in der Newenwelt America gelegen*.

Stam, Robert. 1997. *Tropical Multiculturalism: A Comparative History of Race in Brazilian Cinema and Culture*. Durham, NC: Duke University Press.

———. 2005. *Literature Through Film: Realism, Magic, and the Art of Adaptation*. Oxford, England: Blackwell.

Stäubli, Willy. 1966. *Brasília*. London: Leonard Hill Books.

Sturtevant, William C. 1976. "First Visual Images of Native America." In *First Images of America*, vol. 1, ed. Fred Chiapelli, 417–457. Berkeley: University of California Press.

Süssekind, Flora. 1990. *O Brasil não é longe daqui: O narrador; A viagem*. São Paulo: Companhia das Letras.

Takahashi. Fábio. 2005. "Brasil dos negros é o 105° de ranking social." *Folha de São Paulo,* November 19.

Taunay, Alfredo d'Escragnolle. 1908. *Reminiscências.* Rio de Janeiro: F. Alves.

———. 1923. *Innocencia.* Boston: D. C. Heath. Originally published in 1872 as *Inocência.*

———. 1928. *Visões do sertão.* São Paulo: Companhia Melhoramentos de S. Paulo.

———. 1998. *Monstros e monstrengos: Ensaio sobre a zoologia fantástica brasileira nos séculos XVII and XVIII,* São Paulo: Companhia das Letras. Originally published 1937.

Thevet, André. 1575. *La cosmographie universelle.* Paris: Pierre l'Huillier.

———. 1944. *Singularidades da França Antártica, a que outros chamam de América.* Trans. Estevão Pinto. São Paulo: Companhia Editora Nacional. Original published in 1557 as *Les Singularités de la France Antarctique.*

Thomas, Tony, and Jim Terry, with Busby Berkeley. 1973. *The Busby Berkeley Book.* Greenwich, NY: New York Graphic Society.

Toussaint-Samson, Adèle. 2001. *A Parisian in Brazil: The Travel Account of a Frenchwoman in Nineteenth-Century Rio de Janeiro.* Trans. Emma Toussaint and ed. June Hahner. Wilmington, DE: Scholarly Resources.

Treece, David. 2000. *Exiles, Allies, Rebels: Brazil's Indianist Movement, Indigenist Politics, and Imperial Nation-State.* Contributions to Latin American Studies 16. Westport, CT: Greenwood Press.

Turner, Doris J. 1976. "A Clarification of Some 'Strange' Chapters in Machado's *Dom Casmurro.*" *Luso-Brazilian Review* 3:55–66.

Underwood, David. 1994. *Oscar Niemeyer and the Architecture of Brazil.* New York: Rizzoli International.

Updike, John. 2005. "Beyond Real." *New York Review of Books,* May 26, 4–7.

Vainfas, Ronaldo. 1989. *Trópico dos pecados: Moral, sexualidade, e inquisição no Brasil.* Rio de Janeiro: Editora Campus.

———, ed. 2002. *Dicionário do Brasil imperial (1822–1889).* Rio de Janeiro: Editora Objetiva.

Varnhagen, Francisco Adolfo de. 1840. *Descobrimento do Brasil: Crônica do fim do décimo-quinto século.* 2d ed. Rio de Janeiro: Tipografia Imp. e Const. de J. Villenueve e Comp.

———. 1981. *História geral do Brasil: Antes da sua separação e independência de Portugal.* 10th ed. Belo Horizonte: Editora Itatiaia. Originally published 1854–1857.

Vasconcelos, Carolina Michaëlis de. 1923. "Carta." In *História da colonização portuguesa do Brasil,* vol. 2, ed. Carlos Malheiro Dias. Oporto, Portugal: Litografia Nacional.

Vasconcelos, Simão de. 2002. *Notícias curiosas e necessárias das coisas do Brasil.* Lisbon: Comissão Nacional para as Comemorações do Descobrimentos. Originally published in 1668.

Vasquez, Pedro Karp. 2001. *Postaes do Brasil 1893–1930.* São Paulo, Metalivros.

Veríssimo, José. 1969. *História da literatura brasileira*. 5th ed. Rio de Janeiro: Livraria José Olympio Editora.

Vespucci, Amerigo. 1509. *Disz büchlin saget wie die zwé durchlüchtigsté herré Her Fernandus K. zu Castelien und Herr Emanuel. K. Zu Portugal haben das weyte mör ersuchet vnnd findet vil Jnsulen, vnnd ein Nüwe welt von Wilden nackenden Leüten, vormals vnbekant*. Strausburg, Germany: Gedruckt durch Johāne Grüniger.

———. 1951. *Amerigo Vespucio: El Nuevo Mundo. Cartas relativas a sus viajes y descubrimientos*. Preliminary study by Robert Levillier. Buenos Aires: Editorial Nova.

Vieira, Antônio. 1959. *Obras completas*. 5 vols. Oporto, Portugal: Lello e Irmão Editores.

———. 2001. *Sermões*. 2 vols. São Paulo: Hedra.

Vigneras, Louis-André. 1976. *La búsqueda del paraiso y las legendarias islas del Atlántico*. Valladolid, Spain: Casa-Museo de Colon.

Wag[e]ner, Zacharias. 1964. *Zoobiblion: Livro de animais do Brasil*, ed. Enrico Schaeffer. Brasiliensia Documenta 4. São Paulo: N.p.

Wasserman, Renata R. Mautner. 1983. "The Red and the White: The 'Indian' Novels of José de Alencar." *PMLA* 98, no. 5 (October): 815–827.

———. 1984. "Re-Inventing the New World: Cooper and Alencar." *Comparative Literature* 36, no. 2 (Spring): 130–145.

Watkins, Thayer. N.d. *Plano de Integração Nacional (PIN): The 1970 Plan for Integration in Brazil*. San Jose, CA: San Jose State University. At www.sjsu.edu/faculty/watkins/PIN.htm.

Welles, Orson, and Peter Bogdanovich. 1992. *This Is Orson Welles*, ed. Jonathan Rosenbaum. New York: HarperCollins.

Whatley, Janet, trans. 1990. Introduction to *History of a Voyage*, by Jean de Léry, xv–xxxviii.

White, Hayden. 1978. *Tropics of Discourse: Essays in Cultural Criticism*. Baltimore, MD: Johns Hopkins University Press.

Williams, Bruce. 1999. "To Serve Godard: Anthropological Processes in Brazilian Cinema." *Literature/Film Quarterly* 27:3 (July): 202–209.

Williams, Daryle. 2001. *Culture Wars in Brazil: The First Vargas Regime, 1930–1945*. Durham, NC: Duke University Press.

Wisnik, José Miguel. 1976. Introduction to *Poemas escolhidos*, by Gregório de Matos, 11–31. São Paulo: Editora Cultrix.

Woll, Allen. L. 1974. "Hollywood's Good Neighbor Policy: The Latin Image in American Film, 1939–1946." *Journal of Popular Film* 3, no. 4 (Fall): 278–293.

Xavier, Alberto, ed. 2003. *Depoimento de uma geração: Arquitetura moderna brasileira*. Rev. ed. São Paulo: Cosac and Naify.

Xavier, Ismail. 1990. "*Iracema*: Transcending Cinema Verité." In *The Social Documentary in Latin America*, ed. Julianne Burton, 361–371. Pittsburgh, PA: University of Pittsburgh Press.

————. 1997. *Allegories of Underdevelopment: Aesthetics and Politics in Modern Brazilian Cinema*. Minneapolis: University of Minnesota Press.

————. 2003. "Brazilian Cinema in the 1990s: The Unexpected Encounter and the Resentful Character." In *The New Brazilian Cinema*, ed. Nagrib, 39–63. London: I. B. Tauris.

Zanini, Walter. 1994. "Two Difficult Decades: The 60s and 70s." *Bienal Brasil século XX*, 306–321.

Zona Latina. 1999. "Telenovelas in Latin America." November 7. www.zonalatina. com/Zldata70.htm.

Zweig, Stefan. 1941. *Brazil, the Land of the Future*. Trans. Andrew St. James. New York: Viking Press.

INDEX